FIRE CONGRESS

THE PEOPLE IMPOSE CONGRESSIONAL
TERM LIMITS

I.S. PETTEICE

SENIOR AUTHOR OF
POLITICAL PERSPECTIVES

PUBLICATION
CONSULTANTS
We Believe In The Power Of Authors

PO Box 221974 Anchorage, Alaska 99522-1974
books@publicationconsultants.com—www.publicationconsultants.com

ISBN 978-1-59433-755-0
eISBN 978-1-59433-756-7
Library of Congress Catalog Card Number: 2017961876

Manufactured in the United States of America.

INDEX

FOREWORD

You start with a cage containing four monkeys and inside the cage you hang a banana on a string, and then you place a set of stairs under the banana. Before long a monkey will go to the stairs and climb toward the banana.

You then spray all the monkeys with cold water. After a while, another monkey makes an attempt. As soon as he touches the stairs, you spray all the monkeys with cold water. Pretty soon, when another monkey tries to climb the stairs, the other monkeys will try to prevent it.

Now, put away the cold water. Remove one monkey from the cage and replace it with a new monkey. The new monkey sees the banana and attempts to climb the stairs. To his shock, all of the other monkeys beat the crap out of him. After another attempt and attack, he knows that if he tries to climb the stairs he will be assaulted.

Next, remove another of the original four monkeys, replacing it with a new monkey. The newcomer goes to the stairs and is attacked. The previous newcomer takes part in the punishment - with enthusiasm - because he is now part of the "team."

Then, replace a third original monkey with a new monkey, followed by the fourth. Every time the newest monkey takes to the stairs, he is attacked. Now, the monkeys that are beating him up have no idea why they were not permitted to climb the stairs.

Neither do they know why they are participating in the beating of the newest monkey. Having replaced all of the original monkeys, none of the remaining monkeys will have ever been sprayed with cold water.

Nevertheless, not one of the monkeys will try to climb the stairway for the banana.

Why, you ask? Because in their minds, that is the way it has always been!

This is how today›s House and Senate operates, and this is why from time to time, all of the monkeys need to be replaced at the same time!

America will have to vote out the corrupt members of Congress. Congress will not vote in term limits because it affords them the ability to become wealthy in a profession where they do not have to do anything but smile and lie to their constituents every two or six years when it is voting time.

You cannot impeach a Senator or Representative because it would have to be done by their fellow members and they will not turn on their own. They rarely investigate their own unless the offense is so gross as to cause great public attention and even then they are forced to resign.

It is the "Good Old Boys Club" of which 435 Representatives and 100 Senators have become life members unless America does the same thing every election cycle as they did in 2016 and everyone goes to the polls and votes for new Senators and Representatives until Congress gets their houses cleaned out.

I

THE 2016 ELECTION

"They [Democrats in Congress] believe in Communism. They believe and have called for a revolution. You're going to have to shoot them in the head. But warning, they may shoot you."
Glenn Beck

Bar Stool Economics

Suppose that every day, ten men go out for beer and the bill for all ten comes to $100. If they paid their bill the way we pay our taxes, it would go something like this:

The first four men (the poorest) would pay nothing.

The fifth would pay $1.

The sixth would pay $3.

The seventh would pay $7.

The eighth would pay $12.

The ninth would pay $18.

The tenth man (the richest) would pay $59.

So, that's what they decided to do. The ten men drank in the bar every day and seemed quite happy with the arrangement, until one day, the owner threw them a curve. "Since you are all such good customers," he said, "I'm going to reduce the cost of your daily beer by $20." Drinks for the ten now cost just $80.

The group still wanted to pay their bill the way we pay our taxes so the first four men were unaffected. They would still drink for free. But what about the other six men - the paying customers? How could they divide the $20 windfall so that everyone would get his "fair share?" They realized that $20 divided by six is $3.33. But if they subtracted that from everybody's share, then the fifth man and the sixth man would each end up being paid to drink his beer. So, the bar owner suggested that it would be fair to reduce each man's bill by roughly the same amount, and he proceeded to work out the amounts each should pay.

And so:

The fifth man, like the first four, now paid nothing (100% savings).

The sixth now paid $2 instead of $3 (33% savings).

The seventh now paid $5 instead of $7 (28% savings).

The eighth now paid $9 instead of $12 (25% savings).

The ninth now paid $14 instead of $18 (22% savings).

The tenth now paid $49 instead of $59 (16% savings).

Each of the six was better off than before. And the first four continued to drink for free. But once outside the restaurant, the men began to compare their savings.

"I only got a dollar out of the 20," declared the sixth man. He pointed to the tenth man, "but he got $10!"

"Yeah, that's right," exclaimed the fifth man. "I only saved a dollar, too. It's unfair that he got ten times more than I!"

"That's true!" shouted the seventh man. "Why should he get $10 back when I got only two? The wealthy get all the breaks!"

"Wait a minute," yelled the first four men in unison. "We didn't get anything at all. The system exploits the poor!"

The nine men surrounded the tenth and beat him up.

The next night the tenth man didn't show up for drinks, so the nine sat down and had beers without him. But when it came time to pay the bill, they discovered something important. They didn't have enough money between all of them for even half of the bill!

And that, boys and girls, journalists and college professors, is how our tax system works. The people who pay the highest taxes get the most benefit from a tax reduction. Tax them too much, attack them for being wealthy, and they just may not show up anymore. In fact, they might start drinking overseas where the atmosphere is somewhat friendlier. "David R. Kamerschen, Ph.D., Professor of Economics, University of Georgia"

For those who understand, no explanation is needed. For those who do not understand, no explanation is possible.

I used to think I was just a regular person, but I was born white and whether I like it or not, that makes me a racist. I am a fiscal and moral conservative, and by today's standards, that makes me a fascist. I am heterosexual, which according to gay folks, that now makes me a homophobic. I am non-union, which makes me a traitor to the working class and an ally of big business. I am a Christian, so that labels me as an infidel. I believe in the 2nd Amendment, which makes me a member of the extensive gun lobby. I am older than 70, which makes me a bit less than I used to be. I think and I reason, therefore I doubt much that the main-stream media tells me, which I suppose must make me a reactionary. I am proud of my heritage and our inclusive American culture, which makes me a xenophobe. I thought I was just a patriot. I value my safety and that of my family and I appreciate the police and the legal system, which makes me a right-wing extremist. I believe in hard work, fair play, and fair compensation according to each individual's merits, which in today's world makes me an anti-socialist. I believe in the defense and protection of our homeland for and by all citizens, which now makes me a militant.

During the last election process, an old woman called me and my friends a "basket of deplorables." I need to thank all my friends for sticking with me through these abrupt, new-found challenges in my life and my way of thinking! I just can't imagine or understand what's happened to me so quickly! Funny . . . it all has just taken place over the last 7 or 8 years! And if all this wasn't enough to deal with, I'm now afraid to go into either restroom in public!

On the day of the election, November 8, 2016, it was not an election at all. It was a revolution of "The People." All of the millions of people who could no longer feed their families and could not afford Obamacare; all the people that lost their jobs because the company they worked for had moved to a foreign country or had just shut down; all of the conservative Americans, "The People," that were just fed up, stood up and went to the polls on election day because a businessman listened to them and heard their voices and did not make "political rhetorical promises," but said with their help we could make America great again.

As Maureen Dowd, a Liberal Columnist said, "The election was a complete repudiation of Barack Obama: his fantasy world of political correctness, the politicization of the Justice Department and the I.R.S., an out-of-control E.P.A., his neutering of the military, his nonsupport of the police and his fixation on things like transgender bathrooms. Since he became president, his party has lost 63 House seats, 10 Senate seats, and 14 governorships."

The People were fed up and pushed back. They pushed back with ballots, not bullets. They pushed back with ballots, not riots. They pushed back with ballots, not lootings. And they pushed back with ballots, not fires.

On that election day the Democratic Party fell and with it, one by one, blue states Ohio, Wisconsin, Pennsylvania, and Iowa turned red and the rest of the country rose up and joined them.

Some of these were the uneducated people of America who got the idea that they still mattered. The Media are still dumb-founded and have still not recovered from the blow.

The Socialists, the Communists, the Liberals, the Marxists, the Medias – they all said, "How dare you? Abortion is now okay. Gay rights are great. Illegal immigration is here to stay. Banning Muslims? What kind of bigots are you? Obama gave us everything we wanted."

We will protest and riot and burn if we lose the election.

And that is the difference between the left and the right. When Obama won the election, the Conservatives accepted their defeat with dignity. They accepted Obama as their President even though they did not like the fact that he wanted to turn America into a Socialist government. They patiently waited for his term to end and a new election process to begin. That is what our Constitution is all about.

However, the Far Left is different. The Left are Democrats, they are Socialists, they are Marxists, and they are Communists. Some are just Libtards and Trolls. Most of them are controlled by one man, George Soros, a rich Billionaire/Communist. He bankrolls different organizations who organizes protests.

If you look at the poorest cities in America, you will find that they have been under Democratic rule for generations. Yet the people in those cities seem not to be intelligent enough to vote someone else in as Governor or Mayor in order to change the system. Chicago, Detroit and Los Angeles are prime examples. Chicago has had a Democratic Mayor since 1931. Detroit has had a Democratic Mayor since 1962. Los Angeles has had a Democratic Mayor since 1973.

Illinois has elected several Democratic Governors, but every time one is elected, they end up going to prison. Michigan can't seem to make up its mind. One term they elect a Republican and the next term they go back and elect another Democrat. I am surprised to learn that California has had mostly Republican Governors, although Jerry Brown is a Democrat.

But in 2016, the Conservatives showed they had enough of Socialism and they got in their vehicles after work and every one of them went to the polls and voted; even some that had never voted before, and some that had not voted since Kennedy ran against Nixon for President. They got off work and went straight to the polls to vote.

No matter what Hillary Clinton said, no matter what Bill Clinton said, no matter what Barack Obama said, The People did not listen. The People had enough of "The Bull" and enough of "Obama's Socialism" and on election day 33 million people turned America upside down and voted against Hillary Clinton and Socialism, and the Democratic Party.

When the Presidential winner was announced you could go to each Socialist/Communist television channel and the announcers were literally weeping. Aren't they supposed to be impartial? The Media – the Journalists – well, they had long since stopped being Journalists. They were crying on national television over the loss of the election of the person they had been championing for the past year.

During the pre-election cycle, they were so obsessed with fulfilling their own forecasts that when their candidate lost, their emotional loss was more than they could bear as was that of the Democratic Party which was made up of Socialists, Communists, Marxists, Libtards, Progressives and every Troll on the internet. They call themselves the elite and educated, or were they the amoral Reds that would destroy this country given half a chance?

This was America's last chance and The People felt that Mr. Trump had heard them. They had hope for the first time in eight years.

Someone once said, "Obama has brought more Americans back to conservatism than anyone since Reagan. In one term, he has rejuvenated the Conservative Movement and brought out to the streets millions of Freedom Loving Americans. Name one other time when you saw your friends and neighbors this interested in taking back America!"

Even after a victorious win by Mr. Trump, instead of the Communist Media rallying behind this President, they still cling to their bitterness and resentment and nitpick every word and action that comes from him.

The left is now preying on the right and saying they are afraid. They should be. The days of Socialism in this country are gone. The days of Communism in this country are gone. The days of Marxism are gone. Well, at least for the next eight years.

As Ronald Reagan said, "Socialism only works in two places: Heaven where they don't need it and hell where they already have it." If you asked Reagan about Liberals, he said, "The trouble with our liberal friends is not that they're ignorant; it's just that they know so much that isn't so."

The People are tired of Political Correctness and offending a Socialist because they are amoral and expect everyone to conform to their ideals. The People want to be able to pray again without fear of offending someone. The People want to be able to say Merry Christmas again without fear of offending someone. Political Correctness is out and Americanism is back in.

Communism has always been pervasive in Hollywood and it still is today. During the 1930's and early 1940's, many actors and actresses were blacklisted and forced into retirement. Many were added to the list up through 1957. It was a long list of many well-known names. After 1957 the list was gradually broken and Hollywood was once again free to "undermine our Constitution." https://en.wikipedia.org/wiki/Hollywood_blacklist

It is the Conservatives in Hollywood that are afraid to speak out now. They are afraid they will not find work if it is known they are a Conservative because Hollywood is overrun with Communism. When an award show is televised the Communists are now brazen enough to speak out because they had no fear as long as Barack Obama was in office.

That may soon change as Mr. Trump has promised to "drain the swamp." Under the first Amendment, they have a right to speak out, but they must be very careful about undermining our Constitution for being treasonous against the government.

Their power is also diminishing since the election as many of The People believe that Hollywood exists for the entertainment of "The People." I received the following in an e-mail and I believe, although a little harsh, it sums up the attitude of the Conservatives these days.

"Dear Hollywood Celebrities

"It's time to wake up now. Get this! The only reason you exist is for my entertainment. Some of you are beautiful. Some of you can deliver a line with such conviction that you bring tears to my eyes. Some of you are so convincing that you scare the crap out of me. And others are so funny you can make me laugh uncontrollably.

"But you all have one thing in common. You only exist and have a place in my world to entertain me. That's it. Nothing else!

"You make your living pretending to be someone else. You play dress-up like a 5-year-old. Your world is a make believe world. It is not real. It doesn't exist. You live for the camera while the rest of us live in the real world. Your entire existence depends on my patronage. I crank the organ grinder, and you dance.

"Therefore, I don't care where you stand on issues. Honestly, your opinion means nothing to me. Just because you had a lead role in a movie about prostitution doesn't mean you know what it's like to be a prostitute. Your view matters far less to me than that of someone living in Timbuktu.

"Believe me or not, the hard truth is that you aren't real. I turn off my TV or shut down my computer, and you cease to exist. Once I am done with you, I go back to the real world until I want you to entertain me again.

"I don't care that you think BP executives deserve the death penalty. I don't care what you think about the environment. I don't care if you believe fracking is bad. I don't care if you call for more gun control. I don't care if you believe in catastrophic human-induced global warming. And I could care less that you supported Hillary for President. Get back into your bubble. I'll let you know when I'm in the mood for something pretty or scary or funny.

"And one other thing. What was with all this "I'll leave the country if Donald Trump wins"? Don't you know how stupid that made you sound? What did you think my reaction was going to be? I better not vote for Trump or we'll lose Whoopi Goldberg? Al Sharpton? Amy

Schumer? Leave. I don't care! And don't let the door hit you in the ass on your way out. Oh, by the way, is Clinton returning any of the money you so generously donated to her election?

"Make me laugh. Make me cry. Even scare me. But realize this, the only words of yours that matter are scripted — just like your pathetic little lives. I may agree with some of you from time to time, but in the final analysis, it doesn't matter. In my world, you exist solely for my entertainment.

"So, shut your mouth and, Dance, Monkey, Dance!" (anonymous)

It has been several months now since the election. Mr. Trump has done his best to fulfill every campaign promise. The lame stream media and the Democrats have never given him a break. Every day they pound the President with their vile uncalled-for vitriol.

The Democrats have made it their goal to see that Mr. Trump gets impeached. They are not interested in making America great. They have a Communist agenda.

II

CONGRESSIONAL TERM LIMITS

Ronald Reagan once said, "I have wondered at times about what the Ten Commandments would have looked like if Moses had run them through the U.S. Congress."

In December 2016, Senator Ted Cruz formally announced that he was introducing a Constitutional Amendment to implement term limits for Congress. Of course, to members of Congress that had been in office a number of years, this was not good news. They had gotten wealthy off of the system and had made a career of being a Senator or a Representative. They had long forgotten that they were elected to work for The People and were instead working for themselves, working for their own prestige, for the two weeks on and two weeks off each month, and the fat paychecks from the lobbyist for their votes on the various bills so they could get rich, and for their campaign funds for their next election. And, of course, for the promise of a job in the event of a loss of an election or retirement.

Taking a page out of Trump's winner's book, Cruz said, "Passing term limits will demonstrate that Congress has actually heard the voice of "The People."

It was Mitch McConnell that said that there would be no vote on term limits. Of course, the Senior Republican Senator who has been in office for 31+ years would oppose term limit legislation. Mitch McConnell will continue to fight against this common sense proposal, so you can be sure he will do everything in his power to make sure this amendment never sees the light of day.

The logic behind term limits is simple: if the people running the government are responsible for its problems, then it makes sense to limit the amount of time they can be in office. It is not surprising that McConnell is against term limits. He has gotten rich and powerful from being a Senior Senator.

McConnell who was worth $12 Million in 2013 is worth $17 Million in 2017.

Harry Reid was worth less than $1 Million when he took office in 1982, but he was worth around $10 Million at the time of his retirement. When Sharon Angle was running against him in 2010 she asked him how he became so wealthy because Reid would never disclose any of his tax returns. Reid said he made some very wise investments.

Representatives and Senators have access to insider information from lobbyists that the ordinary citizen does not have.

Such a new Constitutional "Drain the Swamp" Amendment such as term limits would ensure that when new members of Congress arrived in Washington that they would be there to work for Americans and the problems that Americans faces. They would not be worried about where they could get money for their re-election fund.

For the past several years, Americans have been calling for Congress to "Drain the Swamp" of the corruption, and to implement term limits for Congress. When this was discussed with different members of Congress, the old members, most of whom are listed in this book as corrupt members, were against it and the more honest members were for it, or so they say to the Media.

We shall see when or if this comes up to a vote. There have been thousands of faxes delivered to Congress about it, as well as e-mails. It is up to us, "The People," to make sure that Senators and Representatives like McConnell and Pelosi fail.

For instance, Congressman Leahy is 74 years old and has been in office 40 years.

Congressman Orin Hatch is 80 years old and has been in office for 38 years. He once made the statement that he would retire if Mitt Romney would run for office.

Congresswoman Mikulski is 78 years old and has held office for 38 years.

Congressman Roberts is 78 years old and has been in office for 34 years.

Congressman Chuck Schumer is 64 years old and has held office for 34 years.

Congressman John McCain is 78 years old and has been in office for 32 years.

Congressman Shelby who is 80 years old has been in office 36 years.

Congressman McConnell who is 73 years old has been in office 30 years.

Congressman Cochran is 77 years old and has been in office 42 years.

Congressman Dick Durbin is 70 years old and has been in office 32 years.

Congressman Chuck Grassley is 80 years old and has been in office for 34 years.

A LETTER TO YOUR CONGRESSMAN

"Senator Patty Murray
Senator Maria Cantwell
Washington, DC 20510

Dear Senators:

I have tried to live by the rules my entire life. My father was a Command Sergeant Major, U.S. Army, who died of combat related stresses shortly after his retirement. It was he who instilled in me those virtues he felt important - honesty, duty, patriotism and obeying the laws of God and of our various governments. I have served my country, paid my taxes, worked hard, volunteered and donated my fair share of the money, time and artifacts.

Today, as I approach my 79th birthday, I am heart-broken when I look at my country and my government. I shall only point out very few things abysmally wrong which you can multiply by a thousand fold. I have calculated that all the money I have paid in income taxes my entire life cannot even keep the Senate barbershop open for one year! Only Heaven and a few tight-lipped actuarial types know what the Senate dining room costs the taxpayers. So please, enjoy your haircuts and meals on us

Last year, the president [Obama] spent an estimated $1.4 billion on himself and his family. The vice president spends $ millions on hotels. They have had 8 vacations so far this year! And our House of Representatives and Senate have become America's answer to the Saudi royal family. You have become the "perfumed princes and princesses" of our country.

In the middle of the night, you voted in the Affordable Health Care Act, a.k.a. "Obamacare," a bill which no more than a handful of senators or representatives read more than several paragraphs, crammed it down our throats, and then promptly exempted yourselves from it substituting your own taxpayer-subsidized golden health care insurance. You live exceedingly well, eat and drink as well as the "one percenters," consistently vote yourselves perks and pay raises while making 3.5 times the average U.S. individual income, and give up nothing while you (as well as the president and veep) ask us to sacrifice due to sequestration (for which, of course, you plan to blame the Republicans, anyway). You understand very well the only two rules you need to know - (1) How to get elected, and (2) How to get re-elected. And you do this with the aid of an eagerly willing and partisan press, speeches permeated with a certain economy of truth, and by buying the votes of the greedy, the ill-informed and under-educated citizens (and non-citizens, too many of whom do vote) who are looking for a handout rather than a job. Your so-called "safety net" has become a hammock for the lazy. And, what is it now, about 49 or 50 million on food stamps - pretty much all Democrat voters - and the program is absolutely rife with fraud and absolutely no congressional oversight?

I would offer that you are not entirely to blame. What changed you is the seductive environment of power in which you have immersed yourselves. It is the nature of both houses of Congress which requires you to subordinate your virtue in order to get anything done until you have achieved a leadership role. To paraphrase President Reagan, it appears that the second oldest profession (politics), bears a remarkably strong resemblance to the oldest.

As the hirsute first Baron John Emerich Edward Dalberg Acton (1834-1902), English historian and moralist, so aptly and accurately stated, "Power tends to corrupt, and absolute power corrupts absolutely. Great men are almost always bad men. I'm only guessing that this applies to the female sex as well. Tell me, is there a more corrupt entity in this country than Congress?

While we middle-class people continue to struggle, our government becomes less and less transparent, more and more bureaucratic, and ever so much more dictatorial, using Czars and Secretaries (just to mention a very few) to tell us what kind of light bulbs we must purchase, how much soda or hamburgers we can eat, what cars we can drive, which gasoline to use, and what health care we must buy. Countless thousands of pages of regulations strangle our businesses costing the consumer more and more every day.

As I face my final year, or so, with cancer, my President and my government tell me "You'll just have to take a pill," while you, Senators, your colleagues, the President, and other exulted government officials and their families will get the best possible health care on our tax dollars until you are called home by your Creator while also enjoying a retirement beyond my wildest dreams, which of course, you voted for yourselves and we pay for.

The chances of you reading this letter are practically zero as your staff will not pass it on, but with a little luck, a form letter response might be generated by them with an auto signature applied, hoping we will believe that you, our senator or representative, has heard us and actually cares. This letter will, however, go on line where many others will have the chance to read one person's opinion, rightly or wrongly, about this government, its administration and its senators and representatives.

I only hope that occasionally you might quietly thank the taxpayer for all the generous entitlements which you have voted yourselves, for which, by law, we must pay, unless, of course, it just goes on the $19 trillion national debt for which your children and ours, and your grandchildren and ours, ad infinitum, must eventually try to pick up the tab.

My final thoughts are that it must take a person who has either lost his or her soul or conscience or both, to seek re-election and continue to destroy the country that I deeply love. You have put it so far in debt that we will never pay it off while your lot improves by the minute, because of your power.

For you, Senator will never stand up to the rascals in your House who constantly deceive the American people. And that, my dear Senator, is how power has corrupted you and the entire Congress. The only answer to clean up this cesspool is term limits. This, of course, will kill the goose that lays your golden eggs. And woe be to him (or her) who would dare to bring it up.

Sincerely,
Bill Schoonover
3096 Angela Lane
Oak Harbor, WA"

III

HOW BAD DID IT GET

" If you do not take an interest in the affairs of your government, then you are doomed to live under the rule of fools." Plato

When Barack Obama was sworn in after his re-election in 2012, the Communist Party USA celebrated and received a write-up by WND as follows:

"The Communist Party USA, which just days ago boasted of its celebration over the election victory by Barack Obama, now is organizing teleconferences and promoting rallies in support of Obama's plans to raise taxes – and to demand full government funding for Social Security, Medicare, Medicaid "and other basic human needs."

"According to a statement from the communists, it is the "will of the voters" that Obama be allowed to "end ... tax breaks for the wealthiest." And the party said no spending cuts should be allowed because they would be borne by the "working class families, starting with children and youth and the most vulnerable."

"Facing the nation right now is the fiscal cliff which was set up by earlier decisions from the White House and Congress not to address longterm budget problems then. The scenario now is that without new legislation immediately on spending cuts, sought by Republicans, or more taxes, demanded by Democrats and the Communist Party

USA, automatic changes will create both spending cuts and new tax liabilities.

"Many Washington observers say, in fact, that's a goal for Obama, in order to allow him to blame the GOP for the nation's ills, and for him to work on tax increases amidst the backlash from Americans facing huge new liabilities.

"The national legislative struggle is the first challenge to continue the deep organizing that resulted in the election victory, in order to win priorities that benefit the 99 percent," the party said in a statement.

"It has organized a teleconference on the fight at 8 p.m. Eastern on Dec. 4, at 605-475-4850 (1053538#) with Art Perlo, chair of the Economics Commission CPUSA. And it is promoting that the AFL-CIO and "hundreds of organizations" will hold a Candlelight Campaign against Cuts on Dec. 10, all in support of the "Five Weeks to Protect Our Future."

"According to preliminary reports from Washington, Obama already has picked up on one of the suggestions from the Communist Party USA National Committee, which wrote a week ago that there needs to be an "enhanced version of the American Jobs Act ... as part of a green New Deal to create millions of jobs for infrastructure, renewable energy, education and support to state and local government services."

"As part of his demands to Congress regarding a compromise to avoid the "fiscal cliff" Obama has proposed $50 billion in new stimulus spending, reports said. He also wants $1.6 trillion in new taxes and the authority to borrow what he pleases.

"The will of the voters is being put to immediate test as the so-called 'fiscal cliff' negotiations play out in Washington. Labor and the broad alliance that re-elected President Obama clearly supported an end to tax breaks for the wealthiest and keeping hands off Social Security, Medicare, Medicaid, and other basic human needs," the party statement said.

"The communists noted that there already was a round of protests held two days after the election, "spearheaded by AFL-CIO and hundreds of organizations."

"The group continued, "Coming out of the election, the big fight is the crisis over the federal budget. Forces representing corporate power and the richest of the 1 percent are trying to achieve their long-held goals of looting Social Security, Medicare and Medicaid and cutting all government programs that help people or serve a public good."

"The national committee of the Communist organization said, "The outcome of this battle will set the framework for the next four years and have impact on the lives of ordinary working people for decades to come. Only the mobilized working people can stop the corporate offensive and begin to meet our needs. The unity of the broad, inclusive and diverse alliance that won this year's election victory should now be directed to reaching out in every community and workplace to bring the message to Congress in a strong and public way. We urge immediate participation in this critical struggle."

"The national committee said, "It is cruel and divisive to whip up hysteria around the so-called 'fiscal cliff' crisis. The calls to make benefit cuts to Social Security and Medicare go in the opposite direction of the mandate delivered by the majority of voters on November 6. The message of the election clearly was: tax the wealthy more and protect Social Security, Medicare, and Medicaid."

"It also said the expiration of the "Bush-era tax cuts for the wealthy" should be only the starting point.

"We support calls for a financial transaction tax, for closing the capital gains loophole and increasing tax rates on millionaires to the level of the prosperous 1960s, and cutting the level of Pentagon spending in order to meet pressing domestic priorities that create jobs."

"WND reported only days ago that the CPUSA called Obama's election results, "an enormous people's victory."

"The comment was in a report to the Communist Party USA National Committee from the party's chairman, Sam Webb.

"We meet on the heels of an enormous people's victory. It was a long and bitterly contested battle in which the forces of inclusive democracy came out on top. The better angels of the American people spread their wings," he wrote in the online report."

http://www.wnd.com/2012/11/communist-party-usa-go-obama-go/#wySqoIpIjMDjISG0.99

So you think our government was or is not run by Communists. Think again. When a politician says they are a socialist or a progressive, that is the politically correct name for Communism. When a politician says that we need to tax the rich more, or take from the rich and give it to the poor, he is a Communist.

This country began so that each man could make a new beginning on equal footing according to his own skills and if he worked hard and was honest and if he plied his trade better than anyone else, he became a success as he defined the word.

Somewhere along the line that philosophy changed because a poor man saw a rich man and became jealous and decided instead of working harder, he thought the rich man owed him something.

Then all of a sudden mothers and fathers use the excuse that children have changed in society. Children haven't changed. Parents have changed. Parents aren't parents anymore. Children don't know anything. Parents try to make their children's lives easier instead of preparing them for the future or for what life is really about. Parents give their children a time-out instead a good old fashioned spanking so that children do not learn the word "respect." Children are not taught responsibility.

So now we have adult children that need to be on their parents' medical insurance until they are 26 and who are still living in mom and dad's basement? What is wrong with mom and dad? Even McDonald's hire constantly and gives promotions. If that doesn't pay enough salary to support Sonny, after his shift is over he can walk across the street and work the next shift at Taco Bell or KFC. Then he can pay you rent and his part of his insurance. It is called responsibility and not a free ride. Many kids do it and gain self-pride in doing so. If he can't get a job and help you out, mom and dad, show some tough love and kick him out. He'll live through it.

Many kids do it and pay their own way through college at the same time.

Someone recently wrote an article on Facebook about feeling sorry for a child that had to work for his lunch at school and how embarrassing that was for him They said we should do away with children having to work for their lunch. I remember as a child working in the cafeteria at school so I could save my allowance to buy clothes. I enjoyed the work. I was not the only child working there and I am appalled to think someone would call it an embarrassment. I call it learning responsibility, learning economics, learning to take care of myself and taking responsibility. And if you think it is an embarrassment, I feel sorry for you. If I thought you were embarrassed for me then I pity you. I was grateful for the opportunity.

What about all the snowflakes that you are paying for a college education that instead of going to class are out protesting and crying about what a tough life they have under Trump. They are not even old enough to vote or did not bother to register to vote and cast a vote in the last election. But someone said America was ready for a woman in the White House and they got on the Band Wagon and mom and dad are Democrats so they're out there breaking windows and starting fires and studying the Koran and Socialism like your liberal teacher expects and your parents or George Soros are paying them to do it.

I do not know what else they are teaching them in college these days but these young adults do not listen to the evening news and have no idea what is going on in the real world today. If you ask them who the Vice President or President is, they have no idea. They know nothing about world history. Don't they advise them to listen to the news in high school anymore?

Now we have an organization called ANTIFA. These are not kids. These are adults in their 20s and 30's and 92% of them are still living with their parents at home. Are these the same people that Congress is worried about when they say kids need to be on their parents' insurance until they are 26 years old? What is wrong with mom and dad? These adults should be going to work instead of going out and protesting, burning and destroying the property of others? Did they learn this from mom and dad? Does mom and dad approve, or don't they know what their adult children are doing?

And if they destroy property they should have to live with the consequence, like getting arrested and having to do community service to pay for the destruction done by them.

Anyone that says they cannot find a job is lying. What they really mean is that working for minimum wage some place until they can find a better job is demeaning to them. If you do not have a job, working at McDonald's and getting a paycheck is a bonus.

IV

LOBBYIST

Many former Representatives and Senators have retired with their pensions that collectively cost American taxpayers about $25 Million per year, and they trade their knowledge and their Washington connections into becoming lobbyists on K Street where they can earn a salary upwards of $750,000 a year.

Representative Steve Israel and Representative Richard Hanna, both representing New York, introduced a Bill attempting to ban former members of Congress who earn more than $1 million a year as lobbyists from collecting their pensions. This would apply only to members who become lobbyists in the future. Israel argues there are no good arguments against his bill, which calls attention to an issue he calls "indefensible."

"Former Rep. Billy Tauzin (R-La.) was paid nearly $20 million lobbying for drug companies from 2006 to 2010, according to reports.

"Tom Daschle (D-S.D.), the former Senate majority leader, disclosed that he earned $2.1 million for lobbying work when President Obama nominated him — unsuccessfully — to serve as secretary of health and human services in 2009.

"Former Rep. Steve Largent (R-Okla.) makes better money lobbying for a trade group of cell phone companies than he did as a Hall of Fame NFL wide receiver. He makes $1.5 million, the group disclosed.

"Ben Nelson, a Democrat who represented Nebraska in the Senate, pockets nearly $1 million a year as head of the National Association of Insurance Commissions, according to reports on his hiring.

"And the Motion Picture Association of America paid former Senator Chris Dodd (D-Conn.) $3.3 million in 2012 to represent Hollywood's interests in Washington.

"Ray LaHood, an Illinois Republican who spent 14 years in the House before serving as President Obama's first transportation secretary, derided the idea he doesn't deserve his pension while he works as an adviser for DLA Piper, an influential Washington law firm.

"I paid into the congressional retirement program for 35 years — as a congressional staffer for 17 years, 14 years as a member of Congress and 41/2 years as a cabinet member," said LaHood, who doesn't have to register as a lobbyist because he only provides advice to his client.

"It seems kind of an idiotic idea that at 68 years old I am not entitled to my retirement when I paid into the retirement system." dfriedman@ nydailynews.com

http://www.nydailynews.com/news/politics/congressman-bank-lobbyists-article-1.1804659

In an article written by Political Scientist Lee Drutman, Drutman politicized "I would say a few magic words: "When you are done working for the Congressman, you should come work for me at my firm."

"With that, assuming the staffer had any interest in leaving Capitol Hill for K Street—and almost 90 percent of them do, I would own him and, consequently, that entire office. No rules had been broken, at least not yet. No one even knew what was happening, but suddenly, every move that staffer made, he made with his future at my firm in mind. His paycheck may have been signed by the Congress, but he was already working for me, influencing his office for my clients' best interests. It was a perfect—and perfectly corrupt—arrangement." I would say a few magic words: "When you are done working for the Congressman, you should come work for me at my firm." http://www.vox.com/2015/4/20/8455235/congress-lobbying-money-statistic

"Drutman also believes if we pay Congress a higher salary that it will keep them from being corrupt.

"On any given weekend, lobbyists in Washington head for the airport to jet off to luxurious locations across the country.

"Destinations include Napa Valley in California for wine tasting, Wyoming for fly fishing and any number of spas, golf courses, even exclusive hunting trips.

"They are invited to these weekend retreats by members of Congress and their political action committees.

"The cost of accepting the invite is a political donation of anywhere from $1,500 to $5,000. And that doesn't include the cost of travel and lodging at some of the poshest resorts in the United States.

"Why go? Lobbyists tell CNN there is no better access to a member of Congress and his or her top staff than spending a relaxing weekend with them, away from Capitol Hill.

"Rep. Duncan Hunter hosted a cocktail party as the sun set over the Pacific. It used to be that lobbyists would take politicians on trips, but when rules were changed and that was outlawed, politicians and their fund-raisers came up with this variation — organize the trips and invite the lobbyists along to pay for them.

"This past August, CNN followed U.S. Rep. Duncan Hunter, R-California, to a lush weekend retreat at the Montage Laguna Beach resort. The weekend was capped off by a seaside cocktail party hosted by the congressman as the sun set over the Pacific.

"The Congressman is under investigation by the Department of Justice because he may have used tens of thousands of dollars from his congressional campaign committee for his personal use, according to an August 2016 report from the Office of Congressional Ethics. The expenses may have included paying for family travel, flights, utilities, health care, school uniforms and tuition, jewelry and groceries. If Congressman Hunter did use funds from his committee, he may have violated House, rules, standards of conduct and Federal law.

"In early September, U.S. Sen. Ben Cardin, D-Maryland, hosted a golf weekend at the Inn at Perry Cabin, a posh resort on the banks of Chesapeake Bay. A Friday night terrace cocktail party included a special appearance by fellow Maryland lawmaker U.S. Rep. Steny Hoyer, D-Maryland, who was one of the first on the links the next morning.

"Both Cardin and Hunter declined interview requests.

"Hunter's aide told us: "The congressman holds events of all types in many different venues and either people choose to support him or they don't, simple as that."

"Cardin's communications director, Sue Walitsky, sent an email explaining that the fund-raiser at the Inn at Perry Cabin was for the senator's leadership PAC, "So none of the funds raised went to support his personal campaign."

"Sen. Ben Cardin welcomed paying guests to the Inn at Perry Cabin, overlooking the Chesapeake Bay.

"She went on to say the weekend also provided the senator "an opportunity to show off one of the many beautiful locations in his home state."

"Want to travel in congressional style? Here's a list of some recent and upcoming trips and their sponsors, compiled by the Sunlight Foundation. All you need is an invite and your checkbook.

- Beach Retreat: Dorado Beach, Puerto Rico, at the Ritz-Carlton Reserve, Sen. Bob Menendez, D-New Jersey, October 22-23, 2014.
  "2017 New Jersey Sen. Bob Menendez was indicted in 2015 on charges of bribery, conspiracy, mail fraud. Menendez faced charges that he accepted bribes worth almost a million dollars and that he used his office to help his friend, Florida doctor, Salomon Melgen." http://nypost.com/2017/03/20/bob-menendez-to-face-trial-on-bribery-and-corruption-charges/
- Beach weekend: Kiawah Island, South Carolina, at The Sanctuary, Sen. Roy Blunt, R-Missouri, October 24-26, 2014
- Fourth annual Disney weekend: Orlando, at the Four Seasons Resort, Sen. David Vitter, R-Louisiana, November 7-9, 2014
  "David Vitter admitted to a past indiscretion to which he received forgiveness from his wife and from God. Apparently, his colleagues have never let go of the rumor and are still seeking details that will never be forthcoming. Vitter also kept his head down. He worked to rehabilitate his image back home in one of the smartest or luckiest (perhaps both) twists of political fate in recent years. He was never criminally charged. The Senate Ethics Committee, chaired by Barbara Boxer, dismissed the case, finding that whatever the conduct was, it occurred "before his Senate

candidacy" in 2004 and "did not involve the use of public office." https://www.washingtonpost.com/lifestyle/style/vitters-efforts-in-the-senate-outlast-the-shadow-of-his-scandal/2013/03/25/f91ad978-90e3-11e2-9cfd-36d6c9b5d7ad_story.html?utm_term=.c54f4f49e800

- Golf/Spa weekend: White Sulphur Springs, West Virginia, at The Greenbrier, Sen. Mike Crapo, R-Idaho, November 14-16, 2014
  "12/23/2012U.S. Sen. Mike Crapo of Idaho was arrested early Sunday morning in a suburb of Washington, D.C. for driving under the influence, according to a statement released by Alexandria, Va. police. Crapo (pronounced Kra-po), a Republican, was stopped after a patrol officer saw his vehicle go through a red light. After failing field sobriety tests, he was arrested at 12:45 a.m. and "taken into custody without incident," according to the statement by Alexandria police. "There was no refusal (to take sobriety tests), no accident, no injuries," Alexandria Police spokesman Jody Donaldson told The Associated Press. "Just a traffic stop that resulted in a DUI." http://firstread.nbcnews.com/_news/2012/12/23/16114019-idaho-sen-mike-crapo-arrested-for-dui?lite

- Ski Weekend: Deer Valley, Utah, Sen. Lisa Murkowski, R-Alaska, December 6, 2014
- Ski weekend: Jackson Hole, Wyoming, Sen. John Barrasso, R-Wyoming, February 20-21, 2015

For a complete list of all fund-raisers, check out the list at the Sunlight Foundation's Politicalpartytime.org.

http://www.cnn.com/2014/10/29/politics/politicians-play-lobbyists-pay/index.html

"These days there is a law that requires a lobbyist to register their names, salaries, organizations they represent, and the amount of money they spent on lobbying. But they still do things that raise questions. Congressmen and women receive personal gifts and go to dinner at the best restaurants in D.C.

"Does a lobbyist have too much influence on a Congressman? What can be done about it? I think they do. When large sums of money are paid into a campaign fund or PAC on behalf of a Congressman or woman, that is just the same as going into his or her pocket. It is known to him or her that this company did a favor for him or her and receiving that money will affect the decision that is made on a vote being made on a legislative process.

"What can be done is to do away with lobbyists altogether. Congress says their input is necessary for making decisions because they are too busy to read every Bill. However, Congress can do like Judges do. Judges have Clerks that do research and write briefs for them. Congress can assign one or two of their aides to read Bills and write or give summations of the Bills. This would assure an unbiased and uncorrupted summary for the Congressman or Congresswoman to vote on. And, of course, they could vote faster, because they would not have to sit around and wait for their check from the lobbyist.

"Or, Congress could work more days that two weeks a month for their $174,000 salary per year plus benefits.

"In 2013 "the NRA and affiliated National Rifle Association of America Institute for Legislative Action together spent over $800,000 lobbying the Federal government during the first quarter — more than any year covering the same period, according to Federal records.

"Such aggressive advocacy preceded a major legislative victory Wednesday for gun advocates, as the U.S. Senate defeated a proposal to expand background checks on gun buyers.

"And it came as gun control advocates — from President Barack Obama and New York Mayor Michael Bloomberg to former Rep. Gabrielle Giffords and the families of children killed last year in Newtown, Conn. — pressured lawmakers to pass laws limiting purchases of firearms."

https://www.publicintegrity.org/2013/04/20/12534/nra-spends-record-money-lobbying-year

Originally published on April 23, 2012, 5:49 pm

"Yesterday, we reported on the fundraisers that lobbyists hold for Congressmen every day in Washington. Today, we hear what happens inside those events. The stories are part of our series on money in politics.

"At a typical event, there's a member of Congress and a member of his or her staff who is in charge of collecting the checks. This person is known as the fundraiser.

"The fundraiser is standing in the room, and the fundraiser has 35,000 bucks in checks sitting in her pocket right now," says Jimmy Williams, a former lobbyist for the real estate industry. "And we're going to talk about public policy while we take the checks."

"How much influence do those checks have over public policy?

"Most of the time, checks don't buy votes, Williams says. But they buy access. They buy an opportunity to make your case.

"The rules are clear: Lobbyists use money from their political action committees to get access to lawmakers.

"One time, Williams says, he took a couple clients to meet a Congressman when his PAC had fallen behind in its donations.

"'I've put in two calls to your PAC director, and I haven't received any return phone calls,' the Congressman said, according to Williams. "Now why am I taking this meeting?"

"The minute he left the office, Williams called his PAC director, and she cut those checks."

http://wamc.org/post/when-lobbyists-pay-meet-congressmen

Former Tax Lobbyists Are Writing the Rules on Tax Dodging
Lee Fang Apr. 27 2016, 7:14 a.m.

"The secret tax-dodging strategies of the global elite in China, Russia, Brazil, the U.K., and beyond were exposed in spectacular fashion by the recent Panama Papers investigation, fueling a worldwide demand for a crackdown on tax avoidance.

"But there is little appetite in Congress for taking on powerful tax dodgers in the U.S., where the practice has become commonplace.

"A request for comment about the Panama Papers to the two congressional committees charged with tax policy — House Ways and Means and the Senate Finance Committee — was ignored.

"The reluctance by congressional leaders to tackle tax dodging is nothing new, especially given that some of the largest companies paying little to no federal taxes are among the biggest campaign contributors in the country. But there's another reason to remain skeptical that Congress will move aggressively on tax avoidance: Former tax lobbyists now run the tax-writing committees.

"We researched the backgrounds of the people who manage the day-to-day operations of both committees and found that a number of lobbyists who represented world-class tax avoiders now occupy top positions as committee staff. Many have stints in and out of government and the lobbying profession, a phenomenon known as the "reverse revolving door." In other words, the lobbyists that help special interest groups and wealthy individuals minimize their tax bills are not only everywhere on K Street, they're literally managing the bodies that create tax law:

"Barbara Angus, the chief tax counsel of the House Ways and Means Committee, became a staff member in January of this year [2016] after leaving her position as a lobbyist with Ernst & Young. Angus, registration documents show, previously helped lobby lawmakers on tax policy on behalf of clients such as General Electric, HSBC, and Microsoft, among other clients.

"Mark Warren, a tax counsel for the Tax Policy Subcommittee of Ways and Means, is a former lobbyist for the Retail Industry Leaders Association, a trade group that includes Coca-Cola, Home Depot, Walgreens, and Unilever. Warren previously lobbied on a range of tax policies, including tax credits and "tax relief."

"Mike Evans became chief counsel for the Senate Finance Committee in 2014 after leaving his job as a lobbyist for K&L Gates, where he lobbied on tax policy for JP Morgan, Peabody Energy, Brown-Forman, BNSF Railway, and other corporate clients.

"Eric Oman, the senior policy adviser for tax and accounting at the Senate Finance Committee, previously worked for Ernst & Young's lobbying office, representing clients on tax policy.

"A request for comment about the role of former lobbyists now working as staffers was also ignored by the committees.

"Wealthy individuals and corporations routinely squirrel away vast sums of money in jurisdictions like Delaware or Wyoming to avoid taxation, a major factor in the current state of affairs that allows those at the top of the economic pyramid to pay an effective tax rate that is often lower than the middle class. Verizon, Boeing, and General Electric, to name a few, paid no federal income taxes in recent years, despite earning a hefty profit margin. The Tax Justice Network ranks the U.S. as the third most problematic tax haven country, a ranking even worse than Panama."

https://theintercept.com/2016/04/27/congress-tax-lobbyists/

I love that phrase "access to lawmakers." Like we are all stupid.
By Kevin Bogardus and Rachel Leven - 06/28/11 09:45 AM EDT

"Some lobbyists who went to work on Capitol Hill took a pay cut of about $100,000, an analysis by The Hill shows.

"A review of financial disclosure reports for lobbyists who were hired as congressional aides in 2011 reveal that they were paid hundreds of thousands, and in some cases millions, of dollars in salaries, bonuses, and severances while working on K Street in 2010.

"Many of those lobbyists agreed to substantial reductions in their annual salary for a chance to work for members of Congress, public records show.

"The Hill found financial disclosure reports revealing K Street salaries for at least 34 new Capitol Hill aides who were registered to lobby last year at the Federal or state level. The analysis relied on data compiled in a joint project between the watchdogs Remapping Debate and the Center for Responsive Politics, as well as salary information from Legistorm.

"The ex-lobbyists who went to work in the House earned, on average, more than $238,000 per year while working on K Street. Those same lobbyists are on pace to make more than $144,000 per year, on average, in the House, which equals an average pay cut of about $94,000.

"Ex-lobbyists who went to work in the Senate last year were earning more than $309,000, on average, in their old jobs, according to financial disclosure forms. They are on pace to take in an average of more than $160,000 as a staffer, for an average pay cut of more than $149,000.

[That is more than the Senators and Representatives make]

"It is difficult to calculate the precise salary of congressional aides due to the way the data is reported. Legistorm compiles salary information from House and Senate spending reports that detail only what aides earned in a reported time period. The pay rate recorded might or might not be the exact rate of pay for the whole year.

"When possible, The Hill used salary information gleaned from congressional committee records and interviews.

"But even with the rough salary estimates available from the data, there is no doubt many lobbyists took a significant pay cut to work for lawmakers.

"Ivan Adler, a principal at the McCormick Group, said lobbyists return to Congress, not for the salary but because it can help polish their résumés.

"'If they have a chance to go back to the Hill to work for leadership or in a senior role at a substantial "money" committee, it's an opportunity to embellish their backgrounds and thus become more valuable," Adler said.

"He said a legislative aide who left Capitol Hill for a midlevel lobbying job at a corporation or trade association could move up a rung in the congressional hierarchy to a position such as a chief of staff or senior aide to the committee. That experience will make them much more valuable should they choose to return to K Street, said Adler, a headhunter for lobbying jobs.

"They become even more valuable coming off the Hill because that's a higher-level position with a different set of contacts. It increases their knowledge of people, process, and policy," Adler said.

"A Republican lobbyist who considered returning to Capitol Hill this Congress, however, said denizens of K Street sometimes just grow bored of the influence industry.

"The older guys can afford to do it. The younger guys are coming back, refreshing their contacts and can come off the Hill and do something else," the lobbyist said. "There is a big boredom factor downtown, and they are excited to be part of a new Republican majority. You are taking a big pay cut coming back. Does it pay off? Probably."

"Some of the lobbyists are likely to see huge pay cuts from the job switch. Howard Cohen, formerly of HC Associates Inc., faces a steep drop in salary now as chief health counsel of the House Energy and Commerce Committee.

"While working at his firm last year, Cohen earned more than $1 million lobbying for clients including Amgen, the Federation of American Hospitals and the Pharmaceutical Research and Manufacturers of America, according to his financial disclosure form. Now in Congress, Cohen has an annual salary of $168,000, according to House records.

"The House Energy and Commerce Committee has been a popular destination for ex-lobbyists. At least four other individuals who were registered to lobby at some point in 2010 now work for the committee: Gary Andres, formerly of Dutko Worldwide; James Barnette, once of Steptoe & Johnson; David McCarthy, who worked for Algenol Biofuels; and Michael Bloomquist, who lobbied while at Wiley Rein.

"A spokeswoman for the House Energy and Commerce Committee said Rep. Fred Upton (R-Mich.), the panel's chairman, requires his staff not to work with their former employers.

"Chairman Upton has a policy that goes above and beyond the requirements of the House rules and requires staff to recuse themselves from working on issues that specifically affect a former employer," said Alexa Marrero, the committee spokeswoman.

"Andres, once a heavyweight at top-earning lobby firm Dutko, reported earning more than $418,000 last year from the firm. Now the former lobbyist will have a $172,500 annual salary, according to House records.

"Some were drawn to Congress for policy reasons. When asked why he went back to Capitol Hill, Barnette, now the committee's general counsel, said via a spokeswoman, "March 23, 2010," referring to the day the healthcare reform law was passed.

"Other former lobbyists had big K Street paydays, records show.

"Cesar Conda made $376,000 from Navigators Global in salary last year, according to his financial disclosure report. He is now Sen. Marco Rubio's (R-Fla.) chief of staff.

"Conda's former colleague at Navigators, Don Kent, now chief of staff to Sen. Ron Johnson (R-Wis.), made more than $227,000 in his bonus and salary last year from the firm.

"And Brett Loper, now the policy director at the House Republican Steering Committee, earned more than $549,000 in his salary and bonus from his lobbying job at the Advanced Medical Technology Association last year.

"Those relationships had to be severed once they came to Capitol Hill.

"Spencer Stokes sold his firm, Stokes Strategies, for more than $1.1 million, which will be paid out in a one-time sum of $135,000 and monthly installments of $17,000 over a five-year period, according to his financial disclosure report. Having earned more than $565,000 last year from his firm, Stokes is on pace to earn more than $169,000 this year as freshman Sen. Mike Lee's (R-Utah) chief of staff, according to a spokeswoman for Lee.

"Stokes said he joined Lee's staff because he was intrigued by public service.

"I felt that it was a good time to give some time to do things that would be beneficial to my kids and grandkids. And it's a fascinating time now," he said.

"Stokes said he didn't know if he would lobby again in the future.

"People say, 'You're just going to take this and parlay it into some federal lobbying career.' I really don't know what I'm going to do after this. I have absolutely no plans," Stokes said. "I'm just going to do the best that I can do at this job and work hard for the senator and for the state of Utah."

"Tim Harris, formerly a state lobbyist for the Indiana Utility Shareholders Association, said he was drawn by his friendship with Rep. Marlin Stutzman (R-Ind.), having served with him in Indiana's statehouse. Harris will actually see a pay increase from his switch to Capitol Hill, having earned more than $101,000 from his trade group last year and now on pace to earn $140,000 as Stutzman's chief of staff, according to Harris.

"Harris said he was bound by ethics rules not to act on behalf of his former clients.

"We actually checked with the ethics office. I certainly can't do anything on their behalf. It's actually a little easier to go from being a lobbyist to a congressional staffer than the opposite," Harris said.

"Harris is right that while former congressional aides are banned for a time from lobbying their ex-Capitol Hill colleagues, there aren't similar restrictions placed on lobbyists who come to work for Congress.

"When we think of the revolving door between government and the lobbying world, it is easy to forget that it spins both ways," said Dave Levinthal, a spokesman for the Center for Responsive Politics. "It does raise the specter of whether allegiances or loyalties to their previous employer or employers will have an impact on their work on Capitol Hill. That is a notoriously difficult thing to track."

"Ex-Lobbyist, former Firm pay Capitol Hill position

"Howard Cohen, HC Associates Inc. $1,015,000.00 Chief Health Counsel, House Energy and Commerce Committee

"Spencer Stokes, Stokes Strategies $565,100.00 Chief of Staff, Sen. Mike Lee (R-Utah)

"Brett Loper, Advanced Medical Technology Association $549,808.82 Policy Director, House Republican Steering Committee

"Phil Kiko, Foley & Lardner $487,000.00 Staff Director, House Administration Committee

"James Barnette, Steptoe & Johnson $461,396.92 General Counsel, House Energy and Commerce Committee

"Dwight Fettig, Porterfield & Lowenthal $448,225.00 Staff Director, Senate Banking Committee

"Robert Lehman, Squire Sanders Public Advocacy $440,000.00 Chief of Staff, Sen. Rob Portman (R-Ohio)

"Gary Andres, Dutko Worldwide $418,479.84 Staff Director, House Energy and Commerce Committee

"Cesar Conda, Navigators Global $376,000.00 Chief of Staff, Sen. Marco Rubio (R-Fla.)

"Michael Bloomquist, Wiley Rein $335,000.00 Deputy general counsel, House Energy and Commerce Committee"

http://thehill.com/business-a-lobbying/168709-lobbyists-took-100k-cut-in-pay-to-work-on-the-hill

Lobbyist Payments Summary by Vaughn Aubuchon

"Here is a list of the top "Lobbyist Payments" in the U.S., paid to congressmen for the purpose of influencing United States government policies. By nature, all lobbyist payments are unethical, but that is how the US government works.

"Rich US special interest groups form Political Action Committees (PACS), to get their way, by paying off the congressmen. Money controls all.

2002 Total Lobbyist Payments $1,550,222,230

Annual Amount of Bribes Paid to each Congressman in 2002 $2,897,611

In this country, you must pay your way. He who pays the most, gets his way. The best government money can buy. We are no longer a democracy. Corporate rule is the very definition of Fascism. Industry controls the government. Lobbyist Payment Sources Summary by descending major category 2002 Major Contributions (millions of $) The Bribers (Who's paying money to the government to get their way?) Category Totals (millions of $)

Finance, Insurance & Real Estate	227,585,638
Accountants	25,815,440
Finance / Credit Companies	86,975,440
Insurance	37,833,009
Savings & Loans	37,154,550

Misc. Business	224,020,183
Beer, Wine & Liquor	68,419,353
Business Associations, including the DMA	13,510,090
Business Services	13,411,053
Indian Gaming	29,920,358
Lodging / Tourism	45,778,595
Prof. Sports, Arenas & Rel.Equip. & Serv.	12,108,768
Health	209,465,591
	48,223,004
Health Services/HMOs	40,051,037
Hospitals & Nursing Homes	96,773,866
Communications / Electronics	200,872,497
	56,766,274
Books, Magazines & Newspapers	35,906,197
Telecom Services & Equipment	42,838,165
Telephone Utilities	29,498,825
Energy & Natural Resources	159,097,819
Alternative Energy Production & Services	78,143,861
Coal Mining	50,051,366
Transportation	137,561,387
	46,020,819
Airlines	36,803,958
Car Dealers, Japanese	23,506,483
Other	102,524,183
	38,870,950
Clergy & Religious Organizations	44,569,333
Ideological / Single-Issue	84,876,808
Democratic/ Liberal	6,797,000
Environment	6,018,947
Gun Control	6,680,759
Gun Rights	14,286,766
Human Rights	41,294,326

Pro-Israel	6,024,761
Agribusiness	77,662,798
	18,687,038
Agricultural Services & Products	9,262,457
Dairy	12,059,241
Meat processing & products	12,223,410
Poultry & Eggs	20,255,525
Defense	60,080,515
	27,790,089
Labor	27,213,962
Building Trade Unions	6,190,661
Misc. Unions	6,799,122
Teachers Unions	8,821,431
Construction	23,015,349
	7,523,028
Building Materials & Equipment	7,398,021
Lawyers & Lobbyists	16,245,500
	12,002,500

Here's a billion five ... have lunch on me ...$1,550,222,230

In 2009, there were over 12,500 lobbyists. Current annual lobbying payments $3.30 Billion. This averages $6.1 Million for every single lawmaker. (source: www.opensecrets.org - In 2012, here are the TOP 20 PAC contributors. http://www.vaughns-1-pagers.com/politics/lobbyist-payments.htm

"Selling out pays. If you're a corporation or lobbyist, what's the best way to "buy" a member of Congress? Secretly promise them a million dollars or more in pay if they come to work for you after they leave office. Once a public official makes a deal to go to work for a lobbying firm or corporation after leaving office, he or she becomes loyal to the future employer. And since those deals are done in secret, legislators are largely free to pass laws, special tax cuts, or earmarks that benefit their future employer with little or no accountability to the public. While campaign contributions and super PACS are a big problem, the everyday bribery of the revolving door may be the most pernicious form of corruption today.

"Unlike some other forms of money in politics, politicians never have to disclose job negotiations while in office, and never have to disclose how much they're paid after leaving office. In many cases, these types of revolving door arrangements drastically shape the laws we all live under. For example, former Senator Judd Gregg (R-NH) spent his last year in office fighting reforms to bring greater transparency to the derivatives marketplace. Almost as soon as he left office, he joined the board of a derivatives trading company and became an "advisor" to Goldman Sachs. Risky derivative trading exacerbated the financial crisis of 2008, yet we're stuck under the laws written in part by Gregg. How much has he made from the deal? Were his actions in office influenced by relationships with his future employers?

"Republic Report combed through the few disclosures that are out there to find out how much lawmakers make when they sell out and lobby for interests they once oversaw as public officials. To be sure, this list only shows the tip of the iceberg (out of the forty-four lawmakers who left office in 2010 for a lobbying-related career, only one is at an organization that discloses his salary).

"Our research effort uncovered the partial salaries of twelve lawmakers-turned-lobbyists. Republic Report's investigation found that lawmakers increased their salary by 1452 percent on average from the last year they were in office to the latest publicly available disclosure:

"Former Congressman Billy Tauzin (R-LA) made $19,359,927 as a lobbyist for pharmaceutical companies between 2006 and 2010. Tauzin retired from Congress in 2005, shortly after leading the passage of President Bush's prescription drug expansion. He was recruited to lead PhRMA, a lobbying association for Pfizer, Bayer, and other top drug companies. During the health reform debate, the former congressman helped his association block a proposal to allow Medicare to negotiate for drug prices, a major concession that extended the policies enacted in Tauzin's original Medicare drug-purchasing scheme. Tauzin left PhRMA in late 2010. He was paid over $11 million in his last year at the trade group. Comparing Tauzin's salary during his last year as a congressman and his last year as head of PhRMA, his salary went up 7110 percent.

"Former Congressman Cal Dooley (D-CA) has made at least $4,719,093 as a lobbyist for food manufacturers and the chemical industry from 2005 to 2009. Republic Report analyzed disclosures from the Grocery Manufacturers Association (GMA), an industry lobby — for companies like Kellogg — where Dooley worked following his retirement from Congress. We also added in Dooley's salary from the American Chemistry Council, where Dooley now works as the president. The Chemistry Council represents Dow Chemical, DuPont, and other chemical interests. Dooley's salary jumped 1357 percent between his last year in the House and his last reported salary for the Chemistry Council in 2009.

"Former Senator Chris Dodd (D-CT) makes approximately $1.5 million a year as the chief lobbyist for the movie industry. Dodd, who retired from the Senate after 2010, was hired by the Motion Picture Association of America, the lobbying association that represents major studios like Warner Bros. and Universal Studios. Although the MPAA would not confirm with Republic Report Dodd's exact salary, media accounts point to $1.5 million, a slightly higher figure than the previous MPAA head, former Secretary of Agriculture Dan Glickman. Dodd received about a 762 percent raise after moving from public office to lobbying.

"Former Congressman Steve Largent (R-OK) has made at least $8,815,741 over the years as a lobbyist for a coalition of cell phone companies and related wireless industry interests. Republic Report analyzed disclosures from CTIA-The Wireless Association, the trade group Largent leads. CTIA counts wireless companies like AT&T, HTC, and Motorola as members. Largent left Congress in 2002 when his pay was about $150,000 as a public official. His move to the CTIA trade association, where he earns slightly more than $1.5 million a year according to the latest disclosure form, raised his salary by 912 percent.

"Former Senator Tom Daschle (D-SD) makes well over $2.1 million as an unregistered lobbyist in addition to earning several hundred thousand a year in speaking fees and consulting gigs. When Daschle lost his seat in the Senate, he went to work for the lobbying/law firm Alston & Bird, while also providing advice to lobbying firms like the Glover Park Group, AHIP, the health insurance lobbying association, and several well-connected private equity and medical device companies. Although Daschle never registered to lobby, his sky-high income became public when President Obama unsuccessfully nominated the former Democratic majority leader to be Secretary of Health and Human Services. Daschle now works at DLA Piper, another major law/lobbying firm, where he likely makes far more than his Alston & Bird salary of $2.1 million given Daschle's significant role in crafting President Obama's health reform proposals. Not counting the speaking fees, Daschle achieved a 1228 percent salary increase by moving through the revolving door.

"Former Congressman Richard Baker (R-LA) made $3,219,255 between 2008 and 2009 as head of a hedge fund lobbying association. Republic Report reviewed disclosures from the Managed Funds Association, a group that represents hedge funds including Caxton Associations, Magnetar Capital, and Third Point LLC. In Congress, as a member of the influential House Financial Services Committee, Baker oversaw efforts to relax regulations governing Wall Street. Baker's salary went up 956 percent after he left office.

"Former Congressman Jim Slattery (D-OK) makes around $585,000 a year as a lobbyist for Wiley Rein. Slattery left Congress in 1994 to run for higher office. He didn't win. Instead, he went to work for the law/lobbying firm Wiley Rein. When Slattery again ran for statewide office in 2008 against Senator Pat Roberts (R-KS), his mandatory financial disclosure revealed that he earned $585,000 in 2007, representing clients like Verizon Communications and Nucor Corp. Comparing his 1994 House salary with his 2007 income from Wiley Rein, Slattery's pay jumped 337 percent.

"Former Congressman James Greenwood (R-PA) made $6,679,935 between 2005 and 2010 as the head of the Biotechnology Industry Organization. Greenwood took the job with BIO in 2004, and still leads the association, which lobbies on a wide variety of issues on behalf of industry, including genetically modified foods and biofuels. BIO members include Amgen, MedImmune, Novo Nordisk, Genentech, and Human Genone Sciences. Greenwood's salary shot up 671 percent between his last year in office and his BIO salary in 2009.

"Former Congressman Glenn English (D-OK) made $9,294,207 between 2004 and 2010 as the head of the National Rural Electric Cooperative Association. English, who represents many coal-dependent electric cooperatives, played a significant role in weakening climate reform legislation in 2009. Although English became head of the

NREOA after 1994, Republic Report only had access to disclosures for a six-year period. Comparing his congressional salary in 1994 and his last reported lobbying salary in 2009, English's pay went up 1504 percent.

"Former Congressman Steve Bartlett (R-TX) has made at least $9,192,761 as the chief lobbyist for an association of investment banks, including Goldman Sachs, Citigroup, and JP Morgan Chase. Bartlett has worked as the head of the Financial Services Roundtable, a trade association he joined in 1999. Republic Report could only obtain disclosures from recent years, providing us an incomplete picture of his salary. Bartlett's salary at the Financial Services Roundtable is 1770 percent higher than his last year in Congress.

"Former Congressman Matt Salmon (R-AZ) makes around $247,523 a year as a registered lobbyist. Salmon, who retired from Congress in 2001, has represented corporate clients like General Motors and Grand Canyon University (a for-profit college) through a lobbying firm he founded, Upstream Consulting Inc. (Although his income boost was lower than most of his fellow Members-turned-lobbyists, Salmon does get props for the witty firm name.) Salmon announced his intention to run again for Congress, so Republic Report reviewed mandatory candidate disclosures filed by the candidate. The forms reveal that Salmon also receives consulting fees from Policy Impact Strategic Communicators, another lobbying company, as well as nearly $50,000 a year from a company called Solid Ground Solutions. At Policy Impact Strategic Communications, Salmon represented the Republic of Kazakhstan. Salmon enjoyed a 75 percent salary boost by moving from Congress to K Street.

"Former Senator Gordon Smith (R-OR) has made at least $1,650,005 as a media broadcasting industry lobbyist since 2009. Smith is president of the National Association of Broadcasters, a trade group for companies like News Corp and Time Warner. Republic Report has not reviewed NAB disclosures from 2011. Smith's last reported broadcasting lobby salary is 742 percent higher than his Senate salary in 2008.

https://www.thenation.com/article/when-congressman-becomes-lobbyist-he-gets-1452-percent-raise-average/

Why So Much Money Gets Spent on Lobbying? Tuesday, September 28, 2010

"Lobbying is a huge business in Washington. What are these gargantuan sums buying? Former Congressman Lee Hamilton explains "Why So Much Money Gets Spent on Lobbying."

"Recently, The New York Times noted that companies and lobbying firms in Washington are stocking up on Republican lobbyists in anticipation of strong GOP gains in Congress this November. The going rate? Salaries now begin at $300,000, the newspaper reported and can go as high as $1 million.

"This might seem like an outlandish amount of money to pay people even if they are unusually persuasive. Yet when you realize that $3.5 billion got spent on lobbying in 2009 and that there were 2000 lobbyists prowling the hallways of Capitol Hill on the financial reform bill alone, you get an inkling of what's up: That much money wouldn't be involved unless lobbying paid off for the people footing the bill.

"It does because over the last few decades there has been a profound shift in attitude toward Washington. Where the most common refrain a member of Congress once heard was, "Get government off my back," today — despite whatever you might read about mistrust of government — it's very much the opposite: "Put government on my side."

"People from all over the country deluge Washington on behalf of their companies, trade associations, non-profit organizations, labor unions, business groups, health associations, environmental causes…. Every industry, cause and, it sometime seems, enterprise and organization in America wants something from Congress or the federal bureaucracy.

"The people they hire to help them get it are very, very good at what they do. Lobbying is hard work: it requires a lot of old-fashioned shoe leather plus close analysis of arcane language, searching for compromises that will benefit a particular client, carving out exceptions from the general rule and then justifying them in ways that suggest it's all in the national interest.

"And while it's easy to be cynical about what lobbyists do, they represent real people with real interests and often play an important role for members of Congress. A good lobbyist will be one of the most knowledgeable people in the country about his or her field. They provide information about the contents of complex and arcane bills, and especially what impact those bills will have on their industry or business and on Americans in general.

"The result is that for a member of Congress trying to bone up on a complex issue, lobbyists often supply information no one else can muster.

"Yet there are aspects to lobbying that make ordinary Americans squirm. It is not a transparent enterprise. It usually takes place beyond our reach: behind closed office doors or over emails, text messages, Blackberries, chance encounters, and cocktail-party conversations on the exclusive DC social circuit.

"Lobbyists ply their trade not just by supplying information, but also by buying access through campaign contributions, contributions to members' favorite charities, and whatever other tactics they can dream up. And though lobbyists say that all they want is a chance to make their case, that's only partly true — what they really want is access as close to the decision-making point as possible, because in the end what they're aiming for is a specific result: a vote for or against a particular provision, or legislative language favoring their cause.

"Lobbyists are not always successful: if they were, this year's financial reform package would have been strangled at birth. When the tide of public opinion is overwhelming, no array of lobbyists can hold it back.

"But every piece of legislation requires compromises, definitions, debate over who gets included or excluded, and tweaks that the public mostly ignores; that's where lobbyists excel. And these issues often last well beyond the legislative debate: they carry over into the explicit rule-making done by federal bureaucrats.

"The first-amendment rights of lobbyists to ply their trade have long been established. So mitigating their influence and amplifying the voice of ordinary Americans is no small task. But it's not impossible. Voters need to be able to know immediately who is lobbying for what, how much they're spending, and who's funding them; the current situation in which special interests often fight disclosure or hide behind innocuous names is unacceptable in a democracy.

"At the same time, the various research arms of Congress — like the highly regarded Congressional Budget Office — ought to be buttressed so they can fully perform their role of providing unbiased, reliable information to decision-makers. Legislators and their staffs need more time than the leadership often gives them to study legislation and come to their own conclusions about it.

"And lobbyists' undoubted influence on elections should be circumscribed: It's time to insist on total disclosure about all aspects of lobbying, to restrict campaign funds to what can mostly be raised within their constituency, and perhaps even to enact public funding of congressional campaigns.

"(Lee Hamilton is Director of the Center on Congress at Indiana University. He was a member of the U.S. House of Representatives for 34 years.)"

http://centeroncongress.org/why-so-much-money-gets-spent-lobbying

May 8, 2010, Source: Open Secrets.org
Title: "Washington Lobbying Grew to $3.2 Billion Last Year, Despite Economy"
Authors: Center for Responsive Politics - Student Researchers: Alan Grady and Leora Johnson
Faculty Evaluator: John Kramer, Ph.D. Sonoma State University

"According to a study by The Center for Responsive Politics, special interests paid Washington lobbyists $3.2 billion in 2008—more than any other year on record. This was a 13.7 percent increase from 2007 (which broke the record by 7.7 percent over 2006).

"The Center calculates that interest groups spent $17.4 million on lobbying for every day Congress was in session in 2008, or $32,523 per legislator per day. Center director Sheila Krumholz says, "The federal government is handing out billions of dollars by the day, and that translates into job security for lobbyists who can help companies and industries get a piece of the payout."

"Health interests spent more on Federal lobbying than any other economic sector. Their $478.5 million guaranteed the crown for the third year, with the finance, insurance, real estate sector a runner-up, spending $453.5 million. The pharmaceutical/health products industry contributed $230.9 million, raising their last eleven-year total to over $1.6 billion. The second-biggest spender among industries in 2008 was electric utilities, which spent $156.7 million on lobbying, followed by insurance, which spent $153.2 million, and oil and gas, which paid lobbyists $133.2 million. Pro-Israel groups, food processing companies, and the oil and gas industry increased their lobbying expenditures the most (as a percentage) between 2007 and 2008.

"Finance, insurance, and real estate companies have been competing to get a piece of the $700 billion bailout package Congress approved late last year. The companies that reduced lobbying the most are those that declared bankruptcy or were taken over by the federal government and stopped their lobbying operations all together. "Even though some financial, insurance and real estate interests pulled back last year, they still managed to spend more than $450 million as a sector to lobby policymakers. That can buy a lot of influence, and it's a fraction of what the financial sector is reaping in return through the government's bailout program," Krumholz said.

"Business and real estate associations and coalitions were among the organizations that ramped up their lobbying expenditures the most last year. The National Association of Realtors increased spending by 25 percent, from $13.9 million to $17.3 million. The American Bankers Association spent $9.1 million in 2008, a 47 percent increase from 2007. Other industry groups that spent more in 2008 include the Private Equity Council, the Mortgage Bankers Association of America and the Financial Services Roundtable.

"The US Chamber of Commerce remained the number one spender on lobbying in 2008, spending nearly $92 million—more than $350,000 every weekday, and a 73 percent increase over 2007—to advocate for its members' interests. Pro-business associations as a whole increased their lobbying 47 percent between 2007 and 2008.

"With record spending on lobbying, some industries face serious cut backs and have put the brakes on spending, but have not discontinued the practice. Automotive companies decreased the amount they paid lobbyists by 7.6 percent, from $70.9 million to $65.5 million. This is a big change from prior years; auto manufacturers and dealers increased lobbying spending by 21 percent between 2006 and 2007. Between 2007 and 2008 the Alliance of Automobile Manufacturers, which testified before Congress with Detroit's Big Three last year, decreased its reported lobbying by 43 percent, from $12.8 million to $7.3 million. Of the Big Three, only one company, Ford, increased its efforts, though not by much: it went from $7.1 million to $7.7 million, an 8 percent increase.

"Among Washington lobbying firms, Patton Boggs reported the highest revenues from registered lobbying for the fifth year in a row: 41.9 million dollars, an increase over 2006 of more than 20 percent. The firm's most lucrative clients included private equity firm Cerberus Capital Management, confection and pet food maker Mars, communication provider Verizon, pharmaceutical manufacturers Bristol-Myers Squibb and Roche, and the American Association for Justice (formerly the Association of Trial Lawyers of America)."

Update by Lindsay Renick Mayer
"It seems like this should be a classified ad: "Laid off and looking for work? The lobbying industry wants you!" Since we posted this story on OpenSecrets.Org. the lobbying industry has only continued to grow, even as industries across the board have continued to shrink, forcing hundreds of thousands of Americans out of work. This growth could be attributed in part to the economy itself—many executives are looking for some help from the government to keep their businesses afloat. Others are simply taking advantage of the opportunities that a spate of government handouts has presented. But as long as there's a federal government calling the shots, lobbyists will be paid more and more each year to hold their clients' fire to lawmakers' feet.

"Year after year we see increases in lobbying expenditures—in fact, 100 percent over the last decade—and the flurry of activity during the first three months of 2009 indicates that the trend won't come to an end any time soon. Based on records from the Senate Office of Public Records, the nonpartisan Center for Responsive Politics found that from January through March, lobbying increased slightly compared to the same period of time last year, by at least $2.4 million. Unions, organizations and companies spent at least $799.7 million so far this year on sending influence peddlers to Capitol Hill, compared to $797.2 million during the same time in 2008. That might seem like a small increase compared to the billions spent each year on this activity, but in a time of economic turmoil, that's a hefty revenue stream for a single industry.

"That said, the industries that have made the most headlines for the help they've asked for or received from the federal government actually decreased the amount they spent on lobbying in the first three months of 2009 compared to 2008. Recipients of cash from the federal government's Troubled Asset Relief Program (TARP) handed out less money to lobbyists than they had in any quarter of 2008, in part, perhaps, because they faced new rules restricting their lobbying contact with officials in connection with the bailout program. CRP found that TARP recipients have spent $13.9 million on lobbying so far this year, compared to $20.2 million in January through March of last year and $17.8 million in the last three months of 2008. With the government doling out billions of dollars, these sums pale in comparison to the benefit the companies are reaping."

To read more about how lobbying and influence peddling are shaping legislation, keep up with CRP's blog at http://www.opensecrets.org/news/."

http://projectcensored.org/6-lobbyists-buy-congress/

"It is a widely accepted truism in Washington that the place to get rich is on "K Street" — that metonymic shorthand for the Washington lobbying business. But how rich?

"In 2012, we estimate that the median active for-hire Washington lobbyist generated $179,667 in lobbying revenue. That's slightly more than what a member of Congress earns ($174,000) — and has been slightly more since 2010, when the median revenue first eclipsed the member salary.

"But clients appear to be willing to pay significantly more for "revolving door lobbyists" (those lobbyists with government experience) than they do for lobbyists without government experience.

"For 2012, we estimate that lobbyists who list a government staff position somewhere in their lobbyist disclosure firms were associated with a median revenue of $300,000. That's almost three times the median revenue we estimate that lobbyists without government experience generated: $112,500.

"A graph showing the median lobbyist revenue in 2012.

"Figure 1. Graphic credit: The Sunlight Foundation.

"Roughly two-thirds of revolving door lobbyists now generate more revenue trying to influence legislation than lawmakers earn for writing legislation. By contrast, less than 40 percent of those who never worked in government appear to earn more money than members of Congress.

"A graphic showing the amount of lobbyists who earn more than a congressperson.

Figure 2. Graphic credit: The Sunlight Foundation.

"(Interestingly, former government staff generate even more money than former members of Congress. One plausible explanation is that members of Congress earn more revenue from vague responsibilities like strategic advisor or "historian" than they do from "lobbying" subject to LDA reporting requirements.)

"While the gap has always existed, it has widened. In 1998, the revolving door premium was closer to twice the non-revolving door premium. And back in 1998, the majority of contract lobbyists didn't have government experience (or, at least, disclosed government experience).

"That "revolving door" lobbyists generate more revenue than their counterparts should not come as a surprise. Lobbyists with Hill experience are valuable. They have personal relationships and friendships with people who still work in Congress, and hence access. They know the quirks of the procedures, the personalities and who responds well to what. And often, they know the policy pretty well, too, having been around it for years.

"These differences are also consistent with previous research. Both this paper and this paper also find that lobbyists who are well-connected earn a premium in the revenue they generate.

"Revolvers are becoming more corporate

"One reason might be that clients, especially corporations, are willing to pay more for the connections.

"Interestingly, if we look at the percentage of lobbyists' revenues coming from corporate clients, we notice an intriguing divergence starting in 2007. Prior to 2007, the overall share of lobbying revenue from corporate clients is slightly higher for revolving door lobbyists, as compared to lobbyists without government experience, but the difference is negligible.

"Starting in 2007, revolving door lobbyists appear to depend more on corporate clients, while lobbyists without government experience start to depend less on corporate clients. By 2011, there is a noticeable eight percentage point gap, with revolvers depending on corporate clients for roughly three-quarters of their lobbying revenues, while lobbyists without government experience only get two-thirds of their revenue from corporate clients.

"A graph showing the share of revenue from corporate lobbying clients. Figure 3. Graphic credit: The Sunlight Foundation.

"By corporate clients, we mean individual corporations, trade associations and business associations. All other interests are considered non-corporate.

"As always, working with publicly available data is subject to some limitations based on how that data is recorded and disclosed. For a detailed look at how we built and analyzed the dataset – and some cautions about how much we can infer - you can read about our methodology here. Graphics by Amy Cesal and Alexander Furnas."

http://sunlightfoundation.com/blog/2014/01/21/revolving-door-lobbyists-government-experience/

"It's no surprise that American corporations spend billions of dollars each year on lobbying, trying to gain favorable treatment from legislators. What some may find a bit unnerving is the industry that's leading the pack in these efforts.

"You might think our nation's defense and aerospace companies, which have legions of hired guns on Capitol Hill, are the leaders. Or perhaps Big Oil, which is perpetually fighting with environmentalists and consequently needs friends in Washington to block what it considers onerous legislation or regulations.

"In both cases, you'd be wrong. It's actually the pharmaceutical industry that spends the most each year to influence our lawmakers, forking over a total of $2.6 billion on lobbying activities from 1998 through 2012, according to OpenSecrets.org. To get some perspective on just how big that number is, consider that oil and gas companies and their trade associations spent $1.4 billion lobbying Congress over the same time frame while the defense and aerospace industry spent $662 million, a fourth of Big Pharma's total.

"(Number two on the OpenSecrets list, by the way, was my old industry, insurance, which spent $1.8 billion. Although health insurers were among the biggest spenders, the list also includes property and casualty and auto insurers.)

"The huge sum of money our nation's drug makers lavish on Congress each year begs the question, what are they seeking in return? Surely it has something to do with the fact that our nation's legislators turn a blind eye as pharmaceutical companies engage in predatory pricing practices while enjoying exclusive rights to manufacture drugs for 20 years or more. All at the same time that drug costs and drug price inflation are among of the main drivers of health care costs for individuals and families and threaten the fiscal health of our public health care programs.

"To get some idea of the impact of all this on the American health care consumer, it is instructive to compare drug prices in the United States to those in other countries, where governments set a limit on price increases. While it's not news that U.S. residents pay more for the same drugs as our foreign counterparts, what is not as well understood is how that gap grows ever larger each year as drug companies around the world dig ever deeper into the pockets of sick Americans to bolster their profits and meet earnings expectations of Wall Street analysts.

"Each year, the Canadian Government's Patented Medicine Prices Review Board releases a study analyzing drug prices around the world, and according to that study prices in the United States have risen an average of 8 percent a year from 2006 through 2011, while drug prices in Canada have remained flat. The impact that has on the divergence in pricing for the U.S. health care consumer is considerable.

"Back in 2006 for example, U.S. consumers paid about 70 percent more than our northern neighbors for prescription drugs still on patent, according to the Canadian board. Five years later, in 2011, that difference had surged to 100 percent. And with drug price inflation in the United States hitting 11 percent in 2011, that gap will undoubtedly grow ever wider in the future.

"The influence that Big Pharma has purchased by lobbying our nation's legislators has an impact that touches virtually every American. Not only does it affect health insurance premiums, but it also impacts the solvency of our Medicare system, which was expanded in 2006 to include a prescription drug benefit. That was good news for Medicare beneficiaries, of course, but even better news for the pharmaceutical industry. That's because the industry's friends in Congress (and the White House at the time) went along with Big Pharma's demand that Medicare not be allowed to negotiate pricing with drug makers to make medicines more affordable to beneficiaries.

"So not only did drug makers get a huge new revenue stream from taxpayers, but they pulled a fast one on us. Insurers and hospitals and even the Department of Veterans Affairs can bargain with drug makers to get better deals on prices. But, incredibly, not the Medicare program.

"The Congressional Budget Office estimates that the government could save \$112 billion over the coming decade if Congress reconsidered its 2006 gift to drug makers and gave Medicare the ability to negotiate prices.

"Remember that the next time you hear a politician say that the only way to keep the program from going broke is to cut benefits and raise the eligibility age for Medicare from 65 to 67.

"In the weeks ahead, in addition to keeping an eye on how health insurers will be seeking to weaken the consumer protections in ObamaCare so they can keep meeting Wall Street's profit expectations, I will explore the many problematic issues that Congress' hands-off attitude toward the pharmaceutical industry has on the American health care consumer — both on pricing and on drug makers' reluctance to invest in new drugs that don't have blockbuster appeal.

"Federal assistance in the United States, Healthcare reform in the United States, Presidency of Lyndon B. Johnson, Medicare, Health Insurance, Patient Protection and Affordable Care Act, Pharmaceutical industry, Health care in the United States, Medicare Part D, Pharmaceuticals policy, Health care prices, Prescription drug prices in the United States, pharmaceutical industry"

https://www.publicintegrity.org/2013/02/11/12175/opinion-big-pharmas-stranglehold-washington

How much lobbying is there in Washington? It's double what you think. by guest author Tim LaPira. Policy - Nov. 25, 2013, 1:27 p.m.

"Tim LaPira, an Assistant Professor of Political Science at James Madison University, is a Sunlight Foundation Academic Fellow.

"With the help of the lobbying industry, Washington's regional economy seems to have weathered the economic storm of recent years. Curiously, though, the seemingly simple question "How much lobbying is there in Washington?" is surprisingly hard to answer. After Congress passed the 1995 Lobbying Disclosure Act (LDA), which ostensibly required all "lobbyists" to report their activities on behalf of paying clients, the answer should be a no-brainer: just find the legally-mandated disclosure forms, and count them up. The Center for Responsive Politics, with support from the Sunlight Foundation, has been doing this (well!) for years.*

"The problem is that just about everybody in the influence world knows that these numbers fall way short of reality. You might even say "under-the-radar," "stealth," or "shadow" lobbying is a bit of an Open Secret in Washington. What we don't know is just how many shadow lobbyists there are.

"The reason for the lack of transparency is clear: the LDA definition of "lobbyist" is too narrow. If lobbyists want, they can fully comply with the law and do virtually the same influence-for-pay as strategic policy consultants or historical advisers and choose not to disclose. Even lobbyists themselves seem to find little meaning in the term "lobbyist." The American League of Lobbyists even dropped the word "lobbyist" from their name to officially become the Association of Government Relations Professionals.

"Estimating the Actual Size of the Lobbying Industry in Washington

"So, to try to get a better estimate of how many lobbyists "government relations professionals" there are, my collaborator Herschel Thomas and I did the next best thing: we bought the lobbyist phonebook. We drew a random sample of people listed in Lobbyist.info, then had student assistants consult a variety of online sources to determine where they used to work (especially inside the federal government) and what jobs they have now.

"We found that about half of those involved in policy advocacy— our all-of-the-above term for people in the private sector getting paid to influence public policy, regardless if they meet the strict LDA definition of "lobbyist"—did NOT report lobbying activities in 2012 (52.3%, ±5.1% at the 95% confidence level). That is, for every one lobbyist who does the public the favor of disclosing his or her activities, there is one shadow lobbyist listed in directory who does not.

"If we assume that the cost of reported and stealth lobbying is the same—that every one person accounts for an unweighted average of about $270,000 in lobbying influence per year—then we estimate that in the calendar year 2012, organized interests spent about $6.7 billion "relating" with the government.

"Let's put that number in perspective: For every one member of Congress, the influence industry produces about $12.5 million in lobbying. By comparison, the average 2012 budget for a member of the House of Representative's office was only $1.3 million. So, in 2012—a presidential election year, in a down economy, during arguably the least productive Congress ever— "government relaters" accounted for more than nine times the typical House member's official operating expenses.

"What's more, the one-year $6.7 billion tally is about $500 million more than all the campaign money spent on the record setting 2012 election cycle. So if we multiply the one-year lobbying industry estimate by two years, then the relatively non-transparent lobbying industry inside the Beltway generated about twice-plus-$1 billion more in 2011 and 2012 than the relatively highly regulated campaign finance system that influences politics outside the Beltway."

Who Discloses, and Who Does Not?
"This is not exactly an easy question to answer because, well, half of these professionals don't disclose what they're up to. But, we can make some general inferences based on where they used to work. To do this, we simply categorize them into those who've gone through the revolving door, and those who haven't.

Who_Discloses_Lobbying
"Revolvers (lobbyists who worked inside the federal government) are more likely to disclose their lobbying, though 41% still choose to hide it. On the other hand, conventional lobbyists (those who were never on the federal payroll) are much more likely to be opaque about their influence activities.

"Which begs the question: Why are revolvers more transparent? Again, we can't say for sure because we don't have good, publicly disclosed data on the kind of influence activities these people are engaged in now. So we look more closely at where they used to work in the federal government for some clues."

Reg_vs_shadow_by branch
"Among revolvers only, those who previously worked in Congress were much more likely to file lobbying disclosure reports ($z = 3.6$, $p < 0.001$). But, those who worked in bureaucracies in the executive branch are much less likely to do so ($z = -3.5$, $p < 0.001$). Apparently, not only is the legal term for "lobbyist" insufficiently narrow, there is little consensus on what it means to be a lobbyist, especially between those who worked on Capitol Hill versus those who worked in a federal agency.

"The take away: it's "lobbying" if lobbyists are lobbying on Dodd-Frank when it was just a bill in Congress, but it's "not-lobbying" if lobbyists are lobbying on Dodd-Frank when it is a proposed regulation at the Commodity Futures Trading Commission. Or the Treasury Department. Or the SEC. Or the FDIC. Or the Fed. Or, if they're lobbying on the thousands of other regulations proposed by federal agencies every year.

"Combine the semantic confusion of what it means to be a "lobbyist," the "Scarlet L" stigma associated with what is an otherwise ethical profession, and the disincentives of the Obama administration's rules against lobbyists working in the administration, we end up with less—not more—transparency about lobbying in Washington.

"Bottom line: it's needlessly hard to figure how much lobbying there actually is in Washington. Now, only if we could get somebody to relate that idea to Congress…one step in the right direction would be to support the Lobbying Disclosure Enhancement Act, which would close the loophole that shadow lobbyists use to avoid disclosure.

Graphics by Amy Cesal and Alexander Furnas.

Lobbying the Judicial Branch

"Interest groups work to influence the courts in a number of ways. Interest groups often file amicus curiae (friend of the court) briefs, presenting an argument in favor of a particular issue. Sometimes interest groups file lawsuits against the government or other parties. For example, the NAACP worked for years to bring civil rights cases to the Supreme Court. The American Civil Liberties Union also makes extensive use of the courts. http://www.sparknotes.com/us-government-and-politics/american-government/interest-groups/section3.rhtml

Lobbyists Help Pay the Bill at Republican Lawmakers' Retreat

January 30, 2014·4:00 PM ET

Heard on All Things Considered

"House Republicans are taking a three-day retreat this week, paid in part by a lobbyist-run institute. Members of the group get access to the lawmakers at the closed-door event on Maryland's Eastern Shore.

ROBERT SIEGEL, HOST:

"House Republicans are midway through their annual retreat. The three-day get-together is happening at a waterside hotel on Maryland's

Eastern Shore. Lawmakers of both parties hold this kind of annual partisan conference to map out legislative strategy. And as usual, there's some controversy over who's footing the bill for them.

Here's NPR's Peter Overby.

"PETER OVERBY, BYLINE: The Republican conference is at the Hyatt Regency in Cambridge, Maryland. The hotel has a championship golf course and four lighted tennis courts. But the temperature is stuck below freezing and the lawmakers have a busy schedule, including sessions on such tough issues as immigration reform and health care. They're also getting advice from a consultant on how to connect with voters. But it's the financing of the GOP retreat that regularly attracts attention. It's made possible by the Congressional Institute, a tax-exempt social welfare organization run by Republican lobbyists.

"MARK STRAND: They've decided, Republicans, that they didn't want to use taxpayer dollars to do these retreats.

"OVERBY: Mark Strand, the institute's president, says that was 27 years ago.

"STRAND: And the Congressional Institute was formed back then and it's been attempting to help with planning and making these conferences work as effectively as possible.

"OVERBY: The Institute covers the event itself.

"STRAND: But the members of Congress pay their own way.

"OVERBY: The Congressional Institute has a board of directors, mostly veteran Republican lobbyists who also have deep experience as congressional staffers. Other lobbyists join the institute as members, and it's their contributions that underwrite the GOP retreat. The institute's lobbyist members aren't allowed in the working sessions, but Strand says they do get to mix with the lawmakers.

"STRAND: The reception and the dinner of the first night they attend, which is typical for, you know, most organizations in Washington, D.C., that have support. So they just attend the reception, just the dinner, and then they go home the next morning.

"OVERBY: As for the House Democrats, they're booked into the same Hyatt Regency two weeks from now. But for financing the event, they take the opposite approach.

"REPRESENTATIVE XAVIER BECERRA: I can speak to what Democrats are doing. We consider this official work.

"OVERBY: This is California Congressman Xavier Becerra. He chairs the Democratic caucus, which pays for its retreat out of its regular budget. That is, taxpayer dollars.

"BECERRA: We consider this an opportunity to discuss issues and we consider it an opportunity to discuss issues with people who have a vote, who are officially elected to do work. We don't invite lobbyists.

"OVERBY: Now, this isn't to say advocates are barred from Democratic retreats. The caucus often hears speakers from liberal think tanks and nonprofit groups. But it doesn't schmooze with lobbyists, at least not at the retreats. Ross Baker is a Rutgers University political scientist and a long-time Congress watcher. He says there are all sorts of congressional retreats.

"ROSS BAKER: They're just for a variety of reasons and I think mostly it's just to kind of get out of town.

"OVERBY: Not that Washington lacks for conference space.

"BAKER: There seems to be a kind of refreshment factor in getting as far away from Washington as possible without going too far.

"OVERBY: In fact, starting in the late 1990s, there were a series of retreats aimed at promoting civility in the House. This came after Democrats had lost their 40-year House majority and a new GOP majority had impeached President Bill Clinton. Some prominent Republicans and Democrats organized bipartisan retreats, first in Hershey, Pennsylvania, and later at The Greenbrier resort in West Virginia. The Congressional Institute was involved in the effort. But each year, attendance shrank. Baker's assessment...

"BAKER: The people who showed up were people who cared about civility. And the people who probably needed to be there weren't there.

"OVERBY: Not like the Republican and Democratic strategy retreats over on the Eastern Shore. These are events where the party leaders are taking roll. Peter Overby, NPR News, Washington."

http://www.npr.org/2014/01/30/268964623/lobbyists-help-pay -the-bill-at-republican-lawmakers-retreat

* In the interest of full, ahem, disclosure: LaPira was the researcher responsible for editing the OpenSecrets' Lobbying Database from 2005-2007.

http://sunlightfoundation.com/blog/2013/11/25/how-much-lobbying-is-there-in-washington-its-double-what-you-think/

What is lobbying?

Federal statute defines lobbying as any communication made on behalf of a client to members of Congress, congressional staffers, the president, White House staff and high-level employees of nearly 200 agencies, regarding the formulation, modification, or adoption of legislation.

Who is a lobbyist?

What is a lobbyist is a person hired directly by an organization or through a firm for services that include making more than one "lobbying contact" on behalf of a client, and who spends at least 20 percent of his or her time during a six-month period engaged in lobbying activity.

- According to the Center for Public Integrity, more than 22,000 companies and organizations have employed 3,500 lobbying firms and more than 27,000 lobbyists since 1998.

Who lobbies?

Corporations, organizations, much of the Fortune 500, universities, environmental and non-profit groups, and even churches lobby the federal government.

- According to the Center for Public Integrity, the most commonly lobbied issue is budget and appropriations.

Who regulates lobbying?

The Secretary of the Senate and the Clerk of the House of Representatives oversee federal lobbying. According to the Lobbying Disclosure Act of 1995, those offices are charged with providing guidance on lobbying disclosure, ensuring the timeliness and accuracy of required reports, and making those reports available to the public.

- According to a Center for Public Integrity report, nearly 14,000 documents that should have been filed periodically with the Senate Office of Public Records are missing.
- Forty-nine out of the top 50 lobbying firms failed to file required forms during the last six years.

Who must register to lobby with the federal government?

Organizations that employ lobbyists in house must register with Congress if their lobbying expenditures exceed $24,500 during a six-month period. Lobbying firms must file a separate registration – at least 45 days after first contact – for each client whose lobbying billings exceed $6,000 for a six-month period.

- According to a Center for Public Integrity report, nearly 300 individuals and entities lobbied without filing proper registration forms.
- In addition, more than 2,000 initial registrations were filed after the 45-day time frame.

What information must organizations lobbying disclose to the federal government?

Organizations must disclose on a semiannual basis: (1) the issues lobbied during that period, including specific bills and regulations; (2) the names of lobbyists employed by the client; and (3) the federal agencies contacted. Lobbying firms filing on behalf of a client must disclose an estimate of the total lobbying-related income earned from the client during the period. Organizations employing their own lobbyists must disclose an estimate of total lobbying-related expenditures for that period.

What are the penalties for non-compliance with lobbying disclosure laws?

- A lobbyist who knowingly fails to comply with any provision of the law may be subjected to a civil fine, the maximum of which can be $50,000.
- The House and Senate office must refer such alleged non-compliers to the U.S. Attorney for the District of Columbia, the principal prosecutor for federal criminal and civil offenses committed in Washington, D.C.

Can a former member of Congress, legislative staff or senior executive branch staff lobby on the Hill (revolving door)?

Government ethics law prohibits former members of Congress, senior legislative staff, and senior executive branch staff from lobbying their former department or agency for one year after leaving government. These officials must report their past positions on their lobbying registration forms for the first two years after leaving government.

- Former members of Congress retain access to the members-only dining facilities, gymnasiums, cloakrooms and the chamber floors—areas not accessible to others.
- According to a Center for Public Integrity report, more than 2,200 former federal employees, including 273 former White House

staffers, and nearly 250 former members of Congress and agency heads have registered as federal lobbyists between 1998 and 2004.

Can relatives of members of Congress work as lobbyists?

Relatives of members of Congress can and do register to lobby. According to the Senate Ethics Manual, "the decision on whether a spouse may lobby the Senate is generally a decision for the Senator and his or her spouse, giving due regard to the potential reflection upon the Senate."

- Relatives of Congress members who have registered to lobby include the wife of Rep. Roy Blunt R-Mo., the wife of former Sen. Tom Daschle, D-S. D and the son of Sen. Harry Reid D-Nev.

Can lobbyists pay for travel for members of Congress?

According to House and Senate Ethics Rules:

- Lawmakers and their employees cannot accept payment for travel from lobbyists or lobbying firms, even if a non-lobbyist client promises later reimbursement.

Can lobbyists arrange travel for members of Congress?

Lobbyists may set up, book, and travel with members of Congress on vacations, as long as they do not use personal or lobbying firm funds to pay for the trip.

Can lobbyists give gifts to members of Congress?

Lobbyists can give gifts (from meals to clothing to rounds of golf) to members of Congress that are less than $50 in value. The total value of gifts given to one member cannot exceed $100 in a year.

- Lobbyists may not contribute to the legal expense funds of members of Congress or the charities controlled by a member of Congress.

Can lobbyists make political donations?

Lobbyists may make political donations under the same guidelines as other Americans. Lobbyists cannot give more than $5,000 to any political action committee per calendar year. They can, however, work on campaigns and serve as the treasurers of political action committees.

- According to a Center for Public Integrity report, federally registered lobbyists served as the treasurers of at least 800 political action committees since 1998.
- These lobbyists led committees have spent more than $525 million to influence the political process since 1998.
- At least 79 members of Congress have appointed lobbyists to head their campaign committees or leadership PACs since 1998.

Can lobbyists write legislation?

Lobbyists can and at times do write legislation, sometimes at the behest of a member of Congress or their staff. Often, lobbyists will submit language to a member who has a working relationship with the industry which the lobbyist represents.

https://www.publicintegrity.org/2006/01/18/6546/lobbying-faq

Who speaks for you in Washington? Odds are, at least one lobbyist. For every member of Congress in 2011, there were 23 lobbyists trying to twist their arms. 12,719 of them, and they spent big money: $3.3 billion in 2011, double what they spent just 10 years before.

By far, the single biggest spender in the lobbying game was the U.S. Chamber of Commerce, which shelled out $66 million. A distant second was General Electric with $26 million.

Looking at whole industries, the pharmaceutical/health products sector far outspent others in 2011 – a critical year when health care reform regulations were being written. The industry spent more than $240 million.

Check out our infographic for more on lobbyists and other big spenders. See "What Do Others Say?" for more views. Then add to the discussion below. Do you think lobbyists play an appropriate role in Washington?

http://www.facethefactsusa.org/facts/power-numbers-lobbyists-have-congress-covered

Where do they lobby?

Where do these former legislators work in their lobbying careers? There are four types of organizations (given with examples from the retirement class of 2014):

- A lobbying firm. That's where, for instance, Pryor and Kingston went to work.
- A private corporation that does its own lobbying. Johanns, who represented the heavily agricultural state of Nebraska and who served on the Senate Agriculture, Nutrition and Forestry Committee, now works for agricultural equipment manufacturer John Deere. Miller now works for the educational technology company Cengage Learning.
- A trade association. For instance, former Congresswoman Jo Ann Emerson, who served on the House Appropriations subcommittee

responsible for rural development while in Congress, is now the director of the National Rural Electric Cooperative Association).

- Or a nonprofit organization. For instance, former Rep. Jo Bonner now lobbies for the University of Alabama.

Of the former members of Congress who go on to lobby after retiring from Congress, the vast majority (78 percent of former House members and 87 percent of former senators) lobby for firms. We do not investigate why this is so, but presumably, firms offer high pay.

But not all former members who lobby go this route. A third of them attempt to start their own firms or join a family firm. For instance, Waxman joined his son's firm, Waxman Strategies.

The "revolving door" that brings lobbyists and high-level government officials into each other's line of work is a huge and growing part of Washington. There are serious normative implications, and plenty of research questions out there to pursue. Before undertaking that research, we need to know which and how many government officials are taking part. This study is an important first step in untangling the web of influence and implications of this relatively recent phenomenon.

Note added on Jan. 20, 2016: Kingston and Waxman are registered lobbyists. However, in a display of how lax lobbying requirements are, neither Miller nor Cantor are registered as lobbyists despite the facts that: both live and work in Washington D.C.; Miller works directly on public policy issues, and Cantor interacts with current members of Congress on a regular basis.

Jeffrey Lazarus is an associate professor of political science at Georgia State University.

https://www.washingtonpost.com/news/monkey-cage/wp/2016/01/15/which-members-of-congress-become-lobbyists-the-ones-with-the-most-power-heres-the-data/

V

CORRUPT MEMBERS OF CONGRESS

" Politics is not a bad profession. If you succeed, there are many rewards; if you disgrace yourself, you can always write a book."
Ronald Reagan

We the people are the rightful masters of both Congress and the Courts, not to overthrow the Constitution, but to overthrow the men who pervert the Constitution. – Abraham Lincoln.

The following was the final column written by Charlie Reese and always bears repeating:

"Charley Reese's final column for the Orlando Sentinel... He was a journalist for 49 years. This was his last column. Be sure to read the Tax List at the end.

"This is about as clear and easy to understand as it can be. The article below is completely neutral, neither anti-republican or democrat. Charlie Reese, a retired reporter for the Orlando Sentinel, has hit the nail directly on the head, defining clearly who it is that in the final analysis must assume responsibility for the judgments made that impact each one of us every day. It's a short but good read. Worth the time. Worth remembering!

"545 vs. 300,000,000 People

"By Charlie Reese

Politicians are the only people in the world who create problems and then campaign against them.

Have you ever wondered, if both the Democrats and the Republicans are against deficits? Why do we have deficits?

Have you ever wondered, if all the politicians are against inflation and high taxes? Why do we have inflation and high taxes?

You and I don't propose a federal budget. The President does.

You and I don't have the Constitutional authority to vote on appropriations. The House of Representatives does.

You and I don't write the tax code, Congress does.

You and I don't set fiscal policy, Congress does.

You and I don't control monetary policy, the Federal Reserve Bank does.

One hundred senators, 435 congressmen, one President, and nine Supreme Court justices equates to 545 human beings out of the 300 million are directly, legally, morally, and individually responsible for the domestic problems that plague this country.

I excluded the members of the Federal Reserve Board because that problem was created by the Congress. In 1913, Congress delegated its Constitutional duty to provide a sound currency to a federally chartered, but private, central bank.

I excluded all the special interests and lobbyists for a sound reason. They have no legal authority. They have no ability to coerce a senator, a congressman, or a President to do one cotton-picking thing. I don't care if they offer a politician $1 million dollars in cash. The politician has the power to accept or reject it. No matter what the lobbyist promises, it is the legislator's responsibility to determine how he votes.

Those 545 human beings spend much of their energy convincing you that what they did is not their fault. They cooperate in this common con regardless of party.

What separates a politician from a normal human being is an excessive amount of gall. No normal human being would have the gall of a Speaker, who stood up and criticized the President for creating deficits. The President can only propose a budget. He cannot force the Congress to accept it.

It seems inconceivable to me that a nation of 300 million cannot replace 545 people who stand convicted — by present facts — of incompetence and irresponsibility. I can't think of a single domestic problem that is not traceable directly to those 545 people. When you fully grasp the plain truth that 545 people exercise the power of the federal government, then it must follow that what exists is what they want to exist.

If the tax code is unfair, it's because they want it unfair.

If the budget is in the red, it's because they want it in the red.

If the Army & Marines are in Iraq and Afghanistan, it's because they want them in Iraq and Afghanistan...

If they do not receive social security but are on an elite retirement plan not available to the people, it's because they want it that way.

There are no insoluble government problems.

Do not let these 545 people shift the blame to bureaucrats, whom they hire and whose jobs they can abolish; to lobbyists, whose gifts and advice they can reject; to regulators, to whom they give the power to regulate and from whom they can take this power. Above all, do not let them con you into the belief that there exists disembodied mystical forces like "the economy," "inflation," or "politics" that prevent them from doing what they take an oath to do.

Those 545 people, and they alone are responsible.

They and they alone have the power.

They and they alone should be held accountable by the people who are their bosses.

Provided the voters have the gumption to manage their own employees...

We should vote all of them out of office and clean up their mess!"

It's true http://www.snopes.com/politics/soapbox/reese.asp

This might be funny if it weren't so true.

Tax his land, Tax his bed, Tax the table, At which he's fed.

Tax his tractor, Tax his mule, Teach him taxes Are the rule.

Tax his work, Tax his pay, He works for peanuts anyway!

Tax his cow, Tax his goat, Tax his pants, Tax his coat.

Tax his ties, Tax his shirt, Tax his work, Tax his dirt.

Tax his tobacco, Tax his drink, Tax him if he Tries to think.

Tax his cigars, Tax his beer if he cries Tax his tears.

Tax his car, Tax his gas, Find other ways to tax his ass.

Tax all he has. Then let him know that you won't be done till he has no dough.

When he screams and hollers; Then tax him some more, Tax him till He's good and sore.

Then tax his coffin, Tax his grave, Tax the sod in Which he's laid...
Put these words Upon his tomb, 'Taxes drove me to my doom...'
When he's gone, do not relax, it's time to apply The inheritance tax.

Plus, Accounts Receivable Tax
Building Permit Tax
CDL license Tax
Cigarette Tax
Marijuana Tax
Corporate Income Tax
Dog License Tax
Excise Taxes
Federal Income Tax
Federal
Unemployment Tax (FUTA)
Fishing License Tax
Food License Tax
Fuel Permit Tax
Gasoline Tax (currently 44.75
cents per gallon)
Gross Receipts Tax
Hunting License Tax
Inheritance Tax
Inventory Tax
IRS Interest Charges IRS
Penalties (tax on top of tax)
Liquor Tax
Luxury Taxes
Marriage License Tax
Medicare Tax
Personal Property Tax
Property Tax

Real Estate Tax
Service Charge Tax
Social Security Tax
Road Usage Tax
Recreational Vehicle Tax
Sales Tax
School Tax
State Income Tax
State
Unemployment Tax (SUTA)
Telephone Federal Excise Tax
Telephone Federal Universal
Service Fee Tax
Telephone Federal, State and
Local Surcharge Taxes
Telephone Minimum
Usage Surcharge Tax
Telephone Recurring and
Nonrecurring Charges Tax
Telephone State and Local Tax
Telephone Usage Charge Tax
Utility Taxes
Vehicle License
Registration Tax
Vehicle Sales Tax
Watercraft Registration Tax
Well Permit Tax
Workers Compensation Tax

Do you still think this is funny? How many more taxes can our government come up with?

Not one of these taxes existed 100 years ago, & our nation was the most prosperous in the world.

We had absolutely no national debt, we had the largest middle class in the world, and Mom stayed home to raise the kids.

What in the heck happened?

Can you spell 'politicians?"

"Gift Rules for Congress

Both houses of Congress have specific regulations concerning gifts that may be accepted by Members and staff. The term "gift" covers any gratuity, favor, discount, entertainment, hospitality, loan, or other item having monetary value. In particular, the term includes services, training, transportation, lodging and meals, whether provided in- kind, by the purchase of a ticket, payment in advance, or reimbursement after the expense has been incurred.

A gift is deemed to be "accepted" if a Member or employee of Congress exercises dominion over or control of the gift. It does not matter whether it would be used personally by the individual or anybody else.

A gift to a family member or any other individual is considered a gift to the Member or employee of Congress if there is reason to believe the gift was given because of his/her official position.

General Provisions

While gifts rules for the House and the Senate tend to be similar, the House on January 4th and 5th, 2007, adopted a new set of gift restrictions, especially as they apply to lobbyists. The Senate is likely to follow suit.

Generally, a Member or employee of Congress may accept a gift only if it is unsolicited and the:

- Gift is valued at less than $50;
- Aggregate value of gifts from one source in a calendar year is less than $100, though no gifts with a value below $10 count toward the $100 annual limit;
- Gift is not cash or a cash equivalent (e.g. stocks and bonds). The only exceptions are gifts made by relatives and parts of an inheritance;
- Gift is not offered under circumstances that might be construed by reasonable persons as influencing the performance of their governmental duties;

- Tickets to sporting and entertainment events must be valued at face value and cannot be artificially lowered to meet the gift limits.

Gift Ban for Lobbyists, Lobbying Organizations and Agents of Foreign Principals

In the House, more stringent gift rules apply to gifts and travel benefits provided by lobbyists, lobbying organization and agents of a foreign principal. A Member or employee of the House may not accept a gift of any value from a registered lobbyist, an organization that employs a registered lobbyist or an agent of a foreign principal, subject to certain exceptions described below. Furthermore, in most situations, the gift ban covers employees of organizations that employ lobbyists, even if the employee is not a lobbyist and pays for the gift with personal funds.

A 501(c)(3) charity may be subject to the gift ban if it employs or retains a lobbyist, except for the following situation. A lawmaker may accept free attendance at a charity event hosted by a 501(c)(3) charity, even if the event is not a widely-attended event and regardless of whether the charity employs a lobbyist. Local transportation and lodging may be included in "free attendance" so long as all of the net proceeds benefit the charity and the travel and lodging expenses are paid for by the charity.

In addition to the gift ban in the House applicable to lobbyists, lobbying organizations and foreign agents, the gift rules of both the House and the Senate have other specific prohibitions for gifts from registered lobbyists and foreign agents. Members and employees of Congress may not accept:

1. Anything provided by a registered lobbyist or a foreign agent to an entity that is maintained or controlled by a Member or employee of Congress;
2. Charitable contributions from lobbyists and foreign agents expressly solicited by a Member or employee (except in lieu of honoraria);
3. Contributions from lobbyists or foreign agents to a conference, retreat, or similar event, sponsored by or affiliated with an official congressional committee or caucus;
4. Contributions from lobbyists and foreign agents to legal defense funds of Members, officers and employees of Congress;

5. Gifts of personal hospitality unless lobbyists or agents of foreign principals qualify as personal friends; and

6. Reimbursements from lobbyists and foreign agents for officially-connected travel. Many of the same restrictions apply to lobbying organizations. (see "Summary of Congressional Travel Rules").

These limitations make the gift rules very strict. However, numerous exceptions dramatically reduce the scope of the regulations. There are 24 exceptions to the gift rules in general, many of which also apply to the gift ban from lobbyists, lobbying organizations, and agents of foreign principals.

Exceptions to Congressional Gift Rules

A Member or employee of Congress may accept gifts that exceed the value limit for individual gifts and annual limit for gifts from one source if they are subject to one of 24 exceptions. Most of these exceptions (unless otherwise noted) also apply to the gift ban for lobbyists, lobbying organizations and agents of a foreign principal. These exceptions are:

1. Anything for which the Member or employee pays the market value, or does not use and promptly returns. If it is not practicable to return the item to the giver because it is perishable, it may be given to an appropriate charity or discarded.

2. Political contributions reported under the law, or attendance at a fundraising event sponsored by a political organization.

3. Gifts from relatives. A "relative" means a father, mother, son, daughter, brother, sister, uncle, aunt, great aunt, great uncle, first cousin, nephew, niece, husband, wife, grandfather, grandmother, grandson, granddaughter, father-in-law, mother-in-law, son-in-law, daughter-in-law, brother-in-law, sister-in-law, stepfather, stepmother, stepson, stepdaughter, stepbrother, stepsister, half-brother, half-sister, or who is the grandfather or grandmother of the spouse of the individual. Fiancés and fiancées are also subject to this exception, which is why engagement rings and other tokens are not counted towards the gift limit

4. Anything, including personal hospitality, provided by an individual on the basis of a personal friendship. However, such gifts may not exceed $250 in value unless the recipient gets approval from the respective Ethics Committee. Though the rule does not explicitly exempt gifts given because of a significant, personal, dating relationship, the Ethics Committees may grant a waiver permitting the recipient to accept such a gift.

5. Contributions or payments to an approved legal expense trust fund. Officeholders may establish this fund to pay for legal expenses associated with official congressional duties. The individual establishing the fund may make unlimited contributions. However, contributions to a legal defense fund maintained by a Member of the House are limited to $5,000 per year and no lobbyist or foreign agent may contribute to such a fund. In the Senate, contributions to a legal defense fund are limited to $10,000 and no lobbyist, foreign agent, congressional staff person, corporation or labor union may contribute to it.

6. Gifts from another Member or employee of Congress. Whereas Members of Congress are allowed to make any gifts to other Members, the situation related to congressional staff is more complicated because federal employees are prohibited by law from giving a gift to a superior without approval of the respective Ethics Committee. However, both Ethics Committees usually permit voluntary gifts given on specific occasions like marriage, retirement, birth of a child, birthday or anniversary. On the other hand, congressional employees are strictly prohibited from making contributions to the campaign of their supervising Member of Congress.

7. Food, refreshments, lodging, and other benefits that result from the outside business or employment of the Member, or employee, or his/her spouse. The benefits should be customarily provided and not offered or enhanced because of the official position of the Member or employee. For example, the exception covers benefits customarily provided by a prospective employer in connection with bona fide employment discussions, or benefits provided by a political

organization in connection with a fundraising or campaign event sponsored by the organization.

8. Pension and other benefits resulting from continued participation in an employee welfare and benefits plan maintained by a former employer. Such benefits are considered earnings from the previous employment rather than a gift. At the same time, neither the former employer nor the recipient may continue to contribute to the pension or the benefit plan.

9. Informational materials, such as books, articles, periodicals, audio or videotapes, sent to the office.

10. Awards or prizes won in contests open to the public. The group of competitors should be chosen on the basis of talent. However, the awards and prizes received under this exception must be disclosed as earned income in the annual disclosure statements.

11. Honorary degrees (and associated travel, food, refreshments, and entertainment) and other bona fide, non-momentary awards presented in recognition of public service. If the value of the award is more than $250, the Member or employee of Congress must disclose acceptance of the award in the annual disclosure form. If the event where a cash award is bestowed is not open too public, the recipient may accept the honor of the award, but the proposed cash award should be given directly to a designated charity, unless the waiver is guaranteed by the respective Ethics Committee.

12. Donations of products from the home state that are intended primarily for promotional purposes. To be covered with this exemption, the gifts must be of minimal value to any individual recipient, come from producers or distributors of the Member's home state and be available to office visitors. However, a loan of art work from home state producers or distributors is not considered a gift.

13. Training in the interest of Congress. Training expenditures, including food and refreshments furnished to all attendees as an integral part of the training, are exempt from the gift limitations. However, the rules don't allow a Member or employee to accept reimbursement for transportation or lodging in connection with the training (but provision of local transportation is permitted).

14. Bequests, inheritances, and other transfers at death.

15. Any item whose receipt is authorized by the Foreign Gifts and Decorations Act, the Mutual Educational and Cultural Exchange Act, or any other statute. MECEA covers only gifts of travel funded by foreign governments. FGDA authorizes Members and employees to accept gifts of minimal value tendered as a souvenir or a mark of courtesy. Under the current regulations, the upper limit of value is $100 for the Senate and $260 for the House. In addition, FGDA allows accepting, but not retaining, a gift of more than the defined the gift would likely cause offense or embarrassment or otherwise adversely affect the foreign relations of the United States. Such gifts are to be accepted on behalf of the United States. Within 60 days the gifts must be turned over to the Clerk of the House or the Secretary of the Senate for disposal. On the other hand, with the consent of the respective Ethics Committee the Member or employee may retain the gift for display in his or her office or other official use.

16. Anything paid for by the Federal government, or secured by the Government under a Government contract. State and local governmental agencies are not exempt from the gift restriction, or the gift ban if they employ a lobbyist. In addition, a Member or employee may accept gifts from Native American groups that are federally recognized.

17. Personal hospitality, other than from a registered lobbyist, lobbying organization or agent of a foreign principal. This exemption covers hospitality in any personal residence that an individual owns or leases under a lease unrelated to the individual's employment. Additionally, personal hospitality must be paid by the individual himself, not by a corporation or firm, even if the corporation or firm is wholly owned by the individual.

18. Free attendance at a widely attended event that is officially related to Congressional duties.

- An event is considered widely attended when at least 25 persons from outside Congress are expected to attend.
- The event should be open to members from a given industry or profession, or to a range of persons interested in an issue.

- Free attendance does not include entertainment collateral to the event, such as tickets to a sporting or some other purely recreational event.
- The exemption also does not cover food or refreshments that are not taken in a group setting with substantially all of the other attendees.
- A ticket to a sporting or recreational event that is not a charity must come within the gift limit of $49.99 and the aggregate limit from the source of $99.99 per year.

  Even lobbyists, lobbying firms or foreign agents may sponsor a widely attended event.

19. Free attendance at a charity event, as long as the charity event is not sponsored or paid for by a registered lobbyist, lobbying organization or agent of a foreign principal. Even free attendance to a charity event provided by a legitimate sponsor that is substantially recreational may be accepted.

20. Opportunities and benefits that are offered because of the Member's or employee's membership in a group that is not defined on the basis of the employment with Congress. This exemption includes benefits or commercial loans available to the public or all federal employees, reduced fees for participation in organization activities offered to all government employees by professional organizations, etc.

21. A plaque, trophy, or other item that is substantially commemorative in nature and that is intended solely for presentation. However, such items whose value exceeds $250 must be listed on annual financial disclosure statements.

22. Anything for which a waiver is granted by the respective Ethics Committee. The waivers are granted in unusual cases and cover wedding gifts, gifts given because of a significant, personal, dating relationship, etc.

23. Food or refreshments of a nominal value offered other than as part of a meal, known as the "toothpick rule." The Ethics Committees distinguishes the provision of "food" from the sharing of a "meal." A reception where the attendees consume food or drink standing up, like a continental style breakfast where coffee and donuts are served, is not considered a meal

and therefore is covered by the exemption. Generally, such reception food should avoid coinciding with lunch time.

The food sent to a congressional office for consumption by a group of the office's employees (commonly known as the 'pizza rule') is subject to different regulations. In the Senate it is regarded as one gift to the Member of Congress and is subject to the $49.99 per single gift limit and $99.99 annual gift limit. This result may not be avoided by having the food divided into separate packages labeled with the names of individual staff members. In the House, however, the value of perishable food shall be allocated among the individual recipients and not to the Member. In the House, such meals may not be accepted from lobbyists, lobbying organizations or agents of a foreign principal.

24. An item of little intrinsic value such as a greeting card or T-shirt.

Ethics Training for Members and Employees of Congress

The congressional ethics committees provide regular ethics training seminars to all Members and employees of Congress, In the House, all employees are required to receive at least one hour of ethics training annually; officers and senior employees must receive at least two hours of ethics training annually. Training seminars are provided in class as well through video replays of live training sessions.

Since pre-approval for offering or receiving gifts is strongly encouraged, Members and employees of Congress, as well as the general public, may seek advice from the House ethics committee's Office of Advice and Education at (202) 225-7103. Similar assistance is expected to be offered by the Senate ethics committee upon final approval of its new gift rules."

http://www.cleanupwashington.org/lobbying/page.cfm?pageid=43

An individual no longer runs for Congress as a patriot, to represent our country, because he or she is a democrat or a republican, because he or she is a career politician, or because they want to represent "the people." They run for Congress to line their pockets and get rich. For this reason, we do need term limits. We need term limits to weed out the corruptors in Washington. We need term limits so that some real work can get done. We need term limits so that we will have

Representatives and Senators instead of politicians. We need term limits so that our Representatives will listen to "*the people.*"

A politician needs money and they need votes. While I may expect the person I vote for to look out for our country's interest and my interest if I vote for him or her, a large campaign contributor may expect that their money will get repaid in the form of favorable legislation, less stringent regulations, perhaps a political appointment, a government contract, or some other form of payback.

Where does all of this money come from? Who is getting the money? Who is donating the money?

A congressman does not stop raising money once he is elected. The first thing on the agenda is to become a member of as many committees as you can. Congressional committees review and revise legislation before it is voted on by the full legislature. Committee members are principal targets for donations from industries and concerns that they regulate.

Committees decide which bills and resolutions move forward for consideration by the House or Senate as a whole. Committee chairmen have enormous influence over this process. There are more than twenty Senate and House Committees and at least five joint Committees.

Republicans and Democrats that received funds from George Soros during the 2016 election cycle are as follows:

Total Contributions

Clinton, Hillary (D) Pres $22,400

Lowey, Nita M (D-NY) House $15,800

Feingold, Russ (D-WI) Senate $13,500

Kander, Jason (D-MO) Senate $11,100

Bennet, Michael F (D-CO) Senate $10,800

Duckworth, Tammy (D-IL) House $10,800

Hassan, Maggie (D-NH) Senate $10,800

McGinty, Katie (D-PA) Senate $10,800

Ryan, Paul (R-WI) House $10,800

Schumer, Charles E (D-NY) Senate $10,800

Teachout, Zephyr (D-NY) House $10,800

Blumenthal, Richard (D-CT) Senate $8,100

Maloney, Sean Patrick (D-NY) House $8,100

Throne-Holst, Anna (D-NY) House $8,100

Ellison, Keith (D-MN) House $5,400

Harris, Kamala D (D-CA) Senate $5,400
Leahy, Patrick (D-VT) Senate $5,400
Masto, Catherine Cortez (D-NV) Senate $5,400
Murphy, Patrick (D-FL) House $5,400
Ross, Deborah (D-NC) Senate $5,400
Strickland, Ted (D-OH) Senate $5,400
Nadler, Jerrold (D-NY) House $5,200
Kaine, Tim (D-VA) Senate $3,700
Graham, Lindsey (R-SC) Senate $3,500
Applegate, Douglas L (D-CA) House $2,700
Bush, Jeb (R) Pres $2,700
Caforio, Bryan (D-CA) House $2,700
Carroll, Morgan (D-CO) House $2,700
Crist, Charlie (D-FL) House $2,700
Derrick, Mike (D-NY) House $2,700
Hartman, Christina (D-PA) House $2,700
Kasich, John (R) Pres $2,700
Kihuen, Ruben (D-NV) House $2,700
Mowrer, Jim (D-IA) House $2,700
Murray, Patty (D-WA) Senate $2,700
Myers, Kim (D-NY) House $2,700
Rubio, Marco (R-FL) Senate $2,700
Santarsiero, Steve (D-PA) House $2,700
Shea-Porter, Carol (D-NH) House $2,700
Vernon, Monica (D-IA) House $2,700
Boehner, John (R-OH) House $2,600
Engel, Eliot L (D-NY) House $2,500
Heck, Joe (R-NV) House $2,500
Lieu, Ted (D-CA) House $2,500
McCain, John (R-AZ) Senate $2,500
Meng, Grace (D-NY) House $2,500
Royce, Ed (R-CA) House $2,500
Adams, Alma (D-NC) House $1,000
Becerra, Xavier (D-CA) House $1,000
Coleman, Bonnie (D-NJ) House $1,000
Curbelo, Carlos (R-FL) House $1,000
Grassley, Chuck (R-IA) Senate $1,000
Johnson, Ron (R-WI) Senate $1,000

Rodgers, Cathy McMorris (R-WA) House $1,000
Van Hollen, Chris (D-MD) House $1,000
Williams, Clyde (D-NY) House $1,000
Canova, Tim (D-FL) House $500
Donovan, Dan (R-NY) House $300

https://libertywriters.com/2017/02/urgent-new-report-exposes-6-top-republicans-george-soros-payroll-guess-whos-paid-stop-trump/

Being on the Soros dole makes these Republicans and Democrats Trump enemies and loyal to Soros.

Figures for the current election cycle are based on data released on February 08, 2017. Feel free to distribute or cite this material, but please credit the Center for Responsive Politics.

How do some Congressmen get elected? For instance, when Representative, Hank Johnson, Democrat, Georgia, testified before the House Armed Services Committee in 2010, he expressed a concern that the island of Guam … "My fear is that the whole island will become so overly populated that it will tip over and capsize," Johnson said.

On June 21, 2016, a longtime Philadelphia Democratic Congressman, Chaka Fattah, was convicted of racketeering, fraud, and money laundering federal grants and nonprofit funds to repay an illegal $1 million campaign loan and help family and friends

Then we have the scandal involving Democratic Rep. Charles Rangel of New York. Rangel was forced to step down from the chairmanship of the powerful, tax-writing House Ways and Means Committee after being admonished—the lightest "penalty" possible—for accepting corporate-sponsored trips to the Caribbean. Even though he was allowed to say his action was only "a leave of absence" as chairman, few Democrats think he will be allowed to return to his post. He faces far more serious charges in another investigation that has dragged on for more than a year. The ethics committee is still digging into allegations he used his House office to raise money for a building named in his honor at a New York college; he failed to pay taxes on a villa he owns in the Dominican Republic; he had to amend his congressional financial disclosure reports to show more than $500,000 in wealth that he had not reported and that he improperly used his rent-controlled apartments for his campaigns.

The Democrats were hit by another scandal when New York Democratic Rep. Eric Massa suddenly resigned his House seat in the wake of assertions that the freshman congressman had sexually harassed a male staffer and had groped other male staffers in multiple incidents that sparked warnings to Democratic leaders last year. A spokesman for the Pelosi camp said concerns over Massa's inappropriate behavior was communicated to Pelosi's office and was referred to the ethics committee.

The House Ethics Committee decided to drop its inquiry because of Massa's resignation. But Republicans want an investigation into how—or even whether—House Democratic leaders responded to the earlier complaints, asking "what did they know and when did they know it?" The House voted 402-1 on a Republican resolution to send the issue to the ethics committee, though it does not appear that the panel will undertake any serious inquiry. Really, were any of the previous complaints investigated?

Pelosi, who aggressively went after Republican transgressions when the GOP was in control of the House, has been supremely indifferent to the Massa sex scandal, dismissing it as a minor matter. "It's another subject people would like to make into a distraction," she said in an interview on MSNBC. "Distraction," seems to be a favorite word in Washington these days.

In Illinois, a state notorious for political corruption, Gov. Rod Blagojevich was impeached and removed from office for misusing his powers as governor of Illinois in an array of wrongdoings, including trying to sell the Senate seat vacated by Barack Obama to the highest bidder. Blagojevich was convicted in 2011 and sentenced to 14 years (2024) in prison.

Until the Blagojevich scandal struck, Obama's Senate seat, seemed safely in Democratic hands. But then, troubling questions were raised by Blagojevich's appointment of Roland Burris to temporarily fill Obama's remaining term, and the Democratic nomination was eventually captured by State Treasurer Alexi Giannoulias who has a notoriously checkered banking background that includes financial transactions with underworld figures who have heavily contributed to his campaign.

One of Giannoulias' top donors is Nick Giannis who was arrested and charged with writing $1.9 million in bad checks from Broadway

Bank, the Giannoulias family business. Giannis gave about $114,000 to Giannoulias' campaigns for State Treasurer and the Senate.

Questionable financial deals have also brought down Connecticut Democratic Sen. Christopher Dodd, who decided in January 2010 not to seek reelection. The Senate Banking Committee Chairman, who has oversight over the U.S. financial industry, has benefited from two sugar (4.5% and 4.25%) home mortgage loans in 2003 from former Countryside Chief Executive Angelo Mozilo. The mortgage deals have reportedly saved Senator Dodd $75,000 over the life of the loans, according to Portfolio Magazine.

Dodd was not the only Democrat to benefit from Countrywide Financial's VIP mortgage program. Sen. Kent Conrad of North Dakota, chairman of the Budget Committee, was one of several other government officials who received favorable loans after making a personal phone call to Mozilo. The scandal caused Dodd's approval polls to plummet in the midst of the housing meltdown and foreclosure crisis, forcing him to give up his bid for re-election to a sixth term, and giving Republicans a shot at the open Senate seat. His occupation now? – Lobbyist.

A jury in Washington, D.C. convicted Alaska Republican Sen. Ted Stevens Federal corruption charges for receiving gifts and making false statements in 2008. His conviction was overturned because of prosecutorial misconduct. He lost his bid for re-election and died in a plane crash in 2010. He was indicted by a federal grand jury on seven counts of making false statements, for allegedly lying on U.S. Senate financial disclosure forms for the years 1999 to 2006.

Prosecutors alleged that Stevens accepted $250,000 in value of gifts, principally from an oil services company now no longer in business named Veco Corp., and its former CEO, Bill Allen. Among the alleged gifts was renovation project that transformed the Senator's Girdwood, Alaska, home from a cabin to a sizeable house, a $2,700 massage chair and a Viking gas grill. Stevens died on August 9, 2010, when a de Havilland Canada DHC-3 Otter he and several others were flying in crashed in route to a private fishing lodge.

In 2015, New Jersey Democrat Robert Menendez was indicted on corruption charges for allegedly using his Senate office to push the business interests of a friend and donor in exchange for gifts. Robert Menendez, a U.S. senator, and Dr. Salomon Melgen, a Florida ophthalmologist, were indicted for one count of conspiracy, one count of violating the travel act, eight counts of bribery and three counts of honest services fraud; Menendez was also charged with one count of making false statements.

In 2012, Senator Lindsay Graham raised more money from lobbyists than any other member of Congress other than Robert Menendez. Graham who is very much in favor of lobbyists and PACs was second.

Rank	Name	Amt. from lobbyist-bundlers	Total contributions
1	Mitt Romney & Romney Victory Fund	$17.3 million	$797 million
2	Dem. Sen. Campaign Com.	$2.80 million	$126 million
3	Rep. Nat'l Com.	$1.06 million	$226 million
4	Nat'l Rep. Sen. Com.	$1.02 million	$88.9 million
5	Dem. Cong. Campaign Com.	$617,119	$141 million
6	Nat'l Rep. Cong. Com.	$455,000	$118 million
7	Sen. Robert Menendez, D-N.J.	$227,118	$11.8 million
8	Sen. Lindsey Graham, R-S.C.	$223,035	$2.16 million
9	Rick Perry, GOP Pres. Candidate	$178,250	$20.3 million
10	Sen. Harry Reid, D-Nev PAC	$141,750	$2.42 million
11	Sen. Sheldon Whitehouse, D-R.I.	$113,150	$2.98 million
12	David Dewhurst, R-Tex. Sen. Cand.	$100,100	$8.95 million

According to FEC filings, Graham's No. 1 lobbyist-bundler during the past two years was SCANA Corp., a South Carolina-based energy company that ranked among Fortune's 500 largest as recently as 2011.

The corporation was credited with bundling $84,650 for Graham and its political action committee gave him an additional $9,000. During the same period, SCANA Corp., with Graham's help, was angling for permission to build new nuclear power generators.

In February 2012, the Nuclear Regulatory Commission approved the first nuclear reactor construction permits in more than three decades. A month later, when it awarded two of them to the South Carolina Electric & Gas Company, a SCANA Corp. subsidiary, Graham hailed the action.

"We worked for years to see these reactors approved, and I'm very pleased this long-sought goal has finally been achieved," he said in a press release at the time.

Kevin Bishop, Graham's communication director, denies that campaign contributions influence the senator's decision-making process.

https://www.publicintegrity.org/2013/04/24/12531/grahams-campaign-collects-bundle-lobbyists

When Jeb Bush was exploring the idea of whether or not to run for President of the United States in 2016, one of the people he hired was DC Insider Richard Hohlt. Various newspapers neglected to mention that Hohlt was an infamous lobbyist from the financial district who was involved with the S&L collapse, assisted Citicorp and other corporate giants. http://www.motherjones.com/politics/2015/01/jeb-bush-richard-hohlt-karl-rove/

Bush, when he entered the 2016 presidential campaign, vowed to wage war on a bloated and self-serving Washington establishment and outlined a wide-ranging plan to rein in the size of the federal government and curb the influence of lobbyists who live off it.

The irony of it all is that in December of 2016 the following article appeared in the Tampa Bay Times: "Former Gov. Jeb Bush (R-Fla.) has signed on with the major Florida lobbying firm Buchanan Ingersoll & Rooney, the firm announced on Monday.

"Bush, a onetime GOP presidential candidate, will not register as a lobbyist. Instead, he will serve as a strategic adviser through his own consulting firm, Jeb Bush & Associates, with a special focus on clients in Florida.

"Those of us who have had the pleasure of working with the Governor in the past now have the opportunity to do so again, and those who haven't can look forward to a truly rewarding experience. This is an exciting development for the firm and for our clients," read a statement from Mac Stipanovich, the firm's top Florida lobbyist and a long-time Bush ally.

"Buchanan Ingersoll represents clients including U.S. Sugar, State Farm, DraftKings and FanDuel, according to the Tampa Bay Times." http://thehill.com/business-a-lobbying/business-a-lobbying/308758-jeb-bush-joining-prominent-florida-lobbying-firm

"While Jeb Bush was criticizing lawmakers who became lobbyists, John Kasich was denouncing Wall Street greed. Yet both Bush and Kasich had worked in the private sector at the Wall Street Investment Bank of Lehman Bros. Bush was a former governor and Kasich was an in-term congressman. Rather than being traditional lobbyists for Lehman, they were known as "door openers."

"Kasich was hired to run Lehman's banking operation in January 2001. By his own admission he had zero knowledge of the business. He did, however, have 18 years in Congress and voted for legislation to eliminate regulations on banks like Lehman.

"The month before Kasich got the job, he sponsored a bill that would allow Social Security money to be invested in financial firms, including Lehmans.

"Kasich was introduced to all bankers as the "person that knows more about Washington than any of us here If anyone wants to work with him there is no charge to you. If you're a young banker and you want to have some gravitas in the room, you might want John."

"Marco Rubio was a registered lobbyist in Washington D.C. for Becker and Poliakoff in 2003. Rubio said it was an error. How do you make an error like that?"

http://thehill.com/business-a-lobbying/business-a-lobbying/308758-jeb-bush-joining-prominent-florida-lobbying-firm

"Two of Marco Rubio's mistresses have been identified and it looks like he has a lot of explaining to do. Wasn't it finally time for Rubio to drop out of the race now that this news was going to rock his campaign to the core? by Charles C. Johnson, Got News

"U.S. Senator Marco Rubio has carried on at least two extramarital affairs since he entered politics.

"GotNews.com can confirm through lobbyist sources in DC and Tallahassee that at least one DC-based lobbyist has had an extra marital affair with the first term U.S. Senator. Still another Florida-based lobbyist has been IDed as carrying on an affair.

"The first woman was Amber Stoner, a 36-year-old woman who worked for Rubio when he was head of the Florida Republican Party.

"Stoner, who later became a lobbyist, traveled with Rubio at least seventeen times, including several resort towns on the GOP credit card. Rubio still hasn't released all of his credit card records from his time heading the party.

"Stoner, who has been a lobbyist for the health care industry—just like Rubio, was suddenly cut off after Rubio ascended to the Speaker of Florida House. She had formerly been the Foursquare Mayor of… Marco Rubio's office.

"An email read to GotNews.com shows Rubio increasingly desperate calls for attention from Stoner after Rubio gave her the cold shoulder. GOP officials opposing Rubio from Florida read the email as that of a spurned lover.

"The second woman is Dana Hudson, a blonde lobbyist based in the Beltway.

"According to two lobbyists in DC in the national security space Hudson has been bragging about having had sex with the senator to other lobbyists.

"Hudson lobbies on Homeland Security issues and is personal friends with the very same corrupt David Rivera who once partied with Rubio.

"Interestingly, despite an ongoing investigation by the FBI, Rivera still manages to find tickets to the GOP debates. Based upon her Twitter feed Hudson and Rivera seem to enjoy each other's company a lot." http://clashdaily.com/2016/03/breaking-rubios-mistresses-have-been-identified-marco-youve-got-some-explaining-to-do/

David Durenberger (R-Minn.) — Indicted for Misuse of public funds, improper reimbursement for nights he spent at home, 1993. Pleaded guilty to five misdemeanors in exchange for dropped felony charges; no jail time.

Harrison, Williams (D – N.J.) — Indicted on bribery as a result of an FBI sting that famously became known as Abscamon, 1981. At trial, Williams was seen promising (on camera) to use his influence to help an Arab sheik, who was in fact an FBI agent. Williams resigned from the Senate before he was expelled and spent 21 months in prison.

Edward Gurney (R-Fla.) — Indicted on bribery and lying to a grand jury, 1974. Acquitted in 1976 but did not seek reelection in 1974.

Larry Craig (R-Ida) — was arrested for lewd conduct in a men's room at the Minneapolis-St. Paul International Airport in 2007. Craig's claim that he simply had a "wide stance" after an undercover officer accused him of trying to initiate a sexual transaction between bathroom stalls was bandied about on headlines and late-night talk shows.

Craig pleaded guilty to a lesser charge of disorderly conduct, but two months later tried to withdraw the plea. even reversing his decision to resign from the Senate. Craig finished out his term and did not run for re-election in 2008. http://deadstate.org/more-gop-politicians-have-been-arrested-for-sexual-misconduct-in-bathrooms-than-trans-people/.

"Corrine Brown (D-FL): Failed to pay unemployment taxes to the state of Florida; sued by several airlines for unpaid bills and falsified travel reports; failed to report sale of her Tallahassee travel agency; improperly reported the sale of her Gainesville travel agency; sued by Whirlpool Corp. for unpaid bills; pursued by the IRS for $14,228 in unpaid taxes; investigations by the House Ethics Committee for possible acceptance of bribes; refused to file reports in the House about potential conflicts of interest while overseeing airlines she dealt with through her travel agencies; charged with money laundering.

Albert Bustamante (Rep. D-TX): Convicted in 1993 of racketeering and accepting an illegal gratuity.

Wes Cooley (Rep. R-OR): Convicted of falsifying VA loan applications. Paid $7,000 in fines plus court costs, and placed on probation. Subsequently tried to gather support to get re-elected to Congress. *

Bob Dornan (Rep. R-CA): In 1983 attempted to leave Grenada with a stolen AK-47. It was confiscated by the Army and destroyed.

Walter Fauntroy (Rep. D-DC): Financial disclosure misdemeanor (1995).

Jesse Helms (Sen. R-NC): In 1990, the Helms campaign sent out 125,000 postcards primarily to black North Carolina voters claiming that they might not be able to vote, and would be prosecuted for voter fraud if they tried. His campaign, the North Carolina Republican party, and four consulting and marketing firms were charged with violations of the Voting Rights Act. The Helms campaign signed an admission of guilt (claiming later that they didn't have the money to fight it in court), but Helms and his staff were never prosecuted.

Carrol Hubbard (D-KY): Convicted in 1994 of misappropriation of funds.

Jay Kim (R-CA): Convicted of accepting illegal campaign contributions from foreign sources.

Gerald Kleczka (Rep. D-WI): Convicted of DUI in 1987; arrested for DUI in 1990 and 1995.

Joe Kolter (Rep. D-PA): Fraud and conspiracy (1996).

Norman Lent (Rep. R-NY): In 1982 tried to have fifty counterfeit Rolex watches mailed to him from Taiwan.

Donald E. "Buz" Lukens (Rep. D-OH): In 1989 was convicted of contributing to the delinquency of a minor.

Nic Mavroules (Rep. D-MA): In 1991 pleaded guilty to charges of bribery and tax evasion.

Edward Mezvinsky (Rep. D-IA): Indicted in March of 2001 on federal fraud charges. Claimed that he developed mental problems after using a malaria drug called Lariam. "Clearly, the responsibility lies with the manufacturers," claimed Mezvinsky's lawyer, Michael Barrett.*

James Moran (Rep. D-VA): Charged with spousal abuse, and assault and battery. A regular instigator of bar fights while mayor of Alexandria, VA, his position made him immune to arrest. Once said he thought about becoming a boxer because "I like to hit people."

Austin J. Murphy (Rep. D-PA): Vote fraud, including forgery, conspiracy, and tampering with federal records (1999). *

Mary Rose Oakar (Rep. D-OH): Charged with seven federal felonies related to financial-disclosure irregularities (1998).

Bob Packwood (Sen. R-OR): Charged with sexual harassment. Oddly enough, many of the women named as harasses defended Senator Packwood.

Carl Perkins (Rep. D-KY): In 1994 pleaded guilty to filing a false financial-disclosure statement, conspiracy to file false statements with the Federal Election Commission, and bank fraud. Sentenced in March of 1995.

Mel Reynolds (Rep. D-IL): In 1995 was convicted of having sex with a minor and obstructing justice.

Charlie Rose (D-NC): Financial disclosure irregularities (1994).

Larry Smith (D-FL): In 1993 was convicted of income tax evasion and campaign-reporting violations.

Pat Swindall (Rep. R-GA): In 1988 was convicted of perjury.

Walter Tucker (Rep. D-CA): Federal extortion charges; convicted of accepting $30,000 worth of bribes while a Congressman, and sentenced to 27 months in the federal penitentiary.

Charles Wilson (D-TX): In 1995 was forced to pay a $90,000 fine to the Federal Election Commission.

Tom DeLay (R-TX): was convicted of two counts of money laundering and conspiracy in 2010 and sentenced to three years

Bob Ney (R-OH) pled guilty to conspiracy and making false statements as a result of his receiving trips from Abramoff in exchange for legislative favors. Ney received 30 months in prison

Duke Cunningham (R-CA) pleaded guilty on November 28, 2005 to charges of conspiracy to commit bribery, mail fraud, wire fraud and tax evasion in what came to be called the Cunningham scandal. Sentenced to over eight years in prison

William J. Jefferson (D-LA) in August 2005 the FBI seized $90,000 in cash from Jefferson's home freezer. He was re-elected anyway, but lost in 2008. He was convicted of 11 counts of bribery and sentenced to 13 years in prison on November 13, 2009.

Bill Janklow (R-SD) convicted of second-degree manslaughter for running a stop sign and killing a motorcyclist. Resigned from the House and given 100 days in the county jail and three years' probation.

Vito Fossella (R-New York) US Congressman convicted of drunken driving in 2008, later appealed but then pled guilty in 2009 to same charge.

Mel Reynolds (D-IL) was convicted of 12 counts of bank fraud. (1997)

Wes Cooley (R-OR), Cooley was convicted of having lied on the 1994 voter information pamphlet about his service in the Army. He was fined and sentenced to two years' probation (1997)

David Durenberger Senator (R-MN), In 1995 he pled guilty to 5 misdemeanor counts of misuse of public funds and was given one years' probation

Richard Kelly (R-FL) Accepted $25K and then claimed he was conducting his own investigation into corruption. Served 13 months

Harrison A. Williams Senator (D-NJ) Convicted on 9 counts of bribery and conspiracy. Sentenced to 3 years in prison."

Number of members of Congress who escaped tickets and/or arrest from a variety of driving offenses ranging from speeding to DUI in 1999 due to Congressional immunity: 217

Number of members of Congress who were released after being pulled over for drunken driving in 1998 by claiming Congressional immunity: 84

http://www.answers.com/Q/How_many_US_senators_and_congressmen_are_convicted_felons

Chuck Schumer (D-NY) – "While Chuck Schumer is the top-dog of the Democrat party, fighting President Trump with every breath, his corruption must never go unnoticed.

"Chuck Schumer is King of "Pay to Play" in the corrupt, rigged system of Washington, D.C. Today's example is how he exploits immigration law for wealthy real estate developers through the EB-5 visa program, which allows investors to pay $500,000 in exchange for a green card, in return for plenty of campaign cash given back to him," New York attorney Wendy Long said.

"The whole idea behind the EB-5 visa was to help create jobs in economically disadvantaged areas. But where big bucks are involved, corruption soon follows, and with Chuck Schumer and the EB-5 visa program, you need to follow the money.

"As Senator Patrick Leahy has correctly observed, the gerrymandered Schumer use of EB-5s benefits wealthy Manhattan condo projects, many of which 'would be pursued regardless of EB-5, calling into question whether the EB-5 capital is creating any jobs at all,'" Long concluded

"Schumer received $1.09 million in campaign donations since 2011 from real estate interests, and his third top donor source was Fragomen, a law firm that has a prominent EB-5 practice, which donated $82,200 to his campaign committee. Fragomen advertises itself as "support[ing] . . . [the] immigration needs' of 'the world's largest companies . . . all over the world.'"

"Schumer also rakes in campaign dollars from real estate companies such as Related Companies and Silverstein Properties, which also raise EB-5 funds.

"This is just proof that the EB-5 system is open to corruption — and Schumer is taking full advantage of it."

http://thetruthdivision.com/2017/01/breaking-chuck-schumer-busted-pay-play-scheme/

"Schumer is trying to bring Mr. Trump down with innuendoes of non-existent meetings with Russia when it is Schumer that has met and entertained Putin. How do you think Russia got their gas stations in the State of New York? What favors did Schumer receive from Putin in order to get through the regulatory obstacles and environmental regulation? It is difficult for a U.S. citizen to start a business. But Russia had no problem opening up gas stations in Schumer's home state?

"Hillary Clinton helped engineer the sale of a business to Russia, which owns 20 percent of the United States' uranium reserves. But as the senior senator from New York, who served alongside then-Sen. Hillary Clinton, also from New York (sort of), this most likely did not happen without Schumer having a hand in the sale of uranium. Therefore, Freedom Watch will find out what Schumer's role was in selling U.S. uranium to Russia, and how he likely benefited." Schumer is presently under further investigation

http://www.wnd.com/2017/03/4-schumer-scandals-ive-begun-to-uncover/#ef5IcTBERpZQuOPy.99

Joe Heck, R-NV. – "RedRock Strategies announced that, former Congressman and US Senate Candidate Joe Heck will join the political consulting firm as their new President of Government Relations. He crashed and burned in the US Senate race last year after publicly withdrawing his support for President Trump. In talking about Social Security, Heck called it a Pyramid Scheme. It is only good for paying people that have a life span of 67 through 80.

"Tucker Carlson tore into Rep. Maxine Waters after she accused him of racism for asking how a lawmaker can afford to live in a $4.3 million home.

"The Daily Caller co-founder first pointed out on his show several weeks ago that Waters, who has served in public office for nearly

40 years, lives in one of the richest neighborhoods in Los Angeles despite representing one of the poorest.

"Waters was asked about the disparity in a New York Times Magazine interview and accusing Carlson of being "racist" for questioning how an African-American woman acquired her wealth.

"Instead of even bothering to engage with the racism argument, Carlson chose to rip into Waters's shady investments and political corruption.

"So where did the money [for the house] come from?" Carlson asked again. "Maybe she borrowed it from family members. Since 2006 she's paid her own daughter $600,000 from campaign funds."

"Then there's her husband who was once the director of One United Bank," he continued. "Never heard of it? Well in 2008 One United Bank got a $12 million tax bill bailout after Waters convince the treasury department to take up the case."

"One liberal group ranked Waters as one of the most corrupt members of Congress. We are withholding judgment on that," Carlson concluded. "We've asked Waters on this show many times to explain and we're going to keep asking."

http://dailycaller.com/2017/07/24/tucker-refuses-to-let-up-on-race-baiting-maxine-waters-video/

Maxine Waters, D-Ca. Representative - Asked Treasury Secretary for meeting in midst of 2008 Financial Crisis. Waters said the meeting was with minority-owned banks to discuss losses. Only bank present was OneUnited, with which Waters has close ties. CEO requested bailout specifically for OneUnited during and after the meeting.

http://www.wrhammons.com/Candidate/waters-congressional-corruption.htm

"In 2014, New York Republican Michael Grimm pled guilty in court to one count of tax evasion and was set to submit to a "statement of facts" that admits to all the conduct alleged in the 20-count federal indictment. Grimm also publicly admitted to hiring undocumented workers, lying under oath while serving in Congress, obstructing federal and state officials, and cheating employees out of employment insurance claims. There are multiple investigations of allegations against Representative Grimm. One is the fundraising allegation; another is whether he violated the Federal campaign finance laws by soliciting and accepting prohibited campaign contributions, causing false information to be included in campaign finance reports, and improperly seeking assistance from a foreign national in soliciting campaign contributions in exchange for offering to use his official position to help that individual obtain a green card. A complaint was also filed with OCE requesting an investigation into Rep. Grimm's improper use of a broadcast of a floor speech in a fundraising e-mail." http://www.crewsmostcorrupt.org/page/-/PDFs/Reports/ Most% 20Corrupt%20Reports/CREW-Most-Corrupt-Members-of-Congress-Report-2013.pdf?nocdn=1

Duke Cunningham, R-Calif Representative, a distinguished Vietnam War veteran, and former Navy pilot, was sentenced to seven years when he admitted to taking $2.4 million in bribes from defense contractors and evading taxes. http://www.npr.org/sections/ thetwo-way/2013/06/04/188667106/former-rep-duke-cunningham-freed-after-bribery-sentence

Jim Traficant, (D-Ohio) In 2002, Traficant was indicted by a federal grand jury for bribery, tax evasion, racketeering, conspiracy, and obstruction of justice. He was found guilty of all charges in April 2002. Traficant opted to represent himself, insisting that the trial was part of a vendetta against him dating back to his 1983 trial. After a two-month federal trial, on April 11, 2002, he was convicted of 10 felony counts including bribery, racketeering, and tax evasion also took bribes while in office. Traficant received support from David Duke, who urged visitors to his personal website to donate to his personal fund. Duke posted a letter written by Traficant stating that he was targeted by the United States Department of Justice for, among other things, defending John Demjanjuk. Traficant also claimed, in the letter, that he knew facts about "Waco, Ruby Ridge, Pan Am Flight 103, Jimmy Hoffa and the John F. Kennedy assassination," which he may divulge in the future. Author Michael Collins Piper, who initially helped circulate Traficant's letter, said that "There's stuff I've written about Traficant that's showing up in places I don't even know. It's like (six) degrees of separation with the Internet now," and denied that Traficant had any direct connections to Duke. https://en.wikipedia. org/wiki/James_Traficant

John McCain R-AZ "I'm proud that the institute is named after me, but I have nothing to do with it — except that they use my name just as the Goldwater Institute uses Goldwater's name." — Sen. John McCain (R-Ariz.), quoted in news report, April 4, 2016 McCain is facing questions about his ties to an eponymous nonprofit, after Bloomberg reported the Saudi government had donated $1 million to the nonprofit's fundraising arm. After a town hall event in Phoenix, McCain answered questions about the donation in a media scrum. McCain at one point distanced himself from the nonprofit, saying he had "nothing to do with it" beyond being its namesake. Is that really the case?

The Facts

"The Royal Embassy of Saudi Arabia gave $1 million to the McCain Institute Foundation in 2014, tax records show. The donation was transferred to the Arizona State University's fundraising arm to benefit the McCain Institute for International Leadership, which is run through the university.

"Foreign campaign contributions to U.S. elections are banned under Federal law. But there's no restriction on donations to nonprofits with ties to candidates or sitting politicians. Companies and foundations, some that have business before Congress, have contributed at least $100,000 each to the foundation, USA Today reported in 2014. Ethics watchdog groups criticize the practice and the laws that allow it, saying such donations provide a means for foreign governments and special-interest groups to exert influence over politicians. "[$1 Million was received from Saudi Arabia.

"A fundraising luncheon held in March at London's Spencer House during McCain's swing through the United Kingdom. An invitation to the event lists Lord Rothschild and Nathaniel Rothschild as hosts, and indicates the event was made possible with their "kind permission". Tickets to the luncheon cost $1,000 to $2,300.

"Judicial Watch president Tom Fitton said: "The question is whether or not the Rothschilds paid for the event, the venue, the catering, or any other related costs."

"The McCain Institute has also accepted contributions of as much as $100,000 from billionaire liberal activist-funder George Soros.]"

"In addition, the Foundation has accepted foreign donations of $100,000 from OCP, S.A., a Moroccan state-owned phosphate company operating in Western Sahara which repeatedly has been accused of worker abuse and exploitation; and McCain Institute has also accepted at least $100,000 from the pro-Iranian Pivotal Foundation, founded by Francis Najafi who owns the private equity and real estate firm Pivotal Group.

"The Pivotal Foundation has in the last three years given $205,000 to the National Iranian-American Council (NIAC), which has been a vocal advocate for the Iranian nuclear deal the Obama administration negotiated."

https://fellowshipoftheminds.com/2017/07/23/john-mccains -foundation-is-funded-by-saudis-rothschilds-soros/

"In April 2012, McCain met with several of his longtime political allies in Sedona, Ariz., to discuss his vision for a nonprofit aimed to preserve his political legacy. Those in attendance included then-Sen. Jon Kyl (R-Ariz.), Sen. Lindsey O. Graham (R-S.C.), then-CIA Director David Petraeus, former U.S. ambassador to NATO Kurt Volker and actor Ben Affleck, the Arizona Republic reported in 2012.

"The McCain Institute for International Leadership was created in December 2012, with an $8.7 million donation in unused funds from McCain's 2008 presidential campaign.

"It was established to promote "character-driven leadership" and focus on issues that shaped McCain's career, such as foreign policy and national security. Its mission statement says it is "guided by values that have animated" McCain's career and his family. The Washington-based McCain Institute runs an internship program and holds events focused on issues like human trafficking and national security.

"For McCain, he thought it was very important to have something that becomes institutional, that will focus on issues and things that he's cared about in his career that goes well beyond his own contribution," Volker, McCain Institute director, told the Arizona Republic in 2014.

"McCain regularly attends events and fundraisers hosted by the McCain Institute. His wife, Cindy McCain, is on the institute's Human Trafficking Advisory Council, working with the nonprofit to raise awareness for her main policy issue. Many of McCain's longtime political allies sit on the nonprofit's board of directors. Tax records show a longtime McCain fundraiser, Carly Eudy, maintains the McCain Institute Foundation's financial records.

"McCain compared his role with the institute to that of his Senate predecessor, Republican Barry Goldwater, with the Goldwater Institute in Arizona. The think tank was founded in 1988 by a group of conservative activists, with the blessing of Goldwater to use his name.

"There's no indication Goldwater himself started the think tank. His widow told the Phoenix New Times in 1999 that Goldwater "had lent his name to the institute in 1988 because he believed its founder, former Northern Arizona University political science professor Michael Sanera, intended it to be an academically oriented policy research organ." But Goldwater was critical of some of the policy positions the institute took, and tried to convince its board to change direction.

"It's clear McCain's role with the McCain Institute is not exactly comparable to Goldwater's. Still, McCain's role appears to be largely honorary, and his name does not appear in the foundation's tax records. The institute's employees report to the ASU president, and McCain has no involvement in its management or operations decisions, Volker told us.

"The Senator's involvement is truly a supportive role to ASU, its goals and thus the Institute," Volker said. "We are incredibly grateful that he attends some of our events and meets with the Institute's ASU students when his schedule allows. Operational decisions made by the Institute are taken by its Executive Director, with counsel from the Institute's advisory Board of Trustees, under the overall authority of the University."

"John McCain has taken tens of millions of dollars from special interests and lobbyists in his senate and presidential campaigns. Now, we have to wonder if he will be able to remain objective on national security matters, as millions pour into his "charity" from oppressive foreign governments.

"More startling, is the fact that Senator McCain has used this charity to honor and promote Vice President Joe Biden and former Secretary of State Hillary Clinton, who attended posh fundraising event for the McCain slush fund. Why is McCain feting the very liberals whose policies are destroying our country's economy and whose immigration policies are making us unsafe while costing us millions?" http://dailycaller.com/2016/04/04/mccain-charity-following-clinton-foundation-style-of-corruption/

Rachael Dean, McCain's spokeswoman, explained McCain meant to express that he has no ties to the Saudi donation.

"Senator McCain intended to convey that he had nothing to do with the solicitation of the Saudi donation to the McCain Institute," Dean said, and confirmed he has no position with the institute or role in its governance. "He is supportive of the University's goals and programs for the Institute, and he is proud to participate in Institute activities as his schedule allows."

"McCain's answer during the media scrum was curious since he helped set up the McCain Institute and clearly still has ties to it. He has a symbolic role with the nonprofit, attends fundraisers and he and his wife are supportive of its efforts. So his role clearly goes beyond how he characterized it – being the namesake of a think tank like Barry Goldwater was for the Goldwater Institute.

"It appears McCain misspoke. According to his spokeswoman, McCain meant to express that he "had nothing to do" with the donation from the Saudi government to the McCain Institute Foundation, rather than with the institute itself. We don't play gotcha at The Fact Checker, and we understand that people make mistakes when they speak off the cuff. But McCain should be held accountable for his inaccurate claim because it ultimately misled the public to believe he had no ties to the institute that he helped create. We award him Two Pinocchios. https://www.washingtonpost.com/news/fact-checker/wp/2016/04/08/john-mccains-claim-he-has-nothing-to-do-with-the-mccain-institute/?utm_term=.76f213f5a906.

"McCain has long been known as a hero, but being in the Senate for the past 32 plus years has taught him how to play the game and reap the rewards from lobbyists and sometimes "taking the bridge too far." Opensecrets.org just revealed that some RINOS are actually traitors.

"The non-profit, non-partisan research group based in Washington, D.C., that tracks the effects of money and lobbying on elections and public policy, revealed that while George Soros is responsible for funding Democrats and causes, he has also bankrolled Senator John McCain and a small but select group of other Republicans.

"Unsurprisingly, all of the names revealed to receive funding from George Soros have a track record of opposition to President Trump."

"John McCain has been especially critical of Trump, even blasting him today for his stern phone call with the Australian Prime Minister. McCain and Graham also attacked Trump for implementing an immigration ban.

"We fear this executive order will become a self-inflicted wound in the fight against terrorism," McCain and Graham said in a joint statement, adding that Trump's executive order "may do more to help terrorist recruitment than improve our security."

"It seems that every move Trump makes, the same characters are quick to delegitimize the president. Now it all makes sense."

https://libertywritersnews.com/2017/02/urgent-new-report-exposes-6-top-republicans-george-soros-payroll-guess-whos-paid-stop-trump/

Dan Rostenkowski, (D-Il) — "Rostenkowski's political career ended in 1994 after a two-year investigation. In elections later that year, after winning the Democratic primary, Rostenkowski lost his seat in a narrow election and retired from political life. Rostenkowski was charged with illegally converting official funds to his personal use and mail fraud. He was accused in 1996 of embezzling $700,000 from the federal government. He was charged with 13 of the original 17 counts against him. He went to prison after serving in Congress and is now back in Washington working as a lobbyist. Charges against Rostenkowski included: keeping "ghost" employees on his payroll (paying salaries at taxpayer expense for no-show "jobs"); using Congressional funds to buy gifts such as chairs and ashtrays for friends; diverting taxpayer funds to pay for vehicles used for personal transportation; tampering with a Grand Jury witness; and trading in officially purchased stamps for cash at the House Post Office. He died at age 82." https://en.wikipedia.org/wiki/Dan_Rostenkowski

Vern Buchanan, R-Fla. Representative – "In 2008, Buchanan was accused of campaign fraud by forcing employees of his dealerships to write checks to his campaign, while reimbursing them from his own pocket. The investigation that was called into action was fueled by members on both sides of the aisle and looked into his participation in several counts of fraud. Despite the investigations being called off, numerous witnesses came forward testifying he had made campaign violations. CREW'S Most Corrupt has named Buchanan as one of the most corrupt members of Congress for 2008, 2009, 2011, and 2012, accusing him of fundraising fraud and tax evasion. Eleven individuals and entities affiliated with Buchanan have been fined for illegal contributions to his campaign. His ethics issues stem from: (1) pressuring partners and employees to make contributions to his campaign committee; (2) reimbursing them from his corporate funds; (3) trying to coerce a partner into signing a false affidavit; (4) improperly using corporate resources for campaign purposes; (5) tax evasion; and (6) lying on his financial disclosure forms. He was included in CREW's 2008, 2009, 2011, and 2012 reports on congressional corruption for related matters." https://en.wikipedia. org/wiki/Vern_Buchanan

http://www.crewsmostcorrupt.org/page/-/PDFs/Reports/Most%20 Corrupt%20Reports/CREW-Most-Corrupt-Members-of-Congress-Report-2013.pdf?nocdn=1

Gregory Meeks, D-NY Representative – "Citizens for Responsibility and Ethics in Washington (CREW) named Meeks one of the most-corrupt members of Congress in 2011. It was subsequently reported that Meeks' continuing ethical and criminal probes would cause his premature exit from Congress; however, Meeks has denied this. Hip hop artist and law school graduate Mike Scala announced in October 2011 to run for office against Meeks. However, Meeks won the Democratic primary and was re-elected with 89.7% of the general election vote in November 2012." https://en.wikipedia.org/ wiki/Gregory_Meeks

Scott DesJarlais, R-Tenn Representative – "a Member of the Tea Party Movement - In October 2012, the watchdog group Citizens for Responsibility and Ethics in Washington (CREW) requested that the Tennessee Board of Health investigate evidence that DesJarlais had had a sexual relationship with a patient, in violation of the Tennessee Medical Practice Act. The complaint was investigated and in May 2013 DesJarlais was formally reprimanded by the Tennessee Board of Medical Examiners for having sex with patients and was fined $500 - calculated by the Board as "$250 per patient" - and $1000 in costs. He did not contest the charges. In November 2012, after further details of the divorce proceedings were published, CREW asked the House of Representatives' Office of Congressional Ethics to investigate whether DesJarlais had violated House ethics rules, asserting that he had "blatantly" lied when he denied having taped the telephone conversation. The inappropriate relationships in which Rep. DesJarlais engaged with patients took place several years before he was elected to Congress and, therefore, were not within the jurisdiction of the House. During his re-election campaign, however, while serving as a member of Congress, Rep. DesJarlais made numerous untrue statements about this past conduct. By lying to the public about his role in taping a telephone conversation with a patient with whom he had a sexual relationship, Rep. DesJarlais acted in a manner that does not reflect creditably on the House. Additionally, if, as it appears, Rep. DesJarlais falsely claimed one of the patients with whom he was involved was never pregnant and did not have an abortion, his conduct does not reflect creditably on the House."

http://www.crewsmostcorrupt.org/page/-/PDFs/Reports/Most%20Corrupt%20Reports/CREW-Most-Corrupt-Members-of-Congress-Report-2013.pdf?nocdn=1 https://en.wikipedia.org/wiki/Scott_DesJarlais

Don Young, R-Alaska Representative – "In March 2013, the House Ethics Committee created another special committee to investigate more allegations that Young improperly accepted gifts, used campaign funds for personal expenses, failed to report gifts in financial disclosure documents, and made false statements to federal officials. On future predictions, Young stated, "It will go forever. I've been under a cloud all my life. I'm sort of like living in Juneau. It rains on you all the time. You don't even notice it." The Ethics Committee formed a sub-committee charged with the duty of determining whether or not Young broke the law. In 2014, the Committee issued a rebuke to Young after finding he had failed to disclose gifts totaling over $60,000 between 2001 and 2013. In 2016, he was once again under scrutiny for failing to report inherited property assets for 25 years, as well as the value of oil and gas leases consummated only seven months after he left his six-year chairmanship of the United States House Committee on Natural Resources. Allegations of campaign fund misuse and earmark misuse. For three years in a row, Young was included in the annual listing of the most corrupt members of Congress compiled by Citizens for Responsibility and Ethics in

Washington. CREW said he had been investigated for using campaign funds for personal expenses and for a $10 million 2005 earmark to build the Coconut Road Interchange on the I-75 in southwest Florida, which benefitted a campaign donor. No charges have been brought for any criminal wrongdoing after investigations by the FBI. After protests, the funding was reallocated for the Bonita Beach Road interchange. The House Ethics Committee found he had improperly used campaign funds for personal expenses. In 2012 there were no less than four federal and congressional investigations into his business and fundraising activities. Allegations were made that Buchanan used his car dealerships for campaign funding through cash swaps." https://en.wikipedia.org/wiki/Don_Young

Robert Andrews, D-N.J. Representative – "Andrews was the subject of a House Ethics Committee investigation over whether he improperly spent campaign cash to pay for personal trips to Scotland and Los Angeles, and over allegations that he used a graduation party for his daughter to raise funds. His resignation ended the investigation. He told a newspaper he was taking a job at a Philadelphia law firm. He was listed by CREWS as one of the most corrupt men in Congress." https://en.wikipedia.org/wiki/Rob_Andrews

Michele Bachmann, R-MN. Representative – "Rep. Bachmann appears to have improperly used her presidential campaign resources to promote her memoir, and the Department of Justice is investigating whether the Bachmann campaign illegally coordinated advertising with a super PAC. Meanwhile, a campaign aide turned whistleblower filed a Federal Election Commission (FEC) complaint alleging Rep. Bachmann improperly paid campaign staff from her leadership PAC. The campaign also allegedly withheld compensation from presidential campaign staffers who did not sign confidentiality agreements. Another former aide alleged the Bachmann campaign stole an email list, a theft that is still under investigation. A four-term member of Congress representing Minnesota's 6th district, Bachmann is under investigation by the Federal Election Commission, House Ethics Committee, and Federal Bureau of Investigation for violating campaign finance laws while running for president by improperly paying staff from her leadership PAC and using her campaign resources to promote her memoir. Under investigation by the Department of Justice for possible illegal coordination between her presidential campaign and a super

PAC. Under investigation by the Urbandale, Iowa police department for the theft of an email list. Cited in CREW's Last Call report on GOP post-presidential primary spending in 2012. After conducting an investigation into several of the allegations against Rep. Bachmann, OCE found substantial reason to believe Rep. Bachmann violated federal campaign finance laws and House rules by using her PAC to support her presidential campaign, using campaign resources to promote her book, and improperly accepting an in-kind contribution from the book's publisher.144 OCE referred Rep. Bachmann's case to the House Ethics Committee on June 13, 2013.145 OCE recommended the House Ethics Committee dismiss the allegation that Rep. Bachmann failed to accurately disclose payments to Sen. Sorenson for serving as the Iowa chairman of her presidential campaign, instead voting to refer that matter to the FEC.146 On September 11, 2013, the House Ethics Committee announced it was extending its review of the matters involving Rep. Bachmann.147 There is no date by which the committee must act. The FBI's public integrity section reportedly is investigating allegations of campaign finance violations by the Bachmann campaign." http://www.crewsmostcorrupt.org/page/-/PDFs/Reports/Most%20Corrupt%20Reports/CREW-Most-Corrupt-Members-of-Congress-Report-2013.pdf?nocdn=1.

http://www.crewsmostcorrupt.org/mostcorrupt/entry/michele-bachmann

Hal Rogers, R-KY Representative – "Rogers has been widely criticized by both liberal and conservative pundits for his priorities when it comes to national security. National Review referred to Rogers as "a national disgrace" and Rolling Stone named him one of America's "Ten Worst Congressmen", calling him "Bin Laden's Best Friend" due to the fact that Rogers steered Federal Homeland Security money away from large cities to his home district, which critics claim is one of the least likely terrorist targets in America because of its lack of any notable monuments or population centers. In 2007, Citizens for Responsibility and Ethics in Washington named Congressman Rogers to its list of the Most Corrupt Members of Congress. On May 14, 2006, the New York Times reported that Rogers had used his legislative position as chairman of the House subcommittee that controls the Homeland Security budget to create "jobs in his home district and profits for companies that are donors to his political causes." The Lexington Herald-Leader in 2005 called Rogers the "Prince of Pork". The Times article reported that Rogers had inserted language ("existing government card issuance centers") into appropriations bills that effectively pushed the federal government into testing at a cost of $4 million older, inappropriate technology for a new fraud-resistant green card for permanent legal immigrants, at a production plant in Corbin, Kentucky, within Rogers' district. The study concluded that the smart card approach was far superior. The Times found that about $100,000 in contributions had come to Rogers from parties with at least some ties to the identification card effort. In response to these critics, Rogers has stated, "It should surprise no one that this article from Rolling Stone regarding my activity in connection with the Transportation Worker Identity Card (TWIC) is grossly incorrect and highly slanderous," the congressman said. "A true and honest analysis would reveal that my sole interest in TWIC is simply to protect America's seaports, airports, and other transportation facilities from terrorist penetration. To purport that my actions have compromised national security in an effort to bring jobs to Kentucky or for personal gain is an absolute lie." After Iran objected to the interim deployment of an Afloat Forward Staging Base to counter their threats to close the Persian Gulf, Rogers cut the funding for the project." https://en.wikipedia.org/wiki/Hal_Rogers

Tim Bishop, D-N.Y. Representative – "Almost immediately after the investor, Eric Semler, obtained the necessary permits to stage a fireworks show in an environmentally fragile area during his son's bar mitzvah, Rep. Bishop's campaign solicited a donation from him. Rep. Bishop's campaign also appears to have backdated the donations in an attempt to skirt federal contribution limits. The House Ethics Committee is investigating Rep. Bishop, and the U.S. Attorney's Office for the Eastern District of New York and the FBI have made inquiries. Six-term member of Congress representing New York's 1st district. Under investigation by the House Ethics Committee for accepting campaign donations tied to an official action; also under investigation by the U.S. Attorney for the Eastern District of New York and the FBI. Previously named to CREW's Most Corrupt in 2012. In early 2013, the U.S. Attorney's Office for the Eastern District of New York requested information about the matter from Rep. Bishop's office. 49 The Federal Bureau of Investigation has also looked into the matter and spoke with Mr. Havermayer in January or February 2013.50. The status of both investigations is unknown."

http://www.crewsmostcorrupt.org/mostcorrupt/entry/tim-bishop

Paul Broun, R-Ga. Representative – "While he was running for Congress in 2007, Rep. Broun made several loans to his campaign that he said were made from his personal funds and carried no interest. Years later, after the campaign was caught making suspect "interest" payments to Rep. Broun, he amended his Federal Election Commission reports to say two of the loans came from a home equity line of credit — which still left many questions unanswered. Mr. Broun is a four-term member of Congress representing Georgia's 10th district. He is under investigation by the Federal Election Commission for concealing the true source and terms of campaign loans and failing to report other loans to the FEC. Previously named to CREW's Most Corrupt in 2012. The status of the FEC's investigation is pending. In November 2012, the Paul Broun Committee responded to a verbal request from the FEC's Reports Analysis Division to list the Schedule Cs it filed related to the three loans covered by the amendments filed in June 2012.26 It is unknown if this request was related to the FEC's investigation." http://www.crewsmostcorrupt.org/page/-/PDFs/Reports/Most%20 Corrupt%20Reports/CREW-Most-Corrupt-Members-of-Congress- Report-2013.pdf?nocdn=1. http://www.crewsmostcorrupt.org/ mostcorrupt/entry/paul-broun

Also on the list is Rep. Paul Ryan (R-Wisc.), now the speaker of the house, with $71,075 and Rep. Peter DeFazio, (D-Ore.), with $56,000 in contributions, both of whom co-sponsored the legislation that included the 2018 deadline, according to McClatchy.

Ryan's wife, "Janna, who is touted as a housewife who raised three children, was a congressional aide and corporate lobbyist in Washington for a decade before marrying Ryan. Her clients included cigar industry, a logging company, drug makers [Pharmaceutical Researchers and Manufacturers Alliance (PhRMA), Wyeth Pharmaceuticals and Novartis], the health insurance industry and a nuclear power plant. Oil industry clients included Conoco and Marathon Oil. Big health insurance companies Blue Cross Blue Shield and Cigna were also on the list.

"Janna Ryan and her then-boyfriend's work appear to have overlapped. In February 2000 while Janna Ryan still was working on behalf of

UPS, Paul Ryan made one of only two corporate-funded trips he took that year, from Milwaukee to Atlanta, where UPS is headquartered. The trip was paid for by UPS, which also flew the congressman back to Washington, according to his financial disclosure reports.

"It is also significant to note that just hours passing the very first bill of the new Congress, newly elected House Speaker Paul Ryan, R-Wisc., celebrated with a corporate lobbying firm, BGR Group, at a fundraiser for his campaign committee.

"Passing the bill would amend existing law to allow Congress to repeal multiple regulations. "The law is believed to be aimed at rolling back a rule designed to deter mining companies from polluting drinking water sources, rules designed to curb hazardous methane emissions from fracking sites, and a rule that extends the threshold for overtime pay to workers, among others."

"BGR Group represents Chevron, Celgene Corp, the Consumer Technology Association, Eli Lilly & Co., Gilead Sciences, Johnson & Johnson, Raytheon, Southern Company, and Xerox, among many other clients, and has helped a number of clients work on regulatory policy.

"This was a high-dollar event which had a $10,000 price tag for each sponsor of the event, $2,500 for each political action committee, and $1,500 per individual, according to an invitation obtained by the Center for Media and Democracy and shared with The Intercept." https://theintercept.com/2017/01/06/paul-ryan-lobbyist/

"Another point you never hear about from the media is the fact that Ryan hired a lobbyist – David Hoppe – to be his Chief of Staff. Hoppe's Corporate Clients consisted of AT&T, Sony, MetLife, the National Venture Capital Association, BlackRock, Cayman Finance, Amazon, Mars, the Coalition to Stop Internet Gambling, Ford Motor, Delta Airlines, and so on — you know, the types of business interests that pay most of the lobbying firm bills everywhere." https://www.vox.com/polyarchy/2015/10/26/9617908/paul-ryan-david-hoppe-lobbyist

Mitch McConnell, R-Ky. Representative, now U.S. Senator – "The recording indicated Sen. McConnell's then-chief of staff and several legislative assistants helped compile opposition research on some of the senator's potential campaign opponents while on the taxpayer's clock. CREW asked the FBI and the Senate Select Committee on Ethics to investigate whether Sen. McConnell broke federal law or Senate rules, which prohibit congressional staff from engaging in campaign activity on official time or using official resources. Five-term U.S. Senator from Kentucky and Senate Minority Leader, McConnell secretly recorded discussing opposition research conducted by his official staff against potential campaign opponents, possibly in violation of federal law and Senate rules. McConnell is One of two members of Congress from Kentucky named to CREW's Most Corrupt. Recording possibly indicated McConnell's staff helped compile oppo on potential opponent Ashley Judd on the taxpayers' clock. Previously named to CREW's Most Corrupt report in 2007, 2008, and 2009 – his second wife is Elaine Chao, the former Secretary of Labor under George W. Bush and nominated as Transportation Secretary under President Donald Trump." http://www.crewsmostcorrupt.org/mostcorrupt/entry/mitch-mcconnell

http://www.wrhammons.com/Candidate/mcconnell-congressional-corruption.htm

Previously named to CREW's Most Corrupt report in 2007, 2008, and 2009 "Senate Minority Leader Mitch McConnell, who faces a competitive re-election race next year, has been named to a watchdog organization's list of the most corrupt members of Congress.

"The nonpartisan group, Citizens for Responsibility and Ethics in Washington, included McConnell in the annual list because of lingering questions over whether he used congressional staff to conduct campaign opposition research. That charge originates from a conversation among McConnell's campaign staff that was secretly recorded earlier this year.

"The recording indicated Sen. McConnell's then-chief of staff and several legislative assistants helped compile opposition research on some of the senator's potential campaign opponents while on the taxpayer's clock," the group said.

"McConnell's office has said any campaign work conducted by congressional staffers was done on weekends or at night, but CREW could not find evidence on McConnell's campaign payroll of the congressional staffers mentioned in the recording.

"Stay abreast of the latest developments from nation's capital and beyond with curated News Alerts from the Washington Examiner news desk and delivered to your inbox.

"The group concludes that "if members of Sen. McConnell's congressional staff were engaged in campaign activities during office hours and using Senate resources, Sen. McConnell likely violated ... Senate ethics rules and federal law."

"McConnell is running for re-election against Kentucky's Democratic Secretary of State Alison Lundergan Grimes. He also faces a Republican primary challenge from businessman Matt Bevin.

"White House slams 'shameful' reports downplaying inauguration crowds. White House slams 'shameful' reports downplaying inauguration crowds."

By Sarah Westwood • 01/21/17 5:56 PM http://www.washingtonexaminer.com/mitch-mcconnell-added-to-groups-list-of-congress-most-corrupt/article/2536007

"Never before in our history has the U.S Senate been as unproductive as the U.S. Senate post-2008. Even the staunchly obstructionist Republicans during FDR's tenure got more done than our current Senate. Most Americans, by and large, regardless of party affiliation, agree that we need more jobs; that veterans need better healthcare; that the current minimum wage is insufficient; that our infrastructure could use some upgrading; that politicians are too beholden to their benefactors; and that there's too much bickering instead of legislating.

"One man has continuously denied the necessary progress to the American people out of sheer political bitterness, and that one man alone can take all the credit for the complete lack of action on all of those fronts — Mitch McConnell.

"Mitch McConnell is the shittiest Senator in the history of Washington. And there are numbers to back that up. Since he became the Republican leader in the Senate, McConnell has filed more than a quarter of all cloture motions ever filed as long as the Senate has existed. To put that in perspective, this means McConnell, in just his most recent term, is responsible for over 25 percent of all the Senate filibusters since 1787. McConnell is literally a cancerous tumor on the Senate, collecting a six-figure paycheck while depleting all hope of progress as long as he's in office.

"On the flip side, McConnell is quite productive if you're willing to write him a fat check. One week after Amgen, a pharmaceutical multinational, hosted a fundraiser for McConnell in December of 2012, one of their lobbyists, who was in charge of monitoring the "fiscal cliff" negotiations, wrote a $3,000 check to McConnell's campaign. By the time the negotiations were finished, McConnell had secured a $500 million Christmas present for Amgen that came directly out of Medicare. But even that wasn't McConnell's foulest moment of corruption.

"This past July, McConnell took time out of his busy day to have a breakfast date with Richard Anderson, the CEO of Delta Airlines, in the exclusive Senate dining room. Just a day after the breakfast, Anderson and his wife wrote over $10,000 worth of checks to McConnell's campaign. McConnell's spokespeople, of course, denied the allegations that McConnell solicited the donations in the Senate dining room, which would be a felony.

"Nevertheless, the donations to McConnell's campaign could be easily interpreted as a quid pro quo in a relationship where McConnell will likely return the favor by continuing to block closing unfair corporate tax loopholes that cost U.S. taxpayers billions each year. Delta Airlines has used an accounting loophole called "deferral," which allows them to carry their losses forward for several years. This means that despite making billions in profit, Delta Airlines pays $0 in taxes on those profits, and is likely to continue dodging all U.S. income taxes for several more years, at least. If McConnell keeps his job after November, the tax dodging will continue, as will the checks Delta's CEO writes to McConnell's campaign.

"Mitch McConnell's position as a politician who puts out depending on how much you're willing to put in is a far cry from what he used to stand for. Ironically, McConnell used to be a proponent of full disclosure when it came to campaign donations several decades ago.

"What we ought to do is eliminate the political action committee contributions, because those are the ones that raise the specter of undue influence. And those can be gone tomorrow. We can pass a bill tomorrow to take care of that problem," McConnell was quoted saying in 1987.

"We Republicans have put together a responsible and Constitutional campaign reform agenda. It would restrict the power of special interest PACS, stop the flow of all soft money, keep wealthy individuals from buying public office," McConnell said in 1988.

"Now, McConnell is the personification of the insidious culture that exists among Washington politicians and their big donors. Thanks to Lauren Windsor's surreptitiously-recorded audio of McConnell's address at a Koch Brothers-funded gathering of GOP politicians and corporate oligarchs this past summer, the Senate minority leader's deference to big money is well-documented. McConnell, who has received over $41,000 from Koch Industries in this campaign cycle, shamelessly genuflected to the oil barons in front of the entire audience, acknowledging their role in keeping the Republican Party well-funded.

"I want to start by thanking you, Charles and David [Koch], for the important work you're doing," McConnell said. "I don't know where we'd be without you."

"At the summit, McConnell assured benefactors of his continued servility, promising not to spend any time on "gosh-darn" minimum wage increases, eases in student loan debt, or extensions of the safety net for the long-term unemployed. Instead, McConnell vowed in his speech to defund the Environmental Protection Agency, eliminate the Consumer Financial Protection Bureau, and repeal the Affordable Care Act — all of which are greatly pleasing to billionaires who profit from polluting air and water, jacking up interest rates on millions of unwitting college students and credit card holders, and denying health insurance to sick and injured people who depend on it. Mitch McConnell can be counted on to make the rich richer, as well as himself, through his votes.

"McConnell increased his own personal wealth from $3.4 million in 2004 to $27.2 million in 2010. Oddly enough, that was a time when most Americans were seeing their wealth dissipate during the greatest recession in modern history. The Washington Post reported that most of McConnell's gains during that time were due to stock trades, though he's also voted to increase his own Congressional salary six times. Interestingly enough, The New York Times reported that the investment portfolios of U.S. senators consistently outperform the rest of the market by a full 10 percentage points, seeing even more growth than hedge fund managers. Given that most Americans were caught completely off guard by the crash resulting from the banks' misleading investors on subprime loans, it's curious that politicians like McConnell reaped such a massive windfall while everyone else saw their life savings get flushed away. It's almost like he knew what would happen ahead of time.

"Even ignoring all allegations of corruption and insider trading, McConnell is still a paragon of sleaziness. CREW (Citizens for Responsibility and Ethics in Washington) has named McConnell to their most corrupt politicians list four times now, most recently over what smells like Congressional aides doing campaign work on taxpayer time. Mother Jones obtained secret recordings of a McConnell campaign strategy meeting in which the senator lauded opposition research on his potential 2014 challengers obtained by his legislative assistants. Had this research been done using McConnell's office resources, during the work week, it would certainly merit, at the very least, an ethics investigation if not an indictment.

"If Kentuckians are still planning to vote for McConnell despite well-documented instances of his serving billionaire donors over citizens, the highly-questionable rapid growth of his net worth during a recession, and potential violations of basic ethics, even his record as a true-blue Kentuckian can be called into question."

opednews.com Headlined to H3 10/7/14

"The Brent Spence Bridge, which connects Covington, Kentucky, to Cincinnati, Ohio, is badly in need of repairs. Many Kentuckians who work in Cincinnati depend on the bridge for their daily commute. However, the Cincinnati Enquirer recently called the bridge "one of the most hazardous bridges in the nation."

"In true Mitch McConnell fashion, the senator opposes allotting new funds to repair the bridge unless a law protecting a prevailing wage for federal contractors is repealed. In other words, Mitch McConnell won't do anything to help workers in Kentucky unless it comes at the expense of screwing workers in Kentucky.

"If that weren't bad enough, McConnell's campaign even mistakenly included footage of the Duke University men's basketball team celebrating its 2010 title win in a campaign ad. His campaign team tried to fix the mistake by splicing in an image of 2013 Kentucky star player Julius Randle where the Duke celebration was. But using a current player's likeness in a political ad is forbidden by the NCAA, so the ad had to be pulled altogether. As a native Kentuckian and UK fan, I know full well that rooting for Duke anywhere in the Commonwealth is a criminal offense. I also know that using the image of a Kentucky Wildcats basketball player for political purposes without his knowledge is sacrilege for Big Blue fans, which is pretty much the entire state outside of Louisville. The icing on the cake? Mitch McConnell doesn't even know the words to "My Old Kentucky Home," our state anthem.

"Kentucky voters, I'm talking to you. It's on you to forcibly remove this disgustingly corrupt, parasitic, cancerous tumor from the Senate this November. He's done literally nothing for anyone who hasn't directly put money in his pocket. And he'll continue to screw you in favor of his corporate sponsors the longer you allow him to collect a paycheck. He's already down in the latest polls. Finish the job, ditch Mitch, and make your nation proud of you."

*Carl Gibson, 26, is co-founder of US Uncut, a nationwide creative direct-action movement that mobilized tens of thousands of activists against corporate tax avoidance and budget cuts in the months leading up to the Occupy Wall Street movement. Carl and other US Uncut activists are featured in the documentary "We're Not Broke," which premiered at the 2012 Sundance Film Festival. He currently lives in Madison, Wisconsin. You can contact him at carl@rsnorg.org, and follow him on twitter at @uncutCG. http://www.opednews.com/articles/2/Mitch-McConnell-Is-the-Can-by-the-web-Corruption_Donations_Ethics_Mitch-Mcconnell-141007-281.html

"Sarah Palin once reminded us that she originally rose to political prominence in Alaska when she took on the self-proclaimed "Corrupt Bastards Club" of establishment Republican politicians who had literally sold the state government to the oil industry. After giving an outstanding analysis of where the whole ObamaCare disaster was heading – single payer socialized medicine – Palin said what was on the minds of millions of limited government constitutional conservatives after the GOP establishment waived the white flag. "You have to wonder whether the permanent political class in D.C. really wants to get rid of Obamacare at all. We're finding out its good business for them."

"And the one establishment Republican politician who arguably came out better than anyone else in the deal to end the stand-off over defunding ObamaCare and imposing real spending reform on the federal government was the Senate's Republican Minority Leader, Senator Mitch McConnell of Kentucky. Michael Patrick Leahy over at Breitbart reports that it turns out the bill to end the government shutdown that was passed by Congress and promptly signed by President Obama included only one earmark for a major public works project—an additional $2.1 billion authorization for the Olmsted Dam Project in McConnell's home state of Kentucky.

"This pet project of McConnell's is already 300% over budget. The project was first authorized by Congress in 1988 in Section 3 (a) (6) of Public Law 100-676, the Water Resources Development Act of 1988 at an original price tag of only $775 million. Two and a half decades later, the federal government has spent just short of $1.7 billion on the project to date, which remains less than half way complete.

"To paraphrase our friends at The Madison Project: If there is one individual who represents the face of the stale, tone-deaf, timid, moss-covered and obtuse leadership of the GOP establishment, it is Mitch McConnell. Mitch McConnell is emblematic of the rudderless leadership, vacuous core, and duplicitous tendencies of the powers that be within the Republican Party."

http://www.conservativehq.com/article/15207-mitch-mcconnell-washington%E2%80%99s-1-corrupt-bastard

"In a move that will surely bring a huge blow to his anti-insider status, President-elect Donald Trump has named Elaine Chao – the wife of Senate Majority Leader, Mitch McConnell – to a high-level cabinet appointment.

"Chao, who is a former Secretary of Labor under George W. Bush, and former Deputy Secretary of Transportation under George H. W. Bush, was tabbed as Trump's Transportation Secretary.

"Because of her marriage to the Senate Majority Leader, Chao will be faced with a rare conflict of interest. According to CNN, "At the Transportation Department, Chao would have a key role in helping Trump get an infrastructure spending bill passed through Congress and start government-backed works projects — a role likely to be complicated by her relationship with McConnell, who will also be a critical player in any infrastructure bill negotiations."

"Chao is the latest in a string of appointments both to Trump's transition team and his cabinet that have been in direct opposition to one of his primary campaign promises, to "drain the swamp." Now we will wait and see whether this unprecedented insider appointment will cause any of his hard-core supporters to second guess their trust in a proven liar — and their vote." But it is bound to also promote cooperation between McConnell and Trump

http://theproudliberal.org/corruption-trump-just-appointed-mitch-mcconnells-wife-to-his-cabinet/

"Cross posted at Hillbilly Report Senator Mitch McConnell will be seeking re-election in 2014, in Kentucky. For me, this isn't about Republicans or Democrats. It's what I really believe is best for Kentucky and America and I don't believe Senator Mitch McConnell fits that bill. I don't say this lightly because I believe this a serious matter that shouldn't be decided by listening to partisan robocalls, watching 30 second partisan political TV ads, taking the word of authority figures religious or secular, and/or reading partisan mail-outs. It's a matter that should be decided by an informed electorate. This is why I've listed 17 reasons why I can't support Senator Mitch McConnell in his 2014 re-election bid in 2014. The 17 Reasons: May 25, 2011, Senator Mitch McConnell voted to privatize Medicare. Senator Mitch McConnell is a big spender (Earmarks). Senator Mitch McConnell finds ways to funnel millions to his corporate friends like Amgen. Senator Mitch McConnell's refusal to answer questions about his Vietnam-era military service. Senator Mitch McConnell's wealth increased from $3.1 million in 2004 to $27.2 million in 2010. A $24.1 increase of wealth during the worst recession since the great depression. Senator Mitch McConnell uses email fear tactics to raise money. Senator Mitch McConnell's priorities. Senator Mitch McConnell's filibuster tactics. Senator Mitch McConnell's support of Senatorial candidates like Richard Mourdock. Senator Mitch McConnell's vote against veterans. Senator Mitch McConnell's ties with American Crossroads and Crossroads GPS. Senator Mitch McConnell's ties with the US Chamber Of Commerce. Senator Mitch McConnell's cronyism. Senator Mitch McConnell's allegiance to Grover Norquist! Senator Mitch McConnell's environmental record! Mitch McConnell's insensitivity for poor folks! Okay, I think that's enough for now. Oh, I have one more. It's kind of personal. Mitch McConnell doesn't know the words to "My Old Kentucky Home!" http://www.dailykos.com/story/2013/03/12/1193125/-17-Reasons-Why-I-Can-t-Support-Senator-Mitch-McConnell-s-2014-Re-Election-Bid

"KDP calls for Ethics investigation into "Most Corrupt" McConnell for selling access to the Senate Dining Room. Posted August 22, 2014

FRANKFORT – Today, the Kentucky Democratic Party calls for a Congressional ethics investigation into reports that Mitch McConnell has abused his public office for political gain by selling access to the Senate dining room in return for campaign contributions. Accordingly, the KDP will file a complaint for the Senate Select Committee on Ethics to investigate whether Sen. Mitch McConnell (R-KY) violated federal law.

"Today, Kentucky Democratic Party released the following statement from KDP Chairman Dan Logsdon:

"It's not a coincidence that just days after treating a corporate bigwig to a meal in the U.S. Senate dining room, Mitch McConnell was repaid with $10,000 to fund his trusted Washington campaign. These reports are serious, erode the public trust, and if true, his actions could be illegal. Without a full ethics investigation into this matter, the Senator's constituents are right to remain skeptical. After 30 years in Washington, Mitch McConnell seems to forget all too often that he works for the taxpayers of Kentucky, not Fortune 500 CEOs."

Background: "McConnell Was Rated "Most Corrupt" In the Senate Four Times. Independent group Citizens for Ethics and Responsibility in Washington wrote, "Senate Minority Leader Mitch McConnell (R-KY) is a five-term senator from Kentucky. His ethics issues stem from his possible use of Senate staff and resources to conduct opposition research for his campaign. He was included in CREW's 2007, 2008, and 2009 reports on congressional corruption for unrelated matters." [CREW, 2013]"

http://kydemocrat.com/news/kdp-calls-ethics-investigation-most-corrupt%E2%80%9D-mcconnell-selling-access-senate-dining-room

"Bill Owens, D-N.Y. Representative – "Rep. Owens and his wife took a trip to Taiwan organized by lobbyists and paid for by the Taiwanese government, violating federal law and House rules. Although Rep. Owens listed the Chinese Culture University as the trip's sponsor, it was in fact planned by the Taiwanese government and its registered foreign agent in Washington. The Office of Congressional Ethics found reason to believe the trip violated House rules and federal law, which prohibit members from accepting payment from foreign governments for the travel of their family members, or for any travel arranged by lobbyists. A three-term member of Congress representing New York's 21st district, Owens is under investigation by the House Ethics Committee for improperly accepting a trip to Taiwan for himself and his wife arranged by lobbyists and paid for by a foreign government. One of four members of Congress from New York named to CREW's Most Corrupt. Appeared in CREW's Family

Affair exposé." http://www.crewsmostcorrupt.org/mostcorrupt/entry/bill-owens

Peter Roskam, R-Il. Representative – "Rep. Roskam and his wife took a trip to Taiwan sponsored by the Taiwanese government, violating federal law and House rules. Although Rep. Roskam listed the Chinese Culture University as the trip's sponsor, the trip was planned by the Taiwan Economic and Cultural Representative Office, Taiwan's de facto embassy in Washington. The Office of Congressional Ethics found reason to believe Rep. Roskam violated House rules and federal law, which prohibit foreign governments from paying travel expenses for the family of members of Congress. Roskam is a four-term member of Congress representing Illinois' 6th district. He is under investigation by the House Ethics Committee for improperly accepting a trip to Taiwan for himself and his wife sponsored by a foreign government. One of two members of Congress from Illinois named to CREW's Most Corrupt."

http://www.crewsmostcorrupt.org/mostcorrupt/entry/peter-roskam\

Aaron Schock, R-Il. Representative – "A grand jury returned a 52-page indictment on Nov. 10 that alleged Schock used money from his campaign accounts and $1 million-plus U.S. House office budget to bankroll a lavish lifestyle. In February 2015, The Washington Post reported that Schock's congressional offices had been lavishly redecorated in a style inspired by the aristocratic homes in the television show Downton Abbey. In response to that story, the watchdog group Citizens for Responsibility and Ethics in Washington (CREW) filed a complaint alleging Schock could have received an improper gift. CREW's executive director, Anne Weismann, stated, "Again and again, Rep. Schock's seeming obsession with his image impedes his ability to conduct himself in [an] ethical manner." Schock dismissed the criticism with the statement "Haters gonna hate," which was in turn criticized for its apparent flippancy. Schock later stated he intended to pay the decorator. Another investigation had discovered he had spent campaign money on workout DVDs.

"Further media scrutiny of Congressional expenditure reports showed that Schock had spent over $100,000 in government funds on office decorating and renovations between January 2009 and late 2014, mostly during his first term. Other media [clarification needed] reported Schock had charged thousands of dollars for private flights, legal expenses, new cars, tickets to the Super Bowl and Country Music Awards, as well as cufflinks, massage, "gold equipment" and cigars to his government-funded office account. The Associated Press accessed the location metadata on Schock's Instagram photos and correlated it with private flight records to identify flights that did not correspond to his campaign finance disclosures. In response, Schock's office stated it had begun an internal review of the reimbursements.

"In March 2015 there were further reports of spending and disclosure irregularities including that Schock had accepted money from an outside group, the Global Poverty Project, to cover the cost of bringing a photographer on an all-expenses-paid trip to India organized to discuss sanitation and access to clean water. Associated Press also reported that much of Schock's personal wealth had been built with the assistance of political donors. Conservative commentators began calling for Schock's replacement. National Review called him "a crook" and stated: "Politics shouldn't be a ticket to a celebrity lifestyle on the public's dime. For a man who has enjoyed such a short and undistinguished career, Illinois's Representative Aaron Schock (R) has sure packed in a lot of corruption."

"On March 16, Politico reported that Schock had requested the federal government and his campaign reimburse him for a total of 170,000 miles that were driven on his personal car, a Chevrolet Tahoe, between January 2010 and July 2014. But when he transferred that car back to the dealer in July 2014, he signed documents saying it had only been driven 80,000 miles. A subsequent investigation by the Chicago Sun-Times of reimbursements on Schock's previous vehicle, a GM Envoy, revealed a similar discrepancy. He bought the Envoy in 2007 while still in the state house. The Envoy had 24,300 miles on its odometer when he bought it. When he sold it in 2009, he'd put an additional 53,100 miles on it in a little over two years. However, during 2009 he billed the federal government and his campaign for a total of 42,300 miles.

"On March 17, 2015, Schock announced his resignation from Congress, effective March 31, 2015. The resignation came less than 12 hours after the Politico report about the questionable reimbursements went online. On the day he announced his resignation, his spokesman said that Schock had refunded all reimbursements he had received for mileage on his car. By resigning, he avoided an impending congressional ethics inquiry. On March 20, the Chicago Tribune reported that federal investigators had opened a "preliminary investigation" into the activities of Schock. In October 2016, Schock agreed to pay a $10,000 civil penalty to the Federal Election Commission for having asked Rep. Eric Cantor to contribute $25,000 to pay for advertisements for Rep. Adam Kinzinger.

"On November 10, 2016, the United States Attorney for the Central District of Illinois announced that a federal grand jury indicted Schock on 24 criminal counts including theft of government funds, fraud, making false statements and filing false tax returns."

http://www.chicagotribune.com/news/local/breaking/ct-aaron-schock-wants-new-venue-met-1128-20161128-story.html https://en.wikipedia.org/wiki/Aaron_Schock

John Tierney, D-Ma Representative – "Rep. Tierney's tax returns and personal financial disclosure forms have a big hole — thousands of dollars in payments his wife received tied to her brother's illegal gambling operation. Rep. Tierney's wife, Patrice Tierney, received over $200,000 from an account she managed for her brother, who was charged with running an illegal gambling business in Antigua. Rep. Tierney may have violated federal law and House rules by leaving the income off his tax returns and financial disclosure forms. Nine-term member of Congress representing Massachusetts' 6th district. Formerly under investigation by the House Ethics Committee for failing to disclose his wife's assets and income on his tax returns and personal financial disclosure forms." http://www.crewsmostcorrupt.org/mostcorrupt/entry/john-tierney

David Valado, R-Ca, Representative – "Rep. Valadao has only been a member of Congress since January, but it appears he has already joined the ranks of those who come to Washington primarily to advance their own financial interests. In June, Rep. Valadao successfully offered an amendment to an appropriations bill that would effectively stall, if not end, the prospect of completing additional segments of California's high-speed rail project. The congressman's family operates Valadao Dairy, which owns hundreds of acres of land along one of the proposed rail lines, and would face reduced property values as a result of the project. When Rep. Valadao offered his amendment and advocated for its adoption, he failed to inform his

House Appropriations Committee colleagues of his financial interest in its passage. In July, CREW asked the Office of Congressional Ethics to investigate Rep. Valadao. First-term member of Congress representing California's 21st district. Abused his position on the House Appropriations Committee to benefit his and his family's financial interests."

http://www.crewsmostcorrupt.org/mostcorrupt/entry/david-valadao

Vance McAllister, R-La. Representative – "On April 7, 2014, the Ouachita Citizen newspaper of West Monroe, posted online a copy of a surveillance video from an anonymous source which shows McAllister kissing a woman in his Monroe district office. The video was recorded in McAllister's Monroe congressional office on December 23, 2013. McAllister's aide Leah Gordon was alleged to have leaked the video to the Ouachita Citizen. The staff member who kissed McAllister was Melissa Anne Hixon Peacock. Both aides resigned in 2014. The woman was subsequently identified as a married, longtime employee of McAllister. McAllister lost his re-election bid." https://en.wikipedia.org/wiki/Vance_McAllister

Jeff Denham, R-Ca. Representative – "State Senate Campaign donated $25K and loaned $200K to veterans' charity • Same charity asked State Senator Denham to serve as a spokesman and appear in ads. Ads provided valuable exposure in Congressional District weeks before 2010 Primary. Charity's ads cost between $100K and $200K to promote concert raising just $100K. Denham forgave $200K in loans to charity two weeks after winning General Election. As State Senate campaign accepted corporate $$, this was money laundering."

http://www.wrhammons.com/Candidate/denham-congressional-corruption.htm

Jared Polis, D-Col. Representative – "One of seven openly gay members of Congress. Listed as one of most corrupt members of Congress. Investments in Medical Tourism company should've ended before swear-in. Investment in Biotech fund benefiting from Obamacare more troubling. Disclosure: Hammons is a former political opponent of Polis."

http://www.wrhammons.com/Candidate/polis-congressional-corruption.htm

Howard "Buck" McKeon, D-Ca. Representative – "Rep. Howard McKeon received a sweetheart mortgage deal through the Countrywide VIP program, and then improperly used his official staff to try to contain the political fallout for his wife's campaign. In January 2012, news reports revealed that the California Republican received favorable terms on a mortgage through Countrywide's VIP program. Rep. McKeon implausibly claimed that he had not known he received a deal under the VIP program, even though the cover letter of his loan package was stamped "VIP" multiple times. After the deal came to light, members of Rep. McKeon's staff circulated a memo discussing strategy against a candidate running against Rep. McKeon's wife, Patricia McKeon, for a State Assembly seat. Ten-term member of Congress representing California's 25th district. Received a sweetheart mortgage deal through the Countrywide VIP program, then used his official staff to try to contain the political fallout for his wife's campaign. Chairman of the House Armed Services Committee. One of three members from California named to CREW's Most Corrupt. Appeared in CREW's Family Affair exposé."

http://www.crewsmostcorrupt.org/mostcorrupt/entry/buck-mckeon

Eddie Johnson, D-TX. Representative – "Johnson awarded 23 scholarships in violation of Congressional Black Caucus Foundation eligibility rules • Eight scholarships awarded to Rep's grandsons and top aide's children. Listed as one of most corrupt members of Congress."

http://www.wrhammons.com/Candidate/johnson-congressional-corruption.htm

Sanford Bishop, D-Ga. Representative – "also listed as one of most corrupt members of Congress, Bishop improperly awarded Congressional Black Caucus Foundation scholarships to family members and employees' relatives. Bishop even awarded a scholarship to his own stepdaughter." http://www.wrhammons.com/Candidate/sbishop-congressional-corruption.htm

Mark Kirk, R-Il. Senator – "Sponsored legislation that benefited alleged mistress / definite girlfriend. Listed as one of most corrupt members of Congress. Got caught on open mike making comment about Lindsey Graham which offended several women and black Senators."

http://www.chicagotribune.com/news/local/breaking/ct-mark-kirk-graham-met-0612-20150611-story.html. http://www.wrhammons.com/Candidate/kirk-congressional-corruption.htm

Nancy Pelosi, D. Cal. Representative – "Then-Speaker Pelosi and husband purchased 5,000 shares of Visa at $44. As bill hurting credit card companies began journey through House Two days after purchase Visa was trading at $85."

http://www.wrhammons.com/Candidate/pelosi-congressional-corruption.htm

"According to Schweizer [Journalist for Breitbart], corporations that wish to build congressional allies will sometimes hand-pick members of Congress to receive IPOs. Pelosi received her Visa IPO almost two weeks after a potentially damaging piece of legislation for Visa, the Credit Card Fair Fee Act, had been introduced in the House. If passed, the bill would have cut into Visa's profits substantially by lowering so-called "interchange fees," the 1% to 3% charge retailers pay Visa when customers use Visa cards for purchases. Interchange fees are a critical source of revenue for the four credit card companies–$48 billion in 2008, to be exact.

"If the Credit Card Fair Fee Act had been passed into effect, it would have amended antitrust laws to require credit card companies to enter negotiations with merchants over interchange fees, and it would have given the Justice Department and the Federal Trade Commission the power to arbitrate if the two sides failed to come to an agreement. For that reason, Visa and the other credit card companies strongly opposed the bill.

"The Credit Card Fair Fee Act was exactly the kind of bill one would think then-Speaker Pelosi would have backed. "She had been outspoken about antitrust problems posed by insurance, oil, and pharmaceutical companies," Schweizer notes, "and she was vocal about the need for controlling interest rates individual banks charged to use their credit cards."

"Nancy Pelosi is hardly the only member of Congress to be given IPOs, but Pelosi has been especially "lucky" at landing them. She and her husband have participated in at least 10 lucrative IPOs throughout her career. In 1993, Pelosi purchased IPO shares in a high-tech company named Gupta, watched the stock price leap 88% in 24 hours, then seized the profits by selling the stock the next day. Pelosis did the same thing with Netscape and UUNet, resulting in a one-day doubling of their initial investment. Other fast and lucrative IPO flips included Remedy Corporation, Opal, Legato Systems, and Act Networks.

"Schweizer says Nancy Pelosi's financial disclosure forms typically mask the precise dates of her stock buys. He cites the Pelosis' December 1999 stock purchase of between $250,000 and $500,000 in shares from high-tech company OnDisplay. A few months later, OnDisplay was bought by Vignette, which resulted in up to $1 million in capital gains for the Pelosis. What was unusual about the transaction is that Vignette's IPO was underwritten by a major campaign contributor and longtime friend of Nancy Pelosi, William Hambrecht."

https://startthinkingright.wordpress.com/2011/11/14/how-nancy-pelosi-got-rich-corruption-abuse-of-power-alert/

"In late September and early October of 2008, after a financial crisis in the home lending industry the United States Senate met and passed HR 1424, the 2008 Economic Stabilization Bill to bail out the industry at a cost of $700,000,000,000. When news of the bill was released it was found to have several controversial earmarks."

"Earmarks include an economic development credit for American Samoa, tax exemptions for makers of wooden bows and arrows for children, funding for wool research, and amendments to the Internal Revenue Code provisions relating to the tax deduction for domestic film and television productions. These were written into the bill before it was presented to the house in March of 2008.

"On October 3, 2008 the San Francisco Chronicle reported. "While crafting a bill intended to rescue the U.S. economy this week, lawmakers couldn't stop themselves from adding billions of dollars in tax breaks that have little to do with restoring confidence in financial markets."

"An eRumor questioning the relationship between the American Samoa earmark and Speaker of the house, Nancy Pelosi, gained momentum the week of October 20, 2008 over past criticism of a minimum wage hike in 2007 that omitted American Samoa.

"On January 12, 2007 the Washington Times wrote an article about Pelosi and the minimum wage law saying," House Republicans yesterday declared 'something fishy' about the major tuna company in

House Speaker Nancy Pelosi's San Francisco district being exempted from the minimum-wage increase that Democrats approved this week."

"The 2007 bill raised the minimum wage from $5.15 to $7.25 per hour and extended for the first time the U.S. territory of the Northern Mariana Islands but exempted American Samoa. Starkist, a division of Del Monte Foods, has facilities in American Samoa with an employee base of about 5,000, roughly 75% of the work force on that island. The company is headquartered in Nancy Pelosi's district and was very much against the raise in wages. A spokesperson for the Speaker of the House said that neither StarKist nor Del Monte had lobbied Pelosi in any way.

"Facts about Pelosi's husbands Starkist/Del Monte stock investments have not been listed in her earnings disclosure.

"According to the Center for Responsive Politics, neither Starkist nor Del Monte were found on the contributor list for Pelosi in donations amounting $10,000 or more.

"The Bill was passed in the House Mar 5, 2008, passed by the Senate Oct 1, 2008 and signed by President Oct 3, 2008." https://www.truthorfiction.com/earmarks-bailout/

John Boehner, R.Ohio. Representative – "Bought health care stocks in 2009 shortly before Public Option dropped from Democratic health care bill."

http://www.wrhammons.com/Candidate/boehner-congressional-corruption.htm

"Boehner, who has a drinking problem, which is ignored by the media, is also an incorrigible skirt chaser who has had numerous affairs. Married since 1973, he was forced to narrow his skirt chasing from three down to one when he found he was in line to become Speaker of the House.

"Voters put Republicans in the House to show some leadership. Instead we got a drunken adulterer."

Spencer Bachus, R. Ala. Representative – "Participated in Sept. '08 closed-door briefing with Treasury Secretary. Topic: high likelihood of economic decline if drastic steps not taken. "Matter of days before the meltdown in global financial system." Next day, Bachus bought "Ultra-Short" options, betting on that decline. Collected a personal profit of thousands of dollars."

http://www.wrhammons.com/Candidate/bachus-congressional-corruption.htm

Joe Barton, R-TX. Representative – "In April 2008, Barton, then Ranking Member of the House Committee on Energy and Commerce, bought an interest in natural gas wells and earned an estimated 200% profit on his investment that year. Barton lied on financial disclosure forms regarding the identity of the seller. Seller Walter Mize died that same year. Barton thus positioned to benefit from increased production of natural gas while co-sponsoring legislation to increase demand for natural gas."

http://www.wrhammons.com/Candidate/barton-congressional-corruption.htm

Darrell Issa, R. Ca Representative – "As Chairman cut off Ranking Member of Oversight Committee at the hearing, publicized specific and extensive details from a wiretap application. Federal law requires apps for communication intercepts kept sealed. Issa allegedly arrived with and displayed a gun while firing an employee. Accused of arson and settled for only $20,000 of $175,000 insurance claim. Source of Issa's initial capital for Steal Stopper a mystery. Accused of and/or arrested for three separate incidents of auto theft. Accused of hitting a woman with his car and fleeing scene; settled the suit. Arrested for carrying a concealed weapon."

http://www.wrhammons.com/Candidate/issa-congressional-corruption.htm

David Vitter, R. La. Senator – "In 2011, attempted to bribe the Secretary of the Interior for drilling permits. DC Madam had Vitter's number, and he hasn't denied all prostitution rumors."

http://www.wrhammons.com/Candidate/vitter-congressional-corruption.htm

Stephen Fincher, R-Tenn. Representative – "Lied about the source of $250,000 loan to his 2010 Congressional Campaign. Also lied to Federal Election Commission about nature of the loan. Impotent Federal Election Commission agreed Fincher broke law."

http://www.wrhammons.com/Candidate/fincher-congressional-corruption.htm

Nick Rahall, R-W.V. Representative – "Introduced legislation that specifically benefited lobbyist sister. The same sister had an inbox for mail in Rahall's Congressional office."

http://www.wrhammons.com/Candidate/rahall-congressional-corruption.htm

Rob Andrews, D.N.J. Representative – "The Office of Congressional Ethics investigated Rep. Andrews and, on April 2, 2012, referred his case to the House Ethics Committee.68 OCE found there was substantial reason to believe Rep. Andrews improperly used congressional campaign and Leadership PAC funds for personal use to pay expenses related to his family's Scotland trip, his daughter's graduation party, and the trips to Los Angeles, as well as other possible misspending.69 On March 19, 2013, the House Ethics Committee announced it was establishing an investigative subcommittee to investigate whether Rep. Andrews improperly used campaign or PAC funds for personal expenses, misused official resources, or made false statements to federal officials. By using campaign funds to pay for his family's trip to Scotland, for a graduation party for his daughter, Jacqueline Andrews, and to subsidize the fledgling acting and singing career of his daughter, Josie Andrews, Rep. Andrews likely violated 2 U.S.C. §§ 439a(b)(2)(E) and (H) and 11 C.F.R. §§ 113.1(g)(1)(i)(F) and (J). Further, if Rep. Andrews' conduct was knowing and willful, he likely violated criminal law." http://www.crewsmostcorrupt.org/page/-/PDFs/Reports/Most%20Corrupt%20Reports/CREW-Most-Corrupt-Members-of-Congress-Report-2013.pdf?nocdn=1

Debbie Wasserman Schultz (Rep. D-Fla) – "Wasserman Schultz employed Pakistani-born Awan and his wife Hina Alvi, and refused to fire either of them even after U.S. Capitol Police said in February 2017 that they were targets of the criminal investigation. She said police wouldn't show her evidence against the couple and, without it, she assumed they might be victims of anti-Muslim profiling.

"Awan's wife left the country for good in March 2017 after taking $12,000 in cash and having hundreds of thousands of dollars waiting for her in Pakistan obtained through mortgage frauds according to FBI Affidavits.

"What services were Awan Alvi providing to Wasserman Schultz for six months that she paid him for before his arrest? His talents were information technology. What information was he providing that was so very important that Schultz would keep him on her payroll?

"In public court documents filed in Fairfax, Va., Awan's stepmother accused him of wiretapping and extortion. "Imran Awan did admit to me that my phone is tapped and there are devices installed in my house" and "Imran Awan threatened that he is very powerful and if I ever call the police again, [he] will ... kidnap my family members back in Pakistan," his stepmother, Samina Gilani, claimed in the documents (p. 21) filed April 14."

http://dailycallernewsfoundation.org/2017/07/29/wasserman-schultz-seemingly-planned-to-pay-suspect-even-while-he-lived-in-pakistan/

John Lewis D. GA. Representative. Rep. John Lewis: "You know, I believe in forgiveness. I believe in trying to work with people. It will be hard. It's going to be very difficult. I don't see this president-elect as a legitimate president."

So here's what we now know:

* John Lewis has said the last two Republican presidents were illegitimate.
* John Lewis has attended just one inauguration of a Republican president since he was first elected to Congress in 1986: that of George H.W. Bush in 1988.

https://www.washingtonpost.com/news/the-fix/wp/2017/01/17/john-lewis-just-committed-a-big-oopsie/?utm_term=.0e0924f66064

Wes Criddle· May 2, 2016 · Mineola, TX · "The US has entered into a contract with a real estate firm to sell 56 buildings that currently house U.S. Post Offices. All 56 were built, operated, and paid for by tax-paying American citizens. Now enjoy reading the rest: The government has decided it no longer needs these buildings, most of which are located on prime land in towns and cities across the country.

"The sale of these properties will fetch about$19 billion!

"A regular real estate commission will be paid to the company that was given the exclusive listing for handling the sales. That company is CRI and it belongs to a man named Richard Blum.

Diane Feinstein – D-Ca. "Richard Blum is the husband of Senator Dianne Feinstein! (Most voters and many of the government people who approved the deal have not made the connection between the two because they have different last names).

"Senator Feinstein and her husband stand to make a fortune, estimated at between $950 million and $1.1 Billion from these transactions!

"His company is the sole real estate agent on the sale!

"CRI will be making a minimum of 2% and as much as 6% commission on each and every sale. All of the properties that are being sold are all fully paid for. They were purchased with U.S. taxpayers' dollars.

"The U.S.P.S. is allowed free and clear, tax exempt use. The only cost to keep them open is the cost to actually keep the doors open and the heat and lights on. The United States Postal Service doesn't even have to pay county property taxes on these subject properties. Question? Would you put your house in foreclosure just because you couldn't afford to pay the electric bill?

"Well, the folks in Washington have given the Post Office the OK to do it! Worse yet, most of the net proceeds of the sales will go back to the U.S.P.S, an organization that is so poorly managed that they have lost $117 billion dollars in the past 10 years!

"No one in the mainstream media is even raising an eyebrow over the conflict of interest and on the possibility of corruption on the sale of billions of dollars' worth of public assets.

"How does a U.S. Senator from San Francisco manage to get away with organizing and lobbying such a sweet deal? Has our government become so elitist that they have no fear of oversight?

"It's no mere coincidence that these two public service crooks have different last names; a feeble attempt at avoiding transparency in these type of transactions."

http://www.truthorfiction.com/.../Blum-Post-Office-Sale-06101...
http://www.snopes.com/politics/business/blum.asp

Anthony D. Weiner (D-N.Y.) Sentenced on September 25, 2017 to 21 months in Federal prison over his exchange of lewd texts with a 15 year old girl.

If this doesn't upset you, don't complain about the corruption and the ineptness in D.C.

These and other Democrat scandals have sharply reduced whatever trust the voters had in their party to clean up corruption in Washington, especially in blue states like Illinois, Pennsylvania, Connecticut, Delaware, and Massachusetts.

A recent Rasmussen poll found that voters still trust Democrats more than Republicans on ethics and corruption by 35% to 28%. Notably, though, 27% now said they were not sure who to trust.

But we may well be hearing a lot more about the Democratic corruption in the future–this time about offering bribes to affect the outcome of Federal elections.

"Democratic Rep. Joe Sestak of Pennsylvania has charged that someone at the White House, he refuses to identify, offered him a Federal job if he agreed to drop out of the Democratic primary battle against Sen. Arlen Specter. That has spurred demands from Republicans for the appointment of a special prosecutor after months of evasion by the Obama Administration.

"If an offer was made, it was not the first time Obama's White House tried to buy off a Democrat with a political bribe to drop out of a party primary.

"The Denver Post reported last year that former Colorado House Speaker Andrew Romanoff was apparently offered a federal job by top Obama "fixer" Jim Messina if the Colorado Democrat would abandon his Democratic primary bid against appointed Sen. Michael Bennet.

"When President Obama promised to change the way Washington worked, Americans weren't picturing allegations of bribery and shady White House cover-ups. President Obama and his administration should come clean immediately," said Amber Marchand, spokesman for the National Republican Senatorial Committee.

"Monroe, La. (AP) — "Republican Congressman Vance McAllister is trying to make up to Louisiana voters for getting too close to a married former employee. The first-term congressman was caught on tape earlier this year kissing a woman, not his wife. Despite saying earlier that he wouldn't seek a new term, McAllister is now asking voters for two more years in the House. He's bringing up the kissing incident during campaign appearances, calling it a "personal mistake." In a campaign ad, his wife says he has owned up to that same "mistake.

"McAllister is one of nine candidates in the race for the seat representing northeast Louisiana. Unless one of them gets a majority of the vote, the top two vote-getters will advance to a runoff on Dec. 6.

"According to Before It's News, Barack Hussein Obama surrendered his law license in 2008 in order to dodge charges that he lied on his bar application.

"His wife Michelle Obama also surrendered her law license back in 1993, after a Federal judge told her she could either surrender her license or be charged with insurance fraud.

"This information was found after experts became suspicious upon finding that both Michelle and Barack had handed over their licenses to practice law under a "voluntary surrender."

"Anyone familiar with law knows that lawyers only execute a "voluntary surrender" when they are about to be accused of something.

"This is just the latest in a long line of sketchy, criminal dealings committed by the Obamas." http://conservativepost. com/breaking-the-real-reason-barack-and-michelle-lost-their-law-licenses-is-exposed/

Rep. Tim Murphy (R-Pa), an anti-abortion lawmaker, who allegedly encouraged his lover to terminate a pregnancy, announced he would be resigning from Congress by the end of the month (Oct. 2017).

By Jim Drinkard, USA TODAY

Washington — A lobbyist can't legally pay for members of Congress to spend a lavish weekend in California's wine country — but a group of lobbyists apparently can.

Six House Democrats and four House Republicans flew to Stuttgart, Germany where they attended a gala dinner for DaimlerChrysler.

German National Tourist Board

If they form a tax-exempt group, a fairly easy exercise under IRS rules, lobbyists, and their employers can get around congressional ethics regulations that forbid lobbyists to pay directly for such trips. That's the model used by America's Trust, a non-profit group formed last year that appears to be financed primarily by lobbyists and other interests with a stake in issues before Congress. Every member of its 12-person board of directors is a Washington lobbyist.

In late April, the group paid for four members of Congress — three of them accompanied by spouses — to hop aboard a corporate jet, bound for the Napa Valley town of St. Helena. The weekend for the two Republicans and two Democrats included luxury accommodations at the Meadowood resort and a series of presentations on issues facing the wine industry. Meals on the three-day trip totaled $458 for each person. The total bill: $46,000.

Congressional rules allow lawmakers and their aides to take trips paid for by private interests, with a few caveats: The travel must relate to their official duties in Washington; it must not be primarily recreational, and it must not be paid for by lobbyists or representatives of a foreign interest. When lawmakers do travel, they must disclose the trip, its purpose and who paid for it.

Lobbyists also are required to report who pays them, how much they are paid and the issues they lobby on, under a 1995 disclosure law. But tax-exempt groups have minimal disclosure requirements. Paying for trips through a tax-exempt organization exploits a seam between tax law and the ethics rules, says Frances Hill of the University of Miami School of Law.

"The ethics rules invite you to set up conduits" for undisclosed money, she says. And the IRS, which oversees tax-exempt groups, "has been remarkably lacking in curiosity about cases like this." The agency is too understaffed to thoroughly review all of the country's 1.5 million tax-exempt organizations, she adds.

Since 2000, members of Congress have taken more than 5,900 privately financed trips at a cost of $17.6 million, according to the non-partisan PoliticalMoneyLine, which analyzes data on money in politics. More than half of the spending has come from tax-exempt groups such as America's Trust.

If this travel is legal, what's the problem? Experts inside and outside Congress point to several concerns: The non-profit groups don't have to disclose their donors; lobbyists, by forming these groups, can evade rules designed to limit their influence; and lawmakers, who are not allowed to accept gifts or meals worth more than $50, get lavish trips and gourmet meals from special-interest groups.

Who paid, traveled most

Top sponsors of privately paid congressional travel, 2000-2005:

1. Aspen Institute $3.1 million
2. Ripon Society $745,626
3. American Israel Public Affairs Committee $673,625
4. International Management and Development Institute $534,492
5. Association of American Railroads $394,312
6. Harvard University $312,788
7. Nuclear Energy Institute $272,877

8. American Association of Airport Executives $242,844
9. Islamic Free Market Institute Foundation $235,839
10. Confederation of Indian Industry $233,456

Top congressional travelers, by dollar amount, 2000-2005:
1. Rep. F. James Sensenbrenner, R-Wis. $176,718
2. Rep. Gene Green, D-Texas $172,764
3. Rep. Robert Wexler, D-Fla. $168,850
4. Sen. John Breaux, D-La. {+1} $162,496
5. Sen. Evan Bayh, D-Ind. $161,083
6. Rep. James Clyburn, D-S.C. $151,951
7. Rep. John Boehner, R-Ohio $151,684
8. Rep. Cal Dooley, D-Calif. {+1} $148,858
9. Rep. Hal Rogers, R-Ky. $148,092
10. Rep. Maxine Waters, D-Calif. $148,018

1 — Retired in January Source: PoliticalMoneyLine

"It's a new way to lobby people in a non-transparent manner," says James Thurber, who teaches lobbying at American University. "It's a way to cover up sources of influence. You get people trapped on a plane or on a trip for several days, and you can change minds."

Non-profits as travel agents

It isn't hard to find examples of lobbyists connected to non-profit groups sponsoring congressional trips:

- The Islamic Free Market Institute Foundation has paid for at least 23 trips by lawmakers since 2000, at a cost of $235,839. Most of the travel was to an annual conference in the Persian Gulf country of Qatar. The group raised $456,777 in 2003, according to its latest federal tax return, but declined to disclose its financial backers. Among the organization's founders in 1998 was Grover Norquist, a Republican activist and anti-tax lobbyist. He no longer is on the institute's board, but the organization shares an office with Norquist's group, Americans for Tax Reform. The Islamic Institute also has worked with another lobbyist, Asim Ghafoor, who represented an association of Islamic banks.
- Two groups, the Korea-U.S. Exchange Council and the Malaysia Exchange Association, set up to promote trade with Asia in part by organizing trips for lawmakers, have ties to the Alexander

Strategy Group, a lobbying firm founded by Rep. Tom DeLay's former chief of staff, Ed Buckham. The groups financed $224,000 in travel for a dozen House members since 2001.

The lobbying firm set up the Korea group in 2001 with the goal of making Korean businessman Seung Youn Kim, chairman of one of Korea's largest conglomerates, the Hanwha Group, "the leading business statesman in U.S.-Korean relations," according to a strategy memo. But because the group registered as an agent of a foreign interest, it could not legally sponsor congressional travel.

The Malaysia organization, which did not register as a foreign agent, sent three House members — Roger Wicker, R-Miss., Earl Pomeroy, D-N.D. and John Doolittle, R-Calif. — to Kuala Lumpur in February "to strengthen the bilateral relationship between the U.S. and Malaysia," according to Pomeroy's trip disclosure.

- The International Management and Development Institute has paid $534,000 during the past five years for 60 congressional trips, most of them to Germany and other Western European destinations. The institute is run by Don Bonker, a former Democratic House member from Washington state and now a lobbyist for APCO Worldwide.

The institute, funded by corporate contributions, shares an office with APCO. It sent six House Democrats and four House Republicans to Stuttgart in February. There, they heard presentations from officials of DaimlerChrysler at the company's headquarters and attended a "gala dinner in the Mercedes-Benz museum," according to an itinerary.

Privately financed congressional travel has become an issue after it was revealed that DeLay, the House majority leader from Texas, took trips that may have been paid for by lobbyist Jack Abramoff and by a registered foreign agent.

The House ethics committee is likely to look into the matter once it resolves an internal dispute over staffing that has business stalled. It may have to expand its inquiry to include other lawmakers alleged to have similar infractions, including Reps. Bob Ney, R-Ohio, and Tom Feeney, R-Fla.

Both took trips to Scotland — Ney in 2002 and Feeney in 2003 — that they said was paid for by the National Center for Public Policy Research, a non-profit that paid for one of DeLay's trips. Abramoff was on the center's board, and DeLay is under scrutiny because some trip expenses appear to have been paid with Abramoff's credit card.

The center says it hasn't sponsored a trip since the one DeLay took at its expense in 2000, and Ney and Feeney now say they don't know who paid for their travel. Since DeLay's trips became an issue, dozens of lawmakers have scrambled to file missing trip disclosures, some of them years late.

Democrats, led by Rep. Marty Meehan of Massachusetts, have proposed tightening rules to bar lobbyists from indirectly sponsoring travel through "front groups." The American League of Lobbyists, a trade group, called for a review of disclosure rules by the Government Accountability Office.

"The system is flawed," says Ney, who has expressed interest in Meehan's bill. "There's got to be a better system."

A USA TODAY/CNN/Gallup Poll conducted April 29-May 1 found that 82% of Americans believe it would be a "very serious" or "moderately serious" ethical matter if their member of Congress went on a trip paid for by a lobbyist.

Abramoff's attorney, Abbe Lowell, complained in a May 23 opinion column in USA TODAY that his client was being condemned for funneling money to groups that sponsor lawmakers' travel.

"What kind of rule is it that lobbyists cannot sponsor travel themselves, but can permissibly get their clients and others to sponsor charitable and education groups?" he asked. His solution: "Officials should travel on public funds when the travel is part of their jobs, and their own funds when it is not."

The wine country trip paid for by America's Trust included $658-a-night rooms for Reps. Jo Ann Emerson, R-Mo., and her husband; John Tanner, D-Tenn., and his wife; Charlie Melancon, D-La., and his wife; Ken Calvert, R-Calif.; and an aide to Emerson, Atalie Ebersole.

Emerson and Tanner are the co-chairs of America's Trust's Congressional Advisory Board; Calvert and Melancon are advisory board members. Emerson is a member of the Appropriations agriculture subcommittee. Tanner deals with trade matters on the House Ways and Means Committee. Melancon is an Agriculture Committee member. Calvert, whose district is home to a growing wine industry, chairs the Resources water subcommittee, which deals with farm irrigation.

Tanner defended the group, saying it has no political agenda. "America's Trust is one of the few organizations in Washington dedicated to information and bipartisan solutions, in a political atmosphere that is otherwise increasingly polarized," he said in a statement. Emerson declined to comment.

Federal tax filings for America's Trust show it raised $122,500 last year, the bulk of which went to pay the $90,000 salary of its director, Dotti Mavromatis, a former Democratic fundraiser. It has raised $51,500 so far this year.

The group's attorney, Judy Corley, said the organization would not disclose its donors but said four of the lobbyist board members — whom she would not specify — were among them.

The group also declined to say whose corporate plane it used for the trip or who accompanied the members of Congress, although it confirmed that one unidentified board member was aboard.

Shanti Stanton, a lobbyist for UST, which owns California vineyards, was with the congressional group in California, as were four other America's Trust board members: President Sandi Stuart, of the lobbying firm Clark & Weinstock; Katreice Banks, a lobbyist for communications company SBC; Steve Judge, who represents the Securities Industry Association; and Mark Seklecki, a lobbyist for the American Hospital Association.

Stuart said America's Trust was formed "to bring members of both parties together to talk about issues of importance and concern that they will be grappling with in the months and years ahead."

Asked whether that includes issues of concern to the group's financial backers, she said, "There certainly could be, but that's not the intent."

http://usatoday30.usatoday.com/news/washington/2005-06-21-lobbyists-cover_x.htm

http://lobbyit.com/

"Lobbyists corrupting America? That's not news. I mean, it's horrible and we should be talking about it more often, but it's a topic with which a lot of Americans are already familiar. What is news is that we've reached the point where lobbyists are outspending the government's own Congressional budget.

"U.S. Congress's budget – including both the Senate and the House – totals about $2 billion. Lobbying firms, meanwhile, are spending a total of $2.6 billion to convince members of Congress how to vote on certain pieces of legislation, or even what kind of legislation to focus on. That difference in spending is undoubtedly critical in shaping lawmakers' opinions.

"Technically, lobbyists started outspending Congress's budget a decade ago, but the amounts were pretty even back then. The gap has gradually widened ever since, and the difference has never been so great.

"The current $2 billion figure for Congress covers all sorts of costs, including salaries for congressional staffers and research expenditures. Elected officials can never be expected to know everything about everything they're called to vote on, which is why they do their best to surround themselves with people who are either knowledgeable or can learn about a given subject on their behalves.

"That's where the lobbyists come in. These helpful people offer up their expertise and advice to members of Congress for free. Alas, when Congress receives most of its information from people paid for by private interests, they're subsequent votes are bound to reflect the source. In a lot of cases, politicians don't have the money and resources to follow up on the information lobbyists provide them with, so there aren't a lot of critical questions asked of them.

"While it's true that not all lobbyists represent corporations, 95 percent of the largest lobbying firms primarily represent big business. Corporate lobbying spends 34 times more than lobbyists for public interest advocacy and labor unions combined. In that sense, the generalization that "lobbyists = corporate shills" is pretty fair.

"Vox's Ezra Klein offers up a potential solution, but I'm warning you, you're not going to want to hear it: Give Congress more of our tax dollars. After bolstering Congress members' staffs and resources, they could be better equipped to make legislative decisions and — theoretically — not have to rely so heavily on lobbyists.

"Considering that Congress makes votes on $4 trillion each year, even doubling the overall congressional budget to $4 billion doesn't seem so ridiculous when we remember what's at stake. After all, spending more money upfront could ultimately save the taxpayers money if kickbacks to lobbying corporations were reduced.

"Then again, lobbyists are likely to raise their own expenditures, too, so throwing more money at a problem that stems from too much money in politics might not be the right fix. Whatever the solution, something needs to be done, though, because letting corporations have this much sway over our lawmakers is not commiserate with a successful democracy."

http://www.care2.com/causes/lobbyists-now-spend-more-on-congress-than-the-government-does.html

"A deadly rail crash that left one person dead and more than 100 injured in New Jersey has led to questions over whether more could have been done to stop such accidents and put a new spotlight on the railroad industry's massive lobbying efforts to delay the implementation of safety measures, namely a computerized system called positive train control, which can intervene in the case of human error — and other scenarios — and stop a train.

"National Transportation Safety Board vice chair Bella Dinh-Zarr brought up that particular security system the day after the Hoboken crash.

"The cause of the Hoboken crash has not been determined, but officials said the train was traveling faster than permitted when it entered the terminal. "The NTSB has been recommending positive train control for 40 years," Dinh-Zarr told reporters last week, although officials also noted that it's not yet clear whether PTC or similar technology would have prevented the Hoboken crash.

"But the railroad industry, led by privately-owned freight lines, spent millions of dollars to get Congress to delay the deadline for PTC, such that the program may not be fully implemented until 2020 — five years later than the original schedule. The program was first mandated by Congress in 2008 to be in place by Dec. 31, 2015.

"According to the Center for Responsive Politics (CRP), railroads and their trade groups spent just under $30 million on lobbying in 2015, which was the year they were supposed to have the train safety program fully implemented.

"The commuter and freight industries made slightly different arguments during the debate over extending the PTC deadline -- and the freight industry spent much more of its own money on lobbying -- but generally, they were both concerned that the necessary technology was still in its nascent stages, the scope of the project was too big to complete in the necessary time, and, more so for the publicly-funded commuter rail lines, the costs were difficult to meet.

"By October 2015, the House and Senate had agreed to extend the deadline to the end of 2018 at the earliest — with an additional, optional two years available to railroads who meet certain requirements. By the end of that month, President Obama signed the extension, which was part of a short-term infrastructure bill, into law.

"What the Railroads have spent in Congress

"Between 2008 and 2015, the industry spent $316 million on lobbying efforts and an additional $24 million on getting members of Congress re-elected, according to the Center for Responsive Politics.

"The railroads also gave more than $7 million in contributions to individual members for the 2015 - 2016 campaign cycle, according to the CRP.

"The top individual beneficiary so far of the 2016 election cycle is Rep. Bill Shuster (R-Penn.), the chairman of the House Transportation Committee, with $146,000, according to Federal Election Commission records compiled by the CRP. Coming in at number seven was Sen. John Thune (R-SD), the chairman of the Senate committee dealing with transportation oversight, with $63,800, the data show.

"It is likely that a portion of the donations were made after President Obama signed the PTC delay into law in October 2015.

"Nobody's saying the industry shouldn't have a seat at the table but often they wield far more influence than is necessary or appropriate," Joshua Stewart, a spokesman for the government transparency group, the Sunlight Foundation, said.

"Shuster and Thune were among the most vocal advocates for blanket delays of PTC until 2018, making the same case as the railways that services would have to be shut down under the original deadline. "I believe, absent Congressional action, we will begin to see the effects of the deadline four to six weeks prior to the December 31st [2015] deadline as railroads begin to cycle traffic off their lines," Thune said during a 2015 hearing.

"A Thune spokesman said his contributions from the railroad industry had no bearing on his support for the deadline extension. Spokespeople for Shuster, DeFazio and Ryan did not respond to requests for comment.

"Still, CRP executive director Sheila Krumholz noted that while railroads have a smaller lobbying operation than many other industries, they're spending money in similar ways. "They spend in a strategic way, in ways that are going to help them promote their legislative agenda," she said.

"The Florida-based freight rail company CSX Transportation spent almost $3 million lobbying members of Congress to push back the 2015 deadline, according to CRP.

"One of the company's top executives testified about the challenges of implementation during a 2015 House Transportation subcommittee hearing.

"This technology is very difficult to implement. The scale proposition that we each have is very challenging," Frank Longero, the vice president of service design, said.

"Despite its opposition to the 2015 deadline, CSX has already made substantial progress in implementing PTC. According to the Federal Railroad Administration (FRA), the company has already trained 94 percent of its employees and acquired the needed radio spectrum that allows trains to transmit information to devices along the track.

"Asked why CSX advocated for the 2018 extension, spokesman Rob Doolittle cited the sheer magnitude of track miles — nearly 10,000 — across which PTC technology must be updated. "It is a large and complicated deployment," he said.

"While freight rail companies are generally making steady progress in installing the train safety system, many publicly-funded commuter rail lines are struggling to pay for the massive undertaking.

"So far, New Jersey Transit, on which the Hoboken train was operating, is one of 14 public rail lines that have posted "0%" progress on a Federal Railroad Agency chart tracking seven key metrics as of June 30 of this year.

"It did install needed hardware on 8 out of 440 trains, but in a report noted that the software for the computers is still under development. It has also scheduled a demonstration on a short section of track.

"New Jersey Transit has not disputed the government's data.

"The day after the Hoboken crash, New Jersey lawmakers and Gov. Chris Christie announced a deal to fund transportation projects by raising the state gas tax for the first time since 1988, although Christie said discussions on the deal began before the crash. It's not yet clear exactly how much of the new fund would go to railroad maintenance and improvement.

"Congress has appropriated about $300 million to help commuter rail lines install PTC, Shuster aides say, but the American Public

Transportation Association, which represents the commuter lines, says the industry's total cost will be about $3.5 billion.

"Our commuter rail properties and the diverse operating environments they're in – from the extremely strained Long Island Rail Road/Metro North to Nashville – they're all operating on very limited budgets and they are responding in kind to a federal mandate on installation of PTC," said Bill Terry, APTA's senior legislative representative.

"They are doing the best they can with what they've got," he added.

"Congressional aides assert they've done enough to provide loans for public commuter systems, and say it's up to them to find other ways to make up the difference, like raising ticket sales or increasing taxpayer contributions.

"Ed Greenberg, of the Association of American Railroads, which represents the freight industry, said it had been "warning Congress for years that the 2015 deadline was impossible to meet, given the complex task of developing, installing and testing this technology."

"Still, the industry has been working to get this revolutionary technology fully implemented as quickly as possible, once again, spending more than $6.5 billion of private money on getting PTC fully installed, and will be spending another $4-to-5 billion on meeting the current deadline as mandated by Congress last year," Greenberg added, noting that in total, the freight rail industry anticipates a price tag of over $10.6 billion.

"With 2018 (and two-year optional extension) officially on the books, both the commuter and freight rail industries insist they'll be on track to honor the Congressionally-mandated deadlines.

"But the FRA is still urging railroads to beat Congress' deadline if they can. In an August report, the agency noted that a total of 25 accidents — 15 freight and 10 passenger — occurred between 2001 and 2008, resulting in 34 deaths and 600 injuries.

"According to the NTSB, all of the accidents were PTC preventable," the FRA said in the report.

"The FRA also warned that since 2008 – when Congress first started down the road of requiring the train safety system – preventable accidents are still happening.

"On June 28, 2016, two BNSF freight trains collided head-on in Panhandle, Texas," the FRA wrote regarding one of the cases.

"Three crew members were killed."

http://abcnews.go.com/Politics/congress-lobbyists-helped-delay-passenger-train-safety-measures/story?id=42554562

"The Walt Disney Company has a reputation for lobbying hard on copyright issues. The 1998 copyright extension has even been dubbed the "Mickey Mouse Protection Act" by activists like Lawrence Lessig that have worked to reform copyright laws.

"This year, the company is turning to its employees to fund some of that battle. Disney CEO Bob Iger has sent a letter to the company's employees, asking for them to open their hearts—and their wallets—to the company's political action committee, DisneyPAC.

"In the letter, which was provided to Ars by a Disney employee, Iger tells workers about his company's recent intellectual property victories, including stronger IP protections in the Trans-Pacific Partnership, a Supreme Court victory that destroyed Aereo, and continued vigilance about the "state of copyright law in the digital environment." It also mentions that Disney is seeking an opening to lower the corporate tax rate.

"Further Reading — Supreme Court puts Aereo out of business

"With the support of the US Government we achieved a win in the Supreme Court against Aereo—an Internet service claiming the right to retransmit our broadcast signals without paying copyright or retransmission consent fees," writes Iger. "In the coming year, we expect Congress and the Administration to be active on copyright regime issues, efforts to enact legislation to approve and implement the Trans-Pacific Partnership trade agreement, tax reform, and more proposals to weaken retransmission consent, to name a few."

"The source who provided the letter to Ars asked to remain anonymous, and they were bothered by the assumption that anyone who worked for Disney would agree with the company's political positions on tax, trade, intellectual property, and other matters.

"It just seems insensitive to folks that support the company but don't necessarily support all of its priorities," the source said. "Especially for something like TPP, which I view as particularly controversial. We do have a company position, but there's going to be a wide variety of opinion [within the company]."

"The letter concludes with a suggested donation to DisneyPAC. Ars is not publishing the suggested amount in case it is personalized to the source's compensation or position at Disney.

"Further Reading — Obama praises Trans-Pacific Partnership accord as full text is released.

"For your convenience, DisneyPAC has implemented a payroll deduction system, through which your contributions to the PAC will be deducted from your weekly paycheck," Iger explains.

"The source received the letter via business mail and doesn't know how many other employees received it.

"I don't know how widely this was distributed," the source said. "Was it to rank and file folks in [theme] parks, to people working in a popcorn stand?"

"Disney didn't respond to Ars' requests for comment about the fundraising letter.

"Not unusual.

"Although Iger's letter was, in the view of this employee, somewhat tone-deaf, such requests are not illegal or even particularly uncommon. In 2012, Reuters reported on Citigroup's request to its employees to give to Citi PAC, a political entity that "contributes to candidates on both sides of the aisle that support a strong private sector and promote entrepreneurship."

"US corporations are allowed to solicit political contributions as long as donations aren't coerced. The relevant law bars any "threat of a detrimental job action, the threat of any other financial reprisal, or the threat of force" when asking for donations.

"The Disney letter has language explicitly reassuring employees that their jobs won't be affected by their decision whether or not to give to DisneyPAC.

"Your contribution is important to all of us, but I want to emphasize that all contributions are voluntary and have no impact on your job status, performance review, compensation, or employment," writes Iger. "Any amount given or the decision not to give will not advantage or disadvantage you."

"Iger's compensation in the last fiscal year was $45 million (£32 million).

"In the 2014 election cycle, the Disney employees' PAC spent about $375,000, according to OpenSecrets.org. During the current cycle with a presidential election on the way, the company will likely spend more. As of last month, the PAC had raised $295,000 and spent $231,000. The contributions are split roughly evenly between

Democrats and Republicans, which is the PAC's policy according to the CEO's letter.

"According to a MapLight analysis of the data, Disney's PAC contributed a total of $2.2 million in all election cycles since 2002. That doesn't include direct employee contributions to candidates, which adds another $1.5 million over the same period.

"DisneyPAC fundraising letter to employees

"Here's the verbatim text of most of Iger's letter to employees:

"As we head into the election year of 2016, the electorate faces significant decisions about the direction of our Nation's future. Besides choosing a new president, we will once again be electing new senators and representatives. These decisions will have a profound impact on the lives of all Americans. The election will also impact issues that affect our company. As such, we will continue to work with our representatives in Congress to ensure that they understand our perspective on critical issues like trade, intellectual property, tax, and travel policies. I write to urge you to consider supporting the Company's efforts through a contribution to DisneyPAC. A well-funded DisneyPAC is an important tool in our efforts to maintain our positive profile in Washington.

"In the past year, we successfully advocated the Company's position on a number of issues that have a significant impact on our business. We played a major role in ensuring that the "Trade Promotion Authority" legislation set high standards for intellectual property (IP) provisions in our trade negotiations, and we helped get that bill through Congress. We used that language in TPA to advocate successfully for a strong IP chapter in the Trans-Pacific Partnership (TPP) trade negotiations. We also pushed for provisions to promote digital trade and to reduce barriers in media and entertainment sectors. TPP will establish a strong baseline of protection for intellectual property while breaking down trade barriers in the Asia Pacific region. In both TPA and TPP we had to overcome significant efforts to weaken respect for IP, pushed not only by foreign governments but also from within our own Congress and the Administration.

"The fight on these issues is far from over. Last year we spent significant time and effort engaged in a series of government reviews of the state of copyright law in the digital environment.

"We also continued to defend our right to be compensated for carriage of our programming by cable and satellite carriers as well as by emerging "over-the-top" services. With the support of the US Government we achieved a win in the Supreme Court against Aereo—an Internet service claiming the right to retransmit our broadcast signals without paying copyright or retransmission consent fees. With respect to tax issues, Congress extended certain provisions that provide favorable tax treatment for film and television production in the US. It also extended this treatment to live theatrical productions. Last year we also worked closely with the Administration on important veterans' employment issues—an issue of critical importance for the men and women who defend our country and an area in which our company is proud to play a leadership role.

"In the coming year, we expect Congress and the Administration to be active on copyright regime issues, efforts to enact legislation to approve and implement the Trans-Pacific Partnership trade agreement, tax reform, and more proposals to weaken retransmission consent, to name a few.

"On the trade front, we will also look to build on our achievements in other negotiations this year. 2016 should see significant activity in negotiations between the US and China over a Bilateral Investment Treaty (BIT), continued negotiations with the European Union over the proposed Transatlantic Trade and Investment Partnership agreement, the 50-country Trade in Services Agreement negotiations, and efforts by the US Government to raise IP standards and break down trade barriers through a variety of means.

"In 2016, Congress will further discuss various tax reform proposals. While comprehensive reform is unlikely, activity in the coming year will lay the foundation for what many expect to be a genuine opportunity for reform in early 2017. We have been active educating Members of Congress on the importance of lowering the corporate tax rate to be competitive with the rest of the world. The US has one of the highest marginal and effective tax rates among developed countries, creating a significant competitive impediment to companies headquartered in the US.

"Congress will continue to be very active on intellectual property issues... After three years of hearings and testimony from 100 witnesses, we now expect the House Judiciary Committee to turn to legislating. We expect significant attention on legislation to modernize the

Copyright Office, a small agency that can have an enormous impact on our interests.

"And the Copyright Office has launched several proceedings involving possible changes to laws governing the accountability of online services and the laws protecting technologies used to secure distribution of digital content. These discussions obviously have significant implications for a business like ours that is dependent on copyright policy in the face of ongoing change in technology and the marketplace.

"We will also need to continue our work to fend off growing and concerted efforts to weaken our ability to freely negotiate the distribution of our broadcast and cable programming. Last year, the FCC teed up several rule makings that could have a significant adverse affect on retransmission consent and how we package and sell our media networks. As the debate becomes much more heated, we will need to remain vigilant.

"With all of the challenges we will face this year, it is important that our PAC be strong. We, therefore, respectfully suggest that you consider making a contribution of [REDACTED]. You may give more or less than the suggested amount (although no contribution can exceed $5000 in any year) and any contribution will be appreciated. As always, 100% of your contribution is used in direct support of candidates and political entities that uphold policies and principles that are consistent with the best interests of our company. DisneyPAC contributes equally to Democrats and Republicans each calendar year. For your convenience, DisneyPAC has implemented a payroll deduction system, through which your contributions to the PAC will be deducted from your weekly paycheck. If you prefer, you may instead make a one-time personal contribution to the PAC. Your contribution is important to all of us, but I want to emphasize that all contributions are voluntary and have no impact on your job status, performance review, compensation, or employment. Any amount given or the decision not to give will not advantage or disadvantage you. You have the right to refuse to contribute without reprisal. Your help is truly appreciated."

http://arstechnica.com/tech-policy/2016/02/disney-ceo-asks
-employees-to-chip-in-to-pay-copyright-lobbyists/

"Frank Underwood of Netflix's "House of Cards" may seem like America's most corrupt politician. He will stop at nothing, not even murder, to advance his political career. But as a political scientist, I know that real-life corruption is much more commonplace — and frankly more boring. Usually it's just a job offer.

"Remember Jack Abramoff, one of the best-connected lobbyists on Capitol Hill during the George W. Bush administration? In 2006, Abramoff was convicted on federal conspiracy, fraud and tax evasion charges. The scandal eventually led to the conviction of or plea bargains from 21 people, including White House officials, fellow lobbyists, congressional staffers and former Rep. Bob Ney (R-Ohio).

"According to Abramoff's playbook on how to gain influence in Washington, you could "own" a congressional office as soon as you said to a top staffer, "You know, when you're done working on the Hill, we'd very much like you to consider working for us."

"Those magic words win access and information more readily than campaign donations. With a job offer on the table, the official or staff member is all but working for the lobbying firm, on the taxpayers' dime.

"This isn't just hypothetical. Political scientist Adolfo Santos has found that public officials who have plans to become lobbyists act differently while in office from their colleagues who don't. Interestingly, they are more successful at passing the bills they introduce than officials who don't go on to be lobbyists. Does this behavior reflect their desire to please their potential future employer or something else? We can't tell. What we do know is that public officials who are no longer thinking about reelection are freed from the sanctioning power of constituents.

"With a job offer on the table, the official or staff member is all but working for the lobbying firm, on the taxpayers' dime.

"Of course, the law recognizes problems with the flow of public officials to lobbying firms. Current law requires a two-year waiting period before a member of Congress or staffer enters the lobbying world. But two years is simply too soon.

"Job offers, usually with much higher salaries, lure powerful public officials and their staff away from public office. Dick Armey, Tom Daschle, Tom Foley and Trent Lott, all once very powerful members of Congress, are among those who became lobbyists. According to OpenSecrets.org, more than 420 former members of Congress are registered lobbyists. (This number does not include former members who influence public policy without registering as lobbyists.) In addition, more than 5,400 former congressional staffers have left Capitol Hill to become federal lobbyists in the last 10 years.

"End the storm at the Los Angeles and Long Beach ports

"One report found that congressional members, on average, get a 1,452% raise when they become lobbyists. And in another finding, from the Sunlight Foundation, lobbyists who list a government staff position on their resumes can command a median salary of $300,000.

"Others earn more. Former Rep. Steve Largent (R-Okla.), for example, makes $1.5 million as a lobbyist for a trade group, more than he made as a Hall of Fame NFL wide receiver.

"That means one can make much more from trying to influence legislation than from writing legislation. (New York Assemblyman Sheldon Silver, accused of earning millions of dollars in kickbacks, may be an exception.) And, interestingly, according to one study, former staff members can generate more revenue (and earn higher salaries) than former members of Congress.

"But don't these public officials see the ethical problem of shifting allegiances from constituents to their potential future bosses? Often the shift can be so subtle that nobody notices, which reinforces an ethical obliviousness.

"Of course, the timing of some hires can raise public suspicions. Take the case of John Pemberton, who was the chief of staff in the Environmental Protection Agency's division on air pollution programs. He raised eyebrows when he announced only one week after the agency eased regulations on air pollution controls that he would be a lobbyist for a company that owns coal power plants.

"But in general, the media have a short attention span, and the public rarely tracks what their representatives do when they leave office. Only those of us with an interest in lobbying tend to keep track.

"Perhaps we'd all keep a closer eye on post-Congress careers if we stopped thinking of corruption as blatant crimes like bribery, blackmail or even murder. That's what corruption looks like on television. What we need to recognize is that a prospective job offer is the moral equivalent of a blank check.

"Two years is too short a time to make officials and staffers wait before they cash in on the personal connections and expertise they acquired as public servants. They should have to wait at least six years, the length of one Senate term. A six-year wait would significantly weaken their connections and diminish their earning power as lobbyists. And that would reduce the temptation to treat public service as a trial job period, acting on behalf of a future boss rather than the constituents.

"Without a longer waiting period, the democratic system as a whole will pay."

http://www.latimes.com/opinion/op-ed/la-oe-dovi-officials-lobbyists-20150217-story.html

"In a scene all too typical in present day Washington, the culmination of Trans-Pacific Partnership negotiations, along with the push for passage of related legislation such as Trade Promotion Authority (or Fast Track) have set off a lobbying frenzy.

"While liberal organizations and members of Congress deride the TPP as the biggest boondoggle since NAFTA and President Obama defends it as "the most progressive trade treaty ever," the influence peddlers who populate K Street see opportunity.

"Policy makers aren't simply facing a lobbying barrage from the typical slate of domestic interest groups. Foreign governments are running sophisticated operations to influence Congress and gather intelligence in Washington as the negotiations proceed.

"This is now "par for the course," according to Lydia Dennett, an investigator at the Project on Government Oversight [POGO], a nonprofit watchdog. "If a certain country wants trade legislation that will be beneficial to them they can hire an American lobbyist to get them the access the need."

"Working at the behest of a foreign government is a lucrative practice area for lobbyists.

"Leading the way among TPP nations seeking to sway American policy makers is Japan, which signed up former Democratic Leader Tom Daschle's firm as well as well-connected public relations firm DCI.

"We won't know the full extent of Mr. Daschle or DCI's work on behalf of Japan until their next series of Foreign Agent Registration Act [FARA] disclosure reports are filed with the Department of Justice in a few months.

"One concern among good government advocates is that a lack of timely FARA reporting could obfuscate some of the lobbying going on at the behest of foreign clients. A 2014 report by POGO found that 46 percent of the reports were filed late. Enforcement is rare for these relatively minor infractions and the DOJ's website states it "seeks to obtain voluntary compliance with the statute." Ms. Dennett called on Congress to add civil penalties to the FARA Act that to encourage more aggressive enforcement of its statutes.

"Common Cause, an open government advocacy organization, sounded similar alarms. "Our concern is in ensuring that the process is fully transparent and that the laws barring foreign nationals from contributing, donating or spending funds in connection with any federal, state, or local election in the United States, either directly or indirectly, are fully observed," said Dale Eisman, the organization's communications director.

"While we don't yet know the extent of Mr. Daschle or DCI's work, filings from other firms working on behalf of Japan, paint a picture of the country's efforts.

"For much of their direct lobbying, Japan relies on Akin, Gump, Strauss Hauer & Feld, whom they paid $388,000 during the most recent six-month reporting period. In that time the firm's lobbyists contacted Congressional offices at least sixty times and engaged in at least eight exchanges with the United States Trade Representative's office specifically focused on the TPP, TPA, and related issues. Seventeen of those contacts were with one particular staffer, Kaitlin Sighinolfi, a trade policy advisor for Republican Louisiana Congressman Charles Boustany.

"Lott Trent Bipartisan Agreement: Foreign Governments Pay Former Senate Leaders to Sell TPPMr. Boustany's office did not respond to a request for comment on these contacts, but they are likely related to the desire of Louisiana farmers to lower tariff barriers, enabling them to export more of goods to Japan.

"Japan's team also includes Hogan Lovells, which was paid $216,895.29 during the last six-month reporting period. The firm's FARA filing states that the law firm "advises and represents the foreign principal [Japan] on general diplomatic representation, laws, regulations, policies, proposed congressional measures, treaties and other international agreements, and actions by the U.S. Congress,

Executive Branch, U.S. Government agencies and certain state and local governments."

"Prior to recruiting Mr. Daschle, the highest profile lobbyist on Japan's team was Tony Podesta, brother of Hillary Clinton's campaign chairman John Podesta. His firm, The Podesta Group, receives $15,000 per month to counsel Japan on U.S. policy.

"Another TPP country, Vietnam, received more hands-on service from the Podesta Group—paying them $180,000 during the same six-month period. On Vietnam's behalf, the firm made contact with government officials at least 90 times. They also engaged with media outlets ranging from The New York Times to the Food Network on behalf of Japan.

"Working at the behest of foreign governments is a lucrative practice area for the Podesta Group which billed a total of $2,096,666.05 to more than nine overseas governments, including Azerbaijan, India, Iraq, Korea, Somalia, and Hong Kong during the last six months of 2014.

"Japan's aggressive lobbying efforts in Washington are part of an overall increase in foreign nations seeking to purchase influence in Washington. According to Frank Samolis, co-chair of the international trade group at DC behemoth Squire Patton Boggs, there has been a measurable "uptick [in business under the Foreign Agent Registration Act] due to TPA and related bills in Congress."

"Mr. Samolis is a veteran of Capitol Hill trade fights. He previously worked on behalf of Korea, Columbia, and Peru during their trade negotiations with the United States. He now represents Temasek, Singapore's Sovereign Wealth Fund, which paid his firm $132,055.72 during the last six-month filing period, as the country engaged in TPP talks.

"SPB represents multiple foreign principals with an interest in the TPP including, China, which paid the firm $392,014.17 over the same period.

"Mr. Samolis explained that when working on behalf of foreign powers, lobbyists "need to find a confluence with [United States government] interests wherever possible."

"US policy makers understand that a client is foreign, so they are aware and need to be convinced how [the clients] interest comports with [United States government] objectives," Samolis told me.

"For that, we need to make a strong legal and policy case, backed up by the facts."

"Insiders like Mr. Samolis play another critical role. "At least half of my time is devoted to providing intel on US developments and likely future actions," he stated.

"This points to the reason Japan and other countries are eager to hire former senior members of Congress and well-connected insiders. The ability to glean information from former colleagues and contacts is just as important as their skill at influencing legislative and administrative outcomes. This expertise is particularly crucial during complex foreign negotiations requiring approval of a finicky and partisan Congress.

"Mr. Samolis' firm has a platoon of ex-lawmakers including former Senate Majority Leader Trent Lott, a Republican, along with former Louisiana Sen. John Breaux, a Democrat. Pocketing money from foreign governments seems to one of the few things both parties agree on.

"With numerous trade treaties on the horizon, Mr. Samolis and his colleagues' workload is only likely to increase because ultimately foreign governments spend significant amounts of money on lobbying and relate activists for the same reason that domestic corporations and other interest groups do. They know in Washington DC influence can be bought."

http://observer.com/2015/06/many-foreign-governments-pay-k-street-big-money-to-peddle-tpp-to-congress/

By Richard Cowan | Washington

"U.S. lawmakers are once again taking advantage of their summer recess to race around the globe on privately financed tours to places like China, the Middle East and Scotland - trips watchdog groups cite as evidence that congressional ethics reforms are unraveling.

"Critics of such trips say it is unseemly for members of the House and Senate to take trips bankrolled by people and organizations with specific legislative desires.

"It's money well spent by lobbying groups, but for the American public, there is no benefit," said Craig Holman, a lobbyist for the consumer group Public Citizen.

"Congress clamped down on such travel in 2007 after disgraced lobbyist Jack Abramoff's influence-peddling scandal tainted many Republicans with close ties to him, contributing to their 2006 election losses in the House of Representatives.

"Abramoff - convicted and imprisoned on fraud and conspiracy charges - paid for lawmakers he was trying to sway on legislative matters, among these casino gambling, to fly away for lavish junkets, including golf outings in Scotland.

"Former Republican congressman Bob Ney and some former congressional and White House aides were also convicted of charges arising from the Abramoff scandal.

"Nearly 5,000 trips, costing lobbyists $10 million, were taken in 2005. This was a peak which fell to 1,846 in 2006 and then further after reforms were put in place.

"Lately, the number of privately financed trips offered by corporate interests, lobbyists, universities and foreign governments, including China, have been rising. Trips this year so far total 1,363, at a cost to the hosts of $3.2 million, according to figures collected by LegiStorm, a nonpartisan watchdog group.

"There are 100 Senators and 435 members of the House.

"Jeff Joseph, a spokesman for the Consumer Electronics Association, which represents corporate giants such as Google, Microsoft, Apple, LG and Samsung, said critics of the travel were "shortsighted."

"Away from the hustle and bustle of Capitol Hill, lawmakers - whose wives often accompany them - have a chance to "talk to our industry about regulatory issues. They can touch and feel the technologies they are going to legislate on," Joseph said.

"Ethics advocates argue that such trips let private groups give members of Congress an earful about their policy positions and that many lawmakers may feel indebted after a week of free food, hotels, tours and transportation.

"Bill Allison, editorial director of the Sunlight Foundation, a group which advocates government openness, said the best arrangement would be to conduct all lawmaker travel "on the taxpayer's dime."

"It really doesn't accomplish the purpose of a fact-finding mission if the facts are being presented by a group with a specific viewpoint," Allison added.

"A 2007 law passed after the Abramoff scandal imposed new disclosure requirements on lobbyists. The Senate and House also adopted new ethics rules that aimed to stop lobbyists from offering free travel to lawmakers and to require pre-approval by ethics committees of any travel.

"The duration of trips was capped at seven days for foreign travel and four days for domestic travel. But the rules contained exceptions, allowing educational and charitable groups to finance trips for lawmakers.

"Lobbying outfits have taken advantage of those exceptions by creating their own nonprofit groups that are able to offer and pay for trips taken by members of Congress. These tax-exempt groups "are providing exactly the Jack Abramoff-types of international travel that we intended to ban in 2007," Holman, of the Public Citizen consumer group, said.

"Friends of Scotland"

"Lawmakers have traveled to a variety of locales this year on trips paid for by private groups and foreign governments, with Turkey the top destination so far, followed by Israel, LegiStorm said. Over many years, Israel's Dead Sea and other resort spots have been popular, along with Tel Aviv and Jerusalem, it added.

"Despite the bad publicity years ago from the Abramoff-sponsored Scottish travel, four House Republicans and one Democrat - all members of the "Friends of Scotland Congressional Caucus" - are traveling this month in Scotland, at the Scottish government's expense.

"Their visit, in the midst of Edinburgh's world-famous international festival, will include meetings with Scottish officials to discuss "business, economics, energy, infrastructure and natural resources," according to the Scottish Affairs office at the British Embassy in Washington.

"The caucus sponsors an annual "Tartan Day" on Capitol Hill.

"Also this month, 10 members of the Congressional Black Caucus visited Beijing, Shanghai and Hong Kong on a trip financed by China. Democratic Representative Marcia Fudge, who heads the caucus, said the trip's purpose was to "increase mutual understanding" between her members and China's government "through an educational and cultural exchange."

"More than 60 House Democrats and Republicans, along with some aides, traveled to Israel and the West Bank on two trips organized and financed by the American Israel Education Foundation. It is an arm of AIPAC, a pro-Israel lobby that pushes for U.S. aid to Israel "to ensure that the Jewish state maintains its qualitative edge over its adversaries."

"This education foundation is one kind of tax-exempt, non-profit organization that lobbying outfits can use to ease the impact of the 2007 travel restrictions.

"Despite the criticisms, there have been no known allegations of illegal activity related to travel following the 2007 reforms.

"Deeper Understanding"

"Representative Steny Hoyer, the No. 2 House Democrat, said the Israel visit helped lawmakers "gain a deeper understanding of American interests in a changing Middle East."

"A spokesman for House Majority Leader Eric Cantor, who was on the Republicans' trip, said meetings were set with Israeli and Palestinian leaders, and the visiting lawmakers would "look at facilities Congress has funded like anti-missile systems."

"On a similar trip to Israel by a group of House Republicans in 2011, one attendee, Representative Kevin Yoder of Kansas, jumped naked into the Sea of Galilee for a night swim.

"One Washington-based lobbyist familiar with past AIPAC trips, who asked not to be named, said the elegant King David Hotel had long been a favorite for U.S. lawmakers and that tours of Jerusalem's Old City and the Western Wall were a "must."

"But some official work is also done, the lobbyist said, adding, "They always meet with President (Shimon) Peres."

"While the two trips this August were primarily for first-term lawmakers, in 2011 the AIPAC group ferried about one-third of all the members of the House to Israel. Records show that these visits can cost around $10,000 per member of Congress.

"Lawmakers stress the travel's fact-finding nature. But Holman of the Public Citizen group sees it simply as "influence-peddling, an extension of lobbying away from Capitol Hill."

"There also is plenty of taxpayer-financed travel by House and Senate members, which is difficult to track.

"LegiStorm said that since 2000, a total of 36,411 privately financed trips cost $83 million. According to 2012 figures, Republicans took 793 trips and Democrats took 604, but their costs were about equal.

"August recess is not the only popular travel season. Winter months are likely to generate "junkets to places like Las Vegas, New Orleans and Miami. You don't see many trips to Altoona (Pennsylvania)," Allison said.

"One of winter's hot tickets, Allison said, was January's Consumer Electronics Association show in Las Vegas. Thirteen lawmakers, 76 aides, all five Federal Communications Commission commissioners and staffers from other federal agencies attended."

(Editing by Marilyn W. Thompson, Will Dunham and David Brunnstrom)

http://www.reuters.com/article/us-usa-congress-ethics-idUSBRE97I0RE20130819

How does the world of lobbyists work and how can these people influence politicians? The USA Today has a story on the topic which explains how non profit groups set up directly by lobbyists are able to sidestep the rules to show members of congress the world.

Here is an excerpt of the article:

"In late April, the group paid for four members of Congress - three of them accompanied by spouses - to hop aboard a corporate jet, bound for the Napa Valley town of St. Helena. The weekend for the two Republicans and two Democrats included luxury accommodations at the Meadowood resort and a series of presentations on issues facing the wine industry. Meals on the three-day trip totaled $458 for each person. The total bill: $46,000.

"Congressional rules allow lawmakers and their aides to take trips paid for by private interests, with a few caveats: The travel must relate to their official duties in Washington; it must not be primarily recreational; and it must not be paid for by lobbyists or representatives of a foreign interest. When lawmakers do travel, they must disclose the trip, its purpose and who paid for it.

"Lobbyists also are required to report who pays them, how much they are paid and the issues they lobby on, under a 1995 disclosure law. But tax-exempt groups have minimal disclosure requirements. Paying for trips through a tax-exempt organization exploits a seam between tax law and the ethics rules, says Frances Hill of the University of Miami School of Law.

"The ethics rules invite you to set up conduits" for undisclosed money, she says. And the IRS, which oversees tax-exempt groups, "has been remarkably lacking in curiosity about cases like this." The agency is too understaffed to thoroughly review all of the country's 1.5 million tax-exempt organizations, she adds.

"Since 2000, members of Congress have taken more than 5,900 privately financed trips at a cost of $17.6 million, according to the non-partisan PoliticalMoneyLine, which analyzes data on money in politics. More than half of the spending has come from tax-exempt groups such as America's Trust.

"It isn't hard to find examples of lobbyists connected to non-profit groups sponsoring congressional trips:

"• The Islamic Free Market Institute Foundation has paid for at least 23 trips by lawmakers since 2000, at a cost of $235,839. Most of the travel was to an annual conference in the Persian Gulf country of Qatar. The group raised $456,777 in 2003, according to its latest federal tax return, but declined to disclose its financial backers. Among the organization's founders in 1998 was Grover Norquist, a Republican activist and anti-tax lobbyist. He no longer is on the institute's board, but the organization shares an office with Norquist's group, Americans for Tax Reform. The Islamic Institute also has worked with another lobbyist, Asim Ghafoor, who represented an association of Islamic banks.

"• Two groups, the Korea-U.S. Exchange Council and the Malaysia Exchange Association, set up to promote trade with Asia in part by organizing trips for lawmakers, have ties to the Alexander Strategy Group, a lobbying firm founded by Rep. Tom DeLay's former chief of staff, Ed Buckham. The groups financed $224,000 in travel for a dozen House members since 2001.

"The lobbying firm set up the Korea group in 2001 with the goal of making Korean businessman Seung Youn Kim, chairman of one of Korea's largest conglomerates, the Hanwha Group, "the leading business statesman in U.S.-Korean relations," according to a strategy memo. But because the group registered as an agent of a foreign interest, it could not legally sponsor congressional travel.

"The Malaysia organization, which did not register as a foreign agent, sent three House members - Roger Wicker, R-Miss., Earl

Pomeroy, D-N.D. and John Doolittle, R-Calif. - to Kuala Lumpur in February "to strengthen the bilateral relationship between the U.S. and Malaysia," according to Pomeroy's trip disclosure.

"• The International Management and Development Institute has paid $534,000 during the past five years for 60 congressional trips, most of them to Germany and other Western European destinations. The institute is run by Don Bonker, a former Democratic House member from Washington state and now a lobbyist for APCO Worldwide."

http://blog.tmcnet.com/blog/rich-tehrani/lobbyists-lobby-taxpayers-pay.html

"When former House Majority Leader Eric Cantor (R-Va.) lost his 2014 primary race and resigned his office, he got a lot of media attention. What he has been up to since then has gotten less attention: He became a managing director at the investment banking firm Moelis & Co., helping to found the company's Washington office.

"Cantor wasn't the only powerful member of the House who left office that year and began lobbying. Henry Waxman (D-Calif.), Jack Kingston (R-Ga.), and George Miller (D-Calif.), all left the chamber after several decades of service and stints as chairmen of powerful committees and subcommittees: Waxman had chaired both the House Committee on Government Reform and Oversight and the Energy and Commerce Committee; Kingston, an Appropriations subcommittee; and Miller, the Education and Labor Committee. All three began lobbying virtually right away.

"This pattern is pretty typical for the House of Representatives. The most powerful members of Congress are also the most likely to become lobbyists later on."

"Which members of the House walk through the revolving door?

"In her forthcoming article in Interest Groups & Advocacy, "Who Walks Through the Revolving Door? Examining the Lobbying Activity of Former Members of Congress," Amy McKay, Lindsey Herbel and I undertake the first systematic examination of which former Congress members are most likely to lobby after leaving Congress. We do this by examining the lobbying activity of every member who left the chamber between 1976 and 2012.

"In the House, we find that the factors that make a member powerful in the chamber are also some of the best predictors of whether a member lobbies after retiring: seniority, being a party leader, being a committee chair, and being a member of a powerful committee. Apparently, lobbying firms are looking to recruit (formerly) powerful House members.

"It's different in the Senate.

"We were surprised to find that this isn't the case in the Senate. For Senators, membership on a powerful committee doesn't predict lobbying activity, nor does seniority. Holding a committee chairmanship does, but only for Democrats. Only holding a party leadership position significantly predicts lobbying activity for all former senators.

"We suspect that this is because institutional power and influence in the Senate are distributed so much more evenly than it is in the House. In the upper chamber, you don't need to be on a powerful committee to be a powerful senator. Every senator can significantly influence what goes on in that chamber.

"As a result, the most senior senators who retired after 2014 did not go into lobbying. Carl Levin (36 years in the Senate, chairman of the Armed Services Committee) now teaches at Wayne State University in his home state of Michigan. John Rockefeller (30 years in the Senate, chair of the Committee on Veterans' Affairs) now holds a position at the Council on Foreign Relations. But 12-year Senator Mark Pryor (D-Ark.) and six-year Senator Mike Johanns (R-Neb.) now lobby for Venable and Deere & Co., respectively.

"Party and ideology don't make a difference.

"A few things that we examined appear to make little difference in whether a member of Congress goes off to lobby.

"For instance, it doesn't matter whether someone served in the House or the Senate; slightly more than a quarter of both chambers' alumni became lobbyists after leaving Congress.

"Party affiliation doesn't make much difference, either. Twenty-nine percent of House Republicans and 26 percent of House Democrats became lobbyists after retiring. In the Senate, the party difference is sharper (38 percent to 25 percent), but still not statistically significant.

"Nor does ideology matter much. Whether we're looking at the divide between liberal and conservative or moderate and extreme, congressional alumni of all ideological stripes appear to become lobbyists at roughly the same rate."

By Kelley Beaucar Vlahos

Published March 20, 2006

"Washington – Editor's Correction: In the original story that ran on March 20, 2006, the writer included former Democratic leaders Tom Daschle and Dick Gephardt in a list of past lawmakers who are now registered lobbyists. However, the two former leaders are not registered lobbyists, according to the Senate Records Office. Daschle is a special policy adviser with the legal firm Alston & Bird. Gephardt works for DLA Piper Rudnick Gray Cary as senior counsel specializing in financial and labor issues.

"The one-year cooling off periods for the former lawmakers to lobby Congress passed in January. If the two do decide to lobby their prior colleagues, their firms are not required to register them with the Senate Records Office until August 2006.

"What do John Ashcroft, Fred Thompson, J.C. Watts, Zell Miller and have in common these days?

"They are all former members of Congress — and they are all registered lobbyists.

"Former members who leave office for the lucrative world of lobbying — the so-called "revolving door" — have received some rare attention recently as former colleagues still in office debate new lobbying reforms. Proposed rule changes could have a major impact on former lawmakers' activities on Capitol Hill.

"The rules are now under scrutiny," said Larry Noble, director of the Center for Responsive Politics. "Former members of Congress can provide two things as lobbyists — they provide an insider's knowledge of the legislative process and how Congress deals with certain issues. And they also provide access. Their calls will be returned."

"Current House and Senate lobbying reform efforts on Capitol Hill have focused in part on restricting some of former members' special privileges, like activities on the House and Senate floor and access to the in-house gym. Proposed Senate reforms also include an extension of the one-year "cooling off period" in which former members can't directly lobby other members after they leave office.

"Sources say it's hard to gauge how often former members choose to use these privileges to lobby, or how useful they are, but many seem convinced that these are just small tools in a broad arsenal of advantages former members have in the influence industry.

"These are the people that really get things done," said Alex Knott, director of the LobbyWatch project at the Washington-based Center for Public Integrity. "There is a premium on them and there is a reason."

"According to a 2005 report detailing the extent of former members' lobbying activities by the public interest group, Public Citizen, more than 300 former members of Congress have registered as lobbyists since 1970.

"Since 1998, 86 members have left Congress only to lobby on behalf of domestic and foreign interests — that's about 43 percent of all retiring members who left for reasons other than moving to another elected office or to the administration, or death.

"What we do know is it's more commonplace than it used to be and the reason is, there is so much more at stake right now," in terms of big-money contracts, federal aid, grants – the big federal pie, said Craig Holman, campaign finance expert for Public Citizen.

"The American public should be wary," he added.

"It's one of the primary avenues for special interests to gain special control and to influence public policy," he said. "This is a way for moneyed interests and special interests to step into the halls of Congress and basically offer lucrative employment to members and their staffs. It makes members think about private interests rather than public service."

"John Fortier, congressional expert with the American Enterprise Institute, said he doesn't think the problem is that intense. "Former members are only a percentage of lobbyists," he said. About 30,000 people are registered lobbyists, according to best estimates, though it is not clear how many of them are active, he said.

"Big Names, Powerful Influence

"Big shots in Congress will naturally demand top dollar as lobbyists, say experts. Former Sen. Robert Dole, R-N.C., who recently made headlines when it was revealed he was hired by Dubai Ports World to help sell its deal to manage U.S. ports after considerable congressional criticism, reportedly signed onto Washington firm, Alston & Bird, for upwards of $1 million last year.

"While rank and file House and Senate members make around $165,000 a year, the average high-level Washington lobbyist makes at least $300,000 a year, with many former members making much more than that, according to reports.

"It's enticing for a lot of them to go over to that side," said Noble.

"And many have. It seems like many lobbyists of today were newsmakers on C-SPAN just yesterday: Sen. Zell Miller, D-Ga., former Homeland Security Department undersecretary and representative Asa Hutchinson and his brother, former Sen. Tim Hutchinson, both Arkansas Republicans; Sen. Ben Nighthorse Campbell, R-Colo., and Sen. John Beaux, D-La.,

"Former Rep. Bob Livingston, R-La., once chairman of the House Appropriations Committee, left office in 1999 in a cloud of controversy over marital infidelities. He went on to create one of the most lucrative lobbying firms in Washington, pulling in almost $40 million since it opened the same year he retired from Congress.

"The Livingston Group is now ranked the 12th largest non-law lobbying firm in Washington, D.C., and has lobbied on behalf of defense contractors like Northrop Grumman and Raytheon, several U.S cities and the foreign countries of Turkey, Morocco and the Cayman Islands.

"According to the Public Citizen report, Livingston's firm helped protect $1 billion in aid to Turkey that was in jeopardy when Ankara refused to let U.S. forces use its bases to stage its entry into Iraq for the 2003 invasion. Livingston declined comment for this story.

"Critics say the real problem with former lawmakers working as lobbyists is the growing perception that members are routinely negotiating future employment with firms and industries while still in elected office.

"Their poster boy for that charge is Rep. W.J "Billy" Tauzin, R-La., former chairman of the House Energy and Commerce Committee, left office in March 2004 after announcing he was suffering from cancer.

"In January 2005, Tauzin took a $2 million position as the head of the Pharmaceutical Research and Manufacturers of America, one of the most influential lobbies in Washington today.

"He left amid accusations that he was already entertaining the job offer from PhRMA in January 2004, shortly after he helped successfully steer the massive Medicare Modernization Act, which Democratic critics say was too friendly to pharmaceutical companies. Tauzin has denied any conflict of interest.

"Billy Tauzin set a record," said Holman, pointing to the $2 million salary.

"Bradley Smith, a law professor for Capital University Law School in Ohio and former Republican Chairman of the Federal Election Commission, said he "can see why people are disturbed" by the so-called "revolving door."

"I think that it comes down to government being too big," offering too many plums to private interests, he said.

"Lobbying is Fairly Hard Work."

"Rick Tyler, spokesman for former House Speaker Newt Gingrich and his firm Gingrich Communications, called the focus on limiting former members' activities on Capitol Hill "plain silliness." He said if reformers really want to combat the unseemliness of big money interests influencing Congress, they could start by reducing the campaign fundraising performed by Washington lobbyists seeking access to the levers of power.

"As for members being accused of using their position to go after lucrative lobbying jobs right after office, Tyler said there seems to be no widespread abuse.

"It's perfectly legitimate for a former member who has an expertise in a certain area, when they step down, to go back into that field," he said. However, "It would be inappropriate for a member who has a conflict of interest to be negotiating a future deal in return for legislation."

"In itself, lobbying is not a dirty word, argues former Rep. Bill Frenzel, R-Minn., who served in the House for 20 years. It is part of the American democratic system, and as long as former members serve ethically and with decorum, they should not be disparaged, he said.

"I have no trouble with it at all," said Frenzel, noting that no one should be surprised that companies and lobbying firms go after former members. "Lobbying is fairly hard work. If you can't get in to see a congressman, you can't get paid as a lobbyist."

http://www.foxnews.com/story/2006/03/20/premium-placed-on-lobbyists-who-served-in-congress.html

VI

GOVERNMENT CORRUPTION

" WASHINGTON, D.C. — A review of FBI Director James Comey's professional history and relationships shows that the Obama cabinet leader — now under fire for his handling of the investigation of Hillary Clinton — is deeply entrenched in the big-money cronyism culture of Washington, D.C. His personal and professional relationships — all undisclosed as he announced the Bureau would not prosecute Clinton — reinforce bipartisan concerns that he may have politicized the criminal probe.

"These concerns focus on millions of dollars that Comey accepted from a Clinton Foundation defense contractor, Comey's former membership on a Clinton Foundation corporate partner's board, and his surprising financial relationship with his brother Peter Comey, who works at the law firm that does the Clinton Foundation's taxes.

"Lockheed Martin

"When President Obama nominated Comey to become FBI director in 2013, Comey promised the United States Senate that he would recuse himself on all cases involving former employers.

"But Comey earned $6 million in one year alone from Lockheed Martin. Lockheed Martin became a Clinton Foundation donor that very year.

"Comey served as deputy attorney general under John Ashcroft for two years of the Bush administration. When he left the Bush administration, he went directly to Lockheed Martin and became vice president, acting as a general counsel.

"How much money did James Comey make from Lockheed Martin in his last year with the company, which he left in 2010? More than $6 million in compensation.

"Lockheed Martin is a Clinton Foundation donor. The company admitted to becoming a Clinton Global Initiative member in 2010.

"According to records, Lockheed Martin is also a member of the American Chamber of Commerce in Egypt, which paid Bill Clinton $250,000 to deliver a speech in 2010.

"In 2010, Lockheed Martin won 17 approvals for private contracts from the Hillary Clinton State Department.

"HSBC Holdings

"In 2013, Comey became a board member, a director, and a Financial System Vulnerabilities Committee member of the London bank HSBC Holdings.

"Mr. Comey's appointment will be for an initial three-year term which, subject to re-election by shareholders, will expire at the conclusion of the 2016 Annual General Meeting," according to HSBC company records.

"HSBC Holdings and its various philanthropic branches routinely partner with the Clinton Foundation. For instance, HSBC Holdings has partnered with Deutsche Bank through the Clinton Foundation to "retrofit 1,500 to 2,500 housing units, primarily in the low- to moderate-income sector" in "New York City."

"Retrofitting" refers to a Green initiative to conserve energy in commercial housing units. Clinton Foundation records show that the Foundation projected "$1 billion in financing" for this Green initiative to conserve people's energy in low-income housing units.

"Who Is Peter Comey?

"When our source called the Chinatown offices of D.C. law firm DLA Piper and asked for "Peter Comey," a receptionist immediately put him through to Comey's direct line. But Peter Comey is not featured on the DLA Piper website.

"Peter Comey serves as "Senior Director of Real Estate Operations for the Americas" for DLA Piper. James Comey was not questioned about his relationship with Peter Comey in his confirmation hearing.

"DLA Piper is the firm that performed the independent audit of the Clinton Foundation in November during Clinton-World's first big push to put the email scandal behind them. DLA Piper's employees taken as a whole represent a major Hillary Clinton 2016 campaign donation bloc and Clinton Foundation donation base.

"DLA Piper ranks #5 on Hillary Clinton's all-time career Top Contributors list, just ahead of Goldman Sachs.

"And here is another thing: Peter Comey has a mortgage on his house that is owned by his brother, James Comey.

"Peter Comey's financial records, obtained by Breitbart News, show that he bought a $950,000 house in Vienna, Virginia, in June 2008. He needed a $712,500 mortgage from First Savings Mortgage Corporation.

"But on January 31, 2011, James Comey and his wife stepped in to become Private Party lenders. They granted a mortgage on the house for $711,000. Financial records suggest that Peter Comey took out two such mortgages from his brother that day.

"This financial relationship between the Comey brothers began prior to James Comey's nomination to became director of the FBI.

"DLA Piper did not answer Breitbart News' question as to whether James Comey and Peter Comey spoke at any point about this mortgage or anything else during the Clinton email investigation.

"Peter Comey Re-Designed the FBI Building

"FBI Director James Comey grew up in the New Jersey suburbs with his brother Peter. Both Comeys were briefly taken captive in 1977 by the "Ramsey rapist," but the boys managed to escape through a window in their home, and neither boy was harmed.

"James Comey became a prosecutor who worked on the Gambino crime family case. He went on to the Bush administration, a handful of private sector jobs, and then the Obama administration in 2013.

"Peter Comey, meanwhile, went into construction.

"After getting an MBA in real estate and urban development from George Washington University in 1998, Peter Comey became an executive at a company that re-designed George Washington University between 2004 and 2007 while his brother was in town working for the Bush administration.

"In January 2009, at the beginning of the Obama administration, Peter Comey became "a real estate and construction consultant" for Procon Consulting.

"Procon Consulting's client list includes "FBI Headquarters Washington, DC.""

"So what did Procon Consulting do for FBI Headquarters? Quite a bit, apparently. According to the firm's records:

"Procon provided strategic project management for the consolidation of over 11,000 FBI personnel into one, high security, facility.

"Since 1972 the Federal Bureau of Investigation has had its headquarters in a purpose built 2.1 million square foot building on Pennsylvania Avenue. Having become functionally obsolete and in need of major repairs, GSA and the FBI were considering ways to meet the space needs required to maintain the Bureau's mission and consolidate over 11,000 personnel.

"Procon assisted GSA in assessing the FBI's space needs and options for fulfilling those needs. Services provided included project management related to site evaluations, budgeting, due diligence, and the development of procurement and funding strategies.

"Those "funding strategies" included talking to "stakeholders": "Worked with stakeholders and key leadership to identify strategic objectives, goals and long range plans for capital and real estate projects."

"Procon Consulting obtained its contract for FBI Headquarters prior to James Comey's nomination to serve as director of the FBI.

"In June 2011, Peter Comey left Procon Consulting to become "Senior Director of Real Estate Operations for the Americas" for DLA Piper.

"Peter Comey has generated some controversy in that role. According to Law360 in May 2013 (the same month that James Comey was confirmed as someone being considered by Obama to become FBI director):

"Two real estate services businesses filed a $10 million suit against the law firm alleging it stiffed them on as much as $760,000 of work done at DLA Piper's Chicago office and improperly gave proprietary information to a competitor.

"The plaintiffs take particular aim at Peter Comey, DLA Piper's senior director of real estate operations. Leasecorp and SpaceLogik include several emails in the complaint that are purportedly from DLA Piper senior real estate partners Jay Epstein and Rich Klawiter and are sharply critical of Comey's handling of the matter. In one email, Epstein wrote that "it's an embarrassment for the firm to be treating someone who we are working with like this."

"In another email allegedly from Klawiter on Feb. 20, the DLA Piper partner informed Leasecorp President Michael Walker, a principal for both plaintiffs, that Comey had sent him and Epstein an email claiming that the real estate services firms were behind on their contractual obligations.

"I just received an email from Peter (Jay was also a recipient) that is so inflammatory I can't even send it or you'll hit the roof," Klawiter said in the email, according to the complaint. "This is not going to end well."

http://www.breitbart.com/2016-presidential-race/2016/09/10/exposed-fbi-director-james-comeys-clinton-foundation-connection/

Did Lynch and Obama make it clear to Comey that if he pressed for an indictment against Hillary Clinton that he would be taking the Democrat nominee for president out of the election? If he failed to get a conviction he would be facing charges of tampering with and changing the outcome of a Federal election, to which he would be facing the rest of his life in prison, and Obama and Lynch, as well as others, would see to it that he did?

Hillary's statement to the FBI was intentionally given without a court reporter present or without any recording of her testimony to prevent her from having any further exposure to legal charges such as perjury. If she lied to Congress, they have no written FBI deposition to confront Hillary with. This was set up to let her walk without fear of being charged with giving False Testimony or being charged with Obstruction of Justice. This is what those in the "legalese world" call a "Straw Man" legal charge.

Hillary Clinton is an arrogant, condescending, political elite who is only interested in lining the Clinton pockets with donations to the Clinton Foundation (wink, wink) from PACS, lobbyists, and foreign nations that buy access and favors. The Clinton Foundation is nothing more than an operation used to launder money for the Clintons and other politicians involved in illegal activities. The Clintons are able to use the information of those participating to obtain cover for their activities, or blackmail those who are laundering money through them. One 2016 Presidential Candidate described her arrogance as breath-taking.

Donald Trump plans on draining the swamp in Washington. So far he has fired James Comey. That is a good start. Time will tell us who all will be investigated. In the meantime, we continue to watch the Democrats and Lame stream Media throw their tantrums as their emotional anxieties and nightmares increase over the conservative changes that keep coming their way each day.

To drain the swamp in Washington, Mr. Trump may need to start with George Soros and all of the organizations funded by Mr. Soros:

The upper portion of this page is devoted to organizations that are funded directly by George Soros and his Open Society Foundations (OSF). The lower portion of the page focuses on organizations which do not receive direct funding from Soros and OSF, but which receive money from one or more groups that do get direct OSF funding.

"Organizations that, in recent years, have received direct funding and assistance from George Soros and his Open Society Foundations (OSF) include the following. (Comprehensive profiles of each are available in the "Groups" section of DiscoverTheNetworks.org):

Advancement Project: This organization works to organize "communities of color" into politically cohesive units while disseminating its leftist worldviews and values as broadly as possible by way of a sophisticated communications department.

Air America Radio: Now defunct, this was a self-identified "liberal" radio network.

Al-Haq: This NGO produces highly politicized reports, papers, books, and legal analyses regarding alleged Israeli human-rights abuses committed against Palestinians.

All of Us or None: This organization seeks to change voting laws — which vary from state to state — so as to allow ex-inmates, parolees, and even current inmates to cast their ballots in political elections.

Alliance for Justice: Best known for its activism vis a vis the appointment of federal judges, this group consistently depicts Republican judicial nominees as "extremists."

America Coming Together: Soros played a major role in creating this group, whose purpose was to coordinate and organize pro-Democrat voter-mobilization programs.

America Votes: Soros also played a major role in creating this group, whose get-out-the-vote campaigns targeted likely Democratic voters.

America's Voice: This open-borders group seeks to promote "comprehensive" immigration reform that includes a robust agenda in favor of amnesty for illegal aliens.

American Bar Association Commission on Immigration Policy: This organization "opposes laws that require employers and persons providing education, health care, or other social services to verify citizenship or immigration status."

American Bridge 21st Century: This Super PAC conducts opposition research designed to help Democratic political candidates defeat their Republican foes.

American Civil Liberties Union: This group opposes virtually all post-9/11 national security measures enacted by the U.S. government. It supports open borders, has rushed to the defense of suspected terrorists and their abettors, and appointed former New Left terrorist Bernardine Dohrn to its Advisory Board.

American Constitution Society for Law and Policy: This Washington, DC-based think tank seeks to move American jurisprudence to the left by recruiting, indoctrinating, and mobilizing young law students, helping them acquire positions of power. It also provides leftist Democrats with a bully pulpit from which to denounce their political adversaries.

American Family Voices: This group creates and coordinates media campaigns charging Republicans with wrongdoing.

American Federation of Teachers: After longtime AFT President Albert Shanker died in 1997, he was succeeded by Sandra Feldman, who slowly "re-branded" the union, allying it with some of the most powerful left-wing elements of the New Labor Movement. When Feldman died in 2004, Edward McElroy took her place, followed by Randi Weingarten in 2008. All of them kept the union on the leftward course it had adopted in its post-Shanker period.

American Friends Service Committee: This group views the United States as the principal cause of human suffering around the world. As such, it favors America's unilateral disarmament, the dissolution of American borders, amnesty for illegal aliens, the abolition of the death penalty, and the repeal of the Patriot Act.

American Immigration Council: This non-profit organization is a prominent member of the open-borders lobby. It advocates expanded rights and amnesty for illegal aliens residing in the U.S.

American Immigration Law Foundation: This group supports amnesty for illegal aliens, on whose behalf it litigates against the U.S. government.

American Independent News Network: This organization promotes "impact journalism" that advocates progressive change.

American Institute for Social Justice: AISJ's goal is to produce skilled community organizers who can "transform poor communities" by agitating for increased government spending on city services, drug interdiction, crime prevention, housing, public-sector jobs, access to healthcare, and public schools.

American Library Association: This group has been an outspoken critic of the Bush administration's War on Terror — most particularly, Section 215 of the USA Patriot Act, which it calls "a present danger to the constitutional rights and privacy rights of library users."

The American Prospect, Inc.: This corporation trains and mentors young leftwing journalists, and organizes strategy meetings for leftist leaders.

Amnesty International: This organization directs a grossly disproportionate share of its criticism for human rights violations at the United States and Israel.

Applied Research Center: Viewing the United States as a nation where "structural racism" is deeply "embedded in the fabric of society," ARC seeks to "build a fair and equal society" by demanding "concrete change from our most powerful institutions."

Arab American Institute Foundation: The Arab American Institute denounces the purportedly widespread civil liberties violations directed against Arab Americans in the post-9/11 period, and characterizes Israel as a brutal oppressor of the Palestinian people.

Aspen Institute: This organization promotes radical environmentalism and views America as a nation plagued by deep-seated "structural racism."

Association of Community Organizations for Reform Now: This group conducts voter mobilization drives on behalf of leftist Democrats. These initiatives have been notoriously marred by fraud and corruption.

Ballot Initiative Strategy Center: This organization seeks to advance "a national progressive strategy" by means of ballot measures—state-level legislative proposals that pass successfully through a petition ("initiative") process and are then voted upon by the public.

Bend The Arc: A Jewish Partnership for Justice: This organization condemns Voter ID laws as barriers that "make it harder for communities of color, women, first-time voters, the elderly, and the poor to cast their vote."

Bill of Rights Defense Committee: This group provides a detailed blueprint for activists interested in getting their local towns, cities, and even college campuses to publicly declare their opposition to the Patriot Act, and to designate themselves "Civil Liberties Safe Zones." The organization also came to the defense of self-described radical attorney Lynne Stewart, who was convicted in 2005 of providing material support for terrorism.

Black Alliance for Just Immigration: This organization seeks to create a unified movement for "social and economic justice" centered on black racial identity.

Blueprint North Carolina: This group seeks to "influence state policy in North Carolina so that residents of the state benefit from more progressive policies such as better access to health care, higher wages, more affordable housing, a safer, cleaner environment, and access to reproductive health services."

Brennan Center for Justice: This think tank/legal activist group generates scholarly studies, mounts media campaigns, files amicus briefs, gives pro bono support to activists, and litigates test cases in pursuit of radical "change."

Brookings Institution: This organization has been involved with a variety of internationalist and state-sponsored programs, including one that aspires to facilitate the establishment of a U.N.-dominated world government. Brookings Fellows have also called for additional global collaboration on trade and banking; the expansion of the Kyoto Protocol; and nationalized health insurance for children. Nine Brookings economists signed a petition opposing President Bush's tax cuts in 2003.

Campaign for America's Future: This group supports tax hikes, socialized medicine, and a dramatic expansion of social welfare programs.

Campaign for Better Health Care: This organization favors a single-payer, government-run, universal health care system.

Campaign for Youth Justice: This organization contends that "transferring juveniles to the adult criminal-justice system leads to higher rates of recidivism, puts incarcerated and detained youth at unnecessary risk, has little deterrence value, and does not increase public safety."

Campus Progress: A project of the Soros-bankrolled Center for American Progress, this group seeks to "strengthen progressive voices on college and university campuses, counter the growing influence of right-wing groups on campus, and empower new generations of progressive leaders."

Casa de Maryland: This organization aggressively lobbies legislators to vote in favor of policies that promote expanded rights, including amnesty, for illegal aliens currently residing in the United States.

Catalist: This is a for-profit political consultancy that seeks "to help progressive organizations realize measurable increases in civic participation and electoral success by building and operating a robust national voter database of every voting-age American."

Catholics for Choice: This nominally Catholic organization supports women's right to abortion-on-demand.

Catholics in Alliance for the Common Good: This political nonprofit group is dedicated to generating support from the Catholic community for leftwing candidates, causes, and legislation.

Center for American Progress: This leftist think tank is headed by former Clinton chief of staff John Podesta, works closely with Hillary Clinton, and employs numerous former Clinton administration staffers. It is committed to "developing a long-term vision of a progressive America" and "providing a forum to generate new progressive ideas and policy proposals."

Center for Community Change: This group recruits and trains activists to spearhead leftist "political issue campaigns." Promoting increased funding for social welfare programs by bringing "attention to major national issues related to poverty," the Center bases its training programs on the techniques taught by the famed radical organizer Saul Alinsky.

Center for Constitutional Rights: This pro-Castro organization is a core member of the open borders lobby, has opposed virtually all post-9/11 anti-terrorism measures by the U.S. government, and alleges that American injustice provokes acts of international terrorism.

Center for Economic and Policy Research: This group opposed welfare reform, supports "living wage" laws, rejects tax cuts, and consistently lauds the professed achievements of socialist regimes, most notably Venezuela.

Center for International Policy: This organization uses advocacy, policy research, media outreach, and educational initiatives to promote "transparency and accountability" in U.S. foreign policy and global relations. It generally views America as a disruptive, negative force in the world.

Center for Reproductive Rights: CRR's mission is to guarantee safe, affordable contraception and abortion-on-demand for all women, including adolescents. The organization has filed state and federal lawsuits demanding access to taxpayer-funded abortions (through Medicaid) for low-income women.

Center for Responsible Lending: This organization was a major player in the subprime mortgage crisis. According to Phil Kerpen (vice president for policy at Americans for Prosperity), CRL "sh[ook] down and harass[ed] banks into making bad loans to unqualified borrowers." Moreover, CRL negotiated a contract enabling it to operate as a conduit of high-risk loans to Fannie Mae.

Center for Social Inclusion: This organization seeks to counteract America's "structural racism" by means of taxpayer-funded policy initiatives.

Center on Budget and Policy Priorities: Reasoning from the premise that tax cuts generally help only the wealthy, this organization advocates greater tax expenditures on social welfare programs for low earners.

Center on Wisconsin Strategy (COWS): Aiming to redistribute wealth by way of higher taxes imposed on those whose incomes are above average, COWS contends that "it is important that state government be able to harness fair contribution from all parts of society – including corporations and the wealthy."

Change America Now: Formed in December 2006, Change America Now describes itself as "an independent political organization created to educate citizens on the failed policies of the Republican Congress and to contrast that record of failure with the promise offered by a Democratic agenda."

Citizens for Responsibility and Ethics in Washington: This group litigates and brings ethics charges against "government officials who sacrifice the common good to special interests" and "betray the public trust." Almost all of its targets are Republicans.

Coalition for an International Criminal Court: This group seeks to subordinate American criminal-justice procedures to those of an international court.

Color Of Change: This organization was founded to combat what it viewed as the systemic racism pervading America generally and conservatism in particular.

Common Cause: This organization aims to bring about campaign-finance reform, pursue media reform resembling the Fairness Doctrine, and cut military budgets in favor of increased social-welfare and environmental spending.

Constitution Project: This organization seeks to challenge the legality of military commissions; end the detainment of "enemy combatants"; condemn government surveillance of terrorists; and limit the President's executive privileges.

Defenders of Wildlife Action Fund: Defenders of Wildlife opposes oil exploration in Alaska's Arctic National Wildlife Refuge. It condemns logging, ranching, mining, and even the use of recreational motorized vehicles as activities that are destructive to the environment.

Democracy Alliance: This self-described "liberal organization" aims to raise $200 million to develop a funding clearinghouse for leftist groups. Soros is a major donor to this group.

Democracy 21: This group is a staunch supporter of the Bipartisan Campaign Reform Act of 2002, also known as the McCain-Feingold Act.

Democracy Now!: Democracy Now! was created in 1996 by WBAI radio news director Amy Goodman and four partners to provide "perspectives rarely heard in the U.S. corporate-sponsored media," i.e., the views of radical and foreign journalists, left and labor activists, and ideological foes of capitalism.

Democratic Justice Fund: DJF opposes the Patriot Act and most efforts to restrict or regulate immigration into the United States — particularly from countries designated by the State Department as "terrorist nations."

Democratic Party: Soros' funding activities are devoted largely to helping the Democratic Party solidify its power base. In a November 2003 interview, Soros stated that defeating President Bush in 2004 "is the central focus of my life" ... "a matter of life and death." He pledged to raise $75 million to defeat Bush, and personally donated nearly a third of that amount to anti-Bush organizations. "America under Bush," he said, "is a danger to the world, and I'm willing to put my money where my mouth is."

Demos: This organization lobbies federal and state policymakers to "addres[s] the economic insecurity and inequality that characterize American society today"; promotes "ideas for reducing gaps in wealth, income and political influence"; and favors tax hikes for the wealthy.

Drum Major Institute: This group describes itself as "a non-partisan, non-profit think tank generating the ideas that fuel the progressive movement," with the ultimate aim of persuading "policymakers and opinion-leaders" to take steps that advance its vision of "social and economic justice."

Earthjustice: This group seeks to place severe restrictions on how U.S. land and waterways may be used. It opposes most mining and logging initiatives, commercial fishing businesses, and the use of motorized vehicles in undeveloped areas.

Economic Policy Institute: This organization believes that "government must play an active role in protecting the economically vulnerable, ensuring equal opportunity, and improving the well-being of all Americans."

Electronic Privacy Information Center: This organization has been a harsh critic of the USA PATRIOT Act and has joined the American Civil Liberties Union in litigating two cases calling for the FBI "to publicly release or account for thousands of pages of information about the government's use of PATRIOT Act powers."

Ella Baker Center for Human Rights: Co-founded by the revolutionary communist Van Jones, this anti-poverty organization claims that "decades of disinvestment in our cities" — compounded by "excessive, racist policing and over-incarceration" — have "led to despair and homelessness."

Emily's List: This political network raises money for Democratic female political candidates who support unrestricted access to taxpayer-funded abortion-on-demand.

Energy Action Coalition: Founded in 2004, this group describes itself as "a coalition of 50 youth-led environmental and social justice groups working together to build the youth clean energy and climate movement." For EAC, this means "dismantling oppression" according to its principles of environmental justice.

Equal Justice USA: This group claims that America's criminal-justice system is plagued by "significant race and class biases," and thus seeks to promote major reforms.

Fair Immigration Reform Movement: This is the open-borders arm of the Center for Community Change.

Faithful America: This organization promotes the redistribution of wealth, an end to enhanced interrogation procedures vis a vis prisoners-of-war, the enactment of policies to combat global warming, and the creation of a government-run heath care system.

Families USA: This Washington-based health-care advocacy group favors ever-increasing government control of the American healthcare system.

Feminist Majority: Characterizing the United States as an inherently sexist nation, this group focuses on "advancing the legal, social and political equality of women with men, countering the backlash to women's advancement, and recruiting and training young feminists to encourage future leadership for the feminist movement in the United States."

Four Freedoms Fund: This organization was designed to serve as a conduit through which large foundations could fund state-based open-borders organizations more flexibly and quickly.

Free Exchange on Campus: This organization was created solely to oppose the efforts of one individual, David Horowitz, and his campaign to have universities adopt an "Academic Bill of Rights," as well as to denounce Horowitz›s 2006 book The Professors. Member organizations of FEC include Campus Progress (a project of the Center for American Progress); the American Association of University Professors; the American Civil Liberties Union; People for the American Way; the United States Student Association; the Center for Campus Free Speech; the American Library Association; Free Press; and the National Association of State Public Interest Research Groups.

Free Press: This "media reform" organization has worked closely with many notable leftists and such organizations as Media Matters for America, Air America Radio, Global Exchange, Code Pink, Fairness and Accuracy in Reporting, the Revolutionary Communist Party, Mother Jones magazine, and Pacifica Radio.

Funding Exchange: Dedicated to the concept of philanthropy as a vehicle for social change, this organization pairs leftist donors and foundations with likeminded groups and activists who are dedicated to bringing about their own version of "progressive" change and social justice. Many of these grantees assume that American society is rife with racism, discrimination, exploitation, and inequity and needs to be overhauled via sustained education, activism, and social agitation.

Gamaliel Foundation: Modeling its tactics on those of the radical Sixties activist Saul Alinsky, this group takes a strong stand against current homeland security measures and immigration restrictions.

Gisha: Center for the Legal Protection of Freedom of Movement: This anti-Israel organization seeks to help Palestinians "exercise their right to freedom of movement."

Global Centre for the Responsibility to Protect: This group contends that when a state proves either unable or unwilling to protect civilians from mass atrocities occurring within its borders, it is the responsibility of the international community to intervene — peacefully if possible, but with military force if necessary.

Global Exchange: Established in 1988 by pro-Castro radical Medea Benjamin, this group consistently condemns America's foreign policy, business practices, and domestic life. Following the 9/11 terrorist attacks, Global Exchange advised Americans to examine "the root causes of resentment against the United States in the Arab world — from our dependence on Middle Eastern oil to our biased policy towards Israel."

Grantmakers Without Borders: GWB tends to be very supportive of leftist environmental, anti-war, and civil rights groups. It is also generally hostile to capitalism, which it deems one of the chief "political, economic, and social systems" that give rise to a host of "social ills."

Green for All: This group was created by Van Jones to lobby for federal climate, energy, and economic policy initiatives.

Health Care for America Now: This group supports a "single payer" model where the federal government would be in charge of financing and administering the entire U.S. healthcare system.

Human Rights Campaign: The largest "lesbian-gay-bisexual-transgender" lobbying group in the United States, HRC supports political candidates and legislation that will advance the LGBT agenda. Historically, HRC has most vigorously championed HIV/AIDS-related legislation, "hate crime" laws, the abrogation of the military's "Don't Ask, Don't Tell" policy, and the legalization of gay marriage.

Human Rights First: This group supports open borders and the rights of illegal aliens; charges that the Patriot Act severely erodes Americans' civil liberties; has filed amicus curiae briefs on behalf of terror suspect Jose Padilla; and deplores the Guantanamo Bay detention facilities.

Human Rights Watch: This group directs a disproportionate share of its criticism at the United States and Israel. It opposes the death penalty in all cases, and supports open borders and amnesty for illegal aliens.

I'lam: This anti-Israel NGO seeks "to develop and empower the Arab media and to give voice to Palestinian issues."

Immigrant Defense Project: To advance the cause of illegal immigrants, the IDP provides immigration law backup support and counseling to New York defense attorneys and others who represent or assist immigrants in criminal justice and immigration systems, as well as to immigrants themselves.

Immigrant Legal Resource Center: This group claims to have helped gain amnesty for some three million illegal aliens in the U.S., and in the 1980s was part of the sanctuary movement which sought to grant asylum to refugees from the failed Communist states of Central America.

Immigrant Workers Citizenship Project: This open-borders organization advocates mass immigration to the U.S.

Immigration Advocates Network: This alliance of immigrant-rights groups seeks to "increase access to justice for low-income immigrants and strengthen the capacity of organizations serving them."

Immigration Policy Center: IPC is an advocate of open borders and contends that the massive influx of illegal immigrants into America is due to U.S. government policy, since "the broken immigration system [...] spurs unauthorized immigration in the first place."

Independent Media Center: This Internet-based, news and events bulletin board represents an invariably leftist, anti-capitalist perspective and serves as a mouthpiece for anti-globalization/anti-America themes.

Independent Media Institute: IMI administers the SPIN Project (Strategic Press Information Network), which provides leftist organizations with "accessible and affordable strategic communications consulting, training, coaching, networking opportunities and concrete tools" to help them "achieve their social justice goals."

Institute for America's Future: IAF supports socialized medicine, increased government funding for education, and the creation of an infrastructure "to ensure that the voice of the progressive majority is heard."

Institute for New Economic Thinking: Seeking to create a new worldwide "economic paradigm," this organization is staffed by numerous individuals who favor government intervention in national economies, and who view capitalism as a flawed system.

Institute for Policy Studies: This think tank has long supported Communist and anti-American causes around the world. Viewing capitalism as a breeding ground for "unrestrained greed," IPS seeks to provide a corrective to "unrestrained markets and individualism." Professing an unquestioning faith in the righteousness of the United Nations, it aims to bring American foreign policy under UN control.

Institute for Public Accuracy: This anti-American, anti-capitalist organization sponsored actor Sean Penn's celebrated visit to Baghdad in 2002. It also sponsored visits to Iraq by Democratic Congressmen Nick Rahall and former Democrat Senator James Abourezk

Institute for Women's Policy Research: This group views the U.S. as a nation rife with discrimination against women, and publishes research to draw attention to this alleged state of affairs. It also advocates unrestricted access to taxpayer-funded abortion-on-demand, stating that "access to abortion is essential to the economic well-being of women and girls."

International Crisis Group: One of this organization's leading figures is its Mideast Director, Robert Malley, who was President Bill Clinton's Special Assistant for Arab-Israeli Affairs. His analysis of the Mideast conflict is markedly pro-Palestinian.

J Street: This anti-Israel group warns that Israel's choice to take military action to stop Hamas' terrorist attacks "will prove counter-productive and only deepen the cycle of violence in the region"

Jewish Funds for Justice: This organization views government intervention and taxpayer funding as crucial components of enlightened social policy. It seeks to redistribute wealth from Jewish donors to low-income communities "to combat the root causes of domestic economic and social injustice." By JFJ's reckoning, chief among those root causes are the inherently negative by-products of capitalism – most notably racism and "gross economic inequality."

Joint Victory Campaign 2004: Founded by George Soros and Harold Ickes, this group was a major fundraising entity for Democrats during the 2004 election cycle. It collected contributions (including large amounts from Soros personally) and disbursed them to two other groups, America Coming Together and the Media Fund, which also worked on behalf of Democrats.

Justice at Stake: This coalition calls for judges to be appointed by nonpartisan, independent commissions in a process known as "merit selection," rather than elected by the voting public.

LatinoJustice PRLDF: This organization supports bilingual education, the racial gerrymandering of voting districts, and expanded rights for illegal aliens.

Lawyers Committee for Civil Rights Under Law: This group views America as an unremittingly racist nation; uses the courts to mandate race-based affirmative action preferences in business and academia; has filed briefs against the Department of Homeland Security's efforts to limit the wholesale granting of green cards and to identify potential terrorists; condemns the Patriot Act; and calls on Americans to "recognize the contribution" of illegal aliens.

Leadership Conference on Civil and Human Rights: This organization views the United States as a nation rife with racism, sexism, and all manner of social injustice; and it uses legislative advocacy to push for "progressive change" that will create "a more open and just society."

League of United Latin American Citizens: This group views America as a nation plagued by "an alarming increase in xenophobia and anti-Hispanic sentiment"; favors racial preferences; supports the legalization of illegal Hispanic aliens; opposes military surveillance of U.S. borders; opposes making English America's official language; favors open borders; and rejects anti-terrorism legislation like the Patriot Act.

League of Women Voters Education Fund: The League supports taxpayer-funded abortion-on-demand; supports "motor-voter" registration, which allows anyone with a driver's license to become a voter, regardless of citizenship status; and supports tax hikes and socialized medicine.

League of Young Voters: This organization seeks to "empowe[r] young people nationwide" to "participate in the democratic process and create progressive political change on the local, state and national level[s]."

Lynne Stewart Defense Committee: IRS records indicate that Soros's Open Society Institute made a September 2002 grant of $20,000 to this organization. Stewart was the criminal-defense attorney who was later convicted for abetting her client, the "blind sheik" Omar Abdel Rahman, in terrorist activities connected with his Islamic Group.

Machsom Watch: This organization describes itself as "a movement of Israeli women, peace activists from all sectors of Israeli society, who oppose the Israeli occupation and the denial of Palestinians' rights to move freely in their land."

Madre: This international women's organization deems America the world's foremost violator of human rights. As such, it seeks to "communicat[e] the real-life impact of U.S. policies on women and families confronting violence, poverty and repression around the world," and to "demand alternatives to destructive U.S. policies." It also advocates unrestricted access to taxpayer-funded abortion-on-demand.

Malcolm X Grassroots Movement: This group views the U.S. as a nation replete with racism and discrimination against blacks; seeks to establish an independent black nation in the southeastern United States; and demands reparations for slavery.

Massachusetts Immigrant and Refugee Advocacy Coalition: This group calls for the expansion of civil rights and liberties for illegal aliens; laments that illegal aliens in America are commonly subjected to "worker exploitation"; supports tuition-assistance programs for illegal aliens attending college; and characterizes the Patriot Act as a "very troubling" assault on civil liberties.

Media Fund: Soros played a major role in creating this group, whose purpose was to conceptualize, produce, and place political ads on television, radio, print, and the Internet.

Media Matters for America: This organization is a "web-based, not-for-profit ... progressive research and information center" seeking to "systematically monitor a cross-section of print, broadcast, cable, radio, and Internet media outlets for conservative misinformation." The group works closely with the Soros-backed Center for American Progress, and is heavily funded by Democracy Alliance, of which Soros is a major financier.

Mercy Corps: Vis a vis the Arab-Israeli conflict, Mercy Corps places all blame for Palestinian poverty and suffering directly on Israel.

Mexican American Legal Defense and Education Fund: This group advocates open borders, free college tuition for illegal aliens, lowered educational standards to accommodate Hispanics, and voting rights for criminals. In MALDEF's view, supporters of making English the official language of the United States are "motivated by racism and anti-immigrant sentiments," while advocates of sanctions against employers reliant on illegal labor seek to discriminate against "brown-skinned people."

Meyer, Suozzi, English and Klein, PC: This influential defender of Big Labor is headed by Democrat operative Harold Ickes.

Midwest Academy: This entity trains radical activists in the tactics of direct action, targeting, confrontation, and intimidation.

Migration Policy Institute: This group seeks to create "a North America with gradually disappearing border controls ... with permanent migration remaining at moderate levels."

Military Families Speak Out: This group ascribes the U.S. invasion of Iraq to American imperialism and lust for oil.

Missourians Organizing for Reform and Empowerment: This group is the rebranded Missouri branch of the now-defunct, pro-socialist, community organization ACORN.

MoveOn.org: This Web-based organization supports Democratic political candidates through fundraising, advertising, and get-out-the-vote drives.

Ms. Foundation for Women: This group laments what it views as the widespread and enduring flaws of American society: racism, sexism, homophobia, and the violation of civil rights and liberties. It focuses its philanthropy on groups that promote affirmative action for women, unfettered access to taxpayer-funded abortion-on-demand, amnesty for illegal aliens, and big government generally.

Muslim Advocates: Opposed to U.S. counter-terrorism strategies that make use of sting operations and informants, MA characterizes such tactics as forms of "entrapment" that are inherently discriminatory against Muslims.

NARAL Pro-Choice America: This group supports taxpayer-funded abortion-on-demand, and works to elect pro-abortion Democrats.

NAACP Legal Defense and Education Fund: The NAACP supports racial preferences in employment and education, as well as the racial gerrymandering of voting districts. Underpinning its support for race preferences is the fervent belief that white racism in the United States remains an intractable, largely undiminished, phenomenon.

The Nation Institute: This nonprofit entity sponsors leftist conferences, fellowships, awards for radical activists, and journalism internships.

National Abortion Federation: This group opposes any restrictions on abortion at either the state or federal levels, and champions the introduction of unrestricted abortion into developing regions of the world.

National Coalition to Abolish the Death Penalty: This group was established in 1976 as the first "fully staffed national organization exclusively devoted to abolishing capital punishment."

National Committee for Responsive Philanthropy: This group depicts the United States as a nation in need of dramatic structural change financed by philanthropic organizations. It overwhelmingly promotes grant-makers and grantees with leftist agendas, while criticizing their conservative counterparts.

National Committee for Voting Integrity: This group opposes "the implementation of proof of citizenship and photo identification requirements for eligible electors in American elections as the means of assuring election integrity."

National Council for Research on Women: This group supports big government, high taxes, military spending cuts, increased social welfare spending, and the unrestricted right to taxpayer-funded abortion-on-demand.

National Council of La Raza: This group lobbies for racial preferences, bilingual education, stricter hate-crime laws, mass immigration, and amnesty for illegal aliens.

National Council of Women's Organizations: This group views the United States as a nation rife with injustice against girls and women. It advocates high levels of spending for social welfare programs, and supports race and gender preferences for minorities and women in business and academia.

National Immigration Forum: Opposing the enforcement of present immigration laws, this organization urges the American government to "legalize" en masse all illegal aliens currently in the United States who have no criminal records, and to dramatically increase the number of visas available for those wishing to migrate to the U.S. The Forum is particularly committed to opening the borders to unskilled, low-income workers, and immediately making them eligible for welfare and social service programs.

National Immigration Law Center: This group seeks to win unrestricted access to government-funded social welfare programs for illegal aliens.

National Lawyers Guild: This group promotes open borders; seeks to weaken America's intelligence-gathering agencies; condemns the Patriot Act as an assault on civil liberties; rejects capitalism as an unviable economic system; has rushed to the defense of convicted terrorists and their abettors; and generally opposes all U.S. foreign policy positions, just as it did during the Cold War when it sided with the Soviets.

National Organization for Women: This group advocates the unfettered right to taxpayer-funded abortion-on-demand; seeks to "eradicate racism, sexism and homophobia" from American society; attacks Christianity and traditional religious values; and supports gender-based preferences for women.

National Partnership for Women and Families: This organization supports race- and sex-based preferences in employment and education. It also advocates for the universal "right" of women to undergo taxpayer-funded abortion-on-demand at any stage of pregnancy and for any reason.

National Priorities Project: This group supports government-mandated redistribution of wealth — through higher taxes and greater expenditures on social welfare programs. NPP exhorts the government to redirect a significant portion of its military funding toward public education, universal health insurance, environmentalist projects, and welfare programs.

National Public Radio: Founded in 1970 with 90 public radio stations as charter members, NPR is today a loose network of more than 750 U.S. radio stations across the country, many of which are based on college and university campuses. (source)

National Security Archive Fund: This group collects and publishes declassified documents obtained through the Freedom of Information Act to a degree that compromises American national security and the safety of intelligence agents.

National Women's Law Center: This group supports taxpayer-funded abortion-on-demand; lobbies against conservative judicial appointees; advocates increased welfare spending to help low-income mothers; and favors higher taxes for the purpose of generating more funds for such government programs as Medicaid, food stamps, welfare, foster care, health care, child-support enforcement, and student loans.

Natural Resources Defense Council: One of the most influential environmentalist lobbying groups in the United States, the Council claims a membership of one million people.

New America Foundation: This organization uses policy papers, media articles, books, and educational events to influence public opinion on such topics as healthcare, environmentalism, energy policy, the Mideast conflict, global governance, and much more.

New Israel Fund: This organization gives support to NGOs that regularly produce reports accusing Israel of human-rights violations and religious persecution.

NewsCorpWatch: A project of Media Matters for America, NewsCorpWatch was established with the help of a $1 million George Soros grant to Media Matters.

Pacifica Foundation: This entity owns and operates Pacifica Radio, awash from its birth with the Socialist-Marxist rhetoric of class warfare and hatred for capitalism.

Palestinian Center for Human Rights: This NGO investigates and documents what it views as Israeli human-rights violations against Palestinians.

Peace and Security Funders Group: This is an association of more than 60 foundations that give money to leftist anti-war and environmentalist causes. Its members tend to depict America as the world's chief source of international conflict, environmental destruction, and economic inequalities.

Peace Development Fund: In PDF's calculus, the United States needs a massive overhaul of its social and economic institutions. "Recently," explains PDF, "we have witnessed the negative effects of neo-liberalism and the globalization of capitalism, the de-industrialization of the U.S. and the growing gap between the rich and poor ..."

People for the American Way: This group opposes the Patriot Act, anti-terrorism measures generally, and the allegedly growing influence of the "religious right."

People Improving Communities Through Organizing: This group uses Alinsky-style organizing tactics to advance the doctrines of the religious left.

Physicians for Human Rights: This group is selectively and disproportionately critical of the United States and Israel in its condemnations of human rights violations.

Physicians for Social Responsibility: This is an anti-U.S.-military organization that also embraces the tenets of radical environmentalism.

Planned Parenthood: This group is the largest abortion provider in the United States and advocates taxpayer-funded abortion-on-demand.

Ploughshares Fund: This public grant making foundation opposes America's development of a missile defense system, and contributes to many organizations that are highly critical of U.S. foreign policies and military ventures.

Prepare New York: This group supported the proposed construction of a Muslim Community Center near Ground Zero in lower Manhattan – a project known as the Cordoba Initiative, headed by Imam Feisal Abdul Rauf.

Presidential Climate Action Project: PCAP's mission is to create a new 21st-century economy, completely carbon-free and based largely on renewable energy. A key advisor to the organization is the revolutionary communist Van Jones.

Prison Moratorium Project: This initiative was created in 1995 for the express purpose of working for the elimination of all prisons in the United States and the release of all inmates. Reasoning from the premise that incarceration is never an appropriate means of dealing with crime, it deems American society's inherent inequities the root of all criminal behavior.

Progressive Change Campaign Committee: This organization works "to elect bold progressive candidates to federal office and to help [them] and their campaigns save money, work smarter, and win more often."

Progressive States Network: PSN's mission is to "pass progressive legislation in all fifty states by providing coordinated research and strategic advocacy tools to forward-thinking state legislators."

Project Vote: This is the voter-mobilization arm of the Soros-funded ACORN. A persistent pattern of lawlessness and corruption has followed ACORN/Project Vote activities over the years.

Pro Publica: Claiming that "investigative journalism is at risk," this group aims to remedy this lacuna in news publishing by "expos[ing] abuses of power and betrayals of the public trust by government, business, and other institutions, using the moral force of investigative journalism to spur reform through the sustained spotlighting of wrongdoing."

Proteus Fund: This foundation directs its philanthropy toward a number of radical leftwing organizations.

Psychologists for Social Responsibility: This anti-capitalist, anti-corporate, anti-military, anti-American organization "uses psychological knowledge and skills to promote peace with social justice at the community, national and international levels."

Public Citizen Foundation: Public Citizen seeks increased government intervention and litigation against corporations — a practice founded on the notion that American corporations, like the capitalist system of which they are a part, are inherently inclined toward corruption.

Public Justice Center: Viewing America as a nation rife with injustice and discrimination, this organization engages in legislative and policy advocacy to promote "systemic change for the disenfranchised."

Rebuild and Renew America Now (a.k.a. Unity '09): Spearheaded by MoveOn.org and overseen by longtime activist Heather Booth, this coalition was formed to facilitate the passage of President Obama's "historic" $3.5 trillion budget for fiscal year 2010.

Res Publica: Seeking to advance far-left agendas in places all around the world, RP specializes in "E-advocacy," or web-based movement-building.

Roosevelt Institute: Proceeding from the premise that free-market capitalism is inherently unjust and prone to periodic collapses caused by its own structural flaws, RI currently administers several major projects aimed at reshaping the American economy to more closely resemble a socialist system.

Secretary of State Project: This project was launched in July 2006 as an independent "527" organization devoted to helping Democrats get elected to the office of Secretary of State in selected swing, or battleground, states.

Sentencing Project: Asserting that prison-sentencing patterns are racially discriminatory, this initiative advocates voting rights for felons.

Social Justice Leadership: This organization seeks to transform an allegedly inequitable America into a "just society" by means of "a renewed social-justice movement."

Shadow Democratic Party: This is an elaborate network of non-profit activist groups organized by George Soros and others to mobilize resources — money, get-out-the-vote drives, campaign advertising, and policy initiatives — to elect Democratic candidates and guide the Democratic Party towards the left.

Sojourners: This evangelical Christian ministry preaches radical leftwing politics. During the 1980s it championed Communist revolution in Central America and chastised U.S. policy-makers for their tendency "to assume the very worst about their Soviet counterparts." More recently, Sojourners has taken up the cause of environmental activism, opposed welfare reform as a "mean-spirited Republican agenda," and mounted a defense of affirmative action.

Southern Poverty Law Center: This organization monitors the activities of what it calls "hate groups" in the United States. It exaggerates the prevalence of white racism directed against American minorities.

State Voices: This coalition helps independent local activist groups in 22 states work collaboratively on a year-round basis, so as to maximize the impact of their efforts.

Talking Transition: This was a two-week project launched in early November 2013 to "help shape the transition" to City Hall for the newly elected Democratic mayor of New York, Bill de Blasio.

Think Progress: This Internet blog "pushes back, daily," by its own account, against its conservative targets, and seeks to transform "progressive ideas into policy through rapid response communications, legislative action, grassroots organizing and advocacy, and partnerships with other progressive leaders throughout the country and the world."

Thunder Road Group: This political consultancy, in whose creation Soros had a hand, coordinates strategy for the Media Fund, America Coming Together, and America Votes.

Tides Foundation and Tides Center: Tides is a major funder of the radical Left.

U.S. Public Interest Research Group: This is an umbrella organization of student groups that support leftist agendas.

Universal Healthcare Action Network: This organization supports a single-payer health care system controlled by the federal government.

Urban Institute: This research organization favors socialized medicine, expansion of the federal welfare bureaucracy, and tax hikes for higher income-earners.

USAction Education Fund: USAction lists its priorities as: "fighting the right wing agenda"; "building grassroots political power"; winning "social, racial and economic justice for all"; supporting a system of taxpayer-funded socialized medicine; reversing "reckless tax cuts for millionaires and corporations" which shield the "wealthy" from paying their "fair share"; advocating for "pro-consumer and environmental regulation of corporate abuse"; "strengthening progressive voices on local, state and national issues"; and working to "register, educate and get out the vote ... [to] help progressives get elected at all levels of government."

Voter Participation Center: This organization seeks to increase voter turnout among unmarried women, "people of color," and 18-to-29-year-olds — demographics that are heavily pro-Democrat.

Voto Latino: This group seeks to mobilize Latin-Americans to become registered voters and political activists.

We Are America Alliance: This coalition promotes "increased civic participation by immigrants" in the American political process.

Working Families Party: An outgrowth of the socialist New Party, WFP seeks to help push the Democratic Party toward the left.

World Organization Against Torture: This coalition works closely with groups that condemn Israeli security measures against Palestinian terrorism.

YWCA World Office, Switzerland: The YWCA opposes abstinence education; supports universal access to taxpayer-funded abortion-on-demand; and opposes school vouchers.

"Secondary" or "Indirect" Affiliates of the George Soros Network
By Discover the Networks

In addition to those organizations that are funded directly by George Soros and his Open Society Foundations (OSF), there are also numerous "secondary" or "indirect" affiliates of the Soros network. These include organizations which do not receive direct funding from Soros and OSF, but which are funded by one or more organizations that do.

Center for Progressive Leadership: Funded by the Soros-bankrolled Democracy Alliance, this anti-capitalist organization is dedicated to training future leftist political leaders.

John Adams Project: This project of the American Civil Liberties Union was accused of: (a) having hired investigators to photograph CIA officers thought to have been involved in enhanced interrogations of terror suspects detained in Guantanamo, and then (b) showing the photos to the attorneys of those suspects, some of whom were senior al-Qaeda operatives.

Moving Ideas Network (MIN): This coalition of more than 250 leftwing activist groups is a partner organization of the

Soros-backed Center for American Progress. MIN was originally a project of the Soros-backed American Prospect and, as such, received indirect funding from the Open Society Institute. In early 2006, The American Prospect relinquished control of the Moving Ideas Network.

New Organizing Institute: Created by the Soros-funded MoveOn. org, this group "trains young, technology-enabled political organizers to work for progressive campaigns and organizations."

Think Progress: This "project" of the American Progress Action Fund, which is a "sister advocacy organization" of the Soros-funded Center for American Progress and Campus Progress, seeks to transform "progressive ideas into policy through rapid response communications, legislative action, grassroots organizing and advocacy, and partnerships with other progressive leaders throughout the country and the world."

Vote for Change: Coordinated by the political action committee of the Soros-funded MoveOn.org, Vote for Change was a group of 41 musicians and bands that performed concerts in several key election "battleground" states during October 2004, to raise money in support of Democrat John Kerry's presidential bid.

Working Families Party: Created in 1998 to help push the Democratic Party toward the left, this front group for the Soros-funded ACORN functions as a political party that promotes ACORN-friendly candidates."

http://www.discoverthenetworks.org/viewSubCategory.asp?id=1237

VII

SOCIAL SECURITY

Let's talk about your Social Security. Up until the 1980s, your Social Security card expressly stated that it was not to be used for identification purposes. At that time, since nearly everyone had a number, it was convenient to use it as an identification, so "Not for Identification" was removed from the card.

When President Franklin Roosevelt, a Democrat, introduced the Social Security (FICA) Program, he promised five things:

That participation in the Program would be completely voluntary (which it is not).

That the participants would only have to pay 1% of the first $1,400 of their annual incomes into the Program (now 7.65% on the first $110,000).

That the money the participants elected to put into the Program would be deductible from their income for tax purposes each year (no longer tax deductible).

That the money would be put into the independent 'Trust Fund' rather than into the general operating fund, and therefore, would only be used to fund the Social Security Retirement Program, and no other Government program. (Under Johnson the money was moved to The General Fund and Spent).

That the annuity payments to the retirees would never be taxed as income. (Under Clinton and Gore up to 85% of your Social Security can be taxed).

It was Lyndon B. Johnson and the Democratically controlled House and Senate that took our Social Security from the independent Trust Fund and placed into the General Fund so that Congress could spend it.

If you ask Congress about it, they have a different story because they talk a different language called "Washington Speak." Here is their justification for why there is no money in the Social Security Fund:

"Q. Did LBJ take social security from the independent trust fund and put it into the general fund so that Congress could spend it?

"There has never been any change in the way the Social Security Program is financed or the way Social Security payroll taxes are used by the federal government. This question comes from a confusion about the way the Social Security Trust Fund is treated in federal budget accounting. Starting in 1969 (due to action by the Johnson Administration in 1968) the transactions to the Trust Fund were included in what is known as the "unified budget." This is sometimes described by saying that the Social Security Trust Funds are "on-budget." This budget treatment of the Social Security Trust Fund continued until 1990 when the Trust Funds were again taken "off-budget." But whether the Trust Funds are "on-budget" or "off-budget" is primarily a question of accounting practices—it has no effect on the actual operations of the Fund itself.

"Today the federal government automatically puts all of the money that should be set aside for the Social Security Trust Fund into the General Fund. Raiding the Social Security Trust Fund was a precedent set in 1968 by another Progressive, President, Lyndon B. Johnson, to help pay for the Viet Nam War. To date, the federal government has borrowed over $2 Trillion from the Social Security Trust Fund to spend on other programs.

"Contrary to what many Americans believe and what Progressives love to say, there is no money in the Trust Fund to pay future benefits. Furthermore, the fundamentally flawed program faces a severe demographic crisis as members of the baby boom generation retire. The mess we face with Social Security, a program so many are now dependent on, is yet another example of a progressive policy where the potential for unintended consequences was ignored at the program's inception." http://www.ontheissues.org/Celeb/Lyndon_Johnson_Social_Security.htm

Remember not only did you and I contribute to our social security, but our employer did too. What happened to all that money from the people that died and did not draw their social security? You say, well his wife drew it. But these days both spouses have jobs and pay into the system. If she draws his, what happens to hers? I guess Congress thinks it belongs to them.

What we and our employer contributed equaled 15% of our income before taxes. If you average conservatively $30,000 a year over your working life, that comes to $220,500. The government is now calling that an entitlement, but it's your money, not an entitlement.

If you calculate the future invested value of $4,500 per year (yours & your employer's contribution) at a simple 5% interest (less than what the Government pays on the money that it borrows), after 49 years of working you'd have $892,919.98. If you took out only 3% per year, you'd receive $26,787.60 per year and it would last better than 30 years (until you're 95 if you retire at age 65) and that's with no interest paid on that final amount on deposit!

If you bought an annuity and it paid 4% per year, you'd have a lifetime income of $2,976.40 per month.

Congress has pulled off a bigger Ponzi scheme than Bernie Madoff ever did. When Harry Reid was asked how to solve the problem because Social Security was running out of money, he said "There can be some tweaks done."

Where does the money really go? The government tells us the money was spent on the Iraq war and the war on terror. We know the government sends a lot of money out on foreign aide. But here is where the money really goes.

The truth about chain emails on illegals and Social Security:

CIS estimated that welfare payments to illegal immigrant households averaged $1,040 per household in 2001, mainly Medicaid "on behalf of their U.S.-born children." But the report did not attempt to come up with a total for all such households.

"$2.2 Billion dollars a year is spent on food assistance programs such as food stamps, WIC, and free school lunches for illegal aliens."

"$2.5 Billion dollars a year is spent on Medicaid for illegal aliens."

"These figures supposedly come from a 2004 report by CIS that estimated the costs to the federal government of households headed by illegal immigrants in 2002. But the CIS report actually put the costs of food stamp, WIC and free school lunch programs to "illegal alien households" at $1.9 billion, not the $2.2 billion... The $2.5 billion figure for Medicaid to such households is quoted accurately, but again, much of this was in benefits for U.S.-born children, who are citizens.

CIS report: Households headed by illegal aliens imposed more than $26.3 billion in costs on the federal government in 2002 and paid only $16 billion in taxes, creating a net fiscal deficit of almost $10.4 billion, or $2,700 per illegal household.

Even CIS' figures have been questioned by other researchers. The Urban Institute reviewed a related 2003 CIS paper and concluded that its "methods overstate the percentage of the population receiving Medicaid and the share of immigrants on Medicaid, resulting in misleading conclusions about welfare use among immigrants."

CIS: Our findings show that many of the preconceived notions about the fiscal impact of illegal households turn out to be inaccurate. In terms of welfare use, receipt of cash assistance programs tends to be very low, while Medicaid use, though significant, is still less than for other households. Only use of food assistance programs is significantly higher than that of the rest of the population. Also, contrary to the perceptions that illegal aliens don't pay payroll taxes, we estimate that more than half of illegals work "on the books."

"$12 Billion dollars a year is spent on primary and secondary school education for children here illegally and they cannot speak a word of English!"

"$17 Billion dollars a year is spent for education for the American-born children of illegal aliens, known as anchor babies."

Both links given to "verify" these claims lead to an April 1, 2006, episode of "Lou Dobbs Tonight" on CNN. During the show, correspondent Christine Romans cited both of these stats and attributed them to FAIR. A FAIR research paper from 2005 does include these cost projections, but a closer look shows that the underlying assumptions are inflated or unsupported.

The FAIR report starts with the presumption that there are "1.5 million school-aged illegal immigrants residing in the United States." That figure is attributed to an Urban Institute presentation that doesn't actually say that. Instead, the Urban Institute said: "We estimate that there are about 1.4 million undocumented children under 18 with about 1.1 million of school age (5 -19)."

The FAIR report also assumes there are 2 million "U.S.-born siblings" of illegal immigrant families. However, the Urban Institute makes no estimates of U.S.-born siblings and FAIR gives no citation for its figure. And in any case, again, those U.S.-born children of illegal immigrants are themselves U.S. citizens and not "illegal aliens."

"$3 Million Dollars a day is spent to incarcerate illegal aliens."

"30% percent of all Federal Prison inmates are illegal aliens."

Both of these claims can be traced back to that same April 1, 2006, episode of "Lou Dobbs Tonight" on CNN, in the same segment, with the same correspondent, Christine Romans. But the e-mail misrepresents what Romans said. She gave figures for people who are "not U.S. citizens," a category that would include legal residents as well as "illegal aliens."

Romans said that "according to the Federal Bureau of Prisons, 30 percent of federal prisoners are not U.S. citizens," adding that "most are thought to be illegal aliens." Actually, the Federal Bureau of Prisons does not keep figures on illegal immigrants. What solid numbers we can find point to a much smaller figure. A Department of Justice report from 2003 found that only 1.6 percent of the state and federal prison populations was under Immigration and Customs Enforcement jurisdiction, and thus known to be illegal immigrants. Half of these prisoners were detained only because they were here illegally, not for other crimes.

The Bureau of Prisons does track prisoners by offense when information is available. By that metric, 10.7 percent of prisoners in federal jails were incarcerated for immigration offenses in 2009. In 2006, when Romans gave her report, the figure was 10.2 percent.

The "$3 million dollar a day" figure is based on the false assumption that thirty percent of all inmates are illegal immigrants, and thus is greatly inflated.

"$90 Billion Dollars a year is spent on illegal aliens for Welfare & social services by the American taxpayers."

The link to "verify" this claim is dead. However, we found a transcript of a Lou Dobbs episode on Oct. 29, 2006, in which Robert Rector of the conservative Heritage Foundation made the following statement:

Robert Rector, Oct. 29, 2006: Well, assuming that we have about 11 million immigrants in the U.S., the net cost or the total cost of services and benefits provided to them, education, welfare, general social services would be about $90 billion a year, and they would pay very little in taxes. It's important to remember that at least half of illegal immigrants are high school dropouts.

We checked with Rector, who said he was referring to both legal and illegal low-skill immigrant households (those headed by someone who doesn't have a high school diploma). His research also looked at many forms of government spending per household, including money spent on parks and transportation.

"$200 Billion Dollars a year in suppressed American wages are caused by the illegal aliens."

Again, this is from that same April 1, 2006, Lou Dobbs episode. On the show, Dobbs said that "estimates by the most authoritative and recent study put the suppressed wages at $200 billion a year, as a result of immigration, both legal and illegal." The e-mail continues its practice of ignoring any distinction between legal and illegal immigration.

We couldn't find any study that supported Dobb's figure.

"During the year of 2005 there were 4 to 10 million illegal aliens that crossed our Southern Border also, as many as 19,500 illegal aliens from Terrorist Countries. Millions of pounds of drugs, cocaine, meth, heroin and marijuana, crossed into the U. S from the Southern border." The link goes to a 2006 report written by the Republican staff of the House Subcommittee on Investigations of the Committee on Homeland Security. To start, the "19,500" number of "illegal aliens from Terrorist Countries" is nowhere to be found in this report. In fact, the report estimates the number of illegal immigrants coming over the southern border from countries known to harbor terrorists to be in the "hundreds." We've seen a similar scare tactic used previously in ads advocating for a border fence.

"And the four million to ten million statistic is extrapolated using some imprecise reasoning. The committee report figures that since "Border Patrol apprehended approximately 1.2 million illegal aliens" in 2005 and since "Federal law enforcement estimates that 10 percent to 30 percent of illegal aliens are actually apprehended," that "therefore, in 2005, as many as ten to four million [sic] illegal aliens crossed into the United States." That simplistic math produces a figure starkly different from more widely accepted estimates. The Pew Hispanic Center estimated that in 2005 there were 11.1 million illegal immigrants total, living in the United States. The center also estimated that about 500,000 illegal immigrants a year came to the U.S. from 2005 to 2008.

"The National Policy Institute, 'estimated that the total cost of mass deportation would be between $206 and $230 billion or an average cost of between $41 and $46 billion annually over a five-year period.'"

"No, it didn't. The National Policy Institute, a group that says it promotes the rights of "white Americans," ironically was citing figures from the liberal Center for American Progress in a report that argued against mass deportation of undocumented workers. CAP said such deportation would cost more per year than the entire Department of Homeland Security budget, illustrating "the false allure of deportation as a response to our broken immigration system."

"The Dark Side of Illegal Immigration: Nearly One Million Sex Crimes Committed by Illegal Immigrants in The United States."

"Once again, the "verify" link is dead. But a little Internet research found the article cited. An independently published, non-peer-reviewed study did estimate that nearly a million sex crimes have been committed by illegal immigrants over a seven-year period, but it employs some highly creative math and interesting assumptions to get there. The "study" is actually a pretty good case study in bad research."

"The author assumes that 2 percent of illegal immigrants are sex offenders after "examining ICE reports and public records," but does not say how that figure was calculated. A bibliography cites miscellaneous Immigration and Customs Enforcement press releases and media accounts of instances of apprehending illegal immigrants who were sex offenders (seemingly manufacturing a "rate" based on anecdotal evidence). The author then makes no distinction between male and female illegal immigrants when estimating the number that are "sex offenders.""

"As we've said before, anonymous chain e-mails making dramatic claims are quite likely to be false. And that goes even for those that may seem to cite legitimate sources. This one is yet another good candidate for the "delete" key."

– Justin Bank - http://cf.factcheck.org/2009/04/cost-of-illegal-immigrants/

"In 2006 a Petition originated by Californians circulated on the internet and was to be sent to President Bush, California Governor Arnold Schwarzenegger, and several members of Congress from

California. It says that the U.S. Senate voted to give Social Security benefits to illegal immigrants and protests it. It asks that citizenship be required for eligibility for Social Services, that no free services or funding be given to illegal immigrants, and that no college education be provided free to illegals either.

"The Truth is the internet petitions have no value. They do not bear the same weight of signed petitions since anybody who wants to take the time could generate them and just make up the names. These petitions also depend on someone to ultimately send them to the right addresses, which is not a reliable way to get them there. Second, let's look at each of the issues in the eRumors.

"The Senate Vote on Social Security that generated this petition was in May, 2006. The effect of that vote was to allow language in other legislation on the issue to proceed. It would not have granted Social Security benefits to all illegal aliens but it would have allowed illegal aliens who had already paid into Social Security to accrue the benefits of their contributions. The Senate went on to pass a controversial immigration bill but it differed greatly from a version passed in the House of Representatives.

"Social Security

"As of this writing, Illegal immigrants are not benefiting much from Social Security. It's technically illegal to hire an undocumented worker so theoretically there should not be any paying into Social Security. But because of so many illegal workers who use bogus Social Security cards to get jobs, billions of dollars of Social Security deductions are made each year as well as employer payments into Social Security on behalf of those workers. Illegals are not supposed to collect on Social Security and because their Social Security numbers are manufactured, they cannot collect so the money has become a part of the controversy over Illegal immigration. There have been some estimates that more than $60 billion a year are being paid into the system because of illegal immigrants, money that would disappear if the immigrants did.

"Immigration reform being debated in Congress could affect all this such as if amnesty is granted to illegal aliens currently residing in the U.S. or if illegal aliens are given some kind of participation in the Social Security system. There is no legislation, however, that would give illegal aliens Social Security payments if they have not paid into Social Security." https://www.truthorfiction.com/petition-illegals/

Can you see now why Congress is doing nothing about immigration? They have all this money coming in that they are spending and don't have to account for.

Can we take all of the illegal Mexican prisoners that we have and put them on a transport plane and take them deep into Southern Mexico and release them?

VIII

IT'S WHO YOU KNOW, NEGOTIATING

I have heard it since I was a child. "It is not what you know, but it is who you know." And that applies in Washington, D.C. You must have personal connections. It is a revolving door.

"PACS (Political Action Committees) control the most corporate money, trade associations, unions, and politicians. A PAC is an organization that pools campaign contributions from a lot of members and donates those funds to campaign for or against a candidate among other things.

"Receiving a financial contribution from the treasury of a union or a corporation is illegal, so they give their money to PACS. A Union PAC may only solicit money from its members. An independent PAC may solicit money from the general public but must pay their own costs from those funds.

"A Federal multi-candidate PAC may contribute $5,000 to a candidate committee for a primary and general election and $15,000 to a political party.

"A Super PAC, also known as "independent-expenditure only committees", may not make contributions to candidate campaigns or parties, but may engage in unlimited political spending independently of the campaigns. They can raise funds from individuals, corporations,

unions, and other groups without any legal limit on donation size."
https://en.wikipedia.org/wiki/Political_action_committee

Election ads used to be just between the candidates. Then the PACS got involved. Now other movements get involved attempting to influence voters. Some of the movements are called 527s after the IRS Code.

One of the things I worried about the most when Donald Trump was elected was he constantly talked about how well he could negotiate. The first thing he did was negotiate Congress. He took one of the most corrupt members of Congress, Mitch McConnell, and negotiated him on his side by making McConnell's wife, Elaine Chao the head of the Department of Transportation. I am not saying she is not qualified, but how better to get McConnell's cooperation in the Senate. Pretty smart move. Problem is that McConnell is also a Soros man.

Mr. Trump is not dumb. The Lame stream Media treat him like he is, but he puts the smartest people he can find in the best positions of government where they are suited.

The Media has a heyday every time Mr. Trump tweets a message or gives a speech. They make fun of him for days. If they would spend that much energy on positive messages and actual reporting maybe we could make America great again.

In some cases, it is big money that you need. In some cases, it is power that you need. So, it is who do you know and what influence do you have without having to flaunt it.

Donald Trump financed his own presidential campaign. He did not accept PAC funds. This means he can't be bought. Hillary Clinton, however was a different matter. Campaign ads alone cost over $61 Million.

I thought you might be interested in how much Hillary spent.

"*By* Kristian Wilson Nov 3 2016

"There's only one week left until the 2016 presidential election, and everyone is crunching the numbers on voting, spending, and odds of winning. So just how much money has Hillary Clinton spent on her campaign? The numbers are staggering.

"Clinton's presidential bid has cost more money than her opponent's, but the two nominees have spent roughly the same percentage of their campaign funds, according to data compiled by Bloomberg. The Democratic candidate has spent 84 percent of the approximately $1.1

billion she has raised during this election cycle, or $897.7 million. Donald Trump has spent 83.9 percent of his campaign funds.

"The campaign spending data comes from the final pre-election report Clinton's super-PAC filed with the Federal Election Commission. That report covered the 2016 Democratic presidential campaign from Oct. 1-19. During that period, Clinton raised $52.4 million and spent $48.4 million."

"Clinton has outspent Trump on campaign ads throughout the election. Media purchases account for $30.3 million of the money the Democratic candidate spent during the first half of October, with media production and online advertising costing Clinton a combined $4.4 million. For that period, she was alone in buying ads in Arizona, Georgia, and Nebraska. In battleground states during early October, Trump only outspent Clinton in Maine and Wisconsin.

"So where did all that money come from? About 19 percent of Clinton's campaign money has come from four super-PACs: Priorities USA Action ($173.3 million), American Bridge 21st Century ($15.2 million), Correct the Record ($9.4 million), and Ready PAC ($3.6 million).

"An additional $750.6 million has come from the Democratic National Committee and Clinton's joint fundraising committees, the Hillary Victory Fund and the Hillary Action Fund.

"The top five individual donors to Clinton's campaign are:
- hedge-fund manager S. Donald Sussman, $21.8 million
- venture capitalists J.B. and Mary Katherine Pritzker, $17.5 million
- Fox Family Channel founder Haim Saban, and his wife, U.S. Mission to the U.N. Senior Advisor Cheryl Saban, $12.5 million
- Open Society Foundations founder George Soros, $11.8 million
- Chicago philanthropist Fred Eychaner, $10.9 million

"As of Oct. 19, Hillary Clinton had spent $897.7 million on her campaign, leaving her with $171.6 million on-hand to spend in the days leading up to the general election."

If you are going to go into politics for a career, you better know someone, because you are going to need a lot of money.

IX

EARMARKS

" During my first term in Congress, I signed a pledge that I will take no more earmarks and I've been faithful to that pledge."
Michele Bachmann

Webster's dictionary traces the American origins of the expression "pork barrel spending" (earmarks) back to around 1905 or 1910 and defines it as "a government appropriation...that provides funds for local improvements designed to ingratiate legislators with their constituents." In a 1936 Baltimore Evening Sun editorial, H. L. Mencken had this practice in mind when he charged that American government is "a broker in pillage and every election is a sort of advance auction sale of stolen goods."

In November 2012 then Speaker of the House John Boehner announced a ban on Earmarks in the House of Representatives. Speaker Boehner said earmarks had "become a symbol of a Congress that has broken faith with the people."

Members of Congress use "soft earmarks" to provide Federal funding to companies, projects, groups, and organizations, often in their district. This database shows how the recipients of Federal earmarks interact with the federal government through lobbying efforts and campaign contributions. Readers may now, for example, determine the degree to which people and political action committees associated with a specific company or organization have donated money to a congressman responsible for giving that company or organization an earmark.

Earmarks come in two forms: Earmarks and "soft earmarks." Regular or "hard" earmarks refer to those found in legislation and are legally binding. It means that funds are directed to a specific project, usually to a foreign country.

Soft earmarks are the ones we hear about the most, or perhaps the ones we do not hear about often enough. Often "tucked" as amendments into the larger annual appropriations bills of the Federal budget, earmark spending projects often come under criticism as being "rushed through" Congress without the full debate and scrutiny devoted to the larger parent bill.

Perhaps most significantly, earmark spending often results in the expenditure of large sums of taxpayer money to help a limited number of people. For example, in 2005, $223 million was earmarked by then Senate Committee on Appropriations chair Ted Stevens (R-Alaska) to build a bridge to connect an Alaskan town of 8,900 to an island with a population of 50, saving a short ferry ride. Creating an uncharacteristic uproar in the Senate, the earmark nicknamed "the Bridge to Nowhere," was removed from the spending bill.

A fan of mine recently sent me a copy of a conversation between the late Davy Crockett and Horatio Bunce. The conversation is worth repeating if not because it should be impressed on the mind of every Congressman in Washington.

"Not Yours to Give

By David Crockett

Davy Crockett-David "Davy" Crockett was a 19th-century American folk hero, frontiersman, soldier and politician. He is commonly referred to in popular culture by the epithet "King of the Wild Frontier." He represented Tennessee in the U.S. House of Representatives, served in the Texas Revolution, and died at the Battle of the Alamo.

One day in the House of Representatives a bill was taken up appropriating money for the benefit of a widow of a distinguished naval officer. Several beautiful speeches had been made in its support. The speaker was just about to put the question when Crockett arose:

"Mr. Speaker — I have as much respect for the memory of the deceased, and as much sympathy for the suffering of the living, if there be, as any man in this House, but we must not permit our respect for the dead or our sympathy for part of the living to lead us into an act of injustice to the balance of the living. I will not go into an argument to prove that Congress has not the power to appropriate this money as an act of charity. Every member on this floor knows it.

"We have the right as individuals, to give away as much of our own money as we please in charity; but as members of Congress we have no right to appropriate a dollar of the public money. Some eloquent appeals have been made to us upon the ground that it is a debt due the deceased. Mr. Speaker, the deceased lived long after the close of the war; he was in office to the day of his death, and I even heard that the government was in arrears to him.

"Every man in this House knows it is not a debt. We cannot without the grossest corruption, appropriate this money as the payment of a debt. We have not the semblance of authority to appropriate it as charity. Mr. Speaker, I have said we have the right to give as much money of our own as we please. I am the poorest man on this floor. I cannot vote for this bill, but I will give one week's pay to the object, and if every member of Congress will do the same, it will amount to more than the bill asks."

"He took his seat. Nobody replied. The bill was put upon its passage, and, instead of passing unanimously, as was generally supposed, and as, no doubt, it would, but for that speech, it received but few votes, and, of course, was lost.

"Later, when asked by a friend why he had opposed the appropriation, Crockett gave this explanation:

"Several years ago I was one evening standing on the steps of the Capitol with some members of Congress when our attention was attracted by a great light over in Georgetown. It was evidently a large fire. We jumped into a hack and drove over as fast as we could. In spite of all that could be done, many houses were burned and many families made houseless, and besides, some of them had lost all but the clothes they had on.

"The weather was very cold, and when I saw so many children suffering, I felt that something ought to be done for them. The next morning a bill was introduced appropriating $20,000 for their relief. We put aside all other business and rushed it through as soon as it could be done.

"The next morning a bill was introduced appropriating $20,000 for their relief.

"The next summer, when it began to be time to think about election I concluded I would take a scout around among the boys of my district. I had no opposition there but, as the election was some time off, I did not know what might turn up. When riding one day in a part of my district in which I was more of a stranger than any other, I saw a man in a field plowing and coming toward the road. I gauged my gait so that we should meet as he came up, I spoke to the man. He replied politely, but as I thought, rather coldly.

"I began: 'Good friend, I am one of those unfortunate beings called candidates and –'

"'Yes I know you; you are Colonel Crockett. I have seen you once before and voted for you the last time you were elected. I suppose you are out electioneering now, but you had better not waste your time or mine, I shall not vote for you again.'

"This was a bookdealer... I begged him tell me what was the matter.

"'Good Colonel, it is hardly worthwhile to waste time or words upon it. I do not see how it can be mended, but you gave a vote last winter which shows that either you have not capacity to understand the Constitution, or that you are wanting in the honesty and firmness to be guided by it. In either case, you are not the man to represent me. But I beg your pardon for expressing it that way. I did not intend to avail myself of the privilege of the constituent to speak plainly to a candidate for the purpose of insulting you or wounding you.

"'I intend by it only to say that your understanding of the constitution is very different from mine; and I will say to you what but for my rudeness, I should not have said, that I believe you to be honest.'

"'But an understanding of the Constitution different from mine I cannot overlook, because the Constitution, to be worth anything, must be held sacred, and rigidly observed in all its provisions. The man who wields power and misinterprets it is dangerous."

"'I admit the truth of all you say, but there must be some mistake. Though I live in the backwoods and seldom go from home, I take the papers from Washington and read very carefully all the proceedings of Congress. My papers say you voted for a bill too appropriate $20,000 to some sufferers by fire in Georgetown. Is that true?"

"'Well my friend; I may as well own up. You have got me there. But certainly nobody will complain that a great and rich country like ours should give the insignificant sum of $20,000 to relieve its suffering women and children, particularly with a full and overflowing treasury, and I am sure, if you had been there, you would have done just the same as I did."

"'It is not the amount, Colonel, that I complain of; it is the principle. In the first place, the government ought to have in the Treasury no more than enough for its legitimate purposes. But that has nothing with the question. The power of collecting and disbursing money at pleasure is the most dangerous power that can be entrusted to man, particularly under our system of collecting revenue by a tariff, which reaches every man in the country, no matter how poor he may be, and the poorer he is the more he pays in proportion to his means.

"What is worse, it presses upon him without his knowledge where the weight centers, for there is not a man in the United States who can ever guess how much he pays to the government. So you see, that while you are contributing to relieve one, you are drawing it from thousands who are even worse off than he.

"If you had the right to give anything, the amount was simply a matter of discretion with you, and you had as much right to give $20,000,000 as $20,000. If you have the right to give at all; and as the Constitution neither defines charity nor stipulates the amount, you are at liberty to give to any and everything which you may believe, or profess to believe, is a charity and to any amount you may think proper. You will very easily perceive what a wide door this would open for fraud and corruption and favoritism, on the one hand, and for robbing the people on the other. No, Colonel, Congress has no right to give charity.

"Individual members may give as much of their own money as they please, but they have no right to touch a dollar of the public money for that purpose. If twice as many houses had been burned in this country as in Georgetown, neither you nor any other member of Congress would have thought of appropriating a dollar for our relief. There are about two hundred and forty members of Congress. If they had shown their sympathy for the sufferers by contributing each one week's pay, it would have made over $13,000. There are plenty of wealthy men around Washington who could have given $20,000 without depriving themselves of even a luxury of life.

"The congressmen chose to keep their own money, which, if reports be true, some of them spend not very creditably; and the people about Washington, no doubt, applauded you for relieving them from necessity of giving what was not yours to give. The people have delegated to Congress, by the Constitution, the power to do certain things. To do these, it is authorized to collect and pay moneys, and for nothing else. Everything beyond this is usurpation, and a violation of the Constitution.

"So you see, Colonel, you have violated the Constitution in what I consider a vital point. It is a precedent fraught with danger to the country, for when Congress once begins to stretch its power beyond the limits of the Constitution, there is no limit to it, and no security for the people. I have no doubt you acted honestly, but that does not make it any better, except as far as you are personally concerned, and you see that I cannot vote for you.'

"It is a precedent fraught with danger to the country, for when Congress once begins to stretch its power beyond the limits of the Constitution, there is no limit to it, and no security for the people."

"I tell you I felt streaked. I saw if I should have opposition, and this man should go to talking and in that district, I was a gone fawn-skin. I could not answer him, and the fact is, I was so fully convinced that he was right, I did not want to. But I must satisfy him, and I said to him:

"'Well, my friend, you hit the nail upon the head when you said I had not sense enough to understand the Constitution. I intended to be guided by it, and thought I had studied it fully. I have heard many speeches in Congress about the powers of Congress, but what you have said here at your plow has got more hard, sound sense in it than all the fine speeches I ever heard. If I had ever taken the view of it that you have, I would have put my head into the fire before I would have given that vote; and if you will forgive me and vote for me again, if I ever vote for another unconstitutional law I wish I may be shot.'

"He laughingly replied; "Yes, Colonel, you have sworn to that once before, but I will trust you again upon one condition. You are convinced that your vote was wrong. Your acknowledgment of it will do more good than beating you for it. If, as you go around the district, you will tell people about this vote, and that you are satisfied it was wrong, I will not only vote for you, but will do what I can to keep down opposition, and perhaps, I may exert some little influence in that way."

"If I don't, said I, "I wish I may be shot; and to convince you that I am in earnest in what I say I will come back this way in a week or ten days, and if you will get up a gathering of people, I will make a speech to them. Get up a barbecue, and I will pay for it."

"'No, Colonel, we are not rich people in this section but we have plenty of provisions to contribute for a barbecue, and some to spare for those who have none. The push of crops will be over in a few days, and we can then afford a day for a barbecue. This Thursday; I will see to getting it up on Saturday week. Come to my house on Friday, and we will go together, and I promise you a very respectable crowd to see and hear you."

"Well I will be here. But one thing more before I say good-bye. I must know your name."

"My name is Bunce."

"Not Horatio Bunce?"

"Yes."

"Well, Mr. Bunce, I never saw you before, though you say you have seen me, but I know you very well. I am glad I have met you, and very proud that I may hope to have you for my friend."

"It was one of the luckiest hits of my life that I met him. He mingled but little with the public, but was widely known for his remarkable intelligence, and for a heart brim-full and running over with kindness and benevolence, which showed themselves not only in words but in acts.

"He was the oracle of the whole country around him, and his fame had extended far beyond the circle of his immediate acquaintance. Though I had never met him, before, I had heard much of him, and but for this meeting it is very likely I should have had opposition, and had been beaten. One thing is very certain, no man could now stand up in that district under such a vote.

"At the appointed time I was at his house, having told our conversation to every crowd I had met, and to every man I stayed all night with, and I found that it gave the people an interest and confidence in me stronger than I had ever seen manifested before.

"Though I was considerably fatigued when I reached his house, and, under ordinary circumstances, should have gone early to bed, I kept him up until midnight talking about the principles and affairs of government and got more real, true knowledge of them than I had got all my life before.

"I have known and seen much of him since, for I respect him — no, that is not the word — I reverence and love him more than any living man, and I go to see him two or three times every year; and I will tell you, sir, if everyone who professes to be a Christian lived and acted and enjoyed it as he does, the religion of Christ would take the world by storm.

"But to return to my story. The next morning we went to the barbecue and, to my surprise, found about a thousand men there. I met a good many whom I had not known before, and they and my friend introduced me around until I had got pretty well acquainted — at least, they all knew me.

"In due time notice was given that I would speak to them. They gathered up around a stand that had been erected. I opened my speech by saying:

"Fellow-citizens — I present myself before you today feeling like a new man. My eyes have lately been opened to truths which ignorance or prejudice or both, had heretofore hidden from my view. I feel that I can today offer you the ability to render you more valuable service than I have ever been able to render before. I am here today more for the purpose of acknowledging my error than to seek your votes. That I should make this acknowledgment is due to myself as well as to you. Whether you will vote for me is a matter for your consideration only.'

"I went on to tell them about the fire and my vote for the appropriation and then told them why I was satisfied it was wrong. I closed by saying:

"And now, fellow-citizens, it remains only for me to tell you that the most of the speech you have listened to with so much interest was simply a repetition of the arguments by which your neighbor, Mr. Bunce, convinced me of my error.

"'It is the best speech I ever made in my life, but he is entitled to the credit for it. And now I hope he is satisfied with his convert and that he will get up here and tell you so.'

"He came up to the stand and said:

"'Fellow-citizens — it affords me great pleasure to comply with the request of Colonel Crockett. I have always considered him a thoroughly honest man, and I am satisfied that he will faithfully perform all that he has promised you today."

"He went down, and there went up from that crowd such a shout for Davy Crockett as his name never called forth before.

"I am not much given to tears, but I was taken with a choking then and felt some big drops rolling down my cheeks. And I tell you now that the remembrance of those few words spoken by such a man, and the honest, hearty shout they produced, is worth more to me than all the honors I have received and all the reputation I have ever made, or ever shall make, as a member of Congress.

"Now, sir," concluded Crockett, "you know why I made that speech yesterday. There is one thing which I will call your attention, you remember that I proposed to give a week's pay. There are in that House many very wealthy men — men who think nothing of spending a week's pay, or a dozen of them, for a dinner or a wine party when they have something to accomplish by it. Some of those same men made beautiful speeches upon the great debt of gratitude which the country owed the deceased — a debt which could not be paid by money — and the insignificance and worthlessness of money, particularly so insignificant a sum as $20,000 when weighed against the honor of the nation. Yet not one of them responded to my proposition. Money with them is nothing but trash when it is to come out of the people. But it is the one great thing for which most of them are striving, and many of them sacrifice honor, integrity, and justice to obtain it."
Regards,
Col. David Crockett
U.S. Representative from Tennessee
Originally published in The Life of Colonel David Crockett by
Edward Sylvester Ellis

https://dallas125.mysitehosted.com:2096/cpsess5172332942
/3rdparty/roundcube/?_task=mail&_caps=pdf%3D1%2Cflash%3D1
%2Ctif%3D1&_uid=772&_mbox=INBOX&_action=show.

It seems that Congress has long forgotten they do not have the right to spend our money foolishly. Earmarks may appear in either the legislative text or report language (committee reports accompanying reported bills and joint explanatory statement accompanying a conference report).

And if you read carefully the explanations given by Horatio Bunce when Col. David Crockett was a U.S. Representative from Tennessee, no matter how callous it may sound today, because we are used to our Congress spending our money to help our citizens, our Congress does not have the right to pass bills for emergency relief for victims such as those from Hurricane Katrina and Hurricane Sandy, and now Hurricane Harvey and the BP Oil Spill. There is nothing in our Constitution that gives them that authority.

Not only does Congress pass these bill, it is the only way they can get pork for their home states in exchange for votes. For instance, you've heard the expression in politics to never let a good crisis go to waste.

During Hurricane Sandy, here is a list of pork that was attached to the Hurricane Sandy Relief package:

- $2 million to repair damage to the roofs of museums in Washington, D.C., while many in Hurricane Sandy's path still have no roof over their own heads.
- $150 million for fisheries as far away from the storm's path as Alaska.
- $125 million for the Department of Agriculture's Emergency Watershed Protection program, which helps restore watersheds damaged by wildfires and drought.
- $20 million for a nationwide Water Resources Priorities Study.
- $15 million for NASA facilities, though NASA itself has called its damage from the hurricane 'minimal.'
- $50 million in subsidies for tree planting on private properties.
- $336 million for taxpayer-supported AMTRAK without any detailed plan for how the money will be spent.
- $5.3 billion for the Army Corps of Engineers – more than the Corps' annual budget – with no statement of priorities about how to spend the money.
- $12.9 billion for future disaster mitigation activities and studies, without identifying a single way to pay for it.

http://www.politisite.com/2013/01/02/hurricane-sandy-pork -what-is-in-the-60-4b-sandy-relief-package/

In 2005 A Hurricane Relief Package was passed by the Senate for the Hurricane Katrina victims that was filled with pork.

Ted Stevens, the Senator from Alaska received $452 Million to spend however he wished.

$40 Billion goes to the Lousiana Pelican Commission which overrides the Army Corps of Engineers and has the say on how to hurricane-proof the Louisiana coast.

$31.7 for state infrastructure for Louisiana.

See more at http://katrinacoverage.com/tag/pork

In 2007 the Senate passed the Water Resources Bill. It too was laden with Pork – Sandy Pork. Several beach replenishing projects had been added to the bill.

$21,000,000 for Imperial Beach, California, beach replenishment;

$101,000, 000 for beach replenishment at Ocean City, Sea Isle City, and contiguous New Jersey seashore resorts;

$59,000,000 for central New Jersey seashore beach replenishment;

$122,000,000 for beach replenishment in northern New Jersey; and

$10,600,000 for beach replenishment on Pawley's Island, South Carolina.

http://www.heritage.org/budget-and-spending/report/the-water-resources-development-act-2007-pork-fest-forwealthy-beach

While the earmark ban may make good politics, in practice it has made bad public policy — and given that Article I, Section 7 of the Constitution gives Congress the power to tax and spend, it is not only bad policy but constitutionally questionable policy.

Earmarks never accounted for a meaningful portion of Federal spending. Non-discretionary funding (such as Social Security and Medicare) accounted for almost two-thirds of the annual budget by 2015, while earmark spending — even at its peak — barely accounted for one percent of the budget.

"In 2011 when Congress decided there would be no more earmarks, one would think there would be a saving, but it did not make a dent in overall Federal spending. A ban did not stop the same dollars from being appropriated — it just shifted the authority for allocating those dollars from Congress to federal agency bureaucrats.

"Do we really believe that the same bureaucrats responsible for the Veterans Affairs scandal, the disastrous health care rollout and the IRS targeting of political opponents should be given 100 percent control over where Federal dollars are allocated? Should they have control over our Social Security funds?

"What is even worse, unlike with the earmark process, decisions are now made without the knowledge of the outside world and without any recourse to rein in waste, fraud, and abuse. With earmarks, we had complete transparency. We knew who proposed the earmark, what is was for, how much it was for and we gave members a chance to vote on it. Often the most "controversial" earmarks were subjects of stand-alone votes in both chambers. This is the complete opposite of how spending is occurring under the earmark ban.

"Banning earmarks have made Congress even more dysfunctional. Polls show that Americans are profoundly unhappy and disappointed with Congress and the President. Some say they need to start working together to tackle the challenges we face as a nation. I say that is political and media speak. I say we need to vote them out and start over. When they become that dysfunctional and corrupt, it is too late for the man in Congress. I have seen how arrogant they can become. I have seen how they believe they are above the law, how they believe their word is the law of the land. How power and greed overtake them." http://www.rollcall.com/news/the_congressional_earmark_ban_the_real_bridge_to_nowhere_commentary-235380-1.html

The earmark ban has been one of several steps taken under Speaker Boehner to change the way Congress works and to make the legislative process more open and accountable. For example:

- The House now posts legislation online at least three days before a vote;
- Legislative data is being posted online in XML at docs. House. gov, in real-time by the House Clerk, and work is underway on providing bulk access.
- The House floor and committee hearings are streamed live online (and are accessible on desktops and mobile devices).
- And much more.

"This earmark ban shows the American people we are listening," said Speaker Boehner, "and we are dead serious about ending business as usual in Washington." http://www.speaker.gov/general/house-republicans-renew-earmark-ban-113th-congress

"The following database is sortable in a variety of ways, including by House and Senate members. It also provides detailed information on the number and value of earmarks members of Congress have requested during fiscal years 2008, 2009 and 2010. If you go to their website and click on the name of a congressional member you can see whether that congressional member has received financial support from the interests for which he or she has sought federal earmarks." http://www.opensecrets.org/earmarks/index.php

House - Earmarks to Contributors

Name	State	Total Earmarks	Total Contributions	Contrib Earmark %	Earmark Rank	All Earmarks	All Earmarks %
MORANJim Moran (D-VA)	VA	$36,565,000	$111,850	0.3%	6	$109,740,000	33.3%
LARSONJohn B. Larson (D-Conn)	CT	$11,700,000	$105,500	0.9%	53	$52,575,000	22.3%
YOUNGC. W. Bill Young (R-Fla)	FL	$30,600,000	$63,250	0.2%	4	$128,834,000	23.8%
ROTHMANSteven R. Rothman (D-NJ)	NJ	$28,862,800	$59,800	0.2%	19	$80,096,800	36.0%
TIAHRTTodd Tiahrt (R-Kan)	KS	$23,600,000	$51,670	0.2%	40	$63,400,000	37.2%
McKeonHoward P. (Buck) Mckeon (R-Calif)	CA	$9,600,000	$50,500	0.5%	135	$30,250,000	31.7%
LOEBSACKDavid Loebsack (D-Iowa)	IA	$7,920,000	$49,769	0.6%	92	$41,109,000	19.3%
COURTNEYJoe Courtney (D-Conn)	CT	$12,300,000	$49,100	0.4%	81	$43,497,000	28.3%

Name	State	Total Earmarks	Total Contributions	Contrib Earmark %	Earmark Rank	All Earmarks	All Earmarks %
GIFFORDSGabrielle Giffords (D-Ariz)	AZ	$4,150,000	$47,200	1.1%	129	$31,162,000	13.3%
DICKSNorm Dicks (D-Wash)	WA	$31,843,000	$43,350	0.1%	7	$107,553,500	29.6%
MURTHAJohn P. Murtha (D-Pa)	PA	$51,650,000	$38,350	0.1%	14	$92,470,000	55.9%
HARMANJane Harman (D-Calif)	CA	$2,800,000	$37,800	1.4%	247	$16,451,000	17.0%
MARKEYEdward J. Markey (D-Mass)	MA	$12,440,000	$37,550	0.3%	41	$61,882,000	20.1%
HOLTRush Holt (D-NJ)	NJ	$7,160,000	$37,125	0.5%	89	$41,660,000	17.2%
KILROYMary Jo Kilroy (D-Ohio)	OH	$3,200,000	$36,100	1.1%	227	$18,215,500	17.6%
ADERHOLTRobert B. Aderholt (R-Ala)	AL	$20,620,000	$35,095	0.2%	17	$81,287,000	25.4%
PASTOREd Pastor (D-Ariz)	AZ	$14,320,000	$34,000	0.2%	34	$66,030,000	21.7%

Name	State	Total Earmarks	Total Contributions	Contrib Earmark %	Earmark Rank	All Earmarks	All Earmarks %
MURPHYTim Murphy (R-Pa)	PA	$8,280,000	$33,550	0.4%	283	$13,535,000	61.2%
HEINRICHMartin Heinrich (D-NM)	NM	$1,920,000	$31,438	1.6%	189	$22,581,000	8.5%
DRIEHAUSSteve Driehaus (D-Ohio)	OH	$2,225,000	$29,092	1.3%	315	$10,937,300	20.3%
DREIERDavid Dreier (R-Calif)	CA	$6,200,000	$28,800	0.5%	218	$19,123,000	32.4%
GRIJALVARaul M. Grijalva (D-Ariz)	AZ	$4,350,000	$28,660	0.7%	38	$63,965,000	6.8%
JOHNSONSam Johnson (R-Texas)	TX	$7,520,000	$26,100	0.3%	269	$14,410,000	52.2%
SCALISESteve Scalise (R-La)	LA	$1,800,000	$25,850	1.4%	237	$17,388,000	10.4%
PETERSGary Peters (D-Mich)	MI	$2,694,800	$25,125	0.9%	296	$12,319,800	21.9%
GRANGERKay Granger (R-Texas)	TX	$6,900,000	$25,000	0.4%	29	$70,360,400	9.8%

Name	State	Total Earmarks	Total Contributions	Contrib Earmark %	Earmark Rank	All Earmarks	All Earmarks %
HINCHEYMaurice Hinchey (D-NY)	NY	$20,265,000	$24,190	0.1%	50	$54,963,000	36.9%
CALVERTKen Calvert (R-Calif)	CA	$6,800,000	$24,000	0.4%	55	$52,185,000	13.0%
COLETom Cole (R-Okla)	OK	$5,550,000	$23,650	0.4%	90	$41,583,000	13.3%
BISHOPTimothy H. Bishop (D-NY)	NY	$8,400,000	$23,050	0.3%	267	$14,558,600	57.7%
SESTAKJoseph A. Sestak Jr (D-Pa)	PA	$8,050,000	$21,800	0.3%	164	$25,841,200	31.2%
BISHOPSanford D. Bishop Jr (D-Ga)	GA	$8,100,000	$21,550	0.3%	42	$60,565,000	13.4%
FRELINGHUYSENRodney Frelinghuysen (R-NJ)	NJ	$9,600,000	$20,800	0.2%	21	$75,700,000	12.7%
ANDREWSRobert E. Andrews (D-NJ)	NJ	$11,040,000	$20,100	0.2%	230	$17,840,000	61.9%
HASTINGSDoc Hastings (R-Wash)	WA	$4,800,000	$20,000	0.4%	160	$26,425,100	18.2%

Name	State	Total Earmarks	Total Contributions	Contrib Earmark %	Earmark Rank	All Earmarks	All Earmarks %
ALTMIREJason Altmire (D-Pa)	PA	$4,900,000	$19,527	0.4%	297	$12,295,000	39.9%
ROGERSMike D. Rogers (R-Ala)	AL	$11,720,000	$19,500	0.2%	76	$44,365,000	26.4%
SUTTONBetty Sue Sutton (D-Ohio)	OH	$6,550,000	$19,200	0.3%	171	$24,672,700	26.5%
HILLBaron Hill (D-Ind)	IN	$2,400,000	$18,931	0.8%	367	$6,179,000	38.8%
PASCRELLBill Pascrell Jr (D-NJ)	NJ	$3,275,000	$18,900	0.6%	258	$15,424,000	21.2%
BOYDAllen Boyd (D-Fla)	FL	$16,125,000	$18,200	0.1%	64	$48,792,000	33.0%
ELLSWORTHBrad Ellsworth (D-Ind)	IN	$5,040,000	$17,800	0.4%	132	$30,695,000	16.4%
TSONGASNiki Tsongas (D-Mass)	MA	$18,994,800	$17,650	0.1%	119	$33,181,300	57.2%
LOBIONDOFrank A. LoBiondo (R-NJ)	NJ	$7,440,000	$17,150	0.2%	118	$33,326,000	22.3%

Name	State	Total Earmarks	Total Contributions	Contrib Earmark %	Earmark Rank	All Earmarks	All Earmarks %
WUDavid Wu (D-Ore)	OR	$14,060,000	$17,150	0.1%	63	$49,184,800	28.6%
MILLERJeff Miller (R-Fla)	FL	$5,600,000	$16,950	0.3%	203	$21,532,000	26.0%
DELAURORosa L. DeLauro (D-Conn)	CT	$9,100,000	$16,400	0.2%	62	$49,283,000	18.5%
WITTMANRob Wittman (R-Va)	VA	$2,000,000	$16,400	0.8%	262	$14,910,000	13.4%
MARKEYBetsy Markey (D-Colo)	CO	$4,555,000	$16,008	0.4%	287	$13,400,000	34.0%
CASTLEMichael N. Castle (R-Del)	DE	$12,240,000	$16,000	0.1%	56	$51,874,600	23.6%
MALONEYCarolyn B. Maloney (D-NY)	NY	$2,825,000	$15,940	0.6%	342	$7,985,875	35.4%
BORENDan Boren (D-Okla)	OK	$3,798,000	$15,800	0.4%	202	$21,599,000	17.6%
BISHOPRob Bishop (R-Utah)	UT	$25,100,000	$15,800	0.1%	12	$93,980,000	26.7%

Name	State	Total Earmarks	Total Contributions	Contrib Earmark %	Earmark Rank	All Earmarks	All Earmarks %
KAPTURMarcy Kaptur (D-Ohio)	OH	$8,625,000	$15,650	0.2%	28	$71,301,300	12.1%
MATHESONJim Matheson (D-Utah)	UT	$3,500,000	$15,000	0.4%	67	$48,400,000	7.2%
KRATOVILFrank M. Kratovil Jr (D-Md)	MD	$10,380,000	$14,800	0.1%	27	$71,416,300	14.5%
RUPPERSBERGERDutch Ruppersberger (D-Md)	MD	$9,650,000	$14,550	0.2%	16	$84,444,850	11.4%
KINGPete King (R-NY)	NY	$4,635,000	$14,400	0.3%	286	$13,427,000	34.5%
KILPATRICKCarolyn Cheeks Kilpatrick (D-Mich)	MI	$10,200,000	$14,300	0.1%	138	$30,055,000	33.9%
CONNOLLYGerry Connolly (D-Va)	VA	$2,550,000	$13,750	0.5%	159	$26,486,400	9.6%
MAFFEIDan Maffei (D-NY)	NY	$4,960,000	$12,650	0.3%	228	$18,124,500	27.4%
MEEKKendrick B. Meek (D-Fla)	FL	$15,230,000	$12,501	0.1%	116	$33,980,000	44.8%

Name	State	Total Earmarks	Total Contributions	Contrib Earmark %	Earmark Rank	All Earmarks	All Earmarks %
SCHULTZDebbie Wasserman Schultz (D-Fla)	FL	$4,000,000	$12,500	0.3%	72	$46,001,000	8.7%
KANJORSKIPaul E. Kanjorski (D-Pa)	PA	$3,000,000	$12,400	0.4%	248	$16,306,000	18.4%
MCNERNYJerry McNerney (D-Calif)	CA	$4,200,000	$12,200	0.3%	143	$29,358,000	14.3%
TONKOPaul Tonko (D-NY)	NY	$2,100,000	$12,200	0.6%	109	$36,145,000	5.8%
MICHAUDMike Michaud (D-Maine)	ME	$10,745,000	$12,050	0.1%	68	$47,946,000	22.4%
ALEXANDERRodney Alexander (R-La)	LA	$2,100,000	$11,825	0.6%	36	$65,395,000	3.2%
POMEROYEarl Pomeroy (D-ND)	ND	$11,750,000	$11,700	0.1%	2	$148,376,350	7.9%
KENNEDYPatrick J. Kennedy (D-RI)	RI	$13,200,000	$11,500	0.1%	13	$93,353,400	14.1%
HARPERGregg Harper (R-Miss)	MS	$8,000,000	$11,200	0.1%	9	$101,267,000	7.9%

Name	State	Total Earmarks	Total Contributions	Contrib Earmark %	Earmark Rank	All Earmarks	All Earmarks %
CARSONAndre Carson (D-Ind)	IN	$4,150,000	$11,158	0.3%	328	$9,825,000	42.2%
LANGEVINJim Langevin (D-RI)	RI	$7,600,000	$11,100	0.1%	23	$73,352,600	10.4%
OLVERJohn W. Olver (D-Mass)	MA	$5,777,000	$10,850	0.2%	74	$45,861,000	12.6%
WOOLSEYLynn Woolsey (D-Calif)	CA	$250,000	$10,850	4.3%	327	$9,959,000	2.5%
BALDWINTammy Baldwin (D-Wis)	WI	$3,110,000	$10,700	0.3%	201	$21,636,800	14.4%
BARTLETTRoscoe G. Bartlett (R-Md)	MD	$7,750,000	$10,500	0.1%	83	$43,060,650	18.0%
FILNERBob Filner (D-Calif)	CA	$2,000,000	$10,250	0.5%	337	$8,564,000	23.4%
MOLLOHANAlan B. Mollohan (D-WVa)	WV	$24,620,000	$10,150	0.0%	49	$55,183,000	44.6%
MANZULLODon Manzullo (R-Ill)	IL	$3,200,000	$10,000	0.3%	343	$7,930,000	40.4%

Name	State	Total Earmarks	Total Contributions	Contrib Earmark %	Earmark Rank	All Earmarks	All Earmarks %
BEANMelissa Bean (D-Ill)	IL	$1,200,000	$10,000	0.8%	370	$5,895,000	20.4%
KINGSTONJack Kingston (R-Ga)	GA	$12,200,000	$9,950	0.1%	32	$66,787,000	18.3%
GINGREYPhil Gingrey (R-Ga)	GA	$3,600,000	$9,600	0.3%	254	$15,800,000	22.8%
ENGELEliot L. Engel (D-NY)	NY	$1,200,000	$9,600	0.8%	322	$10,378,000	11.6%
SMITHAdam Smith (D-Wash)	WA	$11,280,000	$9,550	0.1%	44	$56,953,600	19.8%
AKINTodd Akin (R-Mo)	MO	$2,640,000	$9,500	0.4%	265	$14,709,000	17.9%
RYANTim Ryan (D-Ohio)	OH	$7,350,000	$9,350	0.1%	111	$35,400,000	20.8%
BROWNCorrine Brown (D-Fla)	FL	$6,200,000	$9,200	0.1%	59	$51,237,000	12.1%
LATHAMTom Latham (R-Iowa)	IA	$11,120,000	$9,150	0.1%	33	$66,190,000	16.8%

Name	State	Total Earmarks	Total Contributions	Contrib Earmark %	Earmark Rank	All Earmarks	All Earmarks %
HALLRalph M. Hall (R-Texas)	TX	$3,200,000	$9,000	0.3%	301	$12,232,000	26.2%
BRIGHTBobby Bright (D-Ala)	AL	$5,640,000	$8,986	0.2%	275	$13,922,000	40.5%
TAYLORGene Taylor (D-Miss)	MS	$2,000,000	$8,950	0.4%	113	$35,034,000	5.7%
MCDERMOTTJim McDermott (D-Wash)	WA	$17,389,000	$8,850	0.1%	43	$58,111,450	29.9%
SCHIFFAdam Schiff (D-Calif)	CA	$1,450,000	$8,850	0.6%	284	$13,497,000	10.7%
WALZTimothy J. Walz (D-Minn)	MN	$1,200,000	$8,650	0.7%	330	$9,712,400	12.4%
KAGENSteve Kagen (D-Wis)	WI	$5,800,000	$8,601	0.1%	233	$17,758,900	32.7%
TURNERMichael R. Turner (R-Ohio)	OH	$2,600,000	$8,500	0.3%	151	$28,113,200	9.2%
LATOURETTESteven C. LaTourette (R-Ohio)	OH	$5,500,000	$8,500	0.2%	156	$27,277,000	20.2%

Name	State	Total Earmarks	Total Contributions	Contrib Earmark %	Earmark Rank	All Earmarks	All Earmarks %
EDWARDSChet Edwards (D-Texas)	TX	$7,500,000	$8,400	0.1%	15	$90,450,000	8.3%
NYEGlenn Nye (D-Va)	VA	$3,400,000	$8,300	0.2%	288	$13,324,200	25.5%
BLUNTRoy Blunt (R-Mo)	MO	$6,800,000	$8,300	0.1%	188	$22,602,000	30.1%
HONDAMike Honda (D-Calif)	CA	$3,590,000	$8,200	0.2%	183	$23,153,000	15.5%
BERKLEYShelley Berkley (D-Nev)	NV	$4,700,000	$8,100	0.2%	77	$44,077,050	10.7%
CHILDERSTravis W. Childers (D-Miss)	MS	$25,500,000	$8,000	0.0%	30	$67,088,000	38.0%
HERSETHStephanie Herseth Sandlin (D-SD)	SD	$11,378,900	$7,650	0.1%	5	$118,399,150	9.6%
CARNEYChris Carney (D-Pa)	PA	$1,700,000	$7,643	0.4%	231	$17,779,000	9.6%
RANGELCharles B. Rangel (D-NY)	NY	$6,450,000	$7,450	0.1%	302	$12,200,000	52.9%

Name	State	Total Earmarks	Total Contributions	Contrib Earmark %	Earmark Rank	All Earmarks	All Earmarks %
MCCARTHYCarolyn McCarthy (D-NY)	NY	$4,800,000	$7,300	0.2%	220	$19,075,000	25.2%
CLYBURNJames E. Clyburn (D-SC)	SC	$15,525,000	$7,250	0.0%	48	$55,874,000	27.8%
LEEBarbara Lee (D-Calif)	CA	$2,350,000	$7,150	0.3%	324	$10,000,000	23.5%
CUMMINGSElijah E. Cummings (D-Md)	MD	$6,200,000	$7,000	0.1%	173	$24,531,200	25.3%
GERLACHJim Gerlach (R-Pa)	PA	$7,200,000	$7,000	0.1%	163	$25,899,000	27.8%
LEWISJerry Lewis (R-Calif)	CA	$14,850,000	$6,800	0.0%	11	$97,583,200	15.2%
LARSENRick Larsen (D-Wash)	WA	$469,000	$6,537	1.4%	125	$31,815,800	1.5%
RAHALLNick Rahall (D-WVa)	WV	$2,000,000	$6,500	0.3%	31	$66,834,000	3.0%
SHUSTERBill Shuster (R-Pa)	PA	$3,900,000	$6,250	0.2%	182	$23,241,250	16.8%

Name	State	Total Earmarks	Total Contributions	Contrib Earmark %	Earmark Rank	All Earmarks	All Earmarks %
DAVISGeoff Davis (R-Ky)	KY	$500,000	$6,000	1.2%	211	$20,275,500	2.5%
SOUDERMark E. Souder (R-Ind)	IN	$3,600,000	$6,000	0.2%	348	$7,550,000	47.7%
FRANKSTrent Franks (R-Ariz)	AZ	$4,800,000	$6,000	0.1%	270	$14,300,000	33.6%
CARTERJohn Carter (R-Texas)	TX	$1,300,000	$6,000	0.5%	87	$42,232,000	3.1%
YOUNGDon Young (R-Alaska)	AK	$2,400,000	$5,900	0.2%	25	$71,905,000	3.3%
ROGERSHal Rogers (R-Ky)	KY	$8,600,000	$5,500	0.1%	10	$98,908,000	8.7%
PALLONEFrank Pallone Jr (D-NJ)	NJ	$4,400,000	$5,400	0.1%	214	$20,070,000	21.9%
CHANDLERBen Chandler (D-Ky)	KY	$2,400,000	$5,250	0.2%	293	$12,589,000	19.1%
SCHAUERMark Schauer (D-Mich)	MI	$876,600	$5,150	0.6%	120	$33,178,600	2.6%

Name	State	Total Earmarks	Total Contributions	Contrib Earmark %	Earmark Rank	All Earmarks	All Earmarks %
LAMBORNDouglas L. Lamborn (R-Colo)	CO	$1,920,000	$5,000	0.3%	252	$16,020,000	12.0%
PRICEDavid Price (D-NC)	NC	$3,600,000	$5,000	0.1%	45	$56,810,000	6.3%
KILDEEDale E. Kildee (D-Mich)	MI	$2,400,000	$5,000	0.2%	75	$44,555,400	5.4%
ETHERIDGEBob Etheridge (D-NC)	NC	$13,150,000	$5,000	0.0%	39	$63,597,000	20.7%
SANCHEZLoretta Sanchez (D-Calif)	CA	$1,700,000	$4,900	0.3%	196	$22,091,000	7.7%
THOMPSONGlenn Thompson (R-Pa)	PA	$2,100,000	$4,900	0.2%	306	$11,936,000	17.6%
REHBERGDenny Rehberg (R-Mont)	MT	$19,804,200	$4,900	0.0%	8	$103,514,200	19.1%
LUJANBen R. Lujan (D-NM)	NM	$400,000	$4,800	1.2%	319	$10,661,000	3.8%
SCHRADERKurt Schrader (D-Ore)	OR	$11,466,000	$4,750	0.0%	86	$42,405,000	27.0%

Name	State	Total Earmarks	Total Contributions	Contrib Earmark %	Earmark Rank	All Earmarks	All Earmarks %
SCHWARTZAllyson Schwartz (D-Pa)	PA	$4,800,000	$4,750	0.1%	279	$13,683,000	35.1%
HOYERSteny H. Hoyer (D-Md)	MD	$1,150,000	$4,700	0.4%	26	$71,854,200	1.6%
HunterDuncan D. Hunter (R-Calif)	CA	$2,400,000	$4,650	0.2%	346	$7,870,000	30.5%
PAYNEDonald M. Payne (D-NJ)	NJ	$3,555,000	$4,580	0.1%	165	$25,353,050	14.0%
KLEINRon Klein (D-Fla)	FL	$2,500,000	$4,550	0.2%	329	$9,731,000	25.7%
FRANKBarney Frank (D-Mass)	MA	$1,235,000	$4,500	0.4%	341	$8,148,000	15.2%
CRENSHAWAnder Crenshaw (R-Fla)	FL	$800,000	$4,500	0.6%	52	$54,424,000	1.5%
HIRONOMazie K. Hirono (D-Hawaii)	HI	$6,053,000	$4,500	0.1%	1	$149,769,900	4.0%
MELANCONCharles Melancon (D-La)	LA	$800,000	$4,350	0.5%	238	$17,380,000	4.6%

Name	State	Total Earmarks	Total Contributions	Contrib Earmark %	Earmark Rank	All Earmarks	All Earmarks %
STEARNSCliff Stearns (R-Fla)	FL	$3,800,000	$4,300	0.1%	257	$15,472,000	24.6%
LEEChristopher J. Lee (R-NY)	NY	$4,400,000	$4,250	0.1%	101	$39,357,000	11.2%
JOHNSONEddie Bernice Johnson (D-Texas)	TX	$1,600,000	$4,250	0.3%	47	$55,975,000	2.9%
BACHUSSpencer Bachus (R-Ala)	AL	$3,750,000	$4,050	0.1%	249	$16,191,000	23.2%
THOMPSONMike Thompson (D-Calif)	CA	$4,400,000	$4,030	0.1%	195	$22,211,000	19.8%
LANCELeonard Lance (R-NJ)	NJ	$4,520,000	$4,000	0.1%	208	$20,752,000	21.8%
REICHERTDave Reichert (R-Wash)	WA	$2,400,000	$4,000	0.2%	295	$12,458,850	19.3%
FORBESJ. Randy Forbes (R-Va)	VA	$400,000	$3,851	1.0%	276	$13,730,000	2.9%
BLUMENAUEREarl Blumenauer (D-Ore)	OR	$4,200,000	$3,776	0.1%	153	$27,805,200	15.1%

Name	State	Total Earmarks	Total Contributions	Contrib Earmark %	Earmark Rank	All Earmarks	All Earmarks %
BOUCHERRick Boucher (D-Va)	VA	$5,988,000	$3,750	0.1%	291	$12,874,000	46.5%
FOSTERBill Foster (D-Ill)	IL	$1,900,000	$3,750	0.2%	332	$9,185,000	20.7%
MORANJerry Moran (R-Kan)	KS	$5,300,000	$3,750	0.1%	222	$18,600,000	28.5%
CULBERSONJohn Culberson (R-Texas)	TX	$8,000,000	$3,650	0.0%	117	$33,792,000	23.7%
MASSAEric Massa (D-NY)	NY	$1,600,000	$3,500	0.2%	236	$17,442,000	9.2%
ROYBALALLARDLucille Roybal-Allard (D-Calif)	CA	$3,200,000	$3,500	0.1%	192	$22,316,000	14.3%
MITCHELLHarry E. Mitchell (D-Ariz)	AZ	$2,400,000	$3,400	0.1%	199	$21,700,000	11.1%
TITUSDina Titus (D-Nev)	NV	$2,200,000	$3,400	0.2%	155	$27,639,850	8.0%
BONNERJo Bonner (R-Ala)	AL	$4,940,000	$3,300	0.1%	200	$21,645,000	22.8%

Name	State	Total Earmarks	Total Contributions	Contrib Earmark %	Earmark Rank	All Earmarks	All Earmarks %
SCOTTRobert C. Scott (D-Va)	VA	$5,000,000	$3,250	0.1%	142	$29,443,500	17.0%
REYESSilvestre Reyes (D-Texas)	TX	$2,300,000	$3,200	0.1%	134	$30,277,000	7.6%
KOSMASSuzanne Kosmas (D-Fla)	FL	$850,000	$3,150	0.4%	310	$11,367,000	7.5%
DENTCharlie Dent (R-Pa)	PA	$6,250,000	$3,150	0.1%	207	$21,112,250	29.6%
POSEYBill Posey (R-Fla)	FL	$4,235,000	$3,150	0.1%	209	$20,673,000	20.5%
JACKSON LEESheila Jackson Lee (D-Texas)	TX	$2,150,000	$3,100	0.1%	271	$14,162,000	15.2%
TEAGUEHarry Teague (D-NM)	NM	$7,914,000	$3,050	0.0%	46	$56,757,740	13.9%
MURPHYChristopher S. Murphy (D-Conn)	CT	$637,000	$3,050	0.5%	167	$25,229,000	2.5%
ACKERMANGary Ackerman (D-NY)	NY	$2,400,000	$3,000	0.1%	340	$8,150,000	29.4%

Name	State	Total Earmarks	Total Contributions	Contrib Earmark %	Earmark Rank	All Earmarks	All Earmarks %
GARRETTScott Garrett (R-NJ)	NJ	$5,040,000	$3,000	0.1%	350	$7,380,000	68.3%
CAPUANOMichael E. Capuano (D-Mass)	MA	$7,200,000	$3,000	0.0%	37	$64,980,000	11.1%
THOMPSONBennie G. Thompson (D-Miss)	MS	$1,165,000	$2,800	0.2%	309	$11,410,000	10.2%
DOYLEMike Doyle (D-Pa)	PA	$3,200,000	$2,750	0.1%	146	$29,038,800	11.0%
JOHNSONHank Johnson (D-Ga)	GA	$1,600,000	$2,650	0.2%	158	$26,688,000	6.0%
ROSLEHTINENIleana Ros-Lehtinen (R-Fla)	FL	$3,600,000	$2,650	0.1%	225	$18,331,000	19.6%
FARRSam Farr (D-Calif)	CA	$3,250,000	$2,601	0.1%	96	$39,930,000	8.1%
OBEYDavid R. Obey (D-Wis)	WI	$5,160,000	$2,600	0.1%	20	$77,620,000	6.6%
LEVINSander Levin (D-Mich)	MI	$1,700,000	$2,600	0.2%	244	$16,675,000	10.2%

Name	State	Total Earmarks	Total Contributions	Contrib Earmark %	Earmark Rank	All Earmarks	All Earmarks %
INSLEEJay Inslee (D-Wash)	WA	$2,400,000	$2,600	0.1%	193	$22,304,000	10.8%
ELLISONKeith Ellison (D-Minn)	MN	$2,800,000	$2,550	0.1%	184	$23,131,000	12.1%
ADLERJohn H. Adler (D-NJ)	NJ	$2,150,000	$2,550	0.1%	114	$34,979,000	6.1%
SLAUGHTERLouise M. Slaughter (D-NY)	NY	$3,600,000	$2,500	0.1%	95	$40,417,000	8.9%
SIRESAlbio Sires (D-NJ)	NJ	$2,520,000	$2,500	0.1%	130	$30,988,000	8.1%
ROSKAMPeter Roskam (R-Ill)	IL	$725,000	$2,500	0.3%	102	$39,086,500	1.9%
ISRAELSteve Israel (D-NY)	NY	$1,700,000	$2,500	0.1%	294	$12,501,000	13.6%
MCGOVERNJames P. McGovern (D-Mass)	MA	$1,525,000	$2,450	0.2%	57	$51,411,000	3.0%
BERMANHoward L. Berman (D-Calif)	CA	$2,000,000	$2,400	0.1%	299	$12,261,000	16.3%

Name	State	Total Earmarks	Total Contributions	Contrib Earmark %	Earmark Rank	All Earmarks	All Earmarks %
MOOREDennis Moore (D-Kan)	KS	$800,000	$2,200	0.3%	317	$10,857,000	7.4%
MURPHYPatrick J. Murphy (D-Pa)	PA	$2,400,000	$2,050	0.1%	307	$11,623,000	20.6%
NEUGEBAUERRandy Neugebauer (R-Texas)	TX	$3,930,000	$2,000	0.1%	312	$11,344,000	34.6%
FUDGEMarcia L. Fudge (D-Ohio)	OH	$2,800,000	$2,000	0.1%	324	$10,000,000	28.0%
CARNAHANRuss Carnahan (D-Mo)	MO	$588,000	$2,000	0.3%	91	$41,532,000	1.4%
CAPPSLois Capps (D-Calif)	CA	$2,300,000	$2,000	0.1%	93	$41,091,000	5.6%
COBLEHoward Coble (R-NC)	NC	$2,400,000	$2,000	0.1%	221	$18,755,000	12.8%
SCHOCKAaron Schock (R-Ill)	IL	$2,100,000	$2,000	0.1%	187	$22,656,000	9.3%
SCOTTDavid Scott (D-Ga)	GA	$1,600,000	$2,000	0.1%	103	$38,828,000	4.1%

Name	State	Total Earmarks	Total Contributions	Contrib Earmark %	Earmark Rank	All Earmarks	All Earmarks %
JACKSONJesse Jackson Jr (D-Ill)	IL	$800,000	$2,000	0.3%	107	$36,368,000	2.2%
HODESPaul W. Hodes (D-NH)	NH	$4,000,000	$2,000	0.1%	60	$51,021,000	7.8%
WATERSMaxine Waters (D-Calif)	CA	$1,760,000	$1,750	0.1%	361	$6,644,000	26.5%
KIRKPATRICKAnn Kirkpatrick (D-Ariz)	AZ	$1,600,000	$1,700	0.1%	272	$14,147,000	11.3%
RODGERSCathy McMorris Rodgers (R-Wash)	WA	$9,758,000	$1,600	0.0%	100	$39,618,000	24.6%
ROYCEEd Royce (R-Calif)	CA	$4,480,000	$1,600	0.0%	363	$6,545,000	68.4%
HOLDENTim Holden (D-Pa)	PA	$2,383,000	$1,550	0.1%	280	$13,667,000	17.4%
LOWEYNita M. Lowey (D-NY)	NY	$132,000	$1,500	1.1%	224	$18,413,500	0.7%
MCINTYREMike McIntyre (D-NC)	NC	$300,000	$1,500	0.5%	191	$22,333,000	1.3%

Name	State	Total Earmarks	Total Contributions	Contrib Earmark %	Earmark Rank	All Earmarks	All Earmarks %
FORTENBERRYJeffrey Lane Fortenberry (R-Neb)	NE	$7,000,000	$1,450	0.0%	246	$16,484,000	42.5%
TOWNSEdolphus Towns (D-NY)	NY	$1,285,000	$1,400	0.1%	219	$19,120,000	6.7%
MILLERGary Miller (R-Calif)	CA	$1,850,000	$1,350	0.1%	216	$19,627,500	9.4%
LUNGRENDan Lungren (R-Calif)	CA	$3,200,000	$1,350	0.0%	239	$17,330,000	18.5%
SALAZARJohn Salazar (D-Colo)	CO	$3,000,000	$1,250	0.0%	133	$30,525,000	9.8%
SARBANESJohn Sarbanes (D-Md)	MD	$150,000	$1,250	0.8%	78	$43,954,400	0.3%
HIMESJim Himes (D-Conn)	CT	$350,000	$1,250	0.4%	212	$20,216,000	1.7%
HIGGINSBrian M. Higgins (D-NY)	NY	$2,000,000	$1,250	0.1%	213	$20,185,000	9.9%

Name	State	Total Earmarks	Total Contributions	Contrib Earmark %	Earmark Rank	All Earmarks	All Earmarks %
BUTTERFIELDG. K. Butterfield (D-NC)	NC	$3,500,000	$1,250	0.0%	166	$25,310,000	13.8%
MACKConnie Mack (R-Fla)	FL	$800,000	$1,200	0.2%	384	$3,517,000	22.7%
LATTARobert E. Latta (R-Ohio)	OH	$500,000	$1,150	0.2%	375	$4,990,000	10.0%
BOCCIERIJohn A. Boccieri (D-Ohio)	OH	$450,000	$1,100	0.2%	347	$7,607,000	5.9%
LOFGRENZoe Lofgren (D-Calif)	CA	$2,010,000	$1,040	0.1%	54	$52,228,000	3.8%
LEWISJohn Lewis (D-Ga)	GA	$100,000	$1,000	1.0%	174	$24,529,000	0.4%
ARCURIMichael Arcuri (D-NY)	NY	$700,000	$1,000	0.1%	144	$29,118,500	2.4%
COHENStephen Ira Cohen (D-Tenn)	TN	$4,585,000	$1,000	0.0%	223	$18,510,000	24.8%
MCHUGHJohn M. McHugh (R-NY)	NY	$4,320,000	$1,000	0.0%	131	$30,727,000	14.1%

Name	State	Total Earmarks	Total Contributions	Contrib Earmark %	Earmark Rank	All Earmarks	All Earmarks %
WILSONJoe Wilson (R-SC)	SC	$4,270,000	$1,000	0.0%	181	$23,334,000	18.3%
MILLERCandice S. Miller (R-Mich)	MI	$100,000	$1,000	1.0%	245	$16,569,000	0.6%
LIPINSKIDaniel Lipinski (D-Ill)	IL	$2,500,000	$1,000	0.0%	304	$11,961,000	20.9%
STUPAKBart Stupak (D-Mich)	MI	$4,000,000	$1,000	0.0%	127	$31,640,600	12.6%
MOOREGwen Moore (D-Wis)	WI	$3,120,000	$1,000	0.0%	186	$22,710,000	13.7%
BROWNHenry Brown (R-SC)	SC	$1,280,000	$1,000	0.1%	197	$21,875,000	5.9%
HALVORSONDeborah Halvorson (D-Ill)	IL	$4,650,000	$1,000	0.0%	194	$22,225,000	20.9%
CASTORKathy Castor (D-Fla)	FL	$800,000	$1,000	0.1%	70	$47,154,000	1.7%
COSTAJim Costa (D-Calif)	CA	$300,000	$1,000	0.3%	69	$47,428,000	0.6%

Name	State	Total Earmarks	Total Contributions	Contrib Earmark %	Earmark Rank	All Earmarks	All Earmarks %
GOHMERTLouis B. Gohmert Jr (R–Texas)	TX	$1,409,000	$950	0.1%	356	$6,799,000	20.7%
ROGERSMike Rogers (R-Mich)	MI	$3,150,000	$900	0.0%	112	$35,275,100	8.9%
PINGREEChellie Pingree (D-Maine)	ME	$5,280,000	$800	0.0%	73	$45,895,000	11.5%
BERRYMarion Berry (D-Ark)	AR	$19,500,000	$750	0.0%	65	$48,777,000	40.0%
BILIRAKISGus Bilirakis (R-Fla)	FL	$450,000	$750	0.2%	281	$13,600,000	3.3%
DINGELLJohn D. Dingell (D-Mich)	MI	$1,600,000	$750	0.0%	147	$29,016,000	5.5%
SPRATTJohn M. Spratt Jr (D-SC)	SC	$600,090	$750	0.1%	108	$36,348,090	1.7%
EMERSONJo Ann Emerson (R-Mo)	MO	$855,000	$750	0.1%	136	$30,134,875	2.8%
MILLERBrad Miller (D-NC)	NC	$1,050,000	$750	0.1%	58	$51,324,000	2.0%

Name	State	Total Earmarks	Total Contributions	Contrib Earmark %	Earmark Rank	All Earmarks	All Earmarks %
DAVISDanny K. Davis (D-Ill)	IL	$3,600,000	$750	0.0%	82	$43,312,000	8.3%
DOGGETTLloyd Doggett (D-Texas)	TX	$1,750,000	$750	0.0%	377	$4,735,000	37.0%
GONZALEZCharlie A. Gonzalez (D-Texas)	TX	$1,600,000	$750	0.0%	157	$27,220,000	5.9%
RICHARDSONLaura Richardson (D-Calif)	CA	$400,000	$650	0.2%	354	$7,054,000	5.7%
SMITHChris Smith (R-NJ)	NJ	$200,000	$600	0.3%	140	$29,835,000	0.7%
MATSUIDoris O. Matsui (D-Calif)	CA	$2,400,000	$600	0.0%	318	$10,855,000	22.1%
ESHOOAnna Eshoo (D-Calif)	CA	$200,000	$500	0.3%	261	$15,024,000	1.3%
BIGGERTJudy Biggert (R-Ill)	IL	$250,000	$500	0.2%	300	$12,250,000	2.0%
DIAZ-BALARTMario Diaz-Balart (R-Fla)	FL	$550,000	$500	0.1%	179	$23,460,000	2.3%

Name	State	Total Earmarks	Total Contributions	Contrib Earmark %	Earmark Rank	All Earmarks	All Earmarks %
DEFAZIOPeter DeFazio (D-Ore)	OR	$12,260,000	$500	0.0%	177	$23,868,900	51.4%
BUCHANANVernon Buchanan (R-Fla)	FL	$1,500,000	$500	0.0%	355	$6,827,000	22.0%
CUELLARHenry Cuellar (D-Texas)	TX	$350,000	$500	0.1%	351	$7,327,000	4.8%
SERRANOJose E. Serrano (D-NY)	NY	$150,000	$500	0.3%	344	$7,927,000	1.9%
MCCOLLUMBetty McCollum (D-Minn)	MN	$2,400,000	$500	0.0%	336	$8,677,000	27.7%
CONAWAYMike Conaway (R-Texas)	TX	$3,325,000	$500	0.0%	206	$21,347,000	15.6%
DIAZBALARTLincoln Diaz-Balart (R-Fla)	FL	$550,000	$500	0.1%	185	$22,999,000	2.4%
DAVISSusan A. Davis (D-Calif)	CA	$1,200,000	$500	0.0%	61	$50,882,000	2.4%
OBERSTARJames L. Oberstar (D-Minn)	MN	$1,200,000	$500	0.0%	24	$72,707,000	1.7%

Name	State	Total Earmarks	Total Contributions	Contrib Earmark %	Earmark Rank	All Earmarks	All Earmarks %
BOSWELLLeonard L. Boswell (D-Iowa)	IA	$350,000	$500	0.1%	88	$41,907,000	0.8%
PELOSINancy Pelosi (D-Calif)	CA	$2,000,000	$500	0.0%	22	$75,384,500	2.7%
BURGESSMichael Burgess (R-Texas)	TX	$3,600,000	$300	0.0%	253	$15,804,400	22.8%
DAHLKEMPERKathleen Dahlkemper (D-Pa)	PA	$2,400,000	$250	0.0%	259	$15,410,000	15.6%
SPACEZachary T. Space (D-Ohio)	OH	$2,000,000	$250	0.0%	277	$13,725,000	14.6%
ORTIZSolomon P. Ortiz (D-Texas)	TX	$2,400,000	$250	0.0%	121	$32,950,000	7.3%
BRALEYBruce Braley (D-Iowa)	IA	$8,900,000	$250	0.0%	122	$32,653,600	27.3%
CAOJoseph Cao (R-La)	LA	$500,000	$250	0.1%	71	$46,822,000	1.1%

Name	State	Total Earmarks	Total Contributions	Contrib Earmark %	Earmark Rank	All Earmarks	All Earmarks %
BARROWJohn Barrow (D-Ga)	GA	$500,000	$250	0.1%	373	$5,350,000	9.3%
MICAJohn L. Mica (R-Fla)	FL	$150,000	$250	0.2%	362	$6,548,000	2.3%
POETed Poe (R-Texas)	TX	$3,200,000	$250	0.0%	345	$7,913,000	40.4%
JENKINSLynn Jenkins (R-Kan)	KS	$2,000,000	$250	0.0%	172	$24,628,000	8.1%
WALDENGreg Walden (R-Ore)	OR	$9,860,000	$250	0.0%	169	$24,861,200	39.7%
BUYERSteve Buyer (R-Ind)	IN	$1,312,000	$250	0.0%	335	$8,812,000	14.9%
PERRIELLOTom Perriello (D-Va)	VA	$500,000	$250	0.1%	255	$15,672,000	3.2%
CLARKEYvette D. Clarke (D-NY)	NY	$400,000	$250	0.1%	240	$17,317,500	2.3%

Criteria to be Considered Earmark Spending

To be classified as an earmark spending, at least one of the following should apply:

- The requested funding is not specifically authorized as necessary for the basic operations of the government in the annual budget.
- The funding is requested by only one chamber of Congress.
- The funding was not included in the President's Budget Request.
- The funding results in a substantial increase over the amounts projected in the president's budget.
- The funding is for a project that will benefit a small population or a narrow special interest.

"Many earmarks make it into the approved budget. In 2005 alone, over 14,000 earmark projects, costing about $27 billion were approved by Congress. The House Appropriations Committee receives about 35,000 earmark spending requests per year. In the ten-year period from 2000 through 2009, the U.S. Congress approved earmark spending projects worth about $208 billion."

"During 2007, earmark spending dropped to $13.2 billion, a significant decrease from the $29 billion spent in 2006. In 2007, nine of the 11 annual spending bills were subject to a moratorium on earmark spending that was enforced by House and Senate Appropriations Committee under the chairmanship of Sen. Byrd and Rep. Obey. In 2008, however, a similar moratorium proposal failed and earmark spending jumped to $17.2 billion." http://usgovinfo.about.com/od/uscongress/a/earmarkspending.htm

"Congressional earmarks are one of the best examples of how Congress' appetite for parochial spending led the nation into our current budgetary hole. Too often, lawmakers have based federal spending decisions on the needs of narrow private interests, rather than appropriating funds... only for effective, efficient programs that deliver taxpayers the greatest value. Though technically banned, earmark spending still exists in different forms, and is just one of many ways Congress sidesteps responsible budgeting and spending.

"Although Congress is responsible for our nation's finances, it continues to fail in its national budgeting, as evidenced by a national debt larger than our entire economy. The way forward lies in the legislative and executive branches working together to establish clear and transparent criteria and metrics for spending. They must ensure that all spending decisions are based on merit, competition, or

well-designed and effective formulas." http://www.taxpayer.net/issues/
earmarks-appropriations#

In the year 1998, Congress spent our money on some of the
following projects:

Selected Earmarks, Fiscal Year 1999 Budget15

FY 1999 Agriculture Appropriations

Agricultural Research Service:

- $250,000 to Alternative Fish Feed, Aberdeen, ID (fish like
  lettuce, peas and brussel sprouts)
- $250,000 to Appalachian Fruit Research Station, Kearneysville,
  WV (to control fruit decay)
- $1,100,000 to Aquaculture Research, AK
- $300,000 to Biological Control of Western Weeds, Albany, CA
- $250,000 to Cereal Crops Research, Madison, WI (developing
  hybrids and improved baking)
- $250,000 to Cotton Ginning, Stoneville, MS
- $750,000 to Grasshopper Research, AK
- $300,000 to Honeybee Research (Varroa/Tracheal Mites),
  Baton Rouge, LA
- $250,000 to Lettuce Geneticist/Breeding, Salinas, CA
- $500,000 to Manure Handling and Disposal, Starkville, MS
- $1,100,000 to National Warmwater Aquaculture
  Center, Stoneville, MS
- $150,000 to Peach Varieties Research, Byron, GA
- $1,000,000 to Peanut Quality Research, Dawson, GA/Raleigh, NC
- $150,000 to Potato Breeder Position, Aberdeen, ID
- $1,400,000 to Rice Research, Stuttgart, AK
- $250,000 to Small Fruits Research, Poplarville, MS
- $500,000 to Subtropical Animal Research Station, Brooksville, FL
- $200,000 to Sugarbeet Research, Ft. Collins, CO
- $500,000 to U.S. Plant Stress and Water Conservation
  Lab, Lubbock, TX
- $200,000 to Vegetable Research, East Lansing, MI

Just the other day (August 2017) my Congressman sent me an email
asking me how I wanted him to vote on some bills. I thought there was
a ban on earmarks, yet there was an immigration bill among them with
an energy bill attached to it. They do this because they know the tacked
on bill will not pass without it being attached to a more popular bill.

X

CONGRESSIONAL PAY

https://www.govtrack.us to track your representatives and senators and get alerts from them.

Not every Congressman believes Congress needs a pay raise. One congressman is trying to reduce congressional pay and eliminate congressional pensions. Rep. Kevin Yoder (R-KS3) thinks members of Congress makes too much money. He introduced two bills in January of 2016 to reform Congressional pay. Elected for... Jul 21, 2016, 3:39 p.m. Rep. Kevin Yoder (R-KS3) thinks members of Congress make too much money. Elected for the first time in 2010 as part of the Tea Party wave, the Republican thinks that reducing Federal spending should start with themselves. But perhaps unsurprisingly, his colleagues aren't exactly signing on in droves.

For years, the first order of business when Congress opened Session, was to give themselves a raise. One of the laws is that even if a congressman serves one term that he receives a life pension. That would be nice if it were true, but it is not.

A report on "Retirement Benefits for Members of Congress outlines how pension benefits are calculated.

No member of Congress is eligible for a pension unless they have served in Congress for at least five years. Senators serve six year terms and House members must seek re-election every two years.

To collect a Congressman or Senator must be any age with at least 25 years of service, or at least age 50 with 20 years of service.

Under the pension program adopted in 1984 the size of the pension is based on the highest three years of a member's salary, the number of years in service, and a multiplier, which is 1.7 percent for the first 20 years of service and 1.0 percent for subsequent years.

Using a rank-and-file twenty-five-year member who just retired, the sum would be the total of two calculations. First multiply $172,443 (the average salary over the last three years) times 20 years' time 0.017. Then multiply $172,443 times 5 years' times 0.01 and add that number to the first calculation. The total: About $67,250 per year.

A three-term Congressman or a one-term Senator who has reached retirement age would be eligible for an annual pension for six years work of $17,588.

The people would also like to see term limitations set for congressmen. A Congressman that is still on the rolls at age 75 (speaking from experience) suffers from a lot of aching bones, probably is not there every day, hopes no one notices that it takes longer to say something because you can't find the right words anymore (probable dementia), disappears down the hall to the lavatory several times more often than other members, wears depends, has to spend more time away on doctor appointments – not to mention all the medications you are taking, and it is a real effort to take a shower every morning. I hate greasy hair on a man.

Most of you know the President receives a salary of $400,000 per year, plus $50,000 for expenses. His salary is set by Congress and may not be reduced during his term. The President is paid a lifetime taxable pension in the amount of $203,700, the same amount that is paid to secretaries to cabinet agencies. This sum begins as soon as the President leaves office.

Each former president and vice president may also take advantage of funds allocated by Congress to help facilitate their transition to private life. These funds are used to provide suitable office space, staff compensation, communications services, and printing and postage associated with the transition. As an example, Congress authorized a total of $1.5 million for the transition expenses of outgoing President George H.W. Bush and Vice President Dan Quayle.

The Secret Service provides lifetime protection for former presidents who entered office before January 1, 1997, and for their spouses. Surviving spouses of former presidents receive protection until remarriage. Legislation enacted in 1984 allows former Presidents or their dependents to decline Secret Service protection.

Former Presidents and their spouses, widows, and minor children are entitled to treatment in military hospitals. Health care costs are billed to the individual at a rate established by the Office of Management and Budget (OMB). Former Presidents and their dependents may also enroll in private health plans at their own expense.

In May 2015, Rep. Jason Chaffetz (R-Utah), introduced a bill that would limit the lifetime pension paid to former presidents at $200,000 and remove the current link between presidential pensions and the salary paid to Cabinet secretaries.

In addition, Sen. Chaffetz's Presidential Allowance Modernization Act would reduce the presidential pension by $1 for every dollar over $400,000 per year earned by former presidents from all sources. For example, under Chaffetz's bill, former President Clinton, who made almost $10 million from speaking fees and book royalties in 2014, would get no government pension or allowance at all.

The bill was passed by the House on January 11, 2016, and passed by the Senate on June 21, 2016. Amendments made by the Senate have been sent back to the House for its consideration.

On July 22, 2016, President Obama vetoed the Presidential Allowance Modernization Act, which would have cut the pensions and allowances paid to former presidents.

In his veto message to Congress, Obama said the bill "would impose onerous and unreasonable burdens on the offices of former presidents."

In an accompanying press release, the White House added that the President had vetoed the bill because it would have "immediately terminated salaries and all benefits to staffers carrying out the official duties of former presidents — leaving no time or mechanism for them to transition to another payroll."

In addition, said the White House, the bill would have made it harder for the Secret Service to protect former presidents and would "immediately terminate leases, and remove furniture from offices of former presidents working to fulfilling their continued public service responsibilities."

The White House added that the President was willing to work with Congress in resolving his issues with the bill.

"If Congress provides these technical fixes, the president would sign the bill," said the White House.

The White House noted that the President had vetoed the bill only after consulting with the four other surviving former presidents and that the veto was "responsive to concerns they raised to us." http://usgovinfo.about.com/od/thepresidentandcabinet/fl/Bill-Would-Cut-Former-Presidentsrsquo-Pension-Allowances.htm

The salary of the Vice President is $237,700.00.

Salary of House/Senate $174,000 for life!

Salary of Speaker of the House $223,500 for life!

Salary of Majority/Minority Leader $193,400 for life!

How much did they really get? According to an April 2014 Congressional Research Service report, the four surviving former presidents received government pension and allowance benefits in 2014 totaling:

Jimmy Carter - $470,000

George H.W. Bush — $837,000

Bill Clinton — $950,000

George W. Bush — $1,287,000

This is really nonsensical. The average Salary of a teacher $40,065

The average Salary of Soldier deployed in Afghanistan is $38,000.

The salary for President Donald J. Trump: $1.00 per year.

But we have a couple of Congressmen that have decided to forego their pensions when they leave office.

78-year-old Rep. Howard Coble of North Carolina has spent twenty-five years in office. "I figured taxpayers pay my salary - not a bad salary," he said. "And I figure that's sufficient. Let me fend for myself after the salary's collected."

"Today, more than 400 retired members of Congress are receiving pensions. For 2009, the bill comes to more than $26 million. Add to that $7.4 million more in taxpayer contributions to current members' future pensions every year.... What might surprise you is that those who have dishonored the office can still get their pensions - even while doing time in prison."

"Duke Cunningham, R-Calif., admitted accepting millions in bribes and is currently serving time. But he is still getting more than $42,000 a year while in prison.

"Jim Traficant, D-Ohio, also took bribes while in office. But he didn't even have to ask for the $323,425 in pension money he received while serving seven years in prison.

"Dan Rostenkowski, D-Ill., served 15 months in prison in the mid-1990s for his role in a corruption scandal. He earned a six-figure pension the whole time. And he currently receives more than $176,000 a year, which includes a $9,000 cost of living increase last year alone. According to public records, he owns three homes and waterfront property on San Marco Island in Florida.

"In all, ... there were ... more than two dozen former members of Congress still eligible for federal pensions, despite being convicted of serious crimes.

"In 2007, Congress passed a law. But constitutionally, it can't apply to crimes that have already been committed.

"That's great news for ex-Congressman William Jefferson, D-La., who was shown taking a bribe in 2005 in an undercover FBI video. He could exit (prison) after 13 years with a roughly $674,000 nest egg.

"Twenty-five years ago, Coble tried to use his sharp pencil to eliminate congressional pensions altogether "to cut down on some of that wasteful spending," he said.

He didn't get much support from his colleagues.

"I was the beneficiary of some rude remarks after that first effort," he said.

"Today, he said it's up to each individual member to decide - like he did - whether they'll take a pension." By Sharyl Attkisson

http://www.cbsnews.com/news/pensions-follow-ex-lawmakers-to-prison/

"The other Senator to decide he will not take a pension was Senator Rand Paul. A massively-sent chain email states, "Many citizens had no idea that members of Congress could retire with the same pay after only one term." Well, maybe many citizens do not have that idea, because it is just flat wrong. Another infamous email demanding passage of a mythical "Congressional Reform Act" claims members of Congress do not pay Social Security taxes. That, too, is wrong

"Salaries and benefits of members of the U.S. Congress have been the source of taxpayer unhappiness and myths over the years. Here are some facts for your consideration.

"As of 2015, the base salary for all rank-and-file members of the U.S. House and Senate is $174,000 per year, plus benefits. Salaries have not been increased since 2009. Compared to private-sector salaries, the salaries of members of Congress is lower than many mid-level executives and managers.

"Pay Increases

"Members of Congress are eligible to receive the same annual cost-of-living increase given to other federal employees, if any. The raise takes effect automatically on January 1 of each year unless Congress, through passage of a joint resolution, votes to decline it, as Congress has done since 2009.

"Benefits Paid to Members of Congress

"You may have read that Members of Congress do not pay into Social Security. Well, that's a myth.

"Prior to 1984, neither Members of Congress nor any other federal civil service employee paid Social Security taxes. Of course, they were also not eligible to receive Social Security benefits. Members of Congress and other federal employees were instead covered by a separate pension plan called the Civil Service Retirement System (CSRS). The 1983 amendments to the Social Security Act required federal employees first hired after 1983 to participate in Social Security. These amendments also required all Members of Congress to participate in Social Security as of January 1, 1984, regardless of when they first entered Congress. Because the CSRS was not designed to coordinate with Social Security, Congress directed the development of a new retirement plan for federal workers. The result was the Federal Employees' Retirement System Act of 1986.

"Members of Congress receive retirement and health benefits under the same plans available to other federal employees. They become vested after five years of full participation.

"Note: Starting in 2014, the only health care coverage made available to members of Congress and their employees by the federal government will be coverage offered through the Health Insurance Exchange created by the Patient Protection and Affordable Care Act - the "Obamacare Act."

"Members elected since 1984 are covered by the Federal Employees' Retirement System (FERS). Those elected prior to 1984 were covered by the Civil Service Retirement System (CSRS). In 1984 all members were given the option of remaining with CSRS or switching to FERS.

"As it is for all other federal employees, congressional retirement is funded through taxes and the participants' contributions. Members of Congress under FERS contribute 1.3 percent of their salary into the FERS retirement plan and pay 6.2 percent of their salary in Social Security taxes.

"Members of Congress are not eligible for a pension until they reach the age of 50, but only if they've completed 20 years of service. Members are eligible at any age after completing 25 years of service or after they reach the age of 62. Please also note that Members of Congress have to serve at least 5 years to even receive a pension.

"The amount of a congressperson's pension depends on the years of service and the average of the highest 3 years of his or her salary. By law, the starting amount of a Member's retirement annuity may not exceed 80% of his or her final salary.

"According to the Congressional Research Service, 413 retired Members of Congress were receiving federal pensions based fully or in part on their congressional service as of Oct. 1, 2006. Of this number, 290 had retired under CSRS and were receiving an average annual pension of $60,972. A total of 123 Members had retired with service under both CSRS and FERS or with service under FERS only. Their average annual pension was $35,952 in 2006.

"Allowances

"Members of Congress are also provided with an annual allowance intended to defray expenses related carrying out their congressional duties, including "official office expenses, including staff, mail, travel between a Member's district or state and Washington, DC, and other goods and services."

"Outside Income

"Many members of Congress retain their private careers and other business interests while they serve. Members are allowed to retain an amount of permissible "outside earned income" limited to no more than 15% of the annual rate of basic pay for level II of the Executive Schedule for federal employees, or $26,550 a year in 2013. However, there is currently no limit on the amount of non-salary income members can retain from their investments, corporate dividends or profits.

"House and Senate rules define what sources of "outside earned income" are permissible. For example, House Rule XXV (112th Congress) limits permissible outside income to "salaries, fees, and other amounts received or to be received as compensation for personal services actually rendered." Members are not allowed to retain compensation arising from fiduciary relationships, except for medical practices. Members are also barred from accepting honoraria - payments for professional services typically provided without charge.

"Perhaps most importantly to voters and taxpayers, member of Congress are strictly prohibited from earning or accepting income that may appear to be intended to influence the way they vote on legislation.

"Tax Deductions

"Members are allowed to deduct up to $3,000 a year from their federal income tax for living expenses while they are away from their home states or congressional districts.

"Along with their salaries, benefits and allowed outside income, the members of the U.S. Congress are provided with various allowances intended to defray expenses related carrying out their congressional duties.

"According to the Congressional Research Service (CRS) report, Congressional Salaries and Allowances, the allowances are provided to cover "official office expenses, including staff, mail, travel between a Member's district or state and Washington, DC, and other goods and services."

"In the House of Representatives

"The Members' Representational Allowance (MRA)

"In the House of Representatives, the Members' Representational Allowance (MRA) is made available to help members defray expenses resulting from three specific components of their "representational duties," those being; the personal expenses component; the office expenses component; and the mailing expenses component.

"Members are not allowed to use their MRA allowance to pay any personal or political campaigning expenses.

"Members must pay any personal or office expenses in excess of the MRA out of their own pockets.

"Each member receives the same amount of MRA funds for personal expenses. Allowances for office expenses vary from member to member based on the distance between the member's home district and Washington, D.C., and average rent for office space in the member's home district. Allowances for mailing vary based on the number of residential mailing addresses in the member's home district as reported by the U.S. Census Bureau.

"The House sets the funding levels for the MRA annually as part of the federal budget process. According to the CRS report, this amount decreased from a total of $660 million for fiscal year 2010 to $573.9 million for fiscal year 2012.

"In 2012, individual representatives received MRA allowances ranging from $1,270,129 to $1,564,613, with an average of $1,353,205.13.

"Most of each member's annual MRA allowance is used to pay their office personnel. In 2012, for example, the office personnel allowance for each member was $944,671.

"Each member is allowed to use their MRA to employ up to 18 full-time, permanent employees and up to four part-time or temporary employees. The annual salary of any employee of a member of the House of Representatives is currently limited to $168,411 (in 2013).

"Some primary responsibilities of the congressional staffs in both the House and Senate include analysis and preparation of proposed legislation, legal research, government policy analysis, scheduling, constituent correspondence, and speech writing.

"All members are required to provide a quarterly report detailing exactly how they spent their MRA allowances. All House MRA expenditures are reported in the quarterly Statement of Disbursements of the House.

"In the Senate

"The Senators' Official Personnel and Office Expense Account (SOPOEA)

"In the U.S. Senate, the Senators' Official Personnel and Office Expense Account (SOPOEA) is made up three separate allowances: the administrative and clerical assistance allowance; the legislative assistance allowance; and the official office expense allowance.

"All Senators receive the same amount for the legislative assistance allowance. The size of the administrative and clerical assistance allowance and the office expense allowance vary based on the population of the state the senators represent, the distance between Washington, D.C. and their home states, and limits authorized by the Senate Committee on Rules and Administration.

"The combined total of the three SOPOEA allowances can be used at the discretion of each Senator to pay for any type of official expenses they incur, including travel, office personnel or office supplies. However, expenses for mailing are currently limited to $50,000 per fiscal year.

"The size of the SOPOEA allowances is adjusted and authorized within the "Contingent Expenses of the Senate," account in the annual legislative branch appropriations bills enacted as part of the annual federal budget process.

"In the fiscal year 2013 legislative branch appropriations bill, the size of the average Senate SOPOEA allowance is $3,209,103, with individual accounts ranging from $2,960,716 to $4,685,632, depending on the population of the senators' states.

"According to the CRS, the total size of the Senate SOPOEA allowance decreased from $422.0 million in fiscal year 2001 to $396.2 million in fiscal year 2012.

"Senators are prohibited from using any portion of their SOPOEA allowance for any personal or political purposes, including campaigning. Payment of any amount spent in excess of a senator's SOPOEA allowance must be paid by the senator.

"Unlike in the House, the size of senators' administrative and clerical assistance staff is not specified. Instead, senators are free to structure their staffs as they choose, as long as they do not spend more than provided to them in the administrative and clerical assistance component of their SOPOEA allowance.

"The fiscal year 2013 legislative branch appropriations report allowed $477,874 for each senator's legislative assistance allowance, stating that this amount was equivalent to three staff members being paid $159,291 each.

"By law, all SOPOEA expenditures of each senator are published in the Semiannual Report of the Secretary of the Senate."

By Michael Roberts Updated January 02, 2016

"Retirement is a common topic of conversation among government employees. Old-timers talk about what they will do in a few years once they are no longer working. Newer workers fantasize about that far off day when they will be the ones boasting about their impending exits.

"While all public servants should keep the three-legged stool of government retirement in mind, the primary source of retirement funding for most public servants is the annuity provided by their retirement systems.

"The calculation of the annuity payment greatly impacts both when an employee can afford to retire and what sort of lifestyle that employee will live in retirement.

"Few people can afford to retire on their retirement eligibility dates. This means employees typically work beyond their retirement eligibility dates and base their actual retirement dates on the amount of their monthly annuity payments.

"Two Variables and One Constant

"In most government retirement systems, two variables determine how much an employee's annuity will be: the employee's salary and the employee's years of service. While age is a factor in determining retirement eligibility, it is rarely used when determining annuity payment amounts.

"Retirement systems need one salary number to plug into their formulas for determining employee's retirement annuity. They use the salary an employee earns in their few highest earning years.

"Most systems use between three and five years in this calculation. They average the salaries to get the single salary number.

"For instance, a retirement system calculates an employee's salary on that employee's three highest earning years. An employee earns $61,000, $62,000, and $66,000 in his three highest-earning years.

"These three numbers are averaged to determine the employee's salary as it relates to a retirement annuity. For the purpose of calculating this employee's retirement annuity, the employee's salary is $63,000: ($61,000 + $62,000 + $66,000) / 3 = $63,000

"Years of service are easier to determine than the single salary number. This number is simply the amount of time an employee contributes to the retirement system. Each pay period an employee contributes to the retirement system earns the employee service credit equal to the amount of time in the pay period.

"There is one other factor in the annuity payment calculation. It is a percentage applied that in essence tells how much of the calculated salary amount shows up in the annuity for each year of service. That is a long and perhaps confusing explanation, but it makes sense in an example.

"Using the $63,000 salary in our example above, let's say the employee has 30 years of service in the retirement system. Let's also say that for each year of service and employee receives 2.0% of the salary number.

"Here is the calculation expressed as a mathematical formula:

Salary X Years X Percentage = Annuity

Here is our example applied to the formula:

$63,000 X 30 X 2.0% = $37,800

"This employee was accustomed to earning around $63,000 per year, but now, this employee receives a government income significantly less. The $37,800 is paid in monthly installments of $3,150. Hopefully, the employee has enough retirement savings and Social Security income to compensate for the reduction.

"Now, let's say the same employee works 40 years instead of retiring after 30. Here is the new calculation:

$63,000 X 40 X 2.0% = $50,400

"By delaying retirement for 10 years, the employee in this example increases his retirement income by $12,600 per year. This translates to an extra $1,050 per month; however, the employee contributes money to the retirement system for 10 more years while forgoing any annuity payment for those 10 years.

"COLAs

"Retirement annuities are fixed income streams. Barring unusual circumstances, the annuity amount an employee is entitled to at retirement is the annuity the employee keeps for life. Annuities can increase with cost-of-living adjustments.

"Retirement systems grant COLAs in one of two ways. The first way is for the system to grant automatic COLAs based on objective data such as the Consumer Price Index for a predetermined date. The other way is for the retirement system's governing board or overseeing legislative body to grant a COLA by vote. When COLAs are subject to politics, proposals are usually based on objective data but can be amended through the legislative process.

"When a company falls on difficult times, one of the things that seems to happen is they reduce their staff and workers. The remaining workers must find ways to continue to do a good job or risk that their job would be eliminated as well.

"Wall street and the media normally congratulate the CEO for making this type of "tough decision".

"Our government should not be immune from similar risks.

"Therefore: Reduce the House of Representatives from the current 435 members to 218 members.

"Reduce Senate members from 100 to 50 (one per State). Then, reduce their remaining staff by 25%.

"Accomplish this over the next 8 years (two steps/two elections) and of course this would require some redistricting.

"Some Yearly Monetary Gains Include:

$44,108,400 for elimination of base pay for congress. (267 members X $165,200 pay/member/yr.)

$437,100,000 for elimination of their staff. (Estimate $1.3 Million in staff per each member of the House, and $3 Million in staff per each member of the Senate every year)

$108,350,000 for the reduction in remaining staff by 25%.

$7,500,000,000 reduction in pork barrel earmarks each year. (Those members whose jobs are gone. Current estimates for total government pork earmarks are at $15 Billion/yr).

"The remaining representatives would need to work smarter and improve efficiencies. It might even be in their best interests to work together for the good of our country!

"We may also expect that smaller committees might lead to a more efficient resolution of issues as well. It might even be easier to keep track of what your representative is doing.

"Congress has more tools available to do their jobs than it had back in 1911 when the current number of representatives was established. (Telephone, computers, cell phones to name a few)

"Note: Congress does not hesitate to head home for extended weekends, holidays and recesses, when what the nation needs is a real fix for economic problems. Also, we had 3 senators who were not doing their jobs for the 18+ months (on the campaign trail) and still they all accepted full pay. Minnesota survived very well with only one senator for the first half of this year. These facts alone support a reduction in senators and congress.

"Summary of opportunity:

$44,108,400 reduction of congress members.

$282,100,000 for elimination of the reduced house member staff.

$150,000,000 for elimination of reduced senate member staff.

$70,850,000 for 25% reduction of staff for remaining house members.

$37,500,000 for 25% reduction of staff for remaining senate members.

$7,500,000,000 reduction in pork added to bills by the reduction of congress members.

88,084,558,400 per year, estimated total savings. (That's 8-BILLION just to start!)

Corporate America does these types of cuts all the time. There's even a name for it.

"Downsizing."

"Also, if Congresspersons were required to serve 20, 25 or 30 years (like everyone else) in order to collect retirement benefits, taxpayers could save a bundle. Now they get full retirement after serving only ONE term.

"Congressional Reform Act of 2016

"1.   Term Limits. 12 years only, one of the possible options below.
    A.   Two Six-year Senate terms
    B.   Six Two-year House terms
    C.   One Six-year Senate term and three Two-Year House terms
"2.   No Tenure / No Pension.
    A Congressman collects a salary while in office and receives no pay when they are out of office.
"3.   Congress (past, present and future) participates in Social Security.
"4.   All funds in the Congressional retirement fund move to the Social Security system immediately. All future funds flow into the Social Security system, and Congress participates with the American people.
"5.   Congress can purchase their own retirement plan, just as all Americans do.
"6.   Congress will no longer get automatic pay raises. Congressional pay will rise by the lower of CPI or 3%.
"7.   Congress loses their current health care system and participates in the same health care system as the American people.
"8.   Congress must equally abide by all laws they impose on the American people.
"9.   All contracts with past and present Congressmen are void effective immediately.

"10. If a Congressman is sentenced to jail or prison, said Congressman loses all rights to his/her pension benefits paid by the people other than social security.

"11. Congress must work forty hours per week, four weeks per month, at their office in Washington, D.C. at the same salary and benefits they are presently receiving.

"12. Any Congressman that is found to be a member of the Socialist or Communist Party and against our United States Constitution is barred from the Capitol Building and shall be dealt with accordingly.

"The American people did not make this contract with Congressmen. Congressmen made all these contracts for themselves.

"Serving in Congress is an honor, not a career. The Founding Fathers envisioned citizen legislators, so ours should serve their term(s), then go home and back to work."

Strange how a man can work his entire life as a police officer and one week before his retirement come up with one small infraction and lose his pension he has worked for his whole life, yet a Congressman can go to jail and never lose his pension. He can run for election to a higher office and miss months from work and still get paid. If he loses he just returns to work. What a privilege it is to be a Congressman.

XI

WHAT WE WANT FROM CONGRESS

After the 2012 election when the Republicans took over Congress, I received a telephone call from someone who asked me what I thought the first thing Congress should do. My response was that they should do what we elected them to do – what we gave them the House and Senate to do – Impeach Obama. The woman was awe struck and could not believe what I was saying. I could hear her suck in her breath over the phone. She then proceeded to hang up on me.

Does this Republican Congress still not know why they were elected? The People have constantly yelled "Impeach" for the last two years Obama was in office and it fell on deaf ears. I wrote to my Congressman several times and he ignored my remarks. They sat back and gave Obama everything he wanted.

"Don't you ever wonder why the GOP has never tried to impeach Obama? Don't you wonder why John Boehner and Mitch McConnell talk a big game, but never actually tried to stop Obama? Don't you wonder why Congress holds the purse strings, yet has never tried to defund Obamacare or Obama's clearly illegal executive action on amnesty for illegal aliens? Bizarre, right? It defies logic, right?

"First, I'd guess many key Republicans are being bribed. Secondly, I believe many key Republicans are being blackmailed. Whether they are having affairs, or secretly gay, or stealing taxpayer money, the National Security Agency knows everything.

"Ask former House Speaker Dennis Hastert about that. The government even knew he was withdrawing large sums of his own money from his own bank account. The NSA, the SEC, the IRS, and all the other three-letter government agencies are watching every Republican political leader. They surveil everything. Thirdly, many Republicans are petrified of being called racists, so they are scared to ever criticize Obama or call out his crimes, let alone demand his impeachment. Fourth , why rock the boat? After defeat or retirement, if you're a good old boy, you've got a $5 million-per-year lobbying job waiting on "K" Street. The big-money interests have the system gamed. Win or lose, they win. Bill Bennett "

There were Impeachment Petitions on file in Congress and they lay there with nothing being done about them. This Republican Congress has been labeled the "Do Nothing Congress." This election I voted for Mr. Trump. I am not ashamed to say that. Like most of America, I am tired of the Liberals; tired of Socialism, tired of all the Communists in Congress. Trump did not appear out of thin air. He came from the last six years of Republican failures. Before he decided to run for President, I was one of the people on Twitter that asked Donald Trump to run for President of the United States.

It is hoped that the corruption in Congress will lessen under the new administration, but unless term limits are placed on Congress, the corruption will not stop. The establishment is frightened of Mr. Trump because they believe he will harm the nation. They are afraid he will upset their taxpayer-subsidized apple carts. While Obama threatens to veto legislation that spends too little, they worry that Mr. Trump will veto legislation that spends too much.

And there is one more thing. They (Republicans and Democrats alike) are afraid of the Clintons. The Clintons have such power in Washington and in politics that everyone is afraid of them. When someone goes after the Clintons, or talks about going after them, they end up as a suicide some place.

We have children crying and protesting in the streets that did not even vote, but they are worried they might have to go to work at a real job because they are working the welfare system. We have children protesting that should be back in school instead of yelling in the street. Where are the parents who are paying for their education when they are skipping class to protest? We have teachers who are encouraging the protests. We have college professors saying things like "All I want is the abolition of imperialists, white supremacists and capitalists heteropatriarchy." And lest we do not forget they called us, the conservatives, deplorables.

Now they are gathering together as Republicans against Trump because they are afraid their days of corruption will end because Mr. Trump became President. They can't buy Donald Trump. They could play their games with Obama and they have, or Obama has played his games with them and that is why he was not impeached.

I read that Obama kept a file on every Senator and every Representative and knew about every phone call they made. There is nothing they do or say Obama didn't know about and that is the hold he had over them. I don't know if that was true or not.

I want Congress to enforce all the laws on the books on immigration. I believe if an illegal immigrant has been in the United States for 20 years and has not applied for citizenship in that twenty-year period, he should be deported. If he hasn't applied for citizenship in twenty years, then he obviously does not want to be a citizen of this country and needs to return to Mexico or whatever country he came from.

Mr. Trump has already set in motion his promises to enforce the immigration laws and the influx of illegal immigration has already decreased.

The President stated he would not allow Islamists to enter this country. People acted like this was something illegal or new to this country. During World War II we did not allow the Japanese to enter this country. As a matter of fact, the Japanese citizens that were already living in this country were pulled from their homes like the Jews in Germany, and put in concentration camps here in the United States until the war was over.

Known as the McCarran-Walter Act, (the Immigration and Nationality Act of 1952 allows for the "Suspension of entry or imposition of restrictions by the President. Whenever the President finds that the entry of aliens or of any class of aliens into the United States would be detrimental to the interests of the United States, the President may, by proclamation, and for such period as he shall deem necessary, suspend the entry of all aliens or any class of aliens as immigrants or non-immigrants or impose on the entry of aliens any restrictions he may deem to be appropriate."

The act was utilized by President Jimmy Carter, no less, in 1979 to keep Iranians out of the United States, but he actually did more. He made all Iranian students already here check in, and then he deported a bunch. Seven thousand were found in violation of their visas, 15,000 Iranians were forced to leave the United States in 1979. It all happened under executive orders #12172 and 12206.

It is of note that the act requires that an applicant for immigration must be of good moral character and "attached to the principles of the Constitution." Since the Quran forbids Muslims to swear allegiance to the U.S. Constitution, technically, all Muslims should be refused immigration. Authenticated at: https://www.gpo.gov/fdsys/pkg/ STATUTE-66/pdf/STATUTE-66-Pg163.pdf

One of the reasons Mr. Trump was elected was because the people wanted Obamacare repealed completely. Each state should have hospitals that give mandatory care to the indigent and the state should pay for that care.

When I turned 75 my standard of medical care changed. When I make a doctor appointment I don't get to see a doctor anymore. I see a PAC instead of a doctor. My standard of care has decreased. But the Democrats, nor Republicans don't care because I am old. Now we have to wait for Obamacare to implode before we can get new healthcare and Americans are partly to blame. They are afraid to let go of what they have even though they are paying exorbitant rates.

The Republicans knew when Obamacare went into effect that the people were asking for it to be repealed and replaced. They even campaigned on repeal and replacing Obamacare. They have had eight years to come up with a new plan and here it is nine years later and they still have nothing to show the American people who still are asking them to repeal and replace Obamacare.

Welfare should be reformed with drug testing up to age 50.

Food stamps should only be given to the person applying for them after an investigation. I know a lady that receives them for herself and her two sons who are in their 40s; one son works, and one son doesn't even look for a job. He plays video games all day. She works and receives her deceased husband's pension. At first, she was eligible because she did not make very much money, but she did not stop the stamps when she started receiving the second income.

I see Mexicans at the grocery store pay for their groceries with food stamps and then go outside and load their groceries into a brand new truck. Yet the husband has a full-time job. Most welfare people make more money per month than a person does making minimum wage, so why should they go out and look for a job?

It's now more profitable to sit at home and watch television than it is to earn an honest day's pay. Hawaii is the biggest offender, where welfare recipients earn $29.13 per hour, or a $60,590 yearly salary, all for doing nothing. Here is the list of the states where the pre-tax equivalent "salary" that welfare recipients receive is higher than having a job:

1. Hawaii: $60,590
2. District of Columbia: $50,820
3. Massachusetts: $50,540
4. Connecticut: $44,370
5. New York: $43,700
6. New Jersey: $43,450
7. Rhode Island: $43,330
8. Vermont: $42,350
9. New Hampshire: $39,750
10. Maryland: $38,160
11. California: $37,160
12. Oregon: $34,300
13. Wyoming: $32,620
14. Nevada: $29,820
15. Minnesota: $29,350
16. Delaware: $29,220
17. Washington: $28,840
18. North Dakota: $28,830
19. Pennsylvania: $28,670
20. New Mexico: $27,900
21. Montana: $26,930
22. South Dakota: $26,610
23. Kansas: $26,490
24. Michigan: $26,430
25. Alaska: $26,400
26. Ohio: $26,200
27. North Carolina: $25,760
28. West Virginia: $24,900
29. Alabama: $23,310

30. Indiana: $22,900
31. Missouri: $22,800
32. Oklahoma: $22,480
33. Louisiana: $22,250
34. South Carolina: $21,91

As a point of reference, the average middle-class annual income today is $50,000, down from $54,000 at the beginning of the Great Recession. Hawaii, DC, and Massachusetts pay more in welfare than the average working folks earn.

Congressional candidates were asked, "Do you vote against hiking the National Debt or Taxes for as long as the U.S. Government is subsidizing the evils of abortion, anti-Semitism, religious/ethical conscience violations or same-sex marriage?" To find the results of that question, please go here: http://www.christian-jewishvoterguides.org/candidate-voter-guides

I want Congress to leave our Constitution and its Amendments alone; that includes the First and Second Amendments.

The Syrian refugees that Obama brought to America should be shipped to Saudi Arabia who has air conditioned tent cities capable of caring for them, or another Arab country capable of caring for them.

"I bought a bird feeder. I hung it on my back porch and filled it with seed. What a beauty of a bird feeder it was, as I filled it lovingly with seed. Within a week we had hundreds of birds taking advantage of the continuous flow of free and easily accessible food.

But then the birds started building nests in the boards of the patio, above the table, and next to the barbecue. Then came the shit. It was everywhere: on the patio tile, the chairs, the table ... everywhere! Then some of the birds turned mean. They would dive bomb me and try to peck me even though I had fed them out of my own pocket.

And others birds were boisterous and loud. They sat on the feeder and squawked and screamed at all hours of the day and night and demanded that I fill it when it got low on food.

After a while, I couldn't even sit on my own back porch anymore. So I took down the bird feeder and in three days the birds were gone. I cleaned up their mess and took down the many nests they had built all over the patio.

Soon, the back yard was like it used to be .... quiet, serene... and no one demanding their rights to a free meal."

Now let's see......Our government gives out free food, subsidized housing, free medical care and free education, and allows anyone born here to be an automatic citizen. Then the illegals came by the tens of thousands. Suddenly our taxes went up to pay for free services; small apartments are housing 5 families; you have to wait 6 hours to be seen by an emergency room doctor; Your child's second-grade class is behind other schools because over half the class doesn't speak English.

Corn Flakes now come in a bilingual box; I have to "press one" to hear my bank talk to me in English, and people waving flags other than "ours" are squawking and screaming in the streets, demanding more rights and free liberties.

Just my opinion, but maybe it's time for the government to take down the bird feeder." [Author unknown]

XII

BUDGET CUTS

PAUL RYAN'S PROPOSED BUDGET CUTS
   A List of Republican Budget Cuts
   Notice S.S. And the military are NOT on this list.
These are all the programs that the new Republican House has proposed cutting.
   * Corporation for Public Broadcasting Subsidy — $445 million annual savings.
   * Save America 's Treasures Program — $25 million annual savings.
   * International Fund for Ireland — $17 million annual savings.
   * Legal Services Corporation — $420 million annual savings.
   * National Endowment for the Arts — $167.5 million annual savings.
   * National Endowment for the Humanities — $167.5 million annual savings.
   * Hope VI Program — $250 million annual savings.
   * Amtrak Subsidies — $1.565 billion annual savings.
   * Eliminate duplicating education programs — H.R. 2274 (in last Congress), authored by Rep. McKeon, eliminates 68 at a savings of $1.3 billion annually.
   * U.S. Trade Development Agency — $55 million annual savings.
   * Woodrow Wilson Center Subsidy — $20 million annual savings.

* Cut in half funding for congressional printing and binding — $47 million annual savings.
* John C. Stennis Center Subsidy — $430,000 annual savings.
* Community Development Fund — $4.5 billion annual savings.
* Heritage Area Grants and Statutory Aid — $24 million annual savings.
* Cut Federal Travel Budget in Half — $7.5 billion annual savings
* Trim Federal Vehicle Budget by 20% — $600 million annual savings.
* Essential Air Service — $150 million annual savings.
* Technology Innovation Program — $70 million annual savings.
*Manufacturing Extension Partnership (MEP) Program — $125 million annual savings.
* Department of Energy Grants to States for Weatherization — $530 million annual savings.
* Beach Replenishment — $95 million annual savings.
* New Starts Transit — $2 billion annual savings.
* Exchange Programs for Alaska Natives, Native Hawaiians, and Their Historical Trading Partners in Massachusetts — $9 million annual savings
* Intercity and High-Speed Rail Grants — $2.5 billion annual savings.
* Title X Family Planning — $318 million annual savings.
* Appalachian Regional Commission — $76 million annual savings.
* Economic Development Administration — $293 million annual savings.
* Programs under the National and Community Services Act — $1.15 billion annual savings.
* Applied Research at Department of Energy — $1.27 billion annual savings.
* Freedom CAR and Fuel Partnership — $200 million annual savings.
* Energy Star Program — $52 million annual savings.
*Economic Assistance to Egypt — $250 million annually.
* U.S. Agency for International Development — $1.39 billion annual savings.
* General Assistance to District of Columbia — $210 million annual savings.
* Subsidy for Washington Metropolitan Area Transit Authority — $150 million annual savings.
*Presidential Campaign Fund — $775 million savings over ten years.

* No funding for federal office space acquisition — $864 million annual savings.

* End prohibitions on competitive sourcing of government services.

* Repeal the Davis-Bacon Act — More than $1 billion annually.

* IRS Direct Deposit: Require the IRS to deposit fees for some services it offers (such as processing payment plans for taxpayers) to the Treasury, instead of allowing it to remain as part of its budget — $1.8 billion savings over ten years.

*Require collection of unpaid taxes by federal employees — $1 billion total savings. That is this about?

* Prohibit taxpayer funded union activities by federal employees — $1.2 billion savings over ten years.

* Sell excess federal properties the government does not make use of — $15 billion total savings.

*Eliminate death gratuity for Members of Congress. WHAT???

* Eliminate Mohair Subsidies — $1 million annual savings.

*Eliminate taxpayer subsidies to the United Nations Intergovernmental Panel on Climate Change — $12.5 million annual savings. WELL ISN'T THAT SPECIAL

* Eliminate Market Access Program — $200 million annual savings.

* USDA Sugar Program — $14 million annual savings.

* Subsidy to Organization for Economic Co-operation and Development (OECD) — $93 million annual savings.

* Eliminate the National Organic Certification Cost-Share Program — $56.2 million annual savings.

*Eliminate fund for Obamacare administrative costs — $900 million savings.

* Ready to Learn TV Program — $27 million savings.

* HUD Ph.D. Program.

* Deficit Reduction Check-Off Act.

*TOTAL SAVINGS: $2.5 Trillion over Ten Years

Some of these same cuts come up every time a budget is proposed, yet they never make the cut.

This was when Obama was President and never presented a budget. Mr. Trump presented a 2018 budget consisting of 49 pages which can be found anywhere on the internet.

One-fourth of the budget was taken away from the food stamp program. According to Bloomberg, the cuts to the food-stamp program in the budget would amount to $193 billion. The program would also phase in a work requirement, according to Mulvaney, so people without dependents would have to be employed to qualify. This will hopefully bring about the agencies investigating more thoroughly how needy the applicant really is. The budget cuts are aimed at reducing poverty.

The budget will call for a $72 billion cut over 10 years to the Social Security Disability Insurance. Mulvaney said this would inspire more people to get off disability and back to work.

"If the folks who are on Social Security Disability Insurance who are not supposed to be, if they go back to work, they're paying into the system, and they're not taking out of the system," Mulvaney told reporters. "So it does make the programs healthier."

"The spending on the border security is $2.6 billion, of which I think $1.6 billion is actual bricks-and-mortar construction," Mulvaney told reporters. "The other $1 billion is infrastructure and technology."

"The budget proposes an additional $610 billion cut to Medicaid, with $250 billion in savings to offset it." http://www.businessinsider.com/trump-white-house-2018-fiscal-year-budget-mick-mulvaney-call-2017-5

XIII

OBAMA AND RUSSIA

" If I have anything to say against Obama, it's not because I'm a racist, it's because I don't like what he has done as President and anybody should be able to feel that way, but what I find now is that if you say anything against him you're called a racist." Angie Harmon

If you ever want to irritate President Obama, just tell him that you own a gun, that you have a job, and that you have read the Constitution.

The real Obama legacy that he leaves behind is:

1. A Republican President
2. A Republican Vice President
3. Republican control of the Senate
4. Republican control of the House
5. A majority of Republican governors – 33 out of 50
6. Republican control of 32 state legislatures
7. Republican control of a majority of county governments
8. Republican control of a majority of city governments
9. Since 2008, the continual, uninterrupted decline in the number of Democrats in the Senate and the House, to their lowest levels since 1929
10. A decimated Democratic party and its leadership.

I have written four books where I gave Barack Obama my undivided attention. Now I would like for him to retire and I am afraid he won't. Obama likes being in the media. He really believes he was a great President in spite of Hillary's loss and all the conservative negative viewpoints against him. Just before the election he was heard to say if he was allowed to run for President again he believed he could win.

When Mr. Bush left the White House he retired gracefully as did previous presidents. But Obama believes the world wants to hear what he has to contribute. While he was President he did nothing in a crisis and now when he should do nothing, he criticizes our current President for saving America from his mistakes.

Mr. Trump and his sons are getting blamed by the Democrats and the Media for all this business about Trump and Russian collusion, but that is all smoke and mirrors to throw you off track as to who the really bad guys are.

"As former FBI Director James Comey's best friend, Robert Mueller, stocks his Seinfeld investigation-about-nothing with every Democratic lawyer and Hillary and/or Obama donor he can find, we are treated to the delicious irony of collusion with Russia being confirmed — and the colluder-in-chief being Ex-president Barack Hussein Obama.

"Even Obama's Democrat supporters are now acknowledging he knew about Russia's hacking of the DNC and Podesta emails. They are acknowledging that he did nothing but are not acknowledging the reason why – that he thought Hillary Clinton was going to succeed him and he wanted to do nothing to offend the Russians to whom he had once famously promised more "flexibility." As Fox News Politics reported:

"President Trump criticized his predecessor for allegedly doing "nothing" about reports that Russia interfered in last year's presidential campaign, in a recent interview. "I just heard today for the first time that (former President) Obama knew about Russia a long time before the election, and he did nothing about it," Trump said in the interview set to air on "Fox & Friends Weekend." "The CIA gave him information on Russia a long time before the election. ... If he had the information, why didn't he do something about it?"

"Even Rep. Adam Schiff, ranking member of the House Intelligence Committee, acknowledged that President Obama's refusal to embarrass his Russian friends by doing nothing was a mistake:

"President Obama's decision to not act sooner on Russian election interference last year was 'a very serious mistake,'" says California Rep. Adam Schiff.

"I think the administration needed to call out Russia earlier, and needed to act to deter and punish Russia earlier and I think that was a very serious mistake," Schiff said in an interview on CNN's "State of the Union" on Sunday.

"Schiff, the top ranking Democrat on the House Intelligence Committee, said that Obama was hesitant to confront Russia over its active measures campaign for fear of being seen as helping Hillary Clinton and of fueling Donald Trump's allegations that the election was being "rigged" against him.

"That is the excuse made by those caught with their hands in the cookie jar. What happened to our democracy being at stake, the sanctity of our electoral process being violated? It was okay to jeopardize our national security through inaction as long as it was thought it might embarrass Hillary? But when Trump won, suddenly it became an issue for which he was responsible?

"As noted, Obama's collusion with the Russians began years earlier when he conspired to gut U.S. missile defense efforts in Europe. As Investor's Business Daily noted over a year ago, President Obama had other plans and his betrayal of our allies was exquisitely ironic:

"Yet within hours of Medvedev's election as president in 2008, the Russian announced that Moscow would deploy SS-26 missiles in his country's enclave of Kaliningrad situated between our NATO allies Poland and Lithuania.

"He wanted the U.S. to abandon plans to deploy missile interceptors in Poland and warning radars in the Czech Republic designed to counter a future threat from Iran.

"What did President Obama do? He caved in and notified the Poles in a midnight phone call on Sept. 17, 2009 — the 70th anniversary of the Soviet Union's invasion of Poland — that we were pulling the plug on that system due to Russian objections.

"Putin then watched in 2012 as Obama promised Medvedev at the Nuclear Security Summit in Seoul, South Korea, that after his re-election he would have more "flexibility" to weaken missile defense, which would help him fulfill his dream of U.S. disarmament.

"Hillary Clinton herself was not above colluding with the Russians, as she did in the Uranium One Deal in which Clinton Foundation donors benefited from her enabling the transfer of 20 percent of our uranium supplies to Russia. That deal was one reason Putin was probably rooting for Hillary, not Trump.

"Instead of investigating Team Trump for collusion and its business dealings with Russia, how about a special counsel to investigate the Uranium one deal? How about a special counsel to investigate Hillary Clinton's illegal email server and destruction of emails under subpoena?

"Instead of President Trump obstructing justice by firing an FBI Director he was constitutionally empowered to fire, how about a special counsel to investigate Loretta Lynch's collusion with the Clinton campaign and obstruction of justice, starting with her meeting with Bill Clinton on the tarmac?

"We know from Comey's testimony that Lynch advised him to call the Clinton investigation a "matter" as the Clinton campaign was calling it. We know that Lynch met on the tarmac with the husband of the subject of a federal investigation. We know that after that meeting, Comey usurped the power of the attorney general and announced that despite all the evidence he himself cited, Hillary would not be prosecuted.

"Coincidence? One thinks not, particularly if reports about Loretta Lynch communicating with former DNC Chair Debbie Wasserman-Shultz that the Clinton investigation wouldn't be allowed to go too far are accurate. As Fox News judicial analyst Judge Andrew Napolitano is contending:

"Judge Andrew Napolitano says former Attorney General Loretta Lynch could be facing jail time for obstruction of justice if emails to former DNC chairwoman Debbie Wasserman Shultz reportedly about furthering DNC interests surface.

"It is alleged, this document has not seen the light of day yet, if it exists that there is one or several emails between Debbie Wasserman Shultz and Loretta Lynch concerning the behavior that Loretta Lynch will take to further the DNC interests while Mrs. Lynch was the Attorney General, that if it happened, would be misconduct in office," he said.

"In all of this there are only two real crimes that we are certain of: James Comey's leak of his memo on his conversation in the

Oval Office and the unmasking and leaking of the name of former National Security Adviser Mike Flynn. As law Professor Jonathan Turley notes:

"... Comey demonstrated a pattern of unethical conduct beginning with his appointment as FBI director during the Obama administration. Specifically, Turley and other constitutional experts have noted that Comey's acquiescence to former Attorney General Loretta Lynch's order for him to refer to the FBI's investigation into Hillary Clinton's illegal handling of classified materials, via an unsecured email server, as a "matter" rather than a criminal investigation proved that he lacked the integrity necessary for someone who treasures the FBI's supposed political independence...

"But the "clearest violation" of federal law that Comey may have committed came after he was fired by the president. During his testimony the former FBI director admitted to leaking his memo to a friend and former colleague at Columbia Law School with, as Turley noted, "the full knowledge that the information would be given to the media." That was extremely odd and inappropriate, given that Trump had asked Comey to investigate and stop various leakers within the government before Comey himself became a leaker.

"Why was releasing the memo potentially a violation of the law? Turley says because it was most likely created using a government computer and because it addressed "a highly sensitive investigation on facts that [Comey] considered material to that investigation." In fact, Comey communicated that information confidentially to top aides, and later noted that we sought to give it to the special counsel (which he helped facilitate with the leak) because he felt it was vital to the ongoing 'Russia' investigation.

"Obstruction of justice? How about President Obama secreting away in his presidential library records regarding former National Security Adviser Susan Rice's involvement in unmasking the names of Team Trump officials in intelligence reports — for five years! From Breitbart News:

"The National Security Council cannot hand over records relating to former National Security Adviser Susan Rice's surveillance of Americans, because they have been moved to the Obama presidential library and may be sealed for as many as five years, conservative watchdog Judicial Watch announced Monday.

"The NSC informed Judicial Watch in a letter dated May 23 that materials related to Rice's requests to know the identities of Americans swept up in surveillance of foreign targets, including any Trump campaign or transition officials, have been moved to the library.

"The NSC's Director of Access Management John Powers said in the letter:

"Documents from the Obama administration have been transferred to the Barack Obama Presidential Library. You may send your request to the Obama Library. However, you should be aware that under the Presidential Records Act, Presidential records remain closed to the public for five years after an administration has left office.

"Judicial Watch earlier this year filed a Freedom of Information Act (FOIA) request for those documents, including of communications between Rice and any intelligence community member or agency regarding any Russian involvement in the 2016 elections, the hacking of Democratic National Committee computers, or any suspected communications between Russia and Trump officials.

"Throw in Loretta Lynch and John Koskinen in the political targeting of the Tea Party and Eric Holder's role in Operation Fast and Furious and withholding of records under executive privilege, and you have a rogues' gallery of felons in the most corrupt administration. The very real possibility exists that James Comey, Susan Rice, Loretta Lynch Lois Lerner, John Koskinen, and even Hillary Clinton herself are guilty of federal crimes and belong in federal prison.

"Of course, if Hillary Clinton had won, we wouldn't be having this conversation. But Hillary lost and the Democrats made a foolish strategic error in pursuing charges of collusion and obstruction of justice based on sheer vengeance. There was no evidence of Trump collusion or obstruction and now the tables are turned. The investigation of Loretta Lynch and other revelations could be the undoing of the Obama administration's criminal enterprise, its trampling of our Constitution and our laws. Reopen the Hillary investigation and expand it to include the Clinton Foundation and Uranium One. Prosecute the lot of them – and lock them all up."

"Daniel John Sobieski is a freelance writer whose pieces have appeared in Investor's Business Daily, Human Events, Reason Magazine and the Chicago Sun-Times among other publications. http://www.americanthinker.com/articles/2017/06/obamas_criminal_enterprise_collapsing.html#ixzz4mXk3fPMt

XIV

CNN

I originally began this chapter with a copy of CNN's Standard Lobbyist Contract. Then I said, "nah!"

CNN is an asset of Turner Broadcasting Company, which is a unit of Time Warner. Jeff Zucker has been the President since 2013. Zucker believes there is a financial incentive for them to move right. He said that studies have repeatedly shown that Fox viewers are less informed than the rest of the country. [I wonder what studies he uses.]

However, Zucker's methods of going after Fox's viewers have backfired. Conservatives do not want to hear right wing stories and negativity about the President we just elected to office. And no we are not uninformed. We know more about what is going on in the world than all the snowflakes that are crying over the loss of the election, missing work or class so they can go out and protest pro-life or whatever George Soros is paying them to protest today.

The only information that the liberals and democrats receive is the fake news they receive on one of the socialist/communist news agencies that no longer report factual news. But apparently that is what they want to hear as they do not complain about the lies, nor do they bother to check the facts.

Time Warner presently has a merger pending with AT&T for $85 Billion. Trump is opposed to it as giving CNN too much network power.

Zucker says regardless of Mr. Trump's war on the network and what the President says is fake news, he is certain that CNN has the trust of the viewers.

Zucker says he wants "to tell different stories in different ways, and add to the news. We are not going to attract new viewers by just feeding CNN onto different platforms." http://pagesix.com/2017/06/19/jeff-zucker-viewers-trust-cnn-more-than-ever/

"In the past, he (Zucker) conceded, CNN has strayed to the left.

"I think it was a legitimate criticism of CNN that it was a little too liberal," he (Zucker) said.

"Since the start of the 2016 election, CNN's audience has nearly tripled in size, which is due largely to its wall-to-wall coverage of billionaire businessman Donald Trump."

"Three senior editorial staffers at CNN—a Pulitzer Prize winning editor, a Pulitzer Prize nominated reporter, and the head of the network's investigative reporting unit—resigned over a week ago as a result of an embarrassing retraction of a very fake news hit piece on President Donald Trump and his associates.

"CNN was forced to retract the faulty hit piece after a Breitbart News investigation discovered the entire piece was untrue. It falsely alleged that associates of President Trump—particularly SkyBridge Capital founder Anthony Scaramucci and Blackstone's Stephen Schwarzman—were under Treasury Department and Senate Intelligence Committee investigation for supposed ties to a Russian fund.

"It turns out that not only did the "meetings" that CNN alleged to have occurred never actually happen, but the Senate Intelligence Committee is not investigating it—and the Treasury Department already looked into the matter but found it to be entirely "without merit," per a senior administration official's comment to Breitbart News.

"CNN retracted the piece after Breitbart News's investigation—and under pressure from the threat of hefty a lawsuit from Scaramucci—and apologized to Scaramucci. CNN has not apologized to President Trump or to Stephen Schwarzman for maligning them, nor has the network apologized to anyone else falsely smeared in the now-retracted hit piece.

"A few days after the embarrassing retraction—reportedly the first of Zucker's tenure at the top of the network—the reporter on the byline, Thomas Frank, resigned, as did the story's editor Eric Lichtblau. Investigative unit chief Lex Haris also resigned.

"From there, the network has spiraled into chaos that has lasted nearly two weeks. The chaos is fueled by further mistakes: a lack of transparency from the network's public relations team and from Zucker, a refusal to course correct away from deep problems with journalistic integrity inside CNN, and by more damning revelations about CNN including from undercover videos of CNN producers and talent published by James O'Keefe's Project Veritas." http://www.breitbart. com/big-government/2017/07/05/while-cnn-burns-network-president-jeff-zucker-rushes-to-new-york-times-for-damage-control/

"Since the 2016 election, MSNBC, NBC, ABC, CBS, The Washington Post, The New York Times, Rolling Stone, Newsweek, Sky News, BBC News, Vice, BI, Time, USA Today, LA Times, Politico and Buzz Feed are Media Outlets that promote fake news. They focus more on alternatives to the truth.

"Mick West, in debunking one of CNN's broadcasts where they are at the Dhrahran International Hotel next to the airport, said the following about CNN: "So what." If it turns out that this was a fake set done as a way to provide coverage without actually sending reporters into harm's way, then so what? What harm is there in that? The problem is that this sets a precedence that it's OK for the media to lie. There's also no logical reason for CNN faking their news reporter being on site in the Gulf. The only logical reason for why CNN would do this is because they in general do not report the news as it occurs but instead produce infotainment as an alternative for the masses in the US. Why? So as to condition the public to accept alternatives to the truth. " https://www.metabunk.org/debunked-cnns-fake-news-broadcasts-charles-jaco-and-the-fake-live-gulf-war-reports.t1140/

XV

MEDIA AND GEORGE SOROS

I t is sort of a disease when you consider yourself some kind of god, the creator of everything, but I feel comfortable about it now since I began to live it out. ~ George Soros, June 3, 1993

Tom Brokaw-George Soros-ACORN Connection

Posted 18/10/2008 by sfcmac in Leftist moonbats, Politics, The Media.

Two Degrees of Separation:

"Meet the Press" interim moderator Tom Brokaw sits on the board of a liberal foundation that has given radical left-wing group ACORN $821,000 and that in turn is funded by liberal uber-donor George Soros, research reveals.

"Conservatives have long considered Brokaw's political views to be somewhere on the left, but these revelations raise new questions about the former NBC News anchor's objectivity.

"Here are the facts. Brokaw sits on the board of the Robin Hood Foundation, a charity that, according to its website, targets poverty in New York City by applying "sound investment principles to philanthropy."

"The foundation awarded ACORN a $456,000 grant in 2003 and a $365,000 grant in 2004. Brokaw does not appear to have played a role in the grants because he didn't become a member of the board until

2005 according to the guidestar.org database, but these are nevertheless the left-wing circles in which he travels.

"The Soros Fund Charitable Foundation, as in George Soros, a major bankroller of the left, gave the Robin Hood Foundation a $9,859,453 community development grant in 2000. The Robin Hood board includes Marian Wright Edelman, president of one of Hillary Clinton's favorite activist groups, the Children's Defense Fund. Hollywood movie mogul Harvey Weinstein and actress Gwyneth Paltrow are also members of the board. As of Dec. 31, 2006, the Robin Hood Foundation had assets of $288,520,098 and income of $159,688,394 (source: guidestar.org). Brokaw has given at least $75,000 to the foundation. (source: "The Emperors of Benevolence," New York Magazine, November 5, 2007) (This post is based on a Capital Research Center blog post.)"

http://www.examiner.com/r-2920389-FLASH__Tom_Brokaw_Involved_in_Soros_Funded_

"On April 8, House Democratic leader Nancy Pelosi headlined a Boston conference on ''media reform." She was joined by four other congressmen, a senator, two FCC commissioners, a Nobel laureate and numerous liberal journalists.

"The 2,500-person event was sponsored by a group called Free Press, one of more than 180 different media-related organizations that receives money from liberal billionaire George Soros.

Soros, who first made a name for himself in investing and currency trading, now makes his name in politics and policy. Since the 2004 election, the controversial financier has used his influence and billions to push a laundry list of left-wing causes. Pick an issue and his Open Society Foundations likely fund the liberal position - pro-abortion, pro-illegal immigration, pro-national health care, pro-drug legalization, pro-Big Government, anti-Israel and, ultimately, anti-America.

"He spent $27 million trying to defeat President Bush just in 2004. That was a drop in the bucket compared to the $8 billion he has donated just to his Open Society Foundations. Soros followed that presidential failure by earning the well-deserved reputation as one of the top liberal contributors. Soon after the election, ''Soros headlined a meeting of 70 millionaires and billionaires in Scottsdale, Ariz., to discuss how to grow the left's ideological assets," explained the Aug. 18, 2005, Christian Science Monitor.

"He continued to lead after the meeting was finished. Through his foundation network, Soros has helped numerous left-wing operations either be born or grow. Many of those are either associated with the media - such as Free Press which pushes for media regulation and government-funded journalism - or have media components to their operation.

"That has given Soros far more influence than even many of his harshest critics realize. He has managed to insinuate himself and his money into the media culture, making connections with the nation's top publishing organizations. He has direct ties to more than 30 mainstream news outlets - including The New York Times, Washington Post, the Associated Press, CNN and ABC. Each one of those operations has employees, often high-level ones, on the boards of Soros-funded media operations.

"It's a connection hard to deny. But Soros does so, blaming the claim on Fox News. ''Another trick is to accuse your opponent of the behavior of which you are guilty, like Fox News accusing me of being the puppet master of a media empire," wrote Soros in the introduction to the new book ''The Philanthropy of George Soros." That book was written by former New York Times reporter Chuck Sudetic who now works for Soros' Open Society Foundations. It is the second such Soros promotional book written by a Times staffer.

"Ties That Bind: Soros and the Top Media Outlets

"When Soros gave $1.8 million to National Public Radio, it became part of the firestorm of controversy that jeopardized NPR's federal funding. That gift only hinted at the widespread influence the controversial billionaire has on the mainstream media. Soros has ties to more than 30 mainstream news outlets.

"Prominent journalists like ABC's Christiane Amanpour and former Washington Post editor and now Vice President Len Downie serve on boards of operations that take Soros cash. This despite the Society of Professional Journalists' ethical code stating: ''avoid all conflicts real or perceived."

"The investigative reporting start-up ProPublica is a prime example. ProPublica, which recently wn its second Pulitzer Prize, initially was given millions of dollars from the Sandler Foundation to ''strengthen the progressive infrastructure" - ''progressive" being code for very liberal.

"In 2010, it also received a two-year contribution of $125,000 each year from the Open Society Foundations. Open Society is Soros' primary foundation and uses the web address www.soros.org. It is a network of more than 30 international foundations, mostly funded by Soros, who has contributed more than $8 billion.

"ProPublica stories are thoroughly researched by top-notch staffers who used to work at some of the biggest news outlets in the nation. But the topics are almost laughably left-wing. The site's proud list of "Our Investigations" includes attacks on oil companies, gas companies, the health care industry, for-profit schools and more. More than 100 stories on the latest lefty cause: opposition to drilling for natural gas by hydraulic fracking. Another 100 on the evils of the foreclosure industry.

"Investigations making the military look bad and one about prisoners at Guantanamo Bay add up to almost the perfect journalism fantasy - a huge budget, lots of major media partners and a liberal agenda unconstrained by advertising.

"The operation has one more thing: a 14-person Journalism Advisory Board, stacked with CNN's David Gergen and representatives from top newspapers, a former publisher of The Wall Street Journal and the editor-in-chief of Simon & Schuster. Several are working journalists, including:

Jill Abramson - New executive editor of The New York Times;

Kerry Smith - The senior vice president for editorial quality of ABC News;

Cynthia A. Tucker - The editor of the editorial page of The Atlanta Journal-Constitution.

ProPublica is far from the only Soros-funded organization that is stacked with members of the supposedly neutral press.

The Center for Public Integrity is another great example. Its board of directors is filled with working journalists like Amanpour from ABC, right alongside blatant liberal media members like Arianna Huffington, of the Huffington Post and now AOL.

"Like ProPublica, the CPI board is a veritable Who's Who of journalism and top media organizations, including:

"Christiane Amanpour - Anchor of ABC's Sunday morning political affairs program, "This Week with Christiane Amanpour." A reliable lefty, she has called tax cuts "giveaways," the Tea Party "extreme," and Obama "very Reaganesque;"

"Matt Thompson - Editorial product manager at National Public Radio and an adjunct faculty member at the prominent Poynter Institute.

The group's Advisory Council features:

"Ben Sherwood - ABC News president and former "Good Morning America" executive producer;

"Kathleen Hall Jamieson - Author and the Walter H. Annenberg Dean of the Annenberg School for Communication of the University of Pennsylvania;

"Michele Norris - Host of NPR's newsmagazine "All Things Considered," public radio's longest-running national program.

"Once again, like ProPublica, the Center for Public Integrity's investigations are mostly liberal - attacks on the coal industry, payday loans and conservatives like Mississippi Gov. Haley Barbour. The center is also more open about its politics, including a detailed investigation into conservative funders David and Charles Koch and their "web of influence." According to the center's own 990 tax forms, the Open Society Institute gave it $651,650 in 2009 alone.

"The well-known Center for Investigative Reporting follows the same template - important journalists on the board and a liberal editorial agenda. Both the board of directors and the advisory board contain journalists from major news outlets. The board features:

Phil Bronstein, director of content development and editor-at-large for Hearst Newspapers;

David Boardman, The Seattle Times;

Len Downie, former Executive Editor of the Washington Post, now VP;

George Osterkamp, CBS News producer.

"Readers of the site are greeted with numerous stories on climate change, illegal immigration and the evils of big companies. It counts among its media partners The Washington Post, Salon, CNN and ABC News. CIR received close to $1 million from Open Society from 2003 to 2009.

"Why does it all matter? Journalists constantly claim to be neutral in their reporting. In almost the same breath, many bemoan the influence of money in politics. It is a maxim of both the left and many in the media that conservatives are bought and paid for by business interests. Yet where are the concerns about where their money comes from?

"Fred Brown, who recently revised the book "Journalism Ethics: A Casebook of Professional Conduct for News Media," argues journalists need to be "transparent" about their connections and "be up front about your relationship" with those who fund you.

"Unfortunately, that rarely happens. While the nonprofits list who sits on their boards, the news outlets they work for make little or no effort to connect those dots. Amanpour's biography page, for instance, talks about her lengthy career, her time at CNN and her many awards. It makes no mention of her affiliation with the Center for Public Integrity.

"$52 Million for Media Is Just the Beginning

"It's a scene journalists dream about - a group of coworkers toasting a Pulitzer Prize. For the team at investigative start-up ProPublica, it was the second time their fellow professionals recognized their work for journalism's top honor.

"For George Soros and ProPublica's other liberal backers, it was again proof that a strategy of funding journalism was a powerful way to influence the American public.

"It's a strategy that Soros has been deploying extensively in media both in the United States and abroad. Since 2003, Soros has spent more than $52 million funding media properties, including the infrastructure of news - journalism schools, investigative journalism and even industry organizations.

"And that number is an understatement. It is gleaned from tax forms, news stories and reporting. But Soros funds foundations that fund other foundations in turn, like the Tides Foundation, which then make their own donations. A complete accounting is almost impossible because a media component is part of so many Soros-funded operations.

"It turns out that Soros' influence doesn't just include connections to top mainstream news organizations such as NBC, ABC, The New York Times and Washington Post. It's bought him connections to the underpinnings of the news business. The Columbia Journalism Review, which bills itself as ''a watchdog and a friend of the press in all its forms," lists several investigative reporting projects funded by one of Soros' foundations.

"The ''News Frontier Database" includes seven different investigative reporting projects funded by Soros' Open Society Institute. Along with ProPublica, there are the Center for Public Integrity, the Center for Investigative Reporting and New Orleans' The Lens. The Columbia School of Journalism, which operates CJR, has received at least $600,000 from Soros, as well.

"Imagine if conservative media punching bags David and Charles Koch had this many connections to journalists. Even if the Kochs could find journalists willing to support conservative media, they would be skewered by the left.

"For Soros, it's news, but nothing new. As one of the world's richest men (No. 46 on Forbes' list), he gets to indulge his dreams. Since those dreams seem to involve controlling media from the ground up, Soros naturally started supporting Columbia University's School of Journalism. Columbia is headed by President Lee Bollinger, who also sits on the Pulitzer Prize board and the board of directors of The Washington Post.

"Bollinger, like some of Soros' other funding recipients, is pushing for journalism to find a new sugar daddy or at least an uncle - Uncle Sam. Bollinger wrote in his book "Uninhibited, Robust, and Wide-Open: A Free Press for a New Century" that government should fund media. A 2009 study by Columbia's journalism program came to the same conclusion, calling for "a national fund for local news."

"Conveniently, Len Downie, the lead author of that piece, is on both the Post's board and the board of the Center for Investigative Reporting, also funded by Soros.

"Soros funds more than just the most famous journalism school in the nation. There are journalism industry associations like:

The National Federation of Community Broadcasters;

The National Association of Hispanic Journalists;

And the Committee to Protect Journalists.

"Readers unhappy with Soros' media influence might be tempted to voice concerns to the Organization of News Ombudsmen - a professional group devoted to "monitoring accuracy, fairness and balance." Perhaps they might consider a direct complaint to PBS's Michael Getler, a director of the organization. Unfortunately, that group is also funded by Soros. At the bottom of the Organization of News Ombudsmen's website front page is the line: "Supported by the Open Society Institute," a Soros foundation. It is the only organization so listed.

The group's membership page lists 57 members from around globe and features:

Deirdre Edgar, readers' representative of The Los Angeles Times;

Brent Jones, standards editor, USA Today;

Kelly McBride, ombudsman, ESPN;

Patrick Pexton, ombudsman, The Washington Post.

"The site doesn't address whether the OSI money creates a conflict of interest. But then, who could readers complain to anyway?

"There's more. The Open Society Institute is one of several foundations funding the Investigative News Network (INN), a collaboration of 53 non-profit news organizations producing what they claim is "non-partisan investigative news." The James L. Knight Foundation also backs the network and is possibly the most-well-known journalism foundation. Knight President and CEO Alberto Ibargüen is on the board of directors for ProPublica.

"INN includes the Investigative Reporting Workshop at American University, the liberal web start-up MinnPost, National Institute for Computer-Assisted Reporting, National Public Radio, and the Wisconsin Center for Investigative Journalism. The network had included the liberal Huffington Post investigative operation among its grants, but HuffPo investigations merged with the possibly even more left-wing Center for Public Integrity, on whose board Arianna Huffington sits. INN hasn't posted its tax forms yet, but in the meantime "the Center for Public Integrity is graciously acting as our fiscal agent."

"Liberal academic programs, left-wing investigative journalism and even supposedly neutral news organizations all paid for by a man who spends tens of millions of dollars openly attacking the right. George Soros is teaching journalists that their industry has a future as long as he opens his wallet.

"Soros' Lifelong Fascination with Journalism

"Media has long been one of the billionaire's interests. According to "Soros: The Life and Times of a Messianic Billionaire," he has been fascinated by media from when he was a boy where early career interests included "history or journalism or some form of writing." He served as "editor-in-chief, publisher, and news vendor of" his own paper, "The Lupa News" and wrote a wall newspaper in his native Hungary before leaving, wrote author Michael T. Kaufman, a 40-year New York Times veteran. The Communist Party "encouraged" such papers.

"But journalists weren't always interested in Soros. He avoided any form of publicity until 1981 when he was subject of a cover story in Institutional Investor called "The World's Greatest Money Manager."

Even in 1983 when he remarried, The New York Times refused to carry the wedding announcement. They were "nobodies." All that changed when he made $1 billion speculating on the British pound. His profile rose a great deal. He was also criticized in the British tabloids including the Daily Mail in 1992 when he was sued by former house staff in England.

"In subsequent years, the Soros connection to journalism has reached all facets of his empire - charity, politics and financial transactions. It might be as sweeping as investments in old media like Times Mirror, new media like AOL or charitable giving like NPR. Or it might be the global reach of Open Society funding journalistic events, awards, grants and travel. Former Times foreign correspondent Michael T. Kaufman, who was later the author of "Soros: The Life and Times of a Messianic Billionaire," discovered Soros had "paid for airfare" for a European speaking engagement. He hadn't even known Soros was funding that trip.

"Now, Soros underwrites journalists, blogs, books, news outlets, TV and radio stations, online operations, start-ups and investigative journalism. The list of media outlets that Soros has helped support reads like a Who's Who of the left. From 2003 to 2009, OSI gave $52 million to roughly 180 media organizations, including the National Federation of Community Broadcasters and the National Association of Hispanic Journalists.

"A Worldwide Media Powerhouse

"The Soros media empire truly spans the globe, but few even realize it because it's decentralized under numerous organizations, funded in turn by more than 30 Open Society Foundations.

"Back in 1997, then-Times writer Judith Miller said much of his charity was focused on the media. "For the past decade, George Soros, the Hungarian-born financier and philanthropist, has spent more than a billion dollars promoting a free press and political pluralism abroad," she wrote.

"The donations have climbed to $8 billion, but he certainly has continued promoting the press, giving himself global influence in the process. Soros has financed bloggers, journalist travel or education, TV shows, Internet start-ups, investigative journalism and even blogs.

"As early as 1994, that empire included "40 independent radio and television stations and publications" just in Eastern Europe, according to the March 10, 1994 Jerusalem Report. At the same time, Soros was backing a post-Communist publication called Transitions, but pulled the plug on it in 1999, according to The New York Times.

"In 1998, Soros was spending money on Russian media. The Oct. 11, 1998 Times explained that "Soros gave $10 million toward an $80 million fund he plans to create to help struggling, independent news organizations in Russia ride out the severe economic downturn in that country.""

"Soros also made investments in Viacom, College Sports TV, journalism awards even backing events at the Frontline Club in London, what the Times called "a popular way station for war correspondents.""

"The charity work is almost impossible to track, but wherever the Open Society Foundations are, their involvement with journalism is not far behind. The foundation has an entire initiative devoted to the media. Its purported goal is "to promote independent and viable media and professional, quality journalism in countries undergoing a process of democratization and building functioning media markets." The site lists 15 different media program coordinators in nations from Afghanistan to the Ukraine.

"In one of its bigger efforts, OSI funded B-92, the Yugoslavia radio network that "urged young Serbs to avoid the draft" and spoke out against the war in Bosnia and Herzegovina. But many operations are smaller. Journalists are chosen to study at Central European University, also funded by Soros. The foundations back the Czech newspaper Lidove Noviny or the Kabul Weekly in Afghanistan.

"Soros-Funded Left-Wing Media Reach More Than 300 Million People Every Month

"The global reach of the Soros media empire means it reaches millions of people. From nakedly partisan left-wing media like Think Progress, the blog for the Center for American Progress, and a TV show on MSNBC (recently canceled), to the supposedly impartial National Public Radio, Soros has impact on the flow of information worldwide.

"It gives him incredible influence. Every month, reporters, writers and bloggers at the many outlets he funds easily reach more than 330 million people around the globe. The U.S. Census estimates the population of the entire United States to be just less than 310 million.

"That's roughly the entire population of the United States with the population of Australia thrown in for good measure - every single month.

"Just counting 13 prominent operations of the 180 media organizations he has funded equals 332 million people each month. Included in that total are big players like NPR, which received $1.8 million from Soros, as well as the little known Project Syndicate and Public News Service, both of which also claim to reach millions of readers.

"And that's really just the beginning. That tally takes into account only a few of the bigger Soros-funded media operations. Many numbers simply aren't available. "Democracy Now!" - "a daily TV/radio news program, hosted by Amy Goodman and Juan Gonzalez" - is known for its left-wing take on global news. Its vitriol ranges from attacks on Blackwater founder Erik Prince and supporters of Andrew Breitbart (whom it calls "Electronic Brownshirts"), to claims the U.S. is opposed to Arab democracy. Just that one Soros-funded operation is heard "on over 900 stations, pioneering the largest community media collaboration in the United States." But it posts no formal audience numbers. Phone calls to "Democracy Now!" were not returned.

"But Soros wildly understates his own impact. It might be through a "media reform" conference with congressmen, a senator, two FCC commissioners, a Nobel laureate and numerous liberal journalists. Or it might be through a radio station in Haiti, which he also supports.

"The media reform event was sponsored by a group called Free Press, which has received $1.4 million from Soros. Free Press has two major agenda items - undermining Internet freedom by pushing so-called "net neutrality," and advocating for government-funded media to the tune of $35 billion a year.

"Many of those attending or speaking were affiliated with Soros-funded operations.

"Free Press is just one of the better funded Soros groups. They also include the Center for American Progress ($7.3 million), which operates the heavily staffed Think Progress blog. That blog "now has 30 writers and researchers," according to Politico. Other well-funded operations include the investigative reporting operations at the Center for Public Integrity ($3.7 million) and Center for Investigative Reporting ($1.1 million), as well as Media Matters ($1.1 million) and the Sundance Institute ($1 million).

"That's not all. "Soros' foundations gave 34 grants from 1997 to 2010 to local NPR member stations and specific programs that have totaled nearly $3.4-million, said the foundations' [spokesperson Maria] Archuleta. Recipients included WNYC and Minnesota Public Radio," wrote now former NPR ombudsman Alicia Shepard.

"In fact, Soros funds nearly every major left-wing media source in the United States. Forty-five of those are financed through his support of the Media Consortium. That organization "is a network of the country's leading, progressive, independent media outlets." The list is predictable - everything from Alternet to the Young Turks, who have since lost their MSNBC show.

"A report by the Media Consortium detailed how progressives had created an "echo chamber" of outlets "in which a message pushes the larger public or the mainstream media to acknowledge, respond, and give airtime to progressive ideas because it is repeated many times." According to the report called "The Big Thaw," "if done well, the message within the echo chamber can become the accepted meme, impact political dynamics, shift public opinion and change public policy."

"That mindset plays out in much of what the consortium's members do. Alternet describes itself as an "award-winning news magazine and online community that creates original journalism and amplifies the best of hundreds of other independent media sources." It hates Tea Parties and complains about "hatemongering" as the "ugly side of Evangelical Christianity." Each month, the site gets 1.5 million unique visitors to its unique view of the world.

"Brave New Films, also funded by the Media Consortium, is run by the same people who run Brave New Foundation. Robert Greenwald and Jim Miller produce and distribute videos attacking businesses and conservatives. The site brags about a 2008 election video "that exposes John McCain's double talk, for instance, and received 9 million views around the world." Their latest effort is yet another attack on Koch Industries, attempting to halt a much-needed pipeline from the Canada to the U.S.

"Then there's the Young Turks and MSNBC host Cenk Uygur. In 2010, he was welcomed to the network with a press release detailing his web impact. "One of YouTube's Top 100 Partners, the irreverent talk show averages over 18 million views per month and has over 320 million views overall on its YouTube Channel."

"The list goes on and on. Project Syndicate calls itself "the world's pre-eminent source of original op-ed commentaries." It has wide reach.

"As of May 2011, Project Syndicate membership included 462 leading newspapers in 150 countries." Its monthly circulation is 72,815,528. Naturally, "support comes from the Open Society Institute," the primary Soros foundation.

"Project Syndicate's columnist line-up, spread to 462 newspapers, is impressively left-leaning or globalist: UN Secretary General Ban Ki-moon, former President Jimmy Carter, former Soviet President Mikhail Gorbachev, as well as lefty economists Jeffrey Sachs and Nobel Prize winner Joseph Stiglitz.

"Public News Service describes itself as "a member-supported news service that advocates journalism in the public interest." It is a "network of state-based news services' in 33 states. It claims it reaches 'a combined national weekly audience of 24 million." PNS is proud of its 2010 success. "Last year the Public News Service produced over 4,000 stories featuring public interest content that were redistributed several hundred thousand times on 6,114 radio stations, 928 print outlets, 133 TV stations and 100s of websites. Nationally, an average of 60 outlets used each story."

"Nearly 30 Soros-funded Media Operations Part of 'War on Fox'

"To hear the left tell it, Fox News has a "history of inciting Islamophobia and racial and ethic animosity" and tries to "race bait its viewers." One staffer is called a "hit man," while his network is accused of "attack politics." A highly questionable study is hyped by numerous outlets claiming that it "confirms that Fox News makes you stupid." Fox is called simply: "The Liars' Network."

"Sure, liberals have it in for Fox News, but that deep-seated, anti-Fox agenda isn't just an organic response from the left. It's a George Soros-funded "echo chamber" "in which a message pushes the larger public or the mainstream media to acknowledge, respond, and give airtime to progressive ideas because it is repeated many times."

"The goal is "Taking Down Fox News," as "Mother Jones," a member of the Media Consortium, described it in a headline. That article, about another Soros-funded operation called Color of Change, explained how "it successfully urged several advertisers, including Best Buy, Wal-Mart, and RadioShack, to pull their ads from Beck's show." Liberals even threw a party to celebrate Beck's departure from Fox News, "drawing hundreds of activists, journalists and political strategists from the nation's capital," according to the Huffington Post.

"It was all part of an organized effort against Fox. In all, nearly 30 organizations have attacked Fox News in the six months since the beginning of December, 2010.

"Think Progress, the heavily Soros-funded blog for the Center for American Progress, slammed Fox more than 30 times in six months. AlterNet, an especially unhinged liberal outlet, went after the network at least 18 times in those months. It is one of 45 organizations aided by Soros' support of the Media Consortium ''a network of the country's leading, progressive, independent media outlets.''

"These outlets are all part of Soros' web of media organizations that mirror his view of Fox as their enemy. That's the way he describes it in the new book, ''The Philanthropy of George Soros.'' ''Those in charge of Fox News, Rupert Murdoch and Roger Ailes, have done well in identifying me as their adversary,'' he wrote. ''They have done less well in the methods they used to attack me: Their lies shall not stand and their techniques shall not endure.''

"That anti-Fox agenda is reflected in plans by another group in Soros' pocket to target the network specifically. Media Matters founder David Brock said his Soros-funded operation ($1.1 million) will ''focus on [News Corp. CEO Rupert] Murdoch and trying to disrupt his commercial interests.''

"The left hating Fox isn't new. But the efforts of the different groups take on an amazing similarity. Take the University of Maryland study that seemed so critical of Fox News. The study itself included this nugget: ''This suggests that misinformation cannot simply be attributed to news sources, but are part of the larger information environment that includes statements by candidates, political ads and so on.'' That didn't stop any of the groups from using it against Fox News. AlterNet, Washington Monthly, Think Progress and The Nation. It quickly moved into the mainstream media from there.

"That's just part of Soros' influence. In the case of Robert Greenwald, he's turned attacking Fox into a mini-industry. Greenwald is founder and president of Brave New Films, also part of the Soros-funded Media Consortium. Greenwald was also behind ''OUTFOXED: Rupert Murdoch's War on Journalism,'' The site for the movie that argues: ''FOX News is on a witch hunt. Fight back.'' The Brave New Films site has an entire section going after Fox called: ''When Fox Attacks.'' It claims: ''Videos from this campaign have been viewed over 8 million times.''

"When Soros was criticized by Fox, multiple pieces of the Soros Empire responded. In one case, Jonathan Schell, a fellow at The Nation Institute, another part of the Media Consortium, made Fox News out to be anti-Semitic for criticizing Soros. An opinion piece titled, "The Protocols of Rupert Murdoch," a reference to the infamous anti-Semitic "Protocols of The Elders of Zion," blasted Glenn Beck.

"Schell claimed Beck's criticism of "the financier and philanthropist George Soros" in effect "recycles, almost in carbon copy, the tropes of the most virulent anti-Semitic ideologues." The column was distributed by another Soros-funded entity, Project Syndicate, which reaches "462 leading newspapers in 150 countries," with a monthly circulation of 72,815,528.

"It's that sort of cooperation that makes the Soros-funded "echo chamber" successful. Go on AlterNet and find articles from The Nation, a rant by Robert Greenwald or an interview by Amy Goodman of Democracy Now! Or go on New America Media's site and find an article from Color Lines.

"The content from the 180 media sites that Soros helps support can be linked, cited or reposted, adding to the sense that there is strong interest in any particular "progressive idea." It's just one more way George Soros influences the media.

"Conclusion

"George Soros is one of the most influential men in the world - in finance, in charity and, yes, in the media. Yet piecing together that influence is difficult because the media are so incurious about his actions.

"When journalists become convinced an outlet is conservative, as they are with Fox News, they become enraged. Stories attacking Fox litter the media landscape. But an extensive and well-funded network of liberal media outlets with deep ties to mainstream news results in almost no coverage.

"That's both unbelievable and unprofessional. Any individual funding more than 180 media outlets, with ties to dozens more through secondary sources, boards and the like, is the very definition of news.

"But journalists don't want to report this story. To do so would mean they would have to be honest about the nature of the profession. They would have to admit:

"Reporters and editors often jump from activist liberal media outlets to mainstream organizations and back again;

"Many of the new journalism start-ups celebrated by the industry from ProPublica to Huffington Post to dozens of investigative journalism operations are all part of a growing liberal news network;

"Prominent journalists at the top outlets in the United States are affiliated with left-wing media outlets and see nothing wrong with such ties.

"The whole infrastructure of journalism - education, industry organizations and news organizations - is intertwined with liberal media outlets. Conservative media organizations have no such ties.

"Any one of these points proves the argument conservatives have long made - that the mainstream media are liberal from top to bottom. Journalists know this and, as their ties to liberal news organizations show, they just don't care.

"Recommendations

"The Business & Media Institute has some recommendations for the media to better handle their obvious conflicts of interest when it comes to Soros:

"Just Say No to Soros Cash: No purportedly ''objective'' journalist should serve on a board or advise any outlet that is financed by Soros. If academics do so, they should be open about their affiliations. But working journalists like Downie, Amanpour and Abramson should divorce themselves from the conflict.

"Question Motivations of News Sources: Reporters and editors should be aware when a story is being deliberately hyped by a network of linked organizations. Such times should always have reporters questioning not just the motives, but the facts of the case - whether it's on the right or the left.

"Spend Time Investigating the Left: Journalists have no trouble finding incentive to do detailed analysis of conservatives, but spend little time questioning the motives or funding of liberal organizations. Reporters should do a more detailed investigation into the Open Society Foundations and their influence throughout the media."

http://www.mrc.org/special-reports/george-soros-media-mogul

"Five major banks agreed to plead guilty to criminal charges brought by the U.S. Department of Justice for manipulating the exchange rates of U.S. dollars and euros. The banks were Citicorp, J.P. Morgan Chase, Barclays, Bank of America, and the Royal Bank of Scotland. A sixth bank, UBS Group, agreed to plead guilty to manipulating interest rates after the Justice Department granted it immunity on the exchange rate criminal charges. The banks will pay an estimated $5.8 billion in fines to the United States. However, only corporations were charged criminally. Not one individual banking executive was indicted in the currency manipulation scam.

"The reason for no personal indictments is simple. George Soros, the man who opened up his checkbook in 2008 and 2012 for Barack Obama's presidential campaign and is estimated to have poured millions of dollars into Obama's coffers, made his hundreds of billions of dollars primarily from the same type of international currency manipulation that landed the five banks into trouble. Had Attorney General Loretta Lynch sought indictments against banking executives, any defense lawyer worth his or her salt would have brought up the fact that Soros, Obama's "money bags", had evaded prosecution for the very same crimes for decades. The cries of uneven application of the law would have been shouted from defense tables at U.S. court houses around the United States.

"Soros's currency manipulation scheming saw its heyday during the Asian financial crisis of the late 1990s. It was during a time when Soros's friend, Bill Clinton, occupied the White House. Although Soros's currency exchange scams rocked stock exchanges around the Pacific Rim, there was no attempt by Clinton's Justice Department to indict Soros, an emigré from Hungary, to justice. One of the worst-hit countries from Soros's currency manipulation was Malaysia, which saw its ringgit plummet in value. Malaysian Prime Minister Mahathir Mohamed thundered that Soros was part of an international Jewish bankers' conspiracy to attack the Malaysian economy. Mohamed said, "We do not want to say that this is a plot by the Jews, but in reality it is a Jew who triggered the currency plunge, and coincidentally Soros is a Jew." Mohamed was condemned for "anti-Semitic" remarks but he was not the only leader to charge Soros with the very same currency speculation that recently landed the "Big 6" banks into criminal trouble. Soros's short-selling the Thai baht resulted in the government of Prime Minister Chavalit Yongchaiyudh calling Soros an "economic war criminal."

"In 1992, Soros dumped £10 billion based on insider information that the pound would be devalued after Britain's withdrawal from the European Exchange Rate Mechanism. Soros became known as "the Man who broke the Bank of England." Soros's attack on pound sterling caused the Chancellor of the Exchequer, Norman Lamont, to borrow £15 billion with an overall cost to Her Majesty's Treasury of £3.4 billion. A few years earlier, in 1988, Soros was convicted of insider trading by the French Bourse regulatory authority. Soros had enough insider information that it enabled him to buy sizable chunks of the shares of four major French companies: Société Générale, Indo-Suez Bank, Paribas, and the Compagnie Générale d'Électricité. Soros's conviction on insider trading was upheld by the European Court of Human Rights in 2006 and the multi-billionaire's appeal of its earlier decision was rejected in 2011.

"Soros's influence not only extends over the Justice Department's decision not to prosecute individual bankers for currency manipulation but also Obama's foreign policy. Soros's Open Society Institute and Foundation, as well as his generous gift, some would say bribe, of $100 million to Human Rights Watch and his sponsorship, along with the U.S. Agency for International Development (USAID)-funded National Endowment for Democracy (NED), of a number of Eastern and Central European front organizations has given the global hedge fund tycoon an inordinate amount of influence over U.S. foreign policy. Soros's fingerprints on manipulation of political parties, media organizations and web sites, "civil society" groups, and governments, sometimes accomplished in league with Radio Free Europe/Radio Liberty, the operations of which Soros inherited from the Central Intelligence Agency, can be seen in "color revolutions" from Georgia and Ukraine to Macedonia and Serbia.

"Soros has supported the independence of Kosovo, the U.S. and NATO protectorate that recently launched terrorist attacks on neighboring Macedonia from its soil. Kosovo and its U.S. military base at Camp Bondsteel serve as logistics points for the allegedly banned Kosovo Liberation Army (KLA), of which Kosovo Foreign Minister Hashim Thaci was once the chief, to attempt to stir up ethnic Albanians who are working with the Soros-funded opposition to overthrow the government of Prime Minister Nikola Gruevski.

"The United States, perhaps representing the interests of Soros and his cabal of "democracy manipulators", was quiet as Macedonia discovered U.S. passports among the dead KLA terrorists found after their foray from Kosovo into the Macedonian town of Kumanovo. The recent attempt to force a revolution in Macedonia was not without the familiar Soros "theme." As anti-government protesters teemed through the central square of Skopje, a female employee of the Soros-financed Helsinki Committee for Human Rights in Macedonia applied a heavy amount of red lipstick on herself and then proceeded to plant a kiss on the riot shield of a policeman. The attempt to stage a Kiev-like "Maidan Revolution" in Skopje became known as the "Lipstick Revolution" as Soros-financed media transmitted the photograph of the kiss imprint to web sites and news organizations around the world. In every case where the Soros organization engages in "democracy manipulation", the Obama-appointed U.S. ambassadors are willing accomplices. This was the case in Kiev with Ambassador Geoffrey Pyatt – and his boss and friend Victoria Nuland, the chief of the State Department's Europe/Eurasia bureau — in Skopje with Ambassador Jess Baily, and in a number of other countries, from Algeria to Zimbabwe and Mongolia to Moldova.

"Soros is a supporter of U.S. and European Union economic sanctions on Russia. However, Soros is also a keen manipulator of economic crises and he has taken advantage of artificial crisis brought about by Western sanctions against Russia to make money on investments designed to bypass Russian gas pipeline projects, such as the Turkish Stream project that is to bring gas from Russia to Turkey, Greece, Macedonia, Serbia, and Hungary. Soros's financial support for the "Lipstick revolutionaries" in Macedonia is a clear attempt to dislodge that country from the Turkish Stream deal. Meanwhile, Soros and his close friend and business associate, Nathaniel Rothschild, have virtually purchased the nation of Montenegro, which, along with Croatia, are being dangled as alternate source of gas from U.S. tankers distributing it from new offshore gas terminals to be built in the Adriatic Sea. Oil and gas exploration companies, in which Soros has vested interests, are drilling in pristine Montenegro and Croatian waters. With Mr. Soros, the so-called defender of freedom, liberty, and the environment, comes phony staged revolutions, inter-ethnic bloodshed and civil wars, and the specter of off-shore platforms, fossil fuel marine terminals, supertankers polluting idyllic maritime regions, from the Adriatic coast to the Gulf of Mexico and the Alaskan Arctic North to Alberta prairies.

"Soros's domination of the Obama administration can be seen in Obama's selections for not only Cabinet-level positions but, more importantly, in the secondary and tertiary levels of government where policy is produced. It is at these levels where Soros's minions concoct foreign, economic, and defense policies that are indistinguishable from those of Soros. However, the Justice Department dared not indict individual bankers for currency manipulation. Had it done so, it would have also had to indict its true master, Mr. Soros."

https://www.infowars.com/does-george-soros-control-the-obama-white-house/

Journalists Exposed on the U.N. Payroll; George Soros, Ted Turner Pay for Journalism Prizes by Cliff Kincaid on February 15, 2005

"When conservative commentator Armstrong Williams was exposed for taking money from the Bush administration, his credibility was cast into doubt and news organizations expressed regrets for having had him on the air to comment on public policy issues. Williams was tainted by a conflict of interest that should have been revealed to the viewing audience. He was said to be a channel for Bush administration propaganda.

"What about U.N. propaganda? It turns out that another Williams, Ian Williams of The Nation magazine, has been on the United Nations payroll, writing articles for the world body and even coaching U.N. officials on how to deal with the press. His financial connection to the U.N. hasn't been entirely concealed (some general information about the relationship is available on his personal website), but it has not been publicly disclosed in connection with his media appearances over the years. The amount of money he has received from the world body is still being closely guarded.

"As the U.N. correspondent for The Nation magazine, Williams has commented on U.N. affairs on ABC, CBC, CNN, BBC, ITN, CNBC, MSNBC and Fox News.

"But Williams is not alone in accepting U.N. payments. Accuracy in Media has learned that the U.N. has been paying journalists here and abroad to spread the U.N. message to an American and international audience.

The Deal

"Williams, a prominent member and past president of the U.N. Correspondents Association (UNCA), advertises himself as someone who "has been on both sides of the camera." His website states that,

"For the last five years, he has played a significant role in training UNDP Resident Representatives and UN reps in media handling, both at HQ [headquarters] and overseas, with a particular emphasis on coaching for interview techniques. The UN's training section also called upon him to help with training senior officials at HQ." UNDP is the U.N. Development Program, a major U.N. agency.

"He is also "a frequent lecturer on the UN and the media at various venues," including the Columbia School of Journalism and the United Nations University.

"Williams strongly insists that his financial relationship with the U.N. does not compromise his role as an independent and objective news professional.

"U.N. correspondents contacted by AIM disagreed, with one saying, "How can you objectively cover an organization while you're taking money from that organization?" Another flatly declared that UNCA and its prominent members were "in bed" with the U.N. "Most of them are pro-U.N.," said one.

"Stephanie Dujarric, Associate Spokesman for U.N. Secretary-General Kofi Annan, insisted that "The United Nations does not pay journalists, openly or surreptitiously, to write pro-UN articles or to appear on news programs to defend the organization."

"However, she said that the U.N. has been paying journalists under some circumstances to go on the U.N.'s World Chronicle television program and to write "public information material," articles, books and pamphlets for the U.N. and its agencies.

"Dujarric asked Susan Markham of the U.N.'s Department of Public Information for further "guidance" before responding to AIM's requests for the names of all the journalists taking money from the U.N. and the amounts.

"As for Williams, she stated that "he is an independent journalist who has written articles for some UN publications. It is up to him to provide the relevant details, should he so choose."

"Williams, a British-born socialist activist based in New York since 1989, does not hide his far-left politics. He is the author of the anti-Bush book, The Deserter: Bush's War on Military Families, Veterans and His Past.

Defending Kofi and Sevan

"His criticism of the U.N., such as it is, comes from the left. In a column posted by The Nation last December, headlined, "The Right's

Assault on Kofi Annan," Williams insisted that the U.N. Secretary-General was coming under fire in the oil-for-food scandal because he opposed the U.S. invasion of Iraq. Williams also declared, "Charges of corruption against UN official Benon Sevan are suspect at best, given that they come via Ahmad Chalabi, who was also the source of the discredited information about Iraq's illusory weapons, as well as the assurances that Iraqis would greet US and British forces as liberators."

"On February 7, however, Annan suspended Sevan, the former head of the oil-for-food program, after an inquiry found that he had repeatedly solicited allocations of oil under the program and had "created a grave and continuing conflict of interest."

"Last May 3, then-UNCA President Tony Jenkins, a reporter for Expresso of Portugal, gave a speech on World Press Freedom Day that included an attack on the American people for being uninformed on world affairs and manipulated by the Bush administration, especially on Iraq. His speech, which also attacked the Bush administration for distributing a "government-produced infomercial" on medical news to the press, was posted on the official website of the U.N. Department of Public Information.

"Expressing outrage over the cost of the Iraq war and saying it could reach $400 billion or more, Jenkins said, "What would have happened if say we had taken just 100 thousand million dollars of that amount and spent it turning Gaza into the Manhattan of the Mediterranean?"

"He criticized the U.S. media, saying, "Why is the coverage of the Middle East so uneven? And so narrow? What is everyone afraid of? You find a broader debate about the policies of the Sharon government in Israel than you do here. It's as if all of American Jewry, in its multifaceted glory, had been hijacked by the Likud."

"Urging U.N. action against Israel, Jenkins said, "Why are so few in the American media explaining that this policy of unilaterally annexing parts of the occupied territories won't work? That we don't live by 19th century rules anymore. That you can't go marching into someone else's land, wipe out all the Indians, build a wall around it and say 'this is mine,' with impunity. That, it was precisely to stop such actions that the United Nations was founded?"

"Jenkins is one of several U.N. correspondents who have appeared on the U.N.'s World Chronicle television program.

No Comment

"While Williams won't discuss the amounts of money he has received, he does not hide the general fact that he has been paid by the U.N. His personal website discloses that "He has produced several booklets for UN agencies, including one on Portugal and aid to Africa, another on ASEAN, and on the International Tribunal on the Law of the Sea and in the past year edited the 2001 UNCTAD report and helped draft the press-kit for the 2002 Arab Human Development Report for UNDP."

"UNCTAD is the U.N. conference on Trade and Development. The Law of the Sea Treaty is currently before the U.S. Senate.

"The World Chronicle U.N. television program, which features interviews with U.N. officials, "is available free of charge to authorized broadcasters who agree to give credit to the United Nations each time a program is aired," its website says. "Guests are interviewed by a panel of journalists from international news organizations accredited to the United Nations," it adds. Guests have included Kofi Annan, Ted Turner and Dan Rather.

"One World Chronicle program, recorded on May 3, 2004, included the topic of global taxes on U.S. citizens. Tony Jenkins was the moderator and James Wurst of U.N. Wire and Louis Hamann of the CBC were on the show to question a U.N. official.

"Hamann asked if a global tax on financial transactions could become a new source of foreign aid. The official replied that we have to pay "much attention" to "innovative financing sources." Hamann pressed, "But do you think the idea of a global tax could ever come to be?" The official said there was no consensus now but that "times may change."

"In the past, U.N. agencies have also sponsored "traveling seminars" for journalists so they write positive stories about U.N. projects. One such trip, said to feature "journalists representing 35 media organizations," was put on by the UNDP.

Stonewall

"When AIM asked Ian Williams for details about his U.N. compensation, he responded, in part: "I am happy to share the details of my other income with you if you will provide in return a complete list of donors to your various organizations and employers, with their names, addresses and affiliations, and your considered opinion on whether they would continue to finance you if you suddenly took a more objective and less hostile attitude to the United Nations."

"But Williams is the one getting money from an international governmental institution that he is supposed to cover objectively.

"AIM also asked James Wurst and Tony Jenkins about financial contributions to UNCA from Ted Turner's U.N. Foundation and the Open Society Institute of George Soros. Wurst is the current UNCA president.

"Turner, a member of the boards of Time Warner and the United Nations Association, has contributed tens of millions of dollars to pro-U.N. causes and the U.N. itself.

"Because of these inquires to current and former UNCA officials, a message distributed by a left-wing website declared that there was underway a "Far-right attack on U.N. correspondents." The message declared, "Several members of the UN Correspondents Association have recently been approached by Cliff Kincaid, veteran UN basher to suggest that their work has been tainted by pro-UN money. His most recent investigative coup, emblazoned across the intellectual deserts of the Far-Right blogs was that an author was corrupted because of accepting money from the UN Foundation and the Better World Foundation to write a book. He is unlikely to win a Pulitzer for it, however, since his source is the author's acknowledgements in the front of the book, published a year ago!"

"The reference is to the book, An Insider's Guide to the U.N., by Linda Fasulo, who covers the U.N. for NBC News, MSNBC and National Public Radio. The book is pro-U.N. to the point of ignoring Annan's documented role in the failure to prevent the 1994 Rwanda genocide.

Big Book Advance

"While Fasulo's book had acknowledged general financial support from the U.N. Foundation and the Rockefeller Brothers Fund, she did not disclose any amounts and refused to do so when asked. AIM was told of payments totaling $26,000 to Fasulo from the U.N. Foundation and the Rockefeller Brothers Fund back in 2001 (the book was published in 2004). NBC has defended her financial arrangement but insists that she is just a "free-lance" correspondent. That is not how she was identified in the book or in the past by NBC News or MSNBC.

"AIM was told that Fasulo had been given $15,000 from the U.N. Foundation, with the other $11,000 coming from the Rockefeller Brothers Fund, channeled through the Philadelphia World Affairs Council. However, the U.N. Foundation's Income Tax Return for that year shows $15,000 going for something called "The UN handbook" and the grant recipient was listed only as "various." This is apparently the Fasulo book because an official of the Rockefeller Brothers Fund said their money was funneled to Fasulo for a book by that same name.

"Fasulo's pro-U.N. bias, so evident in the lavish praise of Annan in her book, was also demonstrated in a March 16, 2004, story posted on the MSNBC website. She reported that Annan "is widely recognized as a man of principle and long-term thinking." Her source for this statement was an anonymous U.N. official.

"Wurst, who works for the Ted Turner-funded U.N. Wire and Global Security Newswire, did not provide any more details about Turner or Soros grants to UNCA. However, UNCA documents on the group's website indicate that the two groups have provided at least $20,000 to underwrite the awarding of journalism prizes for covering the U.N.

"Wurst, Jenkins and Williams say the money doesn't have any influence. "We owe allegiance to no one and nothing but good, hard, critical—but fact based-reporting," they said. "We are a proud, feisty and independent association of journalists."

"But one journalist who submitted articles for consideration for a prize from UNCA said they were rejected because they were considered too critical of the U.N. He was told they should be "more positive" about the U.N.'s efforts to fix problems.

The Winner Is

"While UNCA presents "Excellence in Journalism Awards" to leading journalists, it also bestows UNCA "Citizen of the World" prizes to U.N. officials and Hollywood celebrities. Winners in the latter category have included movie stars Angelina Jolie and Nicole Kidman, and U.N. officials Hans Blix and Lakhdar Brahimi.

"One U.N. correspondent said there is a purpose behind the UNCA prizes. The agenda is "let's promote people who can make us look good," he said.

"If a big name newspaper has done anything remotely connected with the U.N., that's going to win because it looks good to be giving prizes to big names," he added. He cited an award given in 2003 to Robin Wright for "overall coverage of events at the U.N." Wright, then with the Los Angeles Times, is now with the Washington Post.

"The same year, a "Special Lifetime Achievement Award" was given by UNCA to Barbara Crossette, the former New York Times U.N. bureau chief who went to work for Turner's U.N. Wire. The U.N.

Foundation reports paying over $12,000 for a "Barbara Crossette Dinner" at the Harvard Club in 2002.

"In a recent dispatch, Crossette spewed venom at the Bush Administration and its supporters. "Four years of ideologically driven, unrealistic, and outdated social policies have turned American foreign aid into a vehicle for the most intractable, irrational, and uninformed elements of the conservative right," she declared.

"In 1995, Ted Turner himself received an UNCA award for CNN's coverage of the U.N. Four years later, CNN's U.N. bureau won a prize.

"As for Soros, his funding of U.N. causes, in addition to underwriting UNCA's awards, has been underway for many years. Those receiving Open Society Institute funding include:

Coalition for an International Criminal Court ($50,000).

United Nations Association ($65,000).

World Federation of United Nations Associations ($10,000).

"In 2003, when Kofi Annan couldn't preside over the UNCA media awards ceremony at U.N. headquarters, UNCA said that the "renowned philanthropist" George Soros took his place."

http://www.aim.org/special-report/journalists-exposed-on-the-un-payroll-george-soros-ted-turner-pay-for-journ/

"According to Glen Beck, who has done an in depth study of George Soros, "these are the five steps Soros uses to economically deconstruct nations while profiting from the effect:

"Step 1: Form a shadow government using humanitarian aid as cover. Remember, the symbol of Fabian Socialism is a wolf in sheep's clothing. Lies and deceit are their modus operandi. Here are just a few of the Soros-created/funded cover groups:

Open Society Institute (OSI)

Tides Foundation

Sojourners (Rev. Jim Wallis)

Center for American Progress (CAP)

Institute for Policy Studies (an adjunct of CAP)

The Apollo Alliance

Human Rights Watch

La Raza

"Step 2: Control the airwaves. Fund existing radio, TV, media outlets and take control of them, or start your own outlets. Soros has done both: Media Matters, National Public Radio, Faith in Public Life and Huffington Post ("Investigative Fund") are just a few of the Soros-OSI funded front groups.

"Step 3: Destabilize the state, weaken the government and build an anti-government kind of feeling in the country. You exploit an economic crisis or take advantage of an existing crisis – pressure from the top and the bottom. This will allow you to weaken the government and build anti-government public sentiment. Soros has done this through front groups like: People for the American Way, MoveOn. org and the Tides Foundation. Tides also supports the Apollo Alliance, Color for Change (Van Jones), Service Employees International Union (Andy Stern's SEIU) and the charitable arm of the radical 1960s student anarchist group, Students for a Democratic Society, of which the Weather Underground is a spin-off group (i.e., Bill Ayers and Bernardine Dorhn, who launched Obama's political career).

"Step 4: Provoke an election crisis. And during the election, you cry voter fraud. Remember Obama, Hillary and Rahm Emanuel's mantra: "Never allow a good crisis go to waste." At the Shadow Party's "Take Back America" conference in Washington on June 3, 2004, following a glowing introduction from Hillary Clinton, Soros gave the decree, "Do something about the distortion of our electoral process by the excessive use of TV advertising."

"A few months later, two progressive politicians took up this cause, aggressively funded and lobbied by Soros, and eventually passed the McCain/Feingold Campaign Finance Reform law, which launched a new era of 501(c)(3) and 527 nonprofits. In a revealing 2004 article by David Horowitz and Richard Poe, "Shadow Party: Part III," the authors wrote: "By pushing McCain-Feingold through Congress, Soros cut off the Democrats' soft-money supply. By forming the Shadow Party, Soros offered the Democrats an alternate money spigot – one which he personally controlled." That's why Beck calls George Soros President Obama's puppet master.

"Step 5: Take power. You stage massive demonstrations, civil disobedience, sit-ins, general strike; you encourage radical activism. You promote voter fraud and tell followers what to do through your radio and television stations. OSI and Soros front groups like ACORN, SEIU (whose union membership program the voting machines), Color for Change (Van Jones) and the Ruckus Society, an environmental justice group known for their aggressive tactics, causes untold havoc in our election cycle every two years.

"George Soros is a very evil man and has perfected the economic deconstruction of nations, which he learned firsthand as a child in Nazi-controlled Hungary and later throughout Communist-controlled Eastern Europe – except Soros needs no bullets for his revolution; he has a much more treacherous and inconspicuous weapon: money and propaganda.

"Because George Soros is an atheist, he has no allusions about a heaven beyond the grave. Therefore, like most socialists, progressives, Darwinists and atheists, he is trying to establish a utopian society here on earth – a one-world centralized government without borders, religion or culture, one currency, one language and one puppet master to pull the strings of the useful idiots in power … while controlling the world from beyond the shadows." Read more at http://www.wnd.com/2010/11/230489/#uQlRHRjb8VTiLJKP.99

XVI

HILLARY

" Hillary Clinton's night on the 9th of November 2016 went from a celebration to an absolute meltdown once the election unexpectedly turned on her, leaving Donald Trump as the victor. Some of the remnants of Hillary Clinton's rampage in the private VIP area was discovered by the hotel custodial staff the day following the election.

"Hillary Clinton's post - election celebration plans included hundreds of thousands of dollars' worth of fireworks, live performances by various celebrities, such as Cher, who came believing that Hillary was going to win the election, a five-hundred-thousand-dollar special effects glass ceiling that she would break through in a dramatic display once she walked out on stage at her Headquarters among millions of dollars' worth of other celebratory preparations, all paid for by the Clinton Foundation in full.

"The most notable damage was located deep in the VIP room of the Clinton camp. A custom 150 inch ultra HD TV, a gift from the Saudi Arabian government, was found with a broken screen. The damage was caused by a $950,000 bottle of champagne that was believed to have been thrown at the screen by the former presidential candidate some time during the election.

"Early in the morning, the custodial staff were greeted by flipped-over tables as the floors were covered with expensive food, drinks, and appetizers. Broken champagne flutes and gilded silverware were also seen scattered around the would-be party room.

"The most telling sign of a massive meltdown was the cake. The pastry that had once proudly displayed the presidential seal, was violently flung against the walls in chunks. A broken topper from the cake in the shape of the White House was discovered lodged firmly into the drywall near the dessert table.

"Clinton's splurge on party supplies was merely an echo of all the left-leaning polls and hype that "confirmed" Hillary Clinton's indubitable win. Misled by just about every prediction, Hillary Clinton personally planned one big party for her assumed victory. Once it became clear that it would not be Clinton's night, however, the mood of the party soured rapidly.

"A former staffer, who was fired during the rampage, said that the atmosphere around Clinton went from "queen of the hour" to "the girl who was dumped on prom night" in only a few moments.

"Report: Hillary Became "Physically Violent After She Realized She Had Lost the Election Clinton had to be "briefly restrained" after trying to attack her own campaign staff: Paul Joseph Watson -November 15, 2016"

"Hillary Clinton reportedly became "physically violent" towards her own campaign staff after she realized she had lost the presidential election, according to radio host Todd Kincannon. "CNN reporter tells me Hillary became physically violent towards Robby Mook and John Podesta around midnight; had to be briefly restrained," tweeted Kincannon.

"It was Podesta who was sent out to talk to Hillary's dejected supporters shortly before Hillary called Donald Trump to concede, with Clinton nowhere to be seen until the following day.

"When asked about rumors that Hillary was drunk on election night, Kincannon responded, "She was. I posted about that too. She was in a "psychotic drunken rage" according to my reporter friend. Doctor added sedatives to the mix."

"Kincannon then claimed that CNN blocked the reporter from publishing what would have been a bombshell story. "The CNN reporter didn't fail to report it. His editors will not let him. CNN has banned all "Hillary in the bunker" stories," he tweeted.

"Secret Service officials and other staff who worked closely alongside Hillary have previously reported her problems with angry tantrums on numerous occasions. Last year it was also reported that Clinton's own campaign staffers feared she could have a serious meltdown and that Hillary had "been having screaming, child-like tantrums that have left staff members in tears and unable to work." (The above was from an email)

"Rumors of Hillary Clinton's many meltdowns, tantrums, and being physically abusive to her staff were common. During an interview with Matt Lauer, Clinton became enraged and threw a glass at a staffer's head.

"Former Secret Serviceman, Gary Byrne, wrote that Clinton was prone to angry outburst and fits of anger in his book "Crisis of Character." Byrne served as an Officer in the West Wing during the Clinton Administration.

"In addition to claims that she became irate, author Ed Klein said a source told him Hillary cried inconsolably to a friend after the results came in, blaming FBI director Comey and President Barack Obama for not doing enough to stop the FBI investigation into her email scandal.

"According to http://www.foxnews.com/politics/2017/04/18/hillary-clinton-apologized-to-obama-on-election-night.html it was not until President Obama called Hillary Clinton and told her that she needed to call Mr. Trump and concede the election that she actually did so and even then it was with trepidation."

"The mystery of Hillary Clinton, milk-carton missing on election night, appears solved.

"A Tuesday of catharsis for Donald Trump voters turned into an evening of rage for Hillary Clinton. The Democratic presidential nominee, anticipating the postelection reaction of many of her supporters, began shouting profanities, banging tables, and turning objects not nailed down into projectiles.

"Sources have told The American Spectator that on Tuesday night, after Hillary realized she had lost, she went into a rage," R. Emmett Tyrrell reports. "Secret Service officers told at least one source that she began yelling, screaming obscenities, and pounding furniture. She picked up objects and threw them at attendants and staff. She was in an uncontrollable rage."

"The appearance of campaign chairman John Podesta at Manhattan's Javitz Center, and the dematerialization of his heretofore ubiquitous charge, perplexed in the first hours of Wednesday.

"They're still counting votes, and every vote should count," Podesta declared to a sad and stunned hall. "Several states are too close to call, so we're not going to have anything more to say tonight."

"As Podesta recalcitrantly refused to recognize reality early Wednesday morning, Hillary Clinton called Donald Trump to offer congratulations. The juxtaposition of the campaign chairman publicly vowing to fight around the time the candidate privately conceded the election left observers scratching their heads.

"Tyrrell's reporting indicates that Mrs. Clinton's mental state made it impossible for her to address her supporters on election night as custom requests. So, instead, Podesta gave a rah-rah speech on a boo-hoo night to cover for the absence of the first woman president, her fireworks, and her victory speech shout-outs to the mothers of the Black Lives Matter martyrs.

"She is not done yet," Podesta claimed. Tyrrell's reporting indicates that, indeed, Clinton remained far from done.

"Her aides could not allow her to come out in public," he writes. "It would take her hours to calm down. So Podesta went out and gave his aimless speech. I wish we could report on Bill's whereabouts but we cannot."

"Bill appeared the following day at Hillary's belated concession speech wearing a purple tie but, thankfully, no purple marks about his face, suggesting experience dictated avoidance the previous evening.

"People say they're amazed Bill's marriage survived," Tyrrell noted to Breitbart. "I'm amazed Bill survived his marriage."

"Tyrrell's reporting remains a thorn in the side of the Clintons more than two decades after the American Spectator published its Troopergate stories detailing Bill Clinton's escapades as told by his Arkansas security detail, stories that first referenced Paula Jones and pushed the president on the road to impeachment. Nearly 19 years after Hillary Clinton imagined a "vast, right-wing conspiracy" out to get her husband, the cabal's charter member again relies on the accounts of the Clintons' long-suffering security to unmask the public faces worn by the power couple now out of power.

"In the '90s, we published several pieces that documented her throwing lamps and books," Tyrrell tells Breitbart. "This happened pretty often. She has such a foul mouth that the Arkansas state troopers learned a thing or two from her. She has a foul mouth and a good throwing arm."

http://www.breitbart.com/big-government/2016/11/15/hillary-clinton-screaming-obscenities-and-throwing-objects-in-election-night-meltdown/

Will Hillary Clinton run for President again? Michael Goodwin, a Fox News Contributor believes she will. Chelsea Clinton believes she won't. I personally hope she does not. At the moment she is still pondering what went wrong.

XVII

GUN CONTROL

" **A** ny man who thinks he can be happy and prosperous by letting the Government take care of him; better take a closer look at the American Indian." Henry Ford

"The U.N. Resolution 2117 lists 21 points dealing with firearms control, but perhaps of most interest is point number 11:

"Calls for member states to support weapons collection and disarmament of all UN countries!"

By a 53-46 vote - The U.S. Senate voted against the U.N. resolution. This is that brief, glorious moment in history when everyone stands around...reloading......

Now, which 46 Senators voted to destroy us? Well, let their names become known! See below. If you vote in one of the states listed with these 46 "legislators" anti-American traitors, then please preserve our rights and vote against them!

In a 53-46 vote, the Senate narrowly passed a measure that will stop the United States from entering into the United Nations Arms Trade Treaty.

The Statement of Purpose from the Senate Bill reads: "To uphold Second Amendment rights and prevent the United States from entering into the United Nations Arms Trade Treaty." The U.N. Small Arms

Treaty, which has been championed by the Obama Administration, would have effectively placed a global ban on the import and export of small firearms. The ban would have affected all private gun owners in the U.S. and had language that would have implemented an international gun registry, now get this, on all private guns and ammo.

Astonishingly, 46 out of our 100 United States Senators were willing to give away our Constitutional rights to a foreign power.

Here are the 46 senators who voted to give your rights to the U.N. They need to go:

Baldwin (D-WI)	Leahy (D-VT)
Baucus (D-MT)	Levin (D-MI) **
Bennett (D-CO)	McCaskill (D-MO)
Blumenthal (D-CT)	Menendez (D-NJ)
Boxer (D-CA)	Merkley (D-OR)
Brown (D-OH).	Mikulski (D-MD)
Cantwell (D-WA)	Murphy (D-CT)
Cardin (D-MD)	Murray (D-WA)
Carper (D-DE)	Nelson (D-FL) **
Casey (D-PA)	Reed (D-RI)
Coons (D-DE)	Reid (D-NV)
Cowan (D-MA)	Rockefeller (D-WV)
Durbin (D-IL)	Sanders (I-VT)
Feinstein (D-CA)	Schatz (D-HI)
Franken (D-MN)	Schumer (D-NY)
Gillibrand (D-NY)	Shaheen (D-NH)
Harkin (D-IA)	Stabenow (D-MI) **
Hirono (D-HI)	Udall (D-CO)
Johnson (D-SD)	Udall (D-NM)
Kaine (D-VA)	Warner (D-VA)
King (I-ME)	Warren (D-MA)
Klobuchar (D-MN)	Whitehouse (D-RI)
Landrieu (D-LA)	Wyden (D-OR)

Folks, these Senators voted to let the UN take our guns. They need to lose their next election. We have been betrayed.

46 Senators voted to give your 2nd Amendment Constitutional Rights to the U.N.

Oh, look, they're all Democrats! Two Independents!

Facts About Gun Control

Some interesting facts about gun control ...

There are slightly over 30,000 gun related deaths per year by firearms in the US. That is not disputed. What is never shown though, is a breakdown of those deaths to put them in perspective, as compared to other causes of death.

- 65% of those deaths are by suicide which would never be prevented by gun laws
- 15% are by law enforcement in the line of duty and justified
- 17% are through criminal activity, gang and drug related or mentally ill persons
- 3% are accidental discharge deaths

So technically, the number of deaths "by gun violence" is not 30,000 annually but drops to 5,100.

Still too many? Well, first, how are those deaths distributed across the nation?

- 480 homicides (9.4%) were in Chicago
- 344 homicides (6.7%) were in Baltimore
- 333 homicides (6.5%) were in Detroit
- 119 homicides (2.3%) were in Washington DC (a 54% increase over prior years)

So basically, 25% of all gun crime happens in just 4 cities. All 4 of those cities have strict gun laws so it is not the lack of law that is the root cause. This basically leaves 3,825 for the entire rest of the nation or about 75 per state. That is an average because some States have much higher rates than others. For example, California had 1,169. Alabama had 1.

Now, who has the strictest gun laws by far? California of course but understand, it is not the tool (guns) driving this. It is a crime rate spawned by the number of criminal persons residing in those cities and states. So if all cities and states are not created equal, then there must be something other than the tool causing the gun deaths.

Are 5,100 deaths per year horrific?

How about in comparison to other deaths?

All death is sad and especially so when it is in the commission of a crime but that is the nature of crime. Robbery, death, rape, assault; all are done by criminals to victims and thinking that criminals will obey laws is ludicrous. That's why they are criminals.

But what of other deaths in the US?

- 40,000+ die from a drug overdose – There is no excuse for that!
- 36,000 people die per year from the flu, far exceeding the criminal gun deaths
- 34,000 people die per year in traffic fatalities (exceeding gun deaths even if you include suicide)

Now it gets really good.

- 200,000+ people die each year (and growing) from preventable medical malpractice.
- You are safer in Chicago than you are in a hospital!
- 710,000 people die per year from heart disease. Time to stop the cheeseburgers!

So what is the point? If Obama and the anti-gun movement had focused their attention on heart disease, even 10% a decrease would save twice the lives annually of all gun related deaths (including suicide, law enforcement, etc.). A 10% reduction in malpractice would be 66% of the total gun deaths or 4 times the number of criminal homicides. Simple, easily preventable 10% reductions!

So you have to ask yourself, in the grand scheme of things, why the focus on guns?

It's pretty simple.

Taking away guns gives control to governments. This is not a conspiracy theory; this is a historical fact.

Why is it impossible for the government to spill over into a dictatorship? Why did the Japanese not even attempt to attack California in WWII? Because as they put it, there is a gun behind every blade of grass.

The founders of this nation knew that regardless of the form of government, those in power may become corrupt and seek to rule as the British did. They too tried to disarm the populace of the colonies because it is not difficult to understand; a disarmed populace is a controlled populace. Thus, the second amendment was proudly and boldly included in the constitution. It must be preserved at all costs.

So the next time someone tries to tell you that gun control is about saving lives, look at these facts and remember these words from Noah Webster:

"Before a standing army can rule, the people must be disarmed; as they are in almost every kingdom in Europe. The supreme power in America cannot enforce unjust laws by the sword; because the whole body of the people are armed, and constitute a force superior to any band of regular troops that can be, on any pretense, raised in the United States. A military force, at the command of Congress, can execute no laws, but such as the people perceive to be just and constitutional; for they will possess the power."

In a gunfight, the most important rule is .... Have a gun!

Here is some shooting advice from various Concealed Carry Instructors.

If you own a gun, you will appreciate these rules. If not, you should get one and learn how to use it — and learn the rules:

RULES:

A — Guns have only two enemies: rust and politicians.

B — It's always better to be judged by 12, than carried by 6.

C — Cops carry guns to protect themselves, not you.

D — Never let someone or something that threatens you get inside arm's length.

E — Never say "I've got a gun". If you need to use deadly force, the first sound they hear should be the safety clicking off.

F — The average response time of a 911 call is 23 minutes; the response time of a .357 magnum is 1400 feet per second.

G — The most important rule in a gunfight is: Always win. A gunfight is a deadly struggle. There is no such thing as a fair fight, so cheat if necessary.

H — Make your attacker advance through a wall of bullets. You may get killed with your own gun, but he'll have to beat you to death with it, because it will be empty.

I — If you're in a gun fight: If you're not shooting, you should be loading. If you're not loading, you should be moving. If you're not moving, you're dead.

J — In a life and death situation, do something. It may be wrong, but do something!

K — If you carry a gun, people may call you paranoid. Nonsense! If you have a gun, what do you have to be paranoid about?

L — You can say 'stop' or any other word, but a large bore muzzle pointed at someone's head is pretty much a universal language.

M — Never leave an enemy behind. If you have to shoot, shoot to kill. If you end up in court, yours will be the only testimony.

N — You cannot save the planet, but you may be able to save yourself and your family.

And always remember this quote from America's premier Founding Father:

"Peace is that brief, glorious moment in history, when everybody stands around reloading". - Thomas Jefferson

XVIII

ISIS AND SHARIA CRUSADE

The first countries to ban Islam:

See how the world is acting fast on the threat posed by Islam and its barbaric Sharia Law.

Japan has always refused Muslims to live permanently in their country and they cannot own any real estate or any type of business, and have banned any worship of Islam. Any Muslim tourist caught spreading the word of Islam will be deported immediately, including all family members. The Japanese have a philosophy of no Muslims, no terrorists.

Their relationship with Muslim countries is primarily based on oil and gas, which Japan imports. Japan's official policy is not to give citizenship to Muslims and permanent residency is given very sparingly. Japan is a country of 126 million people with only 10,000 Muslim living there.

Cuba rejects plans for first mosque. Shortly after Fidel Castro took over Cuba in 1959 he issued a prohibition on all religion. "Catholic churches were shuttered, religious schools of all kinds were forced to pack up and leave the island and everyday Cubans took to praying to God in private.

"As the years passed, Cuba's government started easing those restrictions. They allowed for a freer expression of Catholicism, the predominant religion on the island, and Santeria, the blend of African, Caribbean and Catholic beliefs that has become popular throughout Cuba.

"Christmas in Cuba

"In recent years, the Islamic faith has also taken hold.

"Pedro Lazo Torres, known as the Imam Yahya, said there used to be so few Muslims in Cuba that they could hold their prayers inside someone's home. As they grew, their prayers spilled out into the street. Torres is now president of Cuba's Islamic League and says the number of Cubans asking to convert continues to increase.

"He now operates out of a mosque that was inaugurated in June of 2015 thanks to funding from Turkey's president, Recep Erdoğan. Located in Old Havana, the mosque sits next to an Islamic museum, known as The Arab House, and has brand new Spanish-Arabic copies of the Koran.

"Torres said the Muslim population has grown in part because of students who travel to Cuba from Chad, Niger, Nigeria and Rwanda. After an earthquake hit Pakistan in 2005, hundreds of Pakistanis resettled in Cuba and were given scholarships by the government.

"But for an island that sees little immigration, most Muslims in Cuba are converts.

"Ninety-nine percent of Cuban Muslims are converted to Islam and not descended of Arabs," said Ahmed Abuero, the mosque's religious leader."

"The African nation of Angola and several other nations have officially banned Islam. Only 1-2% of the population are Muslim, or 90,000 Muslims in the Country.

"Record number of Muslims, (over 2,000) deported from Norway as a way of fighting crime. Since these Muslim criminals have been deported, crime has dropped by a staggering 72%. Prison Officials are reporting that nearly half of their jail cells are now vacant, and courtrooms nearly empty. Police are now free to attend to other matters, mainly traffic offenses to keep their roads and highways safe and assisting the public in as many ways as they can." http://toprightnews.com/heres-what-happened-when-one-nation-started-deporting-radical-muslims/

"In Germany alone in the last year there were 81 violent attacks targeting mosques.

"Austrian police arrested 13 men targeting suspected jihad recruiters. Vienna (AFP) – Austrian police arrested 13 people and raided homes, prayer rooms and mosques around the country early Friday in a mass operation targeting suspected jihad recruiters, prosecutors said.

"The operation in Vienna and the cities of Graz and Linz was reportedly one of the biggest ever for the country, involving some 900 police officers.

"It followed a two-year investigation into several people suspected of recruiting young people to fight in Syria, the prosecutors said." https://www.jihadwatch.org/2014/11/austria-police-raid-mosques-arrest-13-for-jihad-recruitment

"A Chinese court sends 22 Muslim Imams to jail for 16 to 20 years for spreading Islam hatred. And have executed eighteen Jihadists. Shanghai – China has executed eight people for "terrorist" attacks in its restive far western region of Xinjiang, including three who "masterminded" a dramatic car crash in the capital's Tiananmen Square in 2013, state media said.

"Xinjiang is the traditional home of Muslim Uighurs who speak a Turkic language, and China has attributed attacks there to Islamist separatists it says seek to establish an independent state called East Turkestan. https://www.hindujagruti.org/news/20474.html

"China campaigns against Separatism (disallowing Islamist to have their own Separate state). Muslim prayers banned in government buildings and Schools in Xinjiang (Western China). Hundreds of Muslim families prepared to leave China for their own safety and return back to their own Middle Eastern countries.

"Muslim refugees beginning to realize that they are not welcome in Christian countries because of their violent ways and the continuing wars in Syria and Iraq whipped up by the hideous IS who are murdering young children and using mothers and daughters as sex slaves.

"British Home Secretary prepares to introduce 'Anti-social Behaviour Order' for extremists and strip dual nationals of their Citizenship.

"Deportation laws also being prepared.

"The Czech Republic blatantly refuses Islam in their country, regarding it as evil.

"Alabama - A new controversial amendment that will ban the recognition of "foreign laws which would include Sharia law". Alabama legislators passed a law 72-28 to protect the state in the future from Sharia Law.

"The Polish Defence League issues a warning to Muslims. 16 States have all Introduced Legislation to Ban Sharia Law.

"Many Muslims in Northern Ireland have announced plans to leave the Country to avoid anti-Islamic violence by Irish locals.

"The announcement comes after an attack on groups of Muslims in the city of Belfast.

"Groups of Irish locals went berserk and bashed teenage Muslim Gangs who were referring to young Irish girls as sluts and should be all gang raped, according to Islam and ''Sharia Law''.

"Even hospital staff were reluctant to treat the battered Muslim patients, the majority were given the Band-Aid treatment and sent home with staff muttering ''Good Riddance.''

"North Carolina bans Islamic "Sharia Law" in the State, regarding it now as a criminal offence.

"Dutch MP's call for removal of all mosques in the Netherlands. One Member of the Dutch Parliament said: "We want to clean Netherlands of Islam". Dutch MP Machiel De Graaf spoke on behalf of the Party for Freedom when he said,

"All mosques in the Netherlands should be shut down.

"Without Islam, the Netherlands would be a wonderful safe country to live in, as it was before the arrival of Muslim refugees".

"All of a sudden, poof, no USA

"We are so asleep and in need of an awakening. Some of these things on the list are NOT "all of a sudden," but have been going on several years already. Some would have been unbelievable a few years ago. May God help us and have mercy.

"Think, all of this in less than 8 years. Before Obama there was virtually no outlandish presence of Islam in America.

"All of a sudden, Islam is taught in schools. Christianity and the Bible are banned in schools.

"All of a sudden we must allow prayer rugs everywhere and allow for Islamic prayer in schools, airports and businesses.

"All of a sudden we must stop serving pork in prisons.

"All of a sudden we are inundated with law suits by Muslims who are offended by American culture.

"All of a sudden we must allow burkas to be worn everywhere even though you have no idea who or what is covered up under them.

"All of a sudden Muslims are suing employers and refusing to do their jobs if they personally deem it conflicts with Sharia Law.

"All of a sudden the Attorney General of the United States vows to prosecute anyone who engages in "anti-Muslim speech."

"All of a sudden, Jihadists who engage in terrorism and openly admit they acted in the name of Islam and ISIS, are emphatically declared they are NOT Islamic by our leaders and/or their actions are determined NOT to be terrorism, but other nebulous terms like 'workplace violence."

"All of a sudden, it becomes Policy that Secular Middle East dictators that were benign or friendly to the West, must be replaced by Islamists and the Muslim Brotherhood.

"All of a sudden our troops are withdrawn from Iraq and the middle east, giving rise to ISIS.

"All of a sudden, America has reduced its nuclear stockpiles to 1950 levels, as Obama's stated goal of a nuke-free America by the time he leaves office continues uninterrupted.

"All of a sudden, a deal with Iran must be made at any cost, with a pathway to nuclear weapons and hundreds of billions of dollars handed over to fund their programs.

"All of a sudden America apologizes to Muslim states and sponsors of terror worldwide for acts of aggression, war and sabotage they perpetrate against our soldiers.

"All of a sudden, the American Navy is diminished to 1917 Pre-World War I levels of only 300 ships. The Army is at pre-1940 levels. The Air Force scraps 500 planes and planned to retire the use of the A-10 Thunderbolt close air support fighter. A further draw down of another 40,000 military personnel is in progress.

"All of a sudden half of our aircraft carriers are recalled for maintenance by Obama rendering the Atlantic unguarded, none are in the Middle East.

"All of a sudden Obama has to empty Guantanamo Bay of captured Jihadists and let them loose in Jihad-friendly Islamic states. He demands to close the facility.

"All of a sudden America will negotiate with terrorists and trade five Taliban commanders for a deserter and Jihad sympathizer.

"All of a sudden there is no money for American poor, disabled veterans, jobless Americans, hungry Americans, or displaced

Americans but there is endless money for Obama's "Syrian refugee" resettlement programs.

"All of a sudden there is an ammunition shortage in the USA.

"All of a sudden, the most important thing for Obama to do after a mass shooting by two Jihadists, is disarm American Citizens.

"All of a sudden, the President of the United States cannot attend the Christian Funerals of a Supreme Court Justice and a former First Lady because of previous (seemingly unimportant) commitments.

"All of a sudden the President of the United States won't attend the funeral of a flag-rank Officer (Gen. Greene) killed in action; he played golf. But he sends a big delegation to Michael Brown's funeral. He sends a minor delegation to Margaret Thatcher's funeral. He won't acknowledge Chris Kyle's murder but he'll fly the Flag at half-mast for Whitney Houston.

"All of a sudden, I'm sick to my stomach. I'm not sure the majority of Americans recognize the seriousness of the situation and how much "progress" has been made by Islam these last 7 years, a very brief time compared to a 75-year lifetime!"

"This is absolutely unthinkable that nobody especially the CIA would have noticed this....

"Mr. Trump is starting to look better all the time.

This information has all been checked, then double checked... it is 100% Correct.

That's why there is such an alarm within US government, since Trump's statement about temporary suspension of migration of Muslims to US until US authorities make sure there is a proper concept of safe penetration of US territory.

People are stunned to learn that the head of the U.S. CIA is a Muslim! I do hope this wakes up some of you!

Until it hits you like a ton of bricks read it again until you understand it!

We have a Muslim government in the US!

When John Brennan was the head of the CIA he converted to Islam while stationed in Saudi Arabia.

Obama's top adviser, Valerie Jarrett, is a Muslim and was born in Iran where her parents still live.

Hillary Clinton's top adviser, Huma Abedin is a Muslim, whose mother and brother are still involved in the now outlawed Muslim Brotherhood in Egypt!

Assistant Secretary for Policy Development for Homeland Security, Arif Aikhan, is a Muslim.

Homeland Security Adviser, Mohammed Elibiary, is a Muslim.

Obama adviser and founder of the Muslim Public Affairs Council, Salam al-Marayati, is a Muslim.

Obama's Sharia Czar, Imam Mohamed Magid, of the Islamic Society of North America is a Muslim.

Advisory Council on Faith-Based Neighborhood Partnerships, Eboo Patel, is a Muslim.

Nancy Pelosi announced she will appoint Rep Andre Carson, D-Ind, a Muslim, as the first Muslim lawmaker on the House of Representatives Permanent Select Committee on Intelligence, of all things! It would make Carson the first Muslim to serve on the committee that receives intelligence on the threat of Islamic militants in the Middle East! He has suggested that U.S. schools should be modeled after Islamic madrassas, where education is based on the Quran!

Last but not least, our closet Muslim himself, Barack Hussein Obama.

It's questionable if Obama ever officially took the oath of office when he was sworn in. He did not repeat the oath properly to defend our nation and our Constitution. Later the Democrats claimed he was given the oath again, in private. Yeah, right.

CIA director John Brennan took his oath on a copy of the Constitution, not a Bible. Is this a real oath and does it show a lack of respect to our traditions and forefathers?

Valarie Jarret wrote her college thesis on how she wanted to change America into a Muslim friendly nation and she is an Obama top advisor!

Congressman, Keith Ellison took his oath on a copy of the Qur'an, NOT the Bible!

Conservative Congresswoman Michele Bachman, R-MN, was vilified and verbally tarred and feathered by Democrats when she voiced her concern about Muslims taking over our government! Since Michigan is a very heavy Muslim populated state, Bachman should know what she is talking about. Some cities in Michigan have been taken over completely by Muslims.

Considering all these appointments, it would explain why Obama and his minions are systematically destroying our nation, supporting radical Muslim groups worldwide, opening our southern border, and turning a blind eye to the genocide being perpetrated on Christians all over Africa and the Middle East!

Our nation and our government has been infiltrated by people who want to destroy us! It can only get worse unless we put a lid on it!

The End

THE CONSTITUTION OF THE UNITED STATES

THE BILL OF RIGHTS AND ALL AMENDMENTS

(Preamble)

We the People of the United States, in Order to form a more perfect Union, establish Justice, insure domestic Tranquility, provide for the common defence, promote the general Welfare, and secure the Blessings of Liberty to ourselves and our Posterity, do ordain and establish this Constitution for the United States of America.

Article I

Section 1. All legislative Powers herein granted shall be vested in a Congress of the United States, which shall consist of a Senate and House of Representatives.

Section 2. The House of Representatives shall be composed of Members chosen every second Year by the People of the several States, and the Electors in each State shall have the Qualifications requisite for Electors of the most numerous Branch of the State Legislature.

No Person shall be a Representative who shall not have attained to the Age of twenty-five years, and been seven years a Citizen of the United States, and who shall not, when elected, be an Inhabitant of that State in which he shall be chosen.

Representatives and direct Taxes shall be apportioned among the several States which may be included within this Union, according to their respective Numbers, which shall be determined by adding to the whole Number of free Persons, including those bound to Service for a Term of Years, and excluding Indians not taxed, three fifths of all other Persons. The actual Enumeration shall be made within three Years after the first Meeting of the Congress of the United States, and within every subsequent

Term of ten Years, in such Manner as they shall by Law direct. The Number of Representatives shall not exceed one for every thirty Thousand, but each State shall have at Least one Representative; and until such enumeration shall be made, the State of New Hampshire shall be entitled to chuse three, Massachusetts eight, Rhode-Island and Providence Plantations one, Connecticut five, New-York six, New Jersey four, Pennsylvania eight, Delaware one, Maryland six, Virginia ten, North Carolina five, South Carolina five, and Georgia three.

When vacancies happen in the Representation from any State, the Executive Authority thereof shall issue Writs of Election to fill such Vacancies.

The House of Representatives shall chuse their Speaker and other Officers; and shall have the sole Power of Impeachment.

Section 3. The Senate of the United States shall be composed of two Senators from each State, chosen by the Legislature thereof, for six Years; and each Senator shall have one Vote.

Immediately after they shall be assembled in Consequence of the first Election, they shall be divided as equally as may be into three Classes. The Seats of the Senators of the first Class shall be vacated at the Expiration of the second Year, of the second Class at the Expiration of the fourth Year, and of the third Class at the Expiration of the sixth Year, so that one third may be chosen every second Year; and if Vacancies happen by Resignation, or otherwise, during the Recess of the Legislature of any State, the Executive thereof may make temporary Appointments until the next Meeting of the Legislature, which shall then fill such Vacancies.

No Person shall be a Senator who shall not have attained to the Age of thirty Years, and been nine Years a Citizen of the United States, and who shall not, when elected, be an Inhabitant of that State for which he shall be chosen.

The Vice President of the United States shall be President of the Senate, but shall have no Vote, unless they be equally divided.

The Senate shall chuse their other Officers, and also a President pro tempore, in the Absence of the Vice President, or when he shall exercise the Office of President of the United States.

The Senate shall have the sole Power to try all Impeachments. When sitting for that Purpose, they shall be on Oath or Affirmation. When the President of the United States is tried, the Chief Justice shall preside: And no Person shall be convicted without the Concurrence of two thirds of the Members present.

Judgment in Cases of impeachment shall not extend further than to removal from Office, and disqualification to hold and enjoy any Office of honor, Trust or Profit under the United States: but the Party convicted shall nevertheless be liable and subject to Indictment, Trial, Judgment and Punishment, according to Law.

Section 4. The Times, Places and Manner of holding Elections for Senators and Representatives, shall be prescribed in each State by the Legislature thereof; but the Congress may at any time by Law make or alter such Regulations, except as to the Places of chusing Senators.

The Congress shall assemble at least once in every Year, and such Meeting shall be on the first Monday in December, unless they shall by Law appoint a different Day.

Section 5. Each House shall be the Judge of the Elections, Returns and Qualifications of its own Members, and a Majority of each shall constitute a Quorum to do Business; but a smaller Number may adjourn from day to day, and may be authorized to compel the Attendance of absent Members, in such Manner, and under such Penalties as each House may provide.

Each House may determine the Rules of its Proceedings, punish its Members for disorderly Behaviour, and, with the Concurrence of two thirds, expel a Member.

Each House shall keep a Journal of its Proceedings, and from time to time publish the same, excepting such Parts as may in their Judgment require Secrecy; and the Yeas and Nays of the Members of either House on any question shall, at the Desire of one fifth of those Present, be entered on the Journal.

Neither House, during the Session of Congress, shall, without the Consent of the other, adjourn for more than three days, nor to any other Place than that in which the two Houses shall be sitting.

Section 6. The Senators and Representatives shall receive a Compensation for their Services, to be ascertained by Law, and paid out of the Treasury of the United States.6 They shall in all Cases, except Treason, Felony and Breach of the Peace, be privileged from Arrest during their Attendance at the Session of their respective Houses, and in going to and returning from the same; and for any Speech or Debate in either House, they shall not be questioned in any other Place.

No Senator or Representative shall, during the Time for which he was elected, be appointed to any civil Office under the Authority of the United States, which shall have been created, or the Emoluments whereof shall have been encreased during such time; and no Person holding any Office under the United States, shall be a Member of either House during his Continuance in Office.

Section 7. All Bills for raising Revenue shall originate in the House of Representatives; but the Senate may propose or concur with Amendments as on other Bills.

Every Bill which shall have passed the House of Representatives and the Senate, shall, before it become a Law, be presented to the President of the United States; If he approves he shall sign it, but if not he shall return it, with his Objections to that House in which it shall have originated, who shall enter the Objections at large on their Journal, and proceed to reconsider it. If after such Reconsideration two thirds of that House shall agree to pass the Bill, it shall be sent, together with the Objections, to the other House, by which it shall likewise be reconsidered, and if approved by two thirds of that House, it shall become a Law. But in all such Cases the Votes of both Houses shall be determined by yeas and Nays, and the Names of the Persons voting for and against the Bill shall be entered on the Journal of each House respectively. If any Bill shall not be returned by the President within ten Days (Sundays excepted) after it shall have been presented to him, the Same shall be a Law, in like Manner as if he had signed it, unless the Congress by their Adjournment prevent its Return, in which Case it shall not be a Law.

Every Order, Resolution, or Vote to which the Concurrence of the Senate and House of Representatives may be necessary (except on a question of Adjournment) shall be presented to the President of the United States; and before the Same shall take Effect, shall be approved by him, or being disapproved by him, shall be repassed by two thirds of the Senate and House of Representatives, according to the Rules and Limitations prescribed in the Case of a Bill.

Section 8. The Congress shall have Power To lay and collect Taxes, Duties, Imposts and Excises, to pay the Debts and provide for the common Defence and general Welfare of the United States; but all Duties, Imposts and Excises shall be uniform throughout the United States;

To borrow Money on the credit of the United States;

To regulate Commerce with foreign Nations, and among the several States, and with the Indian Tribes;

To establish an uniform Rule of Naturalization, and uniform Laws on the subject of Bankruptcies throughout the United States;

To coin Money, regulate the Value thereof, and of foreign Coin, and fix the Standard of Weights and Measures;

To provide for the Punishment of counterfeiting the Securities and current Coin of the United States;

To establish Post Offices and post Roads;

To promote the Progress of Science and useful Arts, by securing for limited Times to Authors and Inventors the exclusive Right to their respective Writings and Discoveries;

To constitute Tribunals inferior to the supreme Court;

To define and punish Piracies and Felonies committed on the high Seas, and Offences against the Law of Nations;

To declare War, grant Letters of Marque and Reprisal, and make Rules concerning Captures on Land and Water;

To raise and support Armies, but no Appropriation of Money to that Use shall be for a longer Term than two Years;

To provide and maintain a Navy;

To make Rules for the Government and Regulation of the land and naval Forces;

To provide for calling forth the Militia to execute the Laws of the Union, suppress Insurrections and repel Invasions;

To provide for organizing, arming, and disciplining, the Militia, and for governing such Part of them as may be employed in the Service of the United States, reserving to the States respectively, the Appointment of the Officers, and the Authority of training the Militia according to the discipline prescribed by Congress;

To exercise exclusive Legislation in all Cases whatsoever, over such District (not exceeding ten Miles square) as may, by Cession of particular States, and the Acceptance of Congress, become the Seat of the Government of the United States, and to exercise like Authority over all Places purchased by the Consent of the Legislature of the State in which the Same shall be, for the Erection of Forts, Magazines, Arsenals, Dock-Yards, and other needful Buildings;—And

To make all Laws which shall be necessary and proper for carrying into Execution the foregoing Powers, and all other Powers vested by this Constitution in the Government of the United States, or in any Department or Officer thereof.

Section 9. The Migration or Importation of such Persons as any of the States now existing shall think proper to admit, shall not be prohibited by the Congress prior to the Year one thousand eight hundred and eight, but a Tax or duty may be imposed on such Importation, not exceeding ten dollars for each Person.

The Privilege of the Writ of Habeas Corpus shall not be suspended, unless when in Cases of Rebellion or Invasion the public Safety may require it.

No Bill of Attainder or ex post facto Law shall be passed.

No Capitation, or other direct, Tax shall be laid, unless in Proportion to the Census or Enumeration herein before directed to be taken. 7

No Tax or Duty shall be laid on Articles exported from any State.

No Preference shall be given by any Regulation of Commerce or Revenue to the Ports of one State over those of another: nor shall Vessels bound to, or from, one State, be obliged to enter, clear, or pay Duties in another.

No Money shall be drawn from the Treasury, but in Consequence of Appropriations made by Law; and a regular Statement and Account of the Receipts and Expenditures of all public Money shall be published from time to time.

No Title of Nobility shall be granted by the United States: And no Person holding any Office of Profit or Trust under them, shall, without the Consent of the Congress, accept of any present, Emolument, Office, or Title, of any kind whatever, from any King, Prince, or foreign State.

Section 10. No State shall enter into any Treaty, Alliance, or Confederation; grant Letters of Marque and Reprisal; coin Money; emit Bills of Credit; make any Thing but gold and silver Coin a Tender in Payment of Debts; pass any Bill of Attainder, ex post facto Law, or Law impairing the Obligation of Contracts, or grant any Title of Nobility.

No State shall, without the Consent of the Congress, lay any Imposts or Duties on Imports or Exports, except what may be absolutely necessary for executing its inspection Laws: and the net Produce of all Duties and Imposts, laid by any State on Imports or Exports, shall be for the Use of the Treasury of the United States; and all such Laws shall be subject to the Revision and Controul of the Congress.

No State shall, without the Consent of Congress, lay any Duty of Tonnage, keep Troops, or Ships of War in time of Peace, enter into any Agreement or Compact with another State, or with a foreign Power, or engage in War, unless actually invaded, or in such imminent Danger as will not admit of delay.

Article II

Section 1. The executive Power shall be vested in a President of the United States of America. He shall hold his Office during the Term of four Years, and, together with the Vice President, chosen for the same Term, be elected, as follows

Each State shall appoint, in such Manner as the Legislature thereof may direct, a Number of Electors, equal to the whole Number of Senators and Representatives to which the State may be entitled in the Congress: but no Senator or Representative, or Person holding an Office of Trust or Profit under the United States, shall be appointed an Elector.

The Electors shall meet in their respective States, and vote by Ballot for two Persons, of whom one at least shall not be an Inhabitant of the same State with themselves. And they shall make a List of all the Persons voted for, and of the Number of Votes for each; which List they shall sign and certify, and transmit sealed to the Seat of the Government of the United States, directed to the President of the Senate. The President of the Senate shall, in the Presence of the Senate and House of Representatives, open all the Certificates, and the Votes shall then be counted. The Person having the greatest Number of Votes shall be the President, if such Number be a Majority of the whole Number of Electors appointed; and if there be more than one who have such Majority, and have an equal Number of Votes, then the House of Representatives shall immediately chuse by Ballot one of them for President; and if no Person have a Majority, then from the five highest on the List the said House shall in like Manner chuse the President. But in chusing the President, the Votes shall be taken by States, the Representation from each State having one Vote; A quorum for this Purpose shall consist of a Member or Members from two thirds of the States, and a Majority of all the States shall be necessary to a Choice. In every Case, after the Choice of the President, the Person having the greatest Number of Votes of the Electors shall be the Vice President. But if there should remain two or more who have equal Votes, the Senate shall chuse from them by Ballot the Vice President.

The Congress may determine the Time of chusing the Electors, and the Day on which they shall give their Votes; which Day shall be the same throughout the United States.

No Person except a natural born Citizen, or a Citizen of the United States, at the time of the Adoption of this Constitution, shall be eligible to the Office of President; neither shall any Person be eligible to that Office who shall not have attained to the Age of thirty-five Years, and been fourteen Years a Resident within the United States.

In Case of the Removal of the President from Office, or of his Death, Resignation, or Inability to discharge the Powers and Duties of the said Office, the Same shall devolve on the Vice President, and the Congress may by Law provide for the Case of Removal, Death, Resignation or Inability, both of the President and Vice President, declaring what Officer shall then act as President, and such Officer shall act accordingly, until the Disability be removed, or a President shall be elected.

The President shall, at stated Times, receive for his Services, a Compensation, which shall neither be increased nor diminished during the Period for which he shall have been elected, and he shall not receive within that Period any other Emolument from the United States, or any of them.

Before he enters on the Execution of his Office, he shall take the following Oath or Affirmation: — "I do solemnly swear (or affirm) that I will faithfully execute the Office of President of the United States, and will to the best of my Ability, preserve, protect and defend the Constitution of the United States."

Section 2. The President shall be Commander in Chief of the Army and Navy of the United States, and of the Militia of the several States, when called into the actual Service of the United States; he may require the Opinion, in writing, of the principal Officer in each of the executive Departments, upon any Subject relating to the Duties of their respective Offices, and he shall have Power to grant Reprieves and Pardons for Offences against the United States, except in Cases of Impeachment.

He shall have Power, by and with the Advice and Consent of the Senate, to make Treaties, provided two thirds of the Senators present concur; and he shall nominate, and by and with the Advice and Consent of the Senate, shall appoint Ambassadors, other public Ministers and Consuls, Judges of the supreme Court, and all other Officers of the United States, whose Appointments are not herein otherwise provided for, and which shall be established by Law: but the Congress may by Law vest the Appointment of such inferior Officers, as they think proper, in the President alone, in the Courts of Law, or in the Heads of Departments.

The President shall have Power to fill up all Vacancies that may happen during the Recess of the Senate, by granting Commissions which shall expire at the End of their next Session.

Section 3

He shall from time to time give to the Congress Information of the State of the Union, and recommend to their Consideration such Measures as he shall judge necessary and expedient; he may, on extraordinary Occasions, convene both Houses, or either of them, and in Case of Disagreement between them, with Respect to the Time of Adjournment, he may adjourn them to such Time as he shall think proper; he shall receive Ambassadors and other public Ministers; he shall take Care that the Laws be faithfully executed, and shall Commission all the Officers of the United States.

Section 4. The President, Vice President and all civil Officers of the United States, shall be removed from Office on Impeachment for, and Conviction of, Treason, Bribery, or other high Crimes and Misdemeanors.

Article III

Section 1 The judicial Power of the United States, shall be vested in one supreme Court, and in such inferior Courts as the Congress may from time to time ordain and establish. The Judges, both of the supreme and inferior Courts, shall hold their Offices during good Behaviour, and shall, at stated Times, receive for their Services, a Compensation, which shall not be diminished during their Continuance in Office.

Section 2 The judicial Power shall extend to all Cases, in Law and Equity, arising under this Constitution, the Laws of the United States, and Treaties made, or which shall be made, under their Authority;—to all Cases affecting Ambassadors, other public Ministers and Consuls;—to all Cases of admiralty and maritime Jurisdiction;—to Controversies to which the United States shall be a Party;—to Controversies between two or more States;—between a State and Citizens of another State; —between Citizens of different States, —between Citizens of the same State claiming Lands under Grants of different States, and between a State, or the Citizens thereof, and foreign States, Citizens or Subjects.

In all Cases affecting Ambassadors, other public Ministers and Consuls, and those in which a State shall be Party, the supreme Court shall have original Jurisdiction. In all the other Cases before mentioned, the supreme Court shall have appellate

Jurisdiction, both as to Law and Fact, with such Exceptions, and under such Regulations as the Congress shall make.

The Trial of all Crimes, except in Cases of Impeachment, shall be by Jury; and such Trial shall be held in the State where the said Crimes shall have been committed; but when not committed within any State, the Trial shall be at such Place or Places as the Congress may by Law have directed.

Section 3 Treason against the United States, shall consist only in levying War against them, or in adhering to their Enemies, giving them Aid and Comfort. No Person shall be convicted of Treason unless on the Testimony of two Witnesses to the same overt Act, or on Confession in open Court.

The Congress shall have Power to declare the Punishment of Treason, but no Attainder of Treason shall work Corruption of Blood, or Forfeiture except during the Life of the Person attainted.

Article IV

Section 1 Full Faith and Credit shall be given in each State to the public Acts, Records, and judicial Proceedings of every other State. And the Congress may by general Laws prescribe the Manner in which such Acts, Records and Proceedings shall be proved, and the Effect thereof.

Section 2 The Citizens of each State shall be entitled to all Privileges and Immunities of Citizens in the several States.

A Person charged in any State with Treason, Felony, or other Crime, who shall flee from Justice, and be found in another State, shall on Demand of the executive Authority of the State from which he fled, be delivered up, to be removed to the State having Jurisdiction of the Crime.

No Person held to Service or Labour in one State, under the Laws thereof, escaping into another, shall, in Consequence of any Law or Regulation therein, be discharged from such Service or Labour, but shall be delivered up on Claim of the Party to whom such Service or Labour may be due.

Section 3 New States may be admitted by the Congress into this Union; but no new State shall be formed or erected within the Jurisdiction of any other State; nor any State be formed by the Junction of two or more States, or Parts of States, without the Consent of the Legislatures of the States concerned as well as of the Congress.

The Congress shall have Power to dispose of and make all needful Rules and Regulations respecting the Territory or other Property belonging to the United States; and nothing in this Constitution shall be so construed as to Prejudice any Claims of the United States, or of any particular State.

Section 4 The United States shall guarantee to every State in this Union a Republican Form of Government, and shall protect each of them against Invasion; and on Application of the Legislature, or of the Executive (when the Legislature cannot be convened) against domestic Violence.

Article V

The Congress, whenever two thirds of both Houses shall deem it necessary, shall propose Amendments to this Constitution, or, on the Application of the Legislatures of two thirds of the several States, shall call a Convention for proposing

Amendments, which, in either Case, shall be valid to all Intents and Purposes, as Part of this Constitution, when ratified by the Legislatures of three fourths of the several States, or by Conventions in three fourths thereof, as the one or the other Mode of Ratification may be proposed by the Congress; Provided that no Amendment which may be made prior to the Year One thousand eight hundred and eight shall in any Manner affect the first and fourth Clauses in the Ninth Section of the first Article; and that no State, without its Consent, shall be deprived of its equal Suffrage in the Senate.

Article VI

All Debts contracted and Engagements entered into, before the Adoption of this Constitution, shall be as valid against the United States under this Constitution, as under the Confederation.

This Constitution, and the Laws of the United States which shall be made in Pursuance thereof; and all Treaties made, or which shall be made, under the Authority of the United States, shall be the supreme Law of the Land; and the Judges in every State shall be bound thereby, any Thing in the Constitution or Laws of any State to the Contrary notwithstanding.

The Senators and Representatives before mentioned, and the Members of the several State Legislatures, and all executive and judicial Officers, both of the United States and of the several States, shall be bound by Oath or Affirmation, to support this Constitution; but no religious Test shall ever be required as a Qualification to any Office or public Trust under the United States.

Article VII

The Ratification of the Conventions of nine States, shall be sufficient for the Establishment of this Constitution between the States so ratifying the Same.

The Word "the", being interlined between the seventh and eight Lines of the first Page, The Word "Thirty" being partly written on an Erazure in the fifteenth Line of the first Page. The Words "is tried" being interlined between the thirty second and thirty third Lines of the first Page and the Word "the" being interlined between the forty third and forty fourth Lines of the second Page.

Done in Convention by the Unanimous Consent of the States present the Seventeenth Day of September in the Year of our Lord one thousand seven hundred and Eighty-seven and of the Independence of the United States of America the Twelfth In witness whereof We have hereunto subscribed our Names,

Attest William Jackson Secretary

Go: Washington -Presidt. and deputy from Virginia

Delaware	Geo: Read
	Gunning Bedford jun
	John Dickinson
	Richard Bassett
	Jaco: Broom
Maryland	James McHenry
	Dan of St Thos. Jenifer
	Danl Carroll.
Virginia	John Blair—
	James Madison Jr.
North Carolina	Wm Blount
	Richd. Dobbs Spaight.
	Hu Williamson
South Carolina J. Rutledge	
	Charles Cotesworth Pinckney
	Charles Pinckney
	Pierce Butler.
Georgia	William Few
	Abr Baldwin
New Hampshire John Langdon	
	Nicholas Gilman
Massachusetts Nathaniel Gorham	
	Rufus King
Connecticut	Wm. Saml. Johnson
	Roger Sherman
New York	Alexander Hamilton
New Jersey	Wil. Livingston
	David Brearley.
	Wm. Paterson.
	Jona: Dayton
Pennsylvania	B Franklin
	Thomas Mifflin
	Robt Morris
	Geo. Clymer
	Thos. FitzSimons
	Jared Ingersoll
	James Wilson.
	Gouv Morris

AMENDMENTS TO THE CONSTITUTION

(The procedure for changing the United States Constitution is Article V - Mode of Amendment)

(The Preamble to The Bill of Rights)

Congress OF THE United States begun and held at the City of New-York, on Wednesday the fourth of March, one thousand seven hundred and eighty-nine.

THE Conventions of a number of the States, having at the time of their adopting the Constitution, expressed a desire, in order to prevent misconstruction or abuse of its powers, that further declaratory and restrictive clauses should be added: And as extending the ground of public confidence in the Government, will best ensure the beneficent ends of its institution.

RESOLVED by the Senate and House of Representatives of the United States of America, in Congress assembled, two thirds of both Houses concurring, that the following Articles be proposed to the Legislatures of the several States, as amendments to the Constitution of the United States, all, or any of which Articles, when ratified by three fourths of the said Legislatures, to be valid to all intents and purposes, as part of the said Constitution; viz.

ARTICLES in addition to, and Amendment of the Constitution of the United States of America, proposed by Congress, and ratified by the Legislatures of the several States, pursuant to the fifth Article of the original Constitution.

(Articles I through X are known as the Bill of Rights) ratified

-

Article the first. .... After the first enumeration required by the first Article of the Constitution, there shall be one Representative for every thirty thousand, until the number shall amount to one hundred, after which, the proportion shall be so regulated by Congress, that there shall be not less than one hundred Representatives, nor less than one Representative for every forty thousand persons, until the number of Representatives shall amount to two hundred, after which the proportion shall be so regulated by Congress, that there shall not be less than two hundred Representatives, nor more than one Representative for every fifty thousand persons.

-

Article the second. .... No law, varying the compensation for the services of the Senators and Representatives, shall take effect, until an election of Representatives shall have intervened. see Amendment XXVII

AMENDMENT I
Freedom of expression and religion
Congress shall make no law respecting an establishment of religion, or prohibiting the free exercise thereof; or abridging the freedom of speech, or of the press; or the right of the people peaceably to assemble, and to petition the Government for a redress of grievances.

AMENDMENT II
Bearing Arms
A well-regulated Militia, being necessary to the security of a free State, the right of the people to keep and bear Arms, shall not be infringed.

AMENDMENT III
Quartering Soldiers
No Soldier shall, in time of peace be quartered in any house, without the consent of the Owner, nor in time of war, but in a manner to be prescribed by law.

AMENDMENT IV
Search and Seizure
The right of the people to be secure in their persons, houses, papers, and effects, against unreasonable searches and seizures, shall not be violated, and no Warrants shall issue, but upon probable cause, supported by Oath or affirmation, and particularly describing the place to be searched, and the persons or things to be seized.

AMENDMENT V
Rights of Persons
No person shall be held to answer for a capital, or otherwise infamous crime, unless on a presentment or indictment of a Grand Jury, except in cases arising in the land or naval forces, or in the Militia, when in actual service in time of War or public danger; nor shall any person be subject for the same offence to be twice put in jeopardy of life or limb; nor shall be compelled in any criminal case to be a witness against himself, nor be deprived of life, liberty, or property, without due process of law; nor shall private property be taken for public use, without just compensation.

AMENDMENT VI
Rights of Accused in Criminal Prosecutions
In all criminal prosecutions, the accused shall enjoy the right to a speedy and public trial, by an impartial jury of the State and district wherein the crime shall

have been committed, which district shall have been previously ascertained by law, and to be informed of the nature and cause of the accusation; to be confronted with the witnesses against him; to have compulsory process for obtaining witnesses in his favor, and to have the Assistance of Counsel for his defence.

AMENDMENT VII
Civil Trials

In Suits at common law, where the value in controversy shall exceed twenty dollars, the right of trial by jury shall be preserved, and no fact tried by a jury, shall be otherwise re-examined in any Court of the United States, than according to the rules of the common law.

AMENDMENT VIII
Further Guarantees in Criminal Cases

Excessive bail shall not be required, nor excessive fines imposed, nor cruel and unusual punishments inflicted.

AMENDMENT IX
Unenumerated Rights

The enumeration in the Constitution, of certain rights, shall not be construed to deny or disparage others retained by the people.

AMENDMENT X
(Reserved Powers)

The powers not delegated to the United States by the Constitution, nor prohibited by it to the States, are reserved to the States respectively, or to the people.
Attest,
John Beckley, Clerk of the House of Representatives.
Sam. A. Otis Secretary of the Senate.
Frederick Augustus Muhlenberg Speaker of the House of Representatives.
John Adams, Vice-President of the United States, and President of the Senate.
(end of the Bill of Rights)

AMENDMENT XI
Suits Against States

The Judicial power of the United States shall not be construed to extend to any suit in law or equity, commenced or prosecuted against one of the United States by Citizens of another State, or by Citizens or Subjects of any Foreign State.

AMENDMENT XII
Election of President

The Electors shall meet in their respective states, and vote by ballot for President and Vice-President, one of whom, at least, shall not be an inhabitant of the same state with themselves; they shall name in their ballots the person voted for as President, and in distinct ballots the person voted for as Vice-President, and they shall make distinct lists of all persons voted for as President, and of all persons voted for as Vice-President, and of the number of votes for each, which lists they shall sign and certify, and transmit sealed to the seat of the government of the United States, directed to the President of the Senate;—The President of the Senate shall, in the presence of the Senate and House of Representatives, open all the certificates and the votes shall then be counted;—The person having the greatest number of votes for President, shall be the President, if such number be a majority of the whole number of Electors appointed; and if no person have such majority, then from the persons having the highest numbers not exceeding three on the list of those voted for as President, the House of Representatives shall choose immediately, by ballot, the President. But in choosing the President, the votes shall be taken by states, the representation from each state having one vote; a quorum for this purpose shall consist of a member or members from two-thirds of the states, and a majority of all the states shall be necessary to a choice. And if the House of Representatives shall not choose a President whenever the right of choice shall devolve upon them, before the fourth day of March next following, then the Vice-President shall act as President, as in the case of the death or other constitutional disability of the President. —The person having the greatest number of votes as Vice-President, shall be the Vice-President, if such number be a majority of the whole number of Electors appointed, and if no person have a majority, then from the two highest numbers on the list, the Senate shall choose the Vice-President; a quorum for the purpose shall consist of two-thirds of the whole number of Senators, and a majority of the whole number shall be necessary to a choice. But no person constitutionally ineligible to the office of President shall be eligible to that of Vice-President of the United States.

AMENDMENT XIII
Slavery and Involuntary Servitude
Neither slavery nor involuntary servitude, except as a punishment for crime whereof the party shall have been duly convicted, shall exist within the United States, or any place subject to their jurisdiction.

Congress shall have power to enforce this article by appropriate legislation.

AMENDMENT XIV
Rights Guaranteed: Privileges and Immunities of Citizenship, Due Process, and Equal Protection)
1: All persons born or naturalized in the United States, and subject to the jurisdiction thereof, are citizens of the United States and of the State wherein they reside. No State shall make or enforce any law which shall abridge the privileges or immunities of citizens of the United States; nor shall any State deprive any person of life, liberty, or property, without due process of law; nor deny to any person within its jurisdiction the equal protection of the laws.

2: Representatives shall be apportioned among the several States according to their respective numbers, counting the whole number of persons in each State, excluding Indians not taxed. But when the right to vote at any election for the choice of electors for President and Vice President of the United States, Representatives in Congress, the Executive and Judicial officers of a State, or the members of the Legislature thereof, is denied to any of the male inhabitants of such State, being twenty-one years of age and citizens of the United States, or in any way abridged, except for participation in rebellion, or other crime, the basis of representation therein shall be reduced in the proportion which the number of such male citizens shall bear to the whole number of male citizens twenty-one years of age in such State

3: No person shall be a Senator or Representative in Congress, or elector of President and Vice President, or hold any office, civil or military, under the United States, or under any State, who, having previously taken an oath, as a member of Congress, or as an officer of the United States, or as a member of any State legislature, or as an executive or judicial officer of any State, to support the Constitution of the United States, shall have engaged in insurrection or rebellion against the same, or given aid or comfort to the enemies thereof. But Congress may by a vote of two-thirds of each House, remove such disability.

4: The validity of the public debt of the United States, authorized by law, including debts incurred for payment of pensions and bounties for services in suppressing insurrection or rebellion, shall not be questioned. But neither the United States nor any State shall assume or pay any debt or obligation incurred in aid of insurrection or rebellion against the United States, or any claim for the loss or emancipation of any slave; but all such debts, obligations and claims shall be held illegal and void.

5: The Congress shall have power to enforce, by appropriate legislation, the provisions of this article.

AMENDMENT XV

Rights of Citizens to Vote

The right of citizens of the United States to vote shall not be denied or abridged by the United States or by any State on account of race, color, or previous condition of servitude.

The Congress shall have power to enforce this article by appropriate legislation.

AMENDMENT XVI

Income Tax

The Congress shall have power to lay and collect taxes on incomes, from whatever source derived, without apportionment among the several States, and without regard to any census or enumeration.

AMENDMENT XVII

Popular Election of Senators

1: The Senate of the United States shall be composed of two Senators from each State, elected by the people thereof, for six years; and each Senator shall have one vote. The electors in each State shall have the qualifications requisite for electors of the most numerous branch of the State legislatures.

2: When vacancies happen in the representation of any State in the Senate, the executive authority of such State shall issue writs of election to fill such vacancies: Provided, That the legislature of any State may empower the executive thereof to make temporary appointments until the people fill the vacancies by election as the legislature may direct.

3: This amendment shall not be so construed as to affect the election or term of any Senator chosen before it becomes valid as part of the Constitution.

AMENDMENT XVIII
Prohibition of Intoxicating Liquors

1: After one year from the ratification of this article the manufacture, sale, or transportation of intoxicating liquors within, the importation thereof into, or the exportation thereof from the United States and all territory subject to the jurisdiction thereof for beverage purposes is hereby prohibited.

2: The Congress and the several States shall have concurrent power to enforce this article by appropriate legislation.

3: This article shall be inoperative unless it shall have been ratified as an amendment to the Constitution by the legislatures of the several States, as provided in the Constitution, within seven years from the date of the submission hereof to the States by the Congress.

AMENDMENT XIX
Women's Suffrage Rights

The right of citizens of the United States to vote shall not be denied or abridged by the United States or by any State on account of sex.

Congress shall have power to enforce this article by appropriate legislation.

AMENDMENT XX
Terms of President, Vice President, Members of Congress: Presidential Vacancy

1: The terms of the President and Vice President shall end at noon on the 20th day of January, and the terms of Senators and Representatives at noon on the 3d day of January, of the years in which such terms would have ended if this article had not been ratified; and the terms of their successors shall then begin.

2: The Congress shall assemble at least once in every year, and such meeting shall begin at noon on the 3d day of January, unless they shall by law appoint a different day.

3: If, at the time fixed for the beginning of the term of the President, the President elect shall have died, the Vice President elect shall become President. If a President shall not have been chosen before the time fixed for the beginning of his term, or if the President elect shall have failed to qualify, then the Vice President elect shall act as President until a President shall have qualified; and the Congress may by law provide for the case wherein neither a President elect nor a Vice President elect shall have qualified, declaring who shall then act as President, or the manner in which one who is to act shall be selected, and such person shall act accordingly until a President or Vice President shall have qualified

4: The Congress may by law provide for the case of the death of any of the persons from whom the House of Representatives may choose a President whenever the right of choice shall have devolved upon them, and for the case of the death of any of the persons from whom the Senate may choose a Vice President whenever the right of choice shall have devolved upon them.

5: Sections 1 and 2 shall take effect on the 15th day of October following the ratification of this article.

6: This article shall be inoperative unless it shall have been ratified as an amendment to the Constitution by the legislatures of three-fourths of the several States within seven years from the date of its submission.

AMENDMENT XXI
Repeal of Eighteenth Amendment
1: The eighteenth article of amendment to the Constitution of the United States is hereby repealed.

2: The transportation or importation into any State, Territory, or possession of the United States for delivery or use therein of intoxicating liquors, in violation of the laws thereof, is hereby prohibited.

3: This article shall be inoperative unless it shall have been ratified as an amendment to the Constitution by conventions in the several States, as provided in the Constitution, within seven years from the date of the submission hereof to the States by the Congress.

AMENDMENT XXII
Presidential Tenure
1: No person shall be elected to the office of the President more than twice, and no person who has held the office of President, or acted as President, for more than two years of a term to which some other person was elected President shall be elected to the office of the President more than once. But this article shall not apply to any person holding the office of President when this article was proposed by the Congress, and shall not prevent any person who may be holding the office of President, or acting as President, during the term within which this article becomes operative from holding the office of President or acting as President during the remainder of such term.

2: This article shall be inoperative unless it shall have been ratified as an amendment to the Constitution by the legislatures of three-fourths of the several states within seven years from the date of its submission to the states by the Congress.

AMENDMENT XXIII
Presidential Electors for the District of Columbia
1: The District constituting the seat of government of the United States shall appoint in such manner as the Congress may direct: A number of electors of President and Vice President equal to the whole number of Senators and Representatives in Congress to which the District would be entitled if it were a state, but in no event more than the least populous state; they shall be in addition to those appointed by the states, but they shall be considered, for the purposes of the election of President and Vice President, to be electors appointed by a state; and they shall meet in the District and perform such duties as provided by the twelfth article of amendment.

2: The Congress shall have power to enforce this article by appropriate legislation.

AMENDMENT XXIV
Abolition of the Poll Tax Qualification in Federal Elections

1. The right of citizens of the United States to vote in any primary or other election for President or Vice President, for electors for President or Vice President, or for Senator or Representative in Congress, shall not be denied or abridged by the United States or any state by reason of failure to pay any poll tax or other tax.

2. The Congress shall have power to enforce this article by appropriate legislation.

AMENDMENT XXV
Presidential Vacancy, Disability, and Inability

1: In case of the removal of the President from office or of his death or resignation, the Vice President shall become President.

2: Whenever there is a vacancy in the office of the Vice President, the President shall nominate a Vice President who shall take office upon confirmation by a majority vote of both Houses of Congress.

3: Whenever the President transmits to the President pro tempore of the Senate and the Speaker of the House of Representatives his written declaration that he is unable to discharge the powers and duties of his office, and until he transmits to them a written declaration to the contrary, such powers and duties shall be discharged by the Vice President as Acting President.

4: Whenever the Vice President and a majority of either the principal officers of the executive departments or of such other body as Congress may by law provide, transmit to the President pro tempore of the Senate and the Speaker of the House of Representatives their written declaration that the President is unable to discharge the powers and duties of his office, the Vice President shall immediately assume the powers and duties of the office as Acting President.

Thereafter, when the President transmits to the President pro tempore of the Senate and the Speaker of the House of Representatives his written declaration that no inability exists, he shall resume the powers and duties of his office unless the Vice President and a majority of either the principal officers of the executive department or of such other body as Congress may by law provide, transmit within four days to the President pro tempore of the Senate and the Speaker of the House of Representatives their written declaration that the President is unable to discharge the powers and duties of his office. Thereupon Congress shall decide the issue, assembling within forty-eight hours for that purpose if not in session. If the Congress, within twenty-one days after receipt of the latter written declaration, or, if Congress is not in session, within twenty-one days after Congress is required to assemble, determines by two-thirds vote of both Houses that the President is unable to discharge the powers and duties of his office, the Vice President shall continue to discharge the same as Acting President; otherwise, the President shall resume the powers and duties of his office.

AMENDMENT XXVI
Reduction of Voting Age Qualification)

1: The right of citizens of the United States, who are 18 years of age or older, to vote, shall not be denied or abridged by the United States or any state on account of age.

2: The Congress shall have the power to enforce this article by appropriate legislation.

AMENDMENT XXVII
Congressional Pay Limitation)

No law varying the compensation for the services of the Senators and Representatives shall take effect until an election of Representatives shall have intervened.

THE DECLARATION OF INDEPENDENCE

IN CONGRESS, July 4, 1776

The unanimous Declaration of the thirteen United States of America,
When in the Course of human events, it becomes necessary for one people to dissolve the political bands which have connected them with another, and to assume among the powers of the earth, the separate and equal station to which the Laws of Nature and of Nature's God entitle them, a decent respect to the opinions of mankind requires that they should declare the causes which impel them to the separation.

We hold these truths to be self-evident, that all men are created equal, that they are endowed by their Creator with certain unalienable Rights, that among these are Life, Liberty and the pursuit of Happiness.—That to secure these rights, Governments are instituted among Men, deriving their just powers from the consent of the governed, —That whenever any Form of Government becomes destructive of these ends, it is the Right of the People to alter or to abolish it, and to institute new Government, laying its foundation on such principles and organizing its powers in such form, as to them shall seem most likely to effect their Safety and Happiness. Prudence, indeed, will dictate that Governments long established should not be changed for light and transient causes; and accordingly all experience hath shewn, that mankind are more disposed to suffer, while evils are sufferable, than to right themselves by abolishing the forms to which they are accustomed. But when a long train of abuses and usurpations, pursuing invariably the same Object evinces a design to reduce them under absolute Despotism, it is their right, it is their duty, to throw off such Government, and to provide new Guards for their future security.—Such has been the patient sufferance of these Colonies; and such is now the necessity which constrains them to alter their former Systems of Government. The history of the present King of Great Britain is a history of repeated injuries and usurpations, all having in direct object the establishment of an absolute Tyranny over these States. To prove this, let Facts be submitted to a candid world.

He has refused his Assent to Laws, the most wholesome and necessary for the public good. He has forbidden his Governors to pass Laws of immediate and pressing importance, unless suspended in their operation till his Assent should be obtained; and when so suspended, he has utterly neglected to attend to them. He has refused to pass other Laws for the accommodation of large districts of people, unless those people would relinquish the right of Representation in the Legislature, a right inestimable to them and formidable to tyrants only. He has called together legislative bodies at places unusual, uncomfortable, and distant from the depository of their public Records, for the sole purpose of fatiguing them into compliance with his measures. He has dissolved Representative Houses repeatedly, for opposing with manly firmness his invasions on the rights of the people. He has refused for a long time, after such dissolutions, to cause others to be elected; whereby the Legislative powers, incapable of Annihilation, have returned to the People at large for their exercise; the State remaining in the meantime exposed to all the dangers of invasion from without, and convulsions within. He has endeavoured to prevent the population of these States; for that purpose obstructing the Laws for Naturalization of Foreigners; refusing to pass others to encourage their migrations hither, and raising the conditions of new Appropriations of Lands. He has obstructed the Administration of Justice, by refusing his Assent to Laws for establishing Judiciary powers. He has made Judges dependent on his Will alone, for the tenure of their offices, and the amount and payment of their salaries. He has erected a multitude of New Offices, and sent hither swarms of Officers to harass our people, and eat out their substance. He has kept among us, in times of peace, Standing Armies without the Consent of our legislatures. He has affected to render the Military independent of and superior to the Civil power. He has combined with others to subject us to a jurisdiction foreign to our constitution, and unacknowledged by our laws; giving his Assent to their Acts of pretended Legislation: For Quartering large bodies of armed troops among us: For protecting them, by a mock Trial, from punishment for any Murders which they should commit on the Inhabitants of these States: For cutting off our Trade with all parts of the world: For imposing Taxes on us without our Consent: For depriving us in many cases, of the benefits of Trial by Jury: For transporting us beyond Seas to be tried for pretended offences, For abolishing the free System of English Laws in a neighbouring Province, establishing therein an Arbitrary government, and enlarging its Boundaries so as to render it at once an example and fit instrument for introducing the same absolute rule into these Colonies: For taking away our Charters, abolishing our most valuable Laws, and altering fundamentally the Forms of our Governments: For suspending our own Legislatures, and declaring themselves invested with power to legislate for us in all cases whatsoever. He has abdicated Government here, by declaring us out of his Protection and waging War against us. He has plundered our seas, ravaged our Coasts, burnt our towns, and destroyed the lives of our people. He is at this time transporting large Armies of foreign Mercenaries to compleat the works of death, desolation and tyranny, already begun with circumstances of Cruelty

& perfidy scarcely paralleled in the most barbarous ages, and totally unworthy the Head of a civilized nation. He has constrained our fellow Citizens taken Captive on the high Seas to bear Arms against their Country, to become the executioners of their friends and Brethren, or to fall themselves by their Hands. He has excited domestic insurrections amongst us, and has endeavoured to bring on the inhabitants of our frontiers, the merciless Indian Savages, whose known rule of warfare, is an undistinguished destruction of all ages, sexes and conditions.

In every stage of these Oppressions We have Petitioned for Redress in the most humble terms: Our repeated Petitions have been answered only by repeated injury. A Prince whose character is thus marked by every act which may define a Tyrant, is unfit to be the ruler of a free people.

Nor have We been wanting in attentions to our Brittish brethren. We have warned them from time to time of attempts by their legislature to extend an unwarrantable jurisdiction over us. We have reminded them of the circumstances of our emigration and settlement here. We have appealed to their native justice and magnanimity, and we have conjured them by the ties of our common kindred to disavow these usurpations, which, would inevitably interrupt our connections and correspondence. They too have been deaf to the voice of justice and of consanguinity. We must, therefore, acquiesce in the necessity, which denounces our Separation, and hold them, as we hold the rest of mankind, Enemies in War, in Peace Friends.

We, therefore, the Representatives of the united States of America, in General Congress, Assembled, appealing to the Supreme Judge of the world for the rectitude of our intentions, do, in the Name, and by Authority of the good People of these Colonies, solemnly publish and declare, That these United Colonies are, and of Right ought to be Free and Independent States; that they are Absolved from all Allegiance to the British Crown, and that all political connection between them and the State of Great Britain, is and ought to be totally dissolved; and that as Free and Independent States, they have full Power to levy War, conclude Peace, contract Alliances, establish Commerce, and to do all other Acts and Things which Independent States may of right do. And for the support of this Declaration, with a firm reliance on the protection of divine Providence, we mutually pledge to each other our Lives, our Fortunes and our sacred Honor.

The 56 signatures on the Declaration

Georgia:	Button Gwinnett
Lyman Hall	
George Walton	
North Carolina:	William Hooper
Joseph Hewes	
John Penn	
South Carolina:	Edward Rutledge
Thomas Heyward, Jr.	
Thomas Lynch, Jr.	
Arthur Middleton	
Massachusetts:	John Hancock
Maryland:	Samuel Chase
William Paca	
Thomas Stone	
Charles Carroll of Carrollton	
Virginia:	George Wythe
Richard Henry Lee	
Thomas Jefferson	
Benjamin Harrison	
Thomas Nelson, Jr.	
Francis Lightfoot Lee	
Carter Braxton	
Pennsylvania:	Robert Morris
Benjamin Rush	
Benjamin Franklin	
John Morton	
George Clymer	
James Smith	
George Taylor	
James Wilson	
George Ross	
Delaware:	Caesar Rodney
George Read	

Thomas McKean

New York: William Floyd

Philip Livingston

Francis Lewis

Lewis Morris

New Jersey: Richard Stockton

John Witherspoon

Francis Hopkinson

John Hart

Abraham Clark

New Hampshire: Josiah Bartlett

William Whipple

Massachusetts: Samuel Adams

John Adams

Robert Treat Paine

Elbridge Gerry

Rhode Island: Stephen Hopkins

William Ellery

Connecticut: Roger Sherman

Samuel Huntington

William Williams

Oliver Wolcott

New Hampshire: Matthew Thornton

Printed and bound by PG in the USA

USA2018PGIL